**Women's Education, Autonomy, and
Reproductive Behaviour**

The International Union for the Scientific Study of Population Problems was set up in 1928, with Dr Raymond Pearl as President. At that time the Union's main purpose was to promote international scientific co-operation to study the various aspects of population problems, through national committees and through its members themselves. In 1947 the International Union for the Scientific Study of Population (IUSSP) was reconstituted into its present form.
It expanded its activities to:
- stimulate research on population
- develop interest in demographic matters among governments, national and international organizations, scientific bodies, and the general public
- foster relations between people involved in population studies
- disseminate scientific knowledge on population.

The principal ways through which the IUSSP currently achieves its aims are:
- organization of worldwide or regional conferences
- operations of Scientific Committees under the auspices of the Council
- organization of training courses
- publication of conference proceedings and committee reports.

Demography can be defined by its field of study and its analytical methods. Accordingly, it can be regarded as the scientific study of human populations primarily with respect to their size, their structure, and their development. For reasons which are related to the history of the discipline, the demographic method is essentially inductive: progress in knowledge results from the improvement of observation, the sophistication of measurement methods, and the search for regularities and stable factors leading to the formulation of explanatory models. In conclusion, the three objectives of demographic analysis are to describe, measure, and analyse.

International Studies in Demography is the outcome of an agreement concluded by the IUSSP and the Oxford University Press. The joint series reflects the broad range of the Union's activities; it is based on the seminars organized by the Union and important international meetings in the field of population and development. The Editorial Board of the series is comprised of:

John Cleland, UK   Henri Leridon, France
John Hobcraft, UK   Richard Smith, UK
Georges Tapinos, France

Women's Education, Autonomy, and Reproductive Behaviour: Experience from Developing Countries

SHIREEN J. JEJEEBHOY

CLARENDON PRESS · OXFORD

*This book has been printed digitally and produced in a standard specification
in order to ensure its continuing availability*

OXFORD
UNIVERSITY PRESS

Great Clarendon Street, Oxford OX2 6DP

Oxford University Press is a department of the University of Oxford.
It furthers the University's objective of excellence in research, scholarship,
and education by publishing worldwide in

Oxford New York

Auckland Bangkok Buenos Aires Cape Town Chennai
Dar es Salaam Delhi Hong Kong Istanbul Karachi Kolkata
Kuala Lumpur Madrid Melbourne Mexico City Mumbai Nairobi
São Paulo Shanghai Singapore Taipei Tokyo Toronto

with an associated company in Berlin

Oxford is a registered trade mark of Oxford University Press
in the UK and in certain other countries

Published in the United States
by Oxford University Press Inc., New York

© Shireen J. Jejeebhoy 1995

The moral rights of the author have been asserted
Database right Oxford University Press (maker)

Reprinted 2002

ISBN 0-19-829033-0

Foreword

In much of the world thus far, little attention has been paid to the education of girls. Huge gaps persist between women's and men's educational achievement. Globally, nearly 600 million women remain illiterate today, compared with about 320 million men. In certain parts of the world, moreover, as many as three in four women are illiterate, and others have received no more than a negligible education. This neglect has had critical consequences for women's well-being, for their empowerment as well as for their reproductive choices and roles.

Through empowerment, women take control of their lives. The education of girls is held to be a key factor in improving family health, reducing infant mortality, and changing reproductive behaviour. With education comes increased confidence and self-esteem. Educated women are more likely to stand up for themselves, participate in the labour force, and seek health care for themselves and their children.

Over the past few years, recognition of the neglect of women's education has grown, both in international forums and in national agendas, with increasing commitments to investments in female education. The Programme of Action adopted at the International Conference on Population and Development (ICPD), held in Cairo, Egypt, in September 1994, reaffirms everyone's right to education and gives special attention to women and the girl child. Terming the eradication of illiteracy 'one of the prerequisites for human development', the Programme of Action recognizes education as a key factor in sustainable development and in the empowerment of women and gives paramount importance to the elimination of illiteracy among women. One of the goals of the ICPD Programme of Action is universal access to primary education before the year 2015. The Programme of Action also urges countries to take steps to keep girls and adolescents in school, in order to close the gender gap in primary and secondary school education by the year 2005. Encouraging attention 'to the quality and type of education, including recognition of traditional values', the Programme of Action urges 'countries that have achieved the goal of universal primary education . . . to extend education and training to, and facilitate access to and completion of education at, secondary school and higher levels.'

Few studies have addressed the myriad linkages among women's education, their autonomy, and their reproductive behaviour. *Women's Education, Autonomy, and Reproductive Behaviour: Experience from Developing Countries* is one step in filling this gap. Synthesizing the available literature from various disciplines and regions, this review addresses such topics as the ways in which educating women affects their lives and their autonomy, as well as the linkages of women's education to reproductive behaviour, distinguishing the pathways in this relationship and, at the same time, synthesizing the volume of data available on aspects of this relationship.

Recognizing the importance of the subject and the paucity of literature, the International Union for the Scientific Study of Population and the United Nations Population Fund jointly supported this book's publication. The subject is of interest to many beyond the population community, and we hope that it will reach a wide audience.

This study provides many significant insights. It bears out the indisputable impact of education on women's lives. In almost every setting, regardless of region, culture, or level of development, well-educated women have a greater say in their lives, including their reproductive lives, and bear fewer children than do uneducated women. In almost every setting where it has been studied, the relationship is genuine and cannot be explained by the fact that educated women marry better educated men or come from wealthier households.

At the same time, the study cautions that a modest amount of education does not necessarily enhance women's autonomy, improve reproductive health, or increase reproductive choices in all contexts. In settings where incomes and literacy are low and where there are wide disparities in literacy between men and women, there appear to be threshold levels of education which must be reached before changes in fertility and other aspects of reproductive behaviour can occur. The results clearly suggest that the impact of women's education is greatest among women with more than five or six years of schooling; it is also greatest when education offers women an expanded role in family decisions and control over resources.

It is my hope that this review of developing-country experience and its implications will help strengthen national and international commitment to women's and girls' education and, more generally, to the enhancement of women's autonomy.

NAFIS SADIK
Executive Director
United Nations Population Fund

Preface

Education means different things to each of us. To one of the few literate women in a remote village in Rajasthan, India: 'Of course, reading and writing are very important to me; they are the only way I can "talk" to my sister.' Through her ability to correspond with her sister, this woman—living in a culture which allows women little freedom of movement and in which women are married into distant families with few opportunities to meet their mothers and sisters—was able to maintain a vital link that would otherwise have been broken. In Zimbabwe, education meant something else to an educated woman who became a teacher. 'Because I also bring income, which everybody, including the in-laws, enjoys, I am valued more, and nobody expects me to have more children.' Through education, this woman found expanded occupational opportunity, enhanced control over economic resources, and greater ability to make choices (M. M. Mhloyi, 'Fertility Transition in Zimbabwe').

These two reactions are part of a wide spectrum of personal benefits that women all over the world attach to education. Whatever the reaction, a common theme is that education empowers women, providing women with autonomy over their lives, including their reproductive lives. Likewise, the literature tends to argue that educated women have greater autonomy and fewer children than less educated women do. Beyond this general assertion, however, confusion prevails. There is little consensus on, for example, how much education is required before changes in autonomy or reproductive behaviour occur; whether the relationship exists in all cultural contexts, at all times, and at all levels of development; and how education affects fertility. Especially neglected is the role of women's autonomy in the overall relationship between education and fertility. How does education affect women's autonomy? And to what extent do the resulting changes in autonomy affect fertility and other aspects of reproductive behaviour? Which aspects of autonomy are important in the education–fertility relationship? Knowledge and exposure to the outside world? Enhanced decision-making? Control over resources?

These kinds of persistent questions led to the idea for this book at the first meeting of the former Committee on Gender and Population of the International Union for the Scientific Study of Population (IUSSP). Committee members agreed on the need for a review of the literature to understand the ways in which educating women affects their lives and their autonomy as well as the linkages of women's education to reproductive behaviour; to distinguish the various pathways in this relationship; and, at the same time, to synthesize the voluminous data on aspects of this relationship. Because this is a topic of interest to many beyond the demographic community, the need was expressed for a book that addressed a general audience.

This work would have been impossible without the insights and support of Committee members Bridgida Garcia, An-Magritt Jensen, Paulina Makinwa-Adebusoye,

Karen Oppenheim Mason, and Catherine S. Pierce. Their confidence in assigning me the task of compiling and synthesizing the literature and their help in accessing materials from various regions, comments on outlines and drafts, encouragement, and friendship form the foundation of this book. I owe a special debt of gratitude to the Committee's co-Chair, Karen Oppenheim Mason, who gave generously of her time reviewing in detail the substance and style of the manuscript.

The United Nations Population Fund (UNFPA) and IUSSP jointly supported the publication of this review. I am grateful to both. Catherine S. Pierce of UNFPA has been unwavering in her interest and support since the project began. At IUSSP, Bruno Remiche has guided the manuscript through reviews, editing, and all the steps to make it ready for publication.

Although I was aware that a great deal of literature existed on the relationship of education to fertility, the volume of the literature, the geographic coverage of what is available, and the diverse methodologies by which the relationship has been studied exceeded all expectations. Thus, I relied on many people to help me search for materials, interpret methodologies, and read and comment upon earlier incarnations of the text. This review would not have seen the light of publication without their support. I am especially grateful to Mary Beth Weinberger and Teresa Castro-Martin of the United Nations Population Division and to Shea Rutstein of Macro International for making unpublished material from the Demographic and Health Surveys available to me. The resources of the libraries of the East–West Center, Honolulu; UNFPA, New York; and the International Institute for Population Sciences, Bombay, were immensely useful. I thank Phyllis Tabusa, David Rose, and R. T. Randeria of those organizations for helping me gather much of the material used in the book. In addition, many authors generously provided unpublished or inaccessible works. I would also like to record my gratitude to the East–West Center for supporting my stay in Honolulu during two trips.

Many colleagues and friends, all over the world, have given of their time reviewing and discussing drafts of this book. Their insights and comments, incorporated in the text, have helped shape the focus of the book and have contributed to a more comprehensive analysis. I am grateful to, in alphabetical order, Brigitta Bucht, Jack Caldwell, Gretchen Condran, Susan Jayne (Cochrane), Cynthia Lloyd, Tom Merrick, Jyoti Moodbidri, Saumya Rama Rao, Zeba Sathar, and Mary Beth Weinberger, as well as to the participants in the United Nations Expert Group Meeting on Women and Development in Gaborone, Botswana, in mid-1992, for their comments on an early paper on this subject.

Others whose assistance greatly facilitated the completion of this book are Shantha Rajgopal, N. V. Kokate, and Mahesh Naik, in Bombay, who provided much needed research and technical support; Irene Grignac of IUSSP in Liège and Victoria Rector of UNFPA in New York, who coped with the many administrative issues related to publication; Barbara Ryan, whose significant editorial contributions and attention to detail have made the book more readable and more precise; and the publication team at OUP, who so ably and painstakingly expedited its publication.

I owe a large debt of gratitude to my teacher and friend Dick Easterlin, whose own work formed the basis upon which this synthesis of the literature has been structured. His criticism has always been constructive and his encouragement unfailing.

Finally, I should like to acknowledge the support of my family—especially Deanna, Geeta, Ratan, and Ayesha—and many friends for their understanding, humour, and affection throughout the course of this project.

S.J.J.

Contents

List of Figures

List of Tables

Appendix tables

List of Boxes

1 Introduction and Framework

Women's access to education has been recognized as a fundamental right, and increasing their access is among the goals of most developing countries. The benefits of educating women are manifold, ranging from improved productivity, income, and economic development on the national level to a better quality of life on the individual level, notably a healthier and better nourished population and greater autonomy among women. Moreover, educating women is important for all kinds of demographic behaviour, affecting mortality, health, fertility, and contraception.[1] In almost every setting, regardless of region, culture, or level of development, well-educated women are observed to have fewer children than do uneducated women.

Yet the patterns in the relationship between women's education and their fertility are diverse,[2] varying by region of the world, by level of socio-economic development, and over time. These patterns also vary by cultural conditions, especially by the position women occupy in the traditional kinship structure and gender system. This complex set of patterns and interrelationships raises questions, in some contexts, about whether and to what extent modest increases in female education unilaterally lead to reductions in fertility.

Considerable evidence about education and fertility has emerged over the last twenty years in the developing world. The aim of this study is to review that evidence, probing the relationships observed between women's education and fertility under various cultural conditions and settings. It also aims at indicating the pathways or intervening variables through which women's education affects fertility in developing countries.

The study addresses three major questions:
- First, is the relationship of women's education to fertility always inverse, that is, does increased education always lead to a decrease in the number of children? If not, what are the conditions under which non-inverse relationships are observed? Is there a threshold level—some minimum amount—of education that a woman must achieve before that inverse relationship of education to fertility becomes apparent?
- Second, what are the critical pathways influencing the relationship of women's education to fertility? Is fertility affected because education leads to changes in the duration of breast-feeding? Because it raises the age at marriage? Because it increases the practice of contraception and the ability to prevent unwanted births? Or because education reduces women's preferences for large numbers of children?
- Third, do improvements in education empower women in other areas of life, such as enhancing their exposure to information, decision-making, control

of resources, or confidence in dealing with family and the outside world? And do these changes have consequences for fertility and its proximate determinants?

Scope of This Study

In 1979, Susan Cochrane reviewed the relationship of education—for both males and females—to fertility.[3] She explored systematically the possibility of exceptions to the generally expected inverse relationship. Since Cochrane's book was published, several developments have occurred, both in the status of women's education and in the knowledge about its links to fertility, suggesting a need for another review. Largely as a result of two rounds of international fertility surveys—the World Fertility Survey (WFS) of the 1970s, which yielded data on the education–fertility relationship in 38 developing countries, and the Demographic and Health Survey (DHS), which by 1992 had yielded corresponding data on the relationship in well over 30 developing countries—a great deal more evidence has become available on how and why women's education fosters changes in fertility.

More and more, evidence suggests that there is something unique about women's education, unexplained by their economic status or their husbands' characteristics, which leads to changes in fertility behaviour. The implication of this finding is that a considerable portion of the education effect is the result of factors unique to women. Discussions of the relationship of education to fertility have, thus far, neglected to explore what these dimensions of women's situation might be. Since Cochrane's review was published, a large field has developed which focuses on women's general status and fertility decline.[4] This review draws upon that literature to outline pathways relating to women's autonomy which mediate or condition the relationship of education to fertility. Hence, a major difference between this study and Cochrane's is the focus on women's autonomy as intervening and conditioning the relationship of women's education to fertility and its proximate determinants.

The evidence reviewed pertains to developing countries from the mid-1970s onwards. Attempts have been made to examine all relevant research throughout this period and to spread a wide geographical net. Even so, the studies are not necessarily representative of each region. Moreover, they range from those using simple methodologies and small samples to those using highly sophisticated methodologies and large samples. In cases where studies refer to more than one date, the most recent point in time is considered; where national and subnational or regional data are given, national-level data are generally preferred. Both quantitative and, to a lesser extent, qualitative data are reviewed. For the most part, only results based on individual and household-level data are considered, on the rationale that the links of education to other aspects of women's status are best represented by individual-level data. (The studies reviewed are summarized in Appendices A through L.)

Focus on women

This study focuses on the links of women's education to fertility, not on links of children's or men's or the community's education to fertility. One scholar has cautioned that a focus on the role of women's education in bringing about declining fertility should not disregard the role of children's education—specifically, the immediate costs of such education to parents—as being instrumental in setting off changes in the parents' fertility behaviour.[5] Mass schooling of children certainly leads to changes in the values and costs of children to parents and a rethinking of parental reproductive goals. At the same time, however, evidence shows that, even in the face of mass schooling, women's education continues to exert a strong effect on fertility as well as on the perceived costs of, and demand for, children. Better educated women have higher aspirations for their children's education and are less likely to expect labour support from their school-going children than are uneducated women. In other words, it may be unnecessary that couples actually have school-going children and experience the deleterious costs of educating them before adjusting their reproductive goals, although this experience may well strengthen their conviction to limit fertility. There are, moreover, fewer data in support of the linkages between children's education and fertility than those between women's education and fertility. For these reasons, this review focuses on women's schooling.

Men's education also plays an important role in determining fertility. Several studies have observed that when controls for urban–rural residence and for husband's education are introduced, the effect of women's education on fertility is typically reduced by half. Nevertheless, considerable evidence suggests that women's education has the greater influence on fertility.[6]

Although this study relates the level of education of individual women in a particular setting to their fertility, evidence suggests that the contextual effect of schooling can be as important as the individual level in determining reproductive behaviour. A modest exposure to education has little impact on fertility in a context in which average levels of women's education are low. In other words, the overall effect of education in a society may be as powerful an influence on the reproductive patterns of individuals as their own level of education.

Focus on formal education

Another limitation of this study is the focus on the effect of formal schooling rather than that of non-formal education, which has become widely available in developing countries. Policy-makers often speculate that non-formal education—ranging from adult education to skill development; information, education, and communication about maternal and child health and family planning; and health and nutrition education—can have consequences for fertility. Unfortunately, however, data on non-formal education and its links to demographic change are sparse. Moreover, the little information that is available on the effect of non-formal education on women's lives or demographic behaviour is hardly convincing.[7] Because non-formal programmes offer only brief exposure covering a specific issue (e.g. agriculture, literacy, and immunization), the prospect of deriving large indirect benefits from adult non-formal programmes seems unpromising.

Focus on duration of education

This study, like other studies addressing the relationship of education to fertility, measures education by the number of years spent in school, rather than by the content of schooling. This is largely a result of the paucity of data on the impact of the content. In addition, the few studies that address the ways in which schooling affects outlook, especially with regard to reproductive behaviour, have mixed findings. It seems likely, however, that the quality of education and its formal content, whether secular or religious, public or private, has some effect on the outlook of the student. For example, women educated in Catholic schools in the United States of America in the 1950s[8] and in Sierra Leone in the 1970s[9] and women in Islamic societies who receive Koranic education do appear to have more traditional attitudes than women educated in secular schools.[10]

Some scholars have argued that it is not the factual content of the curriculum so much as its value content that is important for fertility.[11] The time spent in school subtly exposes students to this value content, teaches them new ideas, leads them to question traditional authority structures, and changes their aspirations, irrespective of quality. The longer and more intensive the exposure to education, the greater is the change in outlook. By examining a variety of intervening variables, discussed below, this study will draw inferences about what it is about attending different levels of school that influences women's reproductive behaviour.

Women's Education in Developing Countries

The developing world is characterized by enormous diversity in every dimension of the variables that this study covers. Fertility varies from extremely high levels in some countries to near-replacement levels in others. Educational status and the disparities in attainments between males and females vary both by region and over time. So, too, do overall economic development and income levels. Women's economic independence outside the home, as well as the extent to which women's voices are heard within the home, varies widely by culture and region.[12]

Notwithstanding these variations, in most of the developing world, women's educational levels are low and gender disparities are wide.[13] In every region, however, literacy rates for women have risen markedly since 1970—by about 20 per cent on average. Nevertheless, there are still regions of the world—North Africa and the Middle East, sub-Saharan Africa, and South Asia—where fewer than half of all women can read and write (Table 1.1).

- Even in 1990, of the 85 countries included in Table 1.1, 21 countries had female adult literacy rates of less than 25 per cent; and

• Overall literacy of females across these countries was only 54 per cent.

Disparities in literacy between females and males, although narrowing considerably from 1970 to 1990, remain everywhere but in Latin America and the Caribbean. The gender gap is greatest in North Africa and the Middle East, sub-Saharan Africa, and South Asia. In South Asia, in 1990, for every 100 literate males, there were 54 literate females (Table 1.1).

Table 1.1. *Adult literacy rates, by region, 1970, 1990*

Region	Literacy rates				Literate females per 100 literate males	
	1970		1990		1970	1990
	Female	Male	Female	Male		
(Number of countries)	(90)	(91)	(85)	(85)	(90)	(85)
Sub-Saharan Africa	15	35	44	64	44	68
North Africa and the Middle East	20	48	46	70	41	65
East and South-East Asia	58	76	66	85	76	77
South Asia	18	44	32	59	42	54
Latin America and the Caribbean	68	75	83	87	91	96
TOTALS	32	53	54	74	62	72

Notes: The following countries were not included because data were unavailable: in sub-Saharan Africa, Ethiopia, Namibia, and South Africa in 1970 and 1990, Mauritania in 1970, and Malawi and Mauritius in 1990; in North Africa, Oman in 1970 and 1990 and Israel in 1990; in East and South-East Asia, Cambodia, China, Democratic People's Republic of Korea, and Viet Nam in 1970, and Mongolia, Singapore, and the Territory of Hong Kong in 1990; in South Asia, Bhutan in 1970; and in Latin America and the Caribbean, Nicaragua and Trinidad and Tobago in 1990.

Source: Literacy rates were obtained from United Nations Children's Fund, *The State of the World's Children, 1992* (Oxford, Oxford University Press, 1992), and weighted by population size in the nearest available year.

Primary-school enrolment ratios—that is, the ratio of students enrolled in particular grades to the number of children in the appropriate age group—are presented for girls and boys in Table 1.2. By the late 1980s, with the exception of sub-Saharan Africa, every region had achieved near universal primary-school enrolment for boys. In contrast, only Latin America and the Caribbean and East and South-East Asia had achieved near universal primary-school enrolment for girls.[14]

Progress at the secondary level since 1960 has been dramatic in some areas; gross enrolment ratios for females increased from an average of 12 per cent in 1960 to 44 per cent in 1988 in lower-middle-income countries and from 25 per cent to 70 per cent in upper-middle-income countries. Even in the late 1980s, however, fewer than half of all eligible boys and about one third of all girls in the eligible ages were enrolled in secondary school. In every region except Latin America and the Caribbean, the gender gap was even wider at the secondary-school level than at the primary-school level. In South Asia and sub-Saharan Africa, for example, only 60 girls were enrolled for every 100 boys in secondary school.[15]

Table 1.2.   *Primary-school enrolment and sex ratios, by region, selected years*

Region	Enrolment ratios				Sex ratio: enrolled females per 100 enrolled males	
	1960		1986–9		1960	1986–9
	Female	Male	Female	Male	1960	1986–9
(Number of countries)	(74)	(74)	(74)	(74)	(74)	(74)
Sub-Saharan Africa	23	46	58	70	51	83
North Africa and the Middle East	45	77	85	101	58	84
East and South-East Asia	69	87	109	112	79	97
South Asia	35	73	76	103	48	73
Latin America and the Caribbean	81	86	109	111	93	99
TOTALS	45	73	83	100	61	83

Notes: The following countries were not included because data were unavailable for either the year 1960 or the period 1986–9: in sub-Saharan Africa, Angola, Congo, Gabon, Guinea-Bissau, Malawi, Namibia, Rwanda, Senegal, Sierra Leone, South Africa, Uganda, and Zimbabwe; in North Africa and the Middle East, Libyan Arab Jamahiriya, Oman, Saudi Arabia, United Arab Republic, and Yemen; in East Asia, China, and Democratic People's Republic of Korea; in South-East Asia, Cambodia and Viet Nam; in South Asia, Bhutan; and in Latin America and the Caribbean, Brazil, El Salvador, Trinidad and Tobago, and Venezuela.

Source: Calculated from ratios provided in United Nations Children's Fund, *The State of the World's Children, 1992* (Oxford, Oxford University Press, 1992), and weighted by population size in the nearest available year.

Less information is available on attendance and retention. Where data are available, it appears that girls are less likely than boys to attend school and to complete each level of education; they are also more likely to drop out, suggesting a wider gap in educational attainment than would be implied by enrolment ratios alone.

From this general profile of women's education in developing countries, three points may help illuminate the situation of women and the likely links to demographic behaviour:

• First, steadily increasing literacy rates and enrolment ratios over time suggest a shift in the educational distribution of women. Although poorly educated women will constitute the majority in much of the developing world, the proportion of uneducated women will continue to decline. This changing distribution itself may have implications for fertility decline, in that overall fertility levels will be shaped largely by the fertility of progressively better educated women;

• Second, despite rising school enrolment ratios in the developing world, gender-related disparities have diminished only moderately. The male advantage in literacy, extent of enrolment, and years of schooling persists in every region and almost every country; and

• Third, enrolment ratios, literacy rates, years of schooling, and the gender gap differ sharply by region. South Asia, North Africa, and sub-Saharan Africa exhibit the lowest female literacy rates and enrolment ratios, the fewest years of schooling, and the sharpest gender disparities. Even in the late 1980s, fewer than three in five eligible girls were enrolled in primary school in sub-Saharan Africa, three in four in South Asia, and four in five in North Africa. At the secondary-school stage, no more than one in six girls in sub-Saharan Africa and about one in four in South Asia were enrolled.[16] 'Education for all' is still a far cry for women in many regions of the developing world.

Framework for Studying the Linkages of Education, Women's Autonomy, and Fertility Behaviour

Women's autonomy

What is important for demographic change is that women be in control of their own lives and have a voice in matters affecting themselves and their families, not how much prestige or esteem they are accorded.[17] In this sense, the commonly used term 'status of women' is unclear, because its interpretation is highly subjective, it varies from setting to setting, and it may be high even where women have little control over their lives. 'Autonomy' is hence a better term to describe the extent to which women have control over their own lives. Autonomy has been defined as 'the ability . . . to obtain information and use it as the basis for making decisions about one's private concerns and those of one's intimates.'[18] In addition, whether women play an active role in the family and in society, whether they have a real say in making and carrying out decisions, whether they are free to develop bonds with their husbands, whether they have the freedom to move about and to interact with the outside world—all constitute their autonomy.

Women's autonomy as individuals is conditioned largely by the extent of gender stratification in their society. Patriarchal or gender-stratified cultures, as defined by A. R. Radcliffe-Brown,[19] are characterized by patrilineal descent, patrilocal residence, inheritance and succession practices which exclude women, and hierarchical relations in which the father or his relatives has authority over family members. In such cultures, gender relations are inegalitarian, and women have little say in their own lives.

There is a growing recognition that reproductive behaviour is strongly conditioned by the degree of gender stratification in a culture.[20] It has been suggested, for example, that the kinship system prevailing in the northern part of the Indian subcontinent is distinctly more gender-stratified and patriarchal than that prevailing in the south and that these cultural forces are important in explaining the fertility differentials observed in these two regions.[21] The Islamic settings of North Africa and the Middle East are characterized by kinship structures similar to those of northern India, with high levels of female seclusion and dependence. Another region, East Asia, is also traditionally gender-stratified, although in the course of economic development it has, to some extent, assumed more egalitarian gender relations. At the other extreme, kinship structures in South-East Asia and Latin America tend to be far more egalitarian than those observed even in South India; in South-East Asia and Latin America, women are rarely secluded, disparities in literacy and economic opportunity are relatively narrow, and son preference is rare. In Thailand, for example, women enjoy near universal literacy, economic independence, control over family finances, egalitarian spousal relations, and the absence of son preference.[22]

Classifying women in sub-Saharan Africa into this schema is more complex. Women tend to have considerable economic independence, access to resources, freedom of movement, and decision-making power with respect to their own land and trading activities. Beyond this, however, sub-Saharan kinship structures tend to be highly gender-stratified. Men control women through subordination within marriage, and women have little decision-making power over reproductive matters.[23]

At the individual level, there is a growing literature measuring autonomy, including the linkages of its various dimensions to demographic change. From the literature on women and demographic change, five separate but interdependent aspects of autonomy are suggested as important in the education-fertility relationship:

- Knowledge autonomy: education typically enhances women's knowledge of, and exposure to, the outside world;
- Decision-making autonomy: education strengthens women's say in family decisions and decisions concerning their own lives and well-being;
- Physical autonomy in interacting with the outside world: educated women face fewer constraints on physical mobility and have more self-confidence in dealing with the outside world and in extracting the most from available services;
- Emotional autonomy: education encourages a shift in loyalties to the conjugal family rather than extended kin and allows for greater bonding or intimacy between spouses and between parents and children and less self-denial among women; and
- Economic and social autonomy and self-reliance: education enhances women's self-reliance in economic matters, enhances their access to and control over economic resources, and increases their self-reliance for social acceptance and status.

These five aspects of autonomy have been incorporated in the framework, with indications of their likely effect on each of the intervening variables.

Not all of these measures of autonomy are unique to women. Some effects, such as enhanced knowledge and exposure to new ideas, may be applicable to both men and women. For women, however, education is perhaps the primary channel for learning new ideas. In contrast, men are exposed to new ideas not only through formal education but also through their wider contacts with the outside world, which they enjoy by virtue of their gender.

The focus here is on the absolute levels of women's autonomy, rather than on the levels relative to the levels enjoyed by men in the household, although the two are strongly related. It is generally assumed that where women have autonomy, gender relations are egalitarian. For want of comparable data, comparisons in this study are between the autonomy of educated women and the autonomy of other women, rather than the autonomy of men.

Another concern is with how education affects autonomy among women during (and not at the end of) their child-bearing years. In many societies, age can confer a great deal of autonomy on women, independent of education; this interaction may confound the overall effect of education on fertility. Even in cultures that are most hostile to women, older women gain considerable decision-making authority and control over household resources simply by virtue of their age and often long after they have completed reproduction. It is important to recognize that a study of the interrelationships of education, autonomy, and fertility refers, by definition, to women's autonomy during their child-bearing years.

Framework for analysis of fertility determination

To classify the complex and multifaceted linkages between women's education and fertility, this analysis relies upon Richard A. Easterlin's framework for fertility determination.[24] The main advantage of this framework, which synthesizes concepts from sociology and economics, is that it allows for the examination of the various biological, attitudinal, and behavioural mechanisms through which education can affect fertility. A second advantage is that it explains a variety of relationships between education and fertility. Education has the potential both to increase fertility and to reduce it; its effects may be either inadvertent or deliberate. The strengths of these opposing effects may vary considerably, depending on the cultural and development contexts.

In the framework, improvements in women's education and in their autonomy cannot affect fertility directly but do so through three sets of intervening pathways:
- Those influencing the supply of children or the number of children a couple can have;
- Those influencing the demand for children or the number of children a couple wants; and
- Those influencing the costs of, and obstacles to, deliberate fertility regulation.

Supply Supply refers to the number of births or surviving children a couple can have under 'natural fertility' conditions,[25] that is, if the couple makes no attempt to limit fertility. Easterlin usually measures supply in terms of surviving children; this review measures supply in terms of births, since data on births are more widely available. From the couple's point of view, factors affecting the supply of children are inadvertent in that they are not intended to affect the number of children a woman has. Education is an important influence on the supply of children because of its association with the following:
- The delay in age at marriage or entry into unions. Although some argue that women who want many children deliberately marry earlier, little evidence from

developing countries substantiates this. By and large, the timing of marriage remains unrelated to fertility intentions;
• Shorter durations of breast-feeding and, consequently, of post-partum amenorrhoea;
• Lower prevalence and duration of post-partum and other abstinence; and
• Lower child and maternal mortality.

Education may reduce the supply of births, mainly through the postponement of marriage or union, thereby shortening the period of exposure to pregnancy. In contrast, shorter periods of breast-feeding and abstinence tend to increase the supply of children by shortening the non-susceptible period. Education may be associated with increased fecundity and lower rates of intra-uterine mortality and infertility by improving women's nutrition and health levels, although there is little evidence of these relationships. What data are available suggest that nutrition is relatively less important in generating differentials in fertility.[26] Finally, education tends to enhance child survival which, especially in conditions of prolonged breast-feeding that characterize much of the developing world, has the effect of lengthening birth intervals. The result is a slowing of the natural pace of child-bearing and a reduction in the number of births. Lower infant and child mortality tends to increase the total number of surviving children.

Demand   The demand for children refers to the number of children a couple wants, the sex composition of this number, or the intensity with which a couple prefers a particular sex. Education affects a number of motives underlying a couple's preferences for number and composition—notably the economic and non-economic returns parents obtain from children as well as the costs associated with child-rearing. It is argued that economic independence—facilitated by education—can reduce women's reliance on children for their support in the form of child labour, as well as for their assistance in emergencies and during the mothers' old age[27] and that it reduces the reliance on children to legitimize women's positions in their marital homes. Education raises aspirations concerning the children, which increases the time and opportunity costs of children in such a way as to make child-rearing a more costly exercise than before.

The link of women's education to desired family size is affected by another intervening variable—the improved child survival experienced by educated women. By virtue of the better prospects that their children will survive, educated women are less likely to want large numbers of children to ensure that some of them survive. In developing countries, however, this effect is observed to be weaker than the mechanical effect through lengthier birth intervals.[28] Hence, child mortality is included here as a variable affecting the supply of children.

Costs of, and obstacles to, fertility regulation   The practice of contraception is associated with both money and time costs as well as with non-economic costs or constraints. These constraints include ignorance of fertility-control methods, negative or fatalistic attitudes towards contraception, and a reluctance, among couples, to discuss contraception or family-size limitation. Education is expected to enhance the acquisition of knowledge of contraception, permit more interspousal communication on contraception, change attitudes to favour contraception, and provide a greater sense of control over child-bearing. In that sense, better educated women are less likely to experience the non-economic costs of contraception than are uneducated women.

The extent to which the potential supply of children exceeds the demand for them indicates the degree of motivation to practise deliberate fertility regulation. By itself, however, motivation is not sufficient to induce contraception. Whether fertility is actually controlled depends on the costs of, and the obstacles to, fertility regulation. As seen, education is expected both to increase the motivation to use contraception and to reduce the costs associated with contraception. As a result, educated women are more likely than uneducated women to practise contraception.

Easterlin's framework has been modified to incorporate one of the major aims of this study, namely, to trace the pathways between education and fertility that involve women's autonomy. Education is expected to set off changes in the situation of women in ways which then impinge on fertility through the supply, demand, and costs of regulation-intervening channels. Table 1.3 sets out the ways in which education and the changes it precipitates in women's autonomy are believed to influence fertility. An additional intermediate stage in the relationship has been introduced, namely, dimensions of the situation of women which are potentially affected by education and which, in turn, are expected to affect the intervening variables and fertility.

Education may affect fertility through more than one variable, and the effects may not be in the same direction. For example, better educated women marry later than lesser educated women (column 2); the references in column 3 suggest that among the factors responsible are educated women's greater involvement in decision-making (b), greater self-confidence in dealing with the outside world (c), greater emotional autonomy (d), and greater economic and social self-reliance (e). The negative sign in column 4 suggests that increased marital age has an inverse effect on the number of children. The negative sign in column 5 suggests that the overall effect of women's education on fertility via marital age is inverse.

Some changes that result from the enhanced autonomy that accompanies education are totally inadvertent; they are not intended to affect the number of children a woman has. For example, the enhanced knowledge, decision-making authority, and conjugal closeness that educated women enjoy may enable them to shorten traditional lengthy breast-feeding patterns and disregard traditional abstinence taboos. The result, other things being equal, could be increased fertility. Greater decision-making power and economic and social self-reliance, not to mention confidence in dealing with the world, may allow women to postpone marriage, thereby reducing the effective length of exposure to pregnancy.

Other changes in women's autonomy that result from education may affect fertility volitionally, through the demand for children and through contraceptive costs. For example, because educated women know more about the world, have

Table 1.3. *Hypothetical effects of women's education on fertility via changes in the situation of women and the intervening variables affecting fertility*

Intervening variable (1)	Effect of women's education on intervening variables		Effect of this intervening variable on number of children ever born (4)	Effect of women's education on number of children ever born via specific intervening variable (5)
	Direction (2)	Through* (3)		
A. Supply of children				
1. Age at marriage	+	b, c, d, e	–	–
2. Breast-feeding	–	a, b, d	–	+
3. Post-partum abstinence	–	a, b, d	–	+
4. Child mortality†	–	a, b, c, d, e	+	–
B. Demand for children				
5. Desired family size	–	a, b, c, d, e	+	–
6. Son preference	–	e	+	–
7. Children's labour contribution in childhood	–	e	+	–
8. Children's financial and residential support in adulthood	–	e	+	–
9. Children as a source of prestige	–	e	+	–
10. Economic costs of children	+	a, b, e	–	–
11. Time and opportunity costs	+	a, b, e	–	–
C. Costs of and obstacles to contraceptive use‡				
12. Method awareness	+	a	–	–
13. Approval	+	b	–	–
14. Spousal communication	+	b, d	–	–
D. Contraceptive use	+	a, b, c, d, e Supply–Demand 12, 13, 14 Child survival	–	–

* Changes in the situation of women are through the following:
   a = knowledge autonomy, exposure to modern world
   b = decision-making autonomy
   c = autonomy in interacting with the outside world
   d = emotional autonomy
   e = economic and social autonomy and self-reliance, control over economic resources

   † The perception and experience of child mortality can also affect the demand for children and contraceptive use.

   ‡ Contraceptive costs as used here mean the subjective or non-economic costs of contraception, rather than the actual money costs of purchasing contraceptives.

Notes: The supply, demand, and costs of intervening variables—those related to the supply of children, the demand for children, costs of and obstacles to contraception, and actual contraceptive use—are listed in the left-hand column. Column 2 presents the direction of the effect of education on each intervening variable. An entry means that education affects that intervening variable in the direction shown: positively (+) or negatively (−). For example, women's education has a positive effect on age at marriage; in other words, marriage age increases as women become better educated. Women's education has a negative effect on the duration of breast-feeding; in other words, the duration of breast-feeding declines as women become better educated. Column 3 highlights the important measures of women's autonomy responsible for this relationship (the empirical justification underlying this is provided in subsequent chapters); column 4 presents the direction of the effect of each intervening variable on the number of children ever born; and column 5 summarizes the effect of women's education on the number of children ever born via each specific intervening variable.

Source: Adapted from Richard A. Easterlin, 'An Economic Framework for Fertility Analysis', *Studies in Family Planning,* 6 (Mar. 1975), 54–63, and 'The Economics and Sociology of Fertility: A Synthesis', in Charles Tilly (ed.), *Historical Studies of Changing Fertility* (Princeton, Princeton University Press, 1978).

greater autonomy in deciding on both the number of children to have and the use of household resources, and exercise greater independent control over the family's and their own resources, they are more likely to be more concerned about the time and money costs of children, and less likely to look upon sons as their social and economic salvation. They are also more confident about the survival prospects of the infants they bear and, therefore, less likely to want many children to ensure the survival of a few.

Similarly, contraceptive use patterns may be affected by these and other changes, such as the closer links between husband and wife and the greater ability of educated women to use health and contraceptive services. Contraceptive use patterns are influenced by the extent to which the supply of children or the number of births a woman can have exceeds the number desired. They are also influenced by the existence of constraints, such as lack of knowledge about methods and negative attitudes.

Some evidence suggests that education in small amounts may play only a weak role in generating changes in women's autonomy. What is critical but difficult to measure is the cultural context. Contextual factors, such as norms of patriarchy and women's traditional position in the economic structure, may well condition the pattern of the relationships. For example, the extent to which education influences women's social and economic self-reliance may depend on how secluded women are in a particular context. Where strong sanctions exist against socializing with men or leaving the home, education may have a much weaker impact on enhancing women's self-reliance and, thereby, a much weaker effect on fertility reduction than it would in contexts without such strong constraints. It may take considerably greater amounts of education in settings with such constraints before women overcome these cultural barriers and gain self-reliance or control over resources. The possibility is that the pre-existing kinship structure will influence the pace at which education can set off changes in the situation of women, in the intervening variables, and in fertility itself.

Notes

1. B. Berelson, 'Beyond Family Planning', *Studies in Family Planning*, 38 (1969), 1–16.
2. S. H. Cochrane, *Fertility and Education: What Do We Really Know?* (Baltimore and London, The Johns Hopkins University Press, 1979) and 'Effects of Education and Urbanization on Fertility', in R. A. Bulatao and R. D. Lee (eds.), *Determinants of Fertility in Developing Countries*, ii (New York, Academic Press, 1983); and United Nations, *Fertility Behaviour in the Context of Development: Evidence from the World Fertility Survey*, Population Studies No. 100 (New York, Department of International Economic and Social Affairs, United Nations, 1987).
3. Cochrane, *Fertility and Education*.
4. K. O. Mason, *The Status of Women: A Review of Its Relationships to Fertility and Mortality* (New York, The Rockefeller Foundation, 1984) and 'The Impact of Women's Position on Demographic Change During the Course of Development: What Do We Know?', in Nora Federici, Karen Oppenheim Mason, and Solvi Sogner (eds.) *Women's Position and Demographic Change* (Oxford, Oxford University Press, 1993).

5. J. C. Caldwell, 'Mass Education as a Determinant of the Timing of Fertility Decline', in J. C. Caldwell (ed.), *Theory of Fertility Decline* (London, Academic Press, 1982).

6. See, for example, United Nations, *Fertility Behaviour*; J. Cleland and G. Rodriguez, 'The Effect of Parental Education on Marital Fertility in Developing Countries', *Population Studies*, 42 (1988), 419–42; and G. Rodriguez and R. Aravena, 'Socio-economic Factors and the Transition to Low Fertility in Less Developed Countries: A Comparative Analysis', paper presented at the Demographic Health Surveys World Conference, Washington, DC, 5–7 Aug. 1991.

7. For example, a study in Bangladesh finds that the incomes and decision-making roles of rural women in vocational training programmes increased marginally, at best, compared with untrained women: 11 per cent of trained women compared with 5 per cent of untrained women participated in household decisions. M. A. Mabud, *Women's Development, Income and Fertility* (Dhaka, Bangladesh, Planning Commission, External Evaluation Unit, 1985).

8. Charles F. Westoff, R. G. Potter, Jr., and Philip C. Sagi, *The Third Child: A Study in the Prediction of Fertility* (Princeton, Princeton University Press, 1963).

9. M. Bailey, 'Differential Fertility by Religious Group in Rural Sierra Leone', *Journal of Biosocial Science*, 18 (1986), 75–85.

10. See, for example, Israel S. L. Sembajwe, *Fertility and Infant Mortality Amongst the Yoruba in Western Nigeria* (Canberra, Australian National University Press, 1981); and United Nations, *Socio-economic Differentials in Child Mortality in Developing Countries* (New York, Department of International Economic and Social Affairs, United Nations, 1985).

11. J. C. Caldwell, 'Mass Education'; and J. Cleland, 'Maternal Education and Child Survival: Further Evidence and Explanations', in J. Caldwell *et al.* (eds.), *What We Know About Health Transition: The Cultural, Social and Behavioural Determinants of Health* (Canberra, The Health Transition Centre, The Australian National University, 1990).

12. An excellent detailed treatment of women's education is provided in E. M. King and M. A. Hill (eds.), *Women's Education in Developing Countries: Barriers, Benefits and Policy* (Washington, DC, The World Bank, Education and Employment Division, Population and Human Resources Department, 1991).

13. For measures of educational attainment, any international comparison of educational data must rely on such measures as literacy rates and enrolment ratios, both of which provide a limited picture of general educational attainment. Frequently, literacy is interpreted as no more than the ability to write one's name, and the enrolment ratio does not necessarily measure attendance in schools and exposure to the school curriculum. One source of meaningful data on educational attainment, providing gender-specific data on mean years of schooling among adults (aged 25 and above) in many developing countries, is the United Nations Development Programme, *Human Development Report 1993* (Oxford and New Delhi, Oxford University Press, 1993).

14. Primary-school enrolment ratios between 1960 and the late 1980s in 74 countries for which data are available at both points in time show impressive increases for both boys (from 73 to 100) and girls (from 45 to 83), accompanied by a narrowing of gender disparities in enrolment. Nevertheless, the enrolment ratios of girls remain much lower than those of boys. See United Nations Children's Fund, *The State of the World's Children, 1992* (Oxford, Oxford University Press, 1992).

15. King and Hill (eds.), *Women's Education*.

16. United Nations Children's Fund, *The State of the World's Children*.

17. Mason, *Status of Women* and 'Impact of Women's Position'; J. D. Kasarda, J. O. Billy, and K. West, *Status Enhancement and Fertility: Reproductive Responses to Social Mobility and Educational Opportunity* (New York, Academic Press, 1986); and A. C. Smock, *Women's Education in Developing Countries: Opportunities and Outcomes* (New York, Praeger Publishers, 1981).
18. Tim Dyson and Mick Moore, 'On Kinship Structure, Female Autonomy and Demographic Behaviour in India', *Population and Development Review*, 9 (March 1983), 35–60.
19. A. R. Radcliffe-Brown, *Structure and Function in Primitive Society* (London, Cohen and West, 1952), 22.
20. Mason, 'Impact of Women's Position'; and Cleland and Rodriguez, 'Effect of Parental Education'.
21. Dyson and Moore, 'On Kinship Structure'. On the basis of such measures as the extent of son preference and gender disparities in infant mortality, levels of women's economic activity and literacy, and the extent of women's seclusion, Dyson and Moore show that women in northern India assume subservient, secluded, and dependent roles both within the family and outside it. In contrast, in the south, which is characterized by more egalitarian gender relations, women play a more decisive role within the family and outside it. Correspondingly, fertility has remained high in the north but has fallen considerably in the south.
22. John Knodel, Aphichat Chamratrithirong, and N. Debavalya, *Thailand's Reproductive Revolution* (Madison, Wisc., University of Wisconsin Press, 1987).
23. M. M. Kritz and D. T. Gurak, 'Women's Status, Education and Family Formation in Sub-Saharan Africa', *International Family Planning Perspectives*, 15/3 (Sept. 1989), 100–5.
24. Richard A. Easterlin, 'The Economics and Sociology of Fertility: A Synthesis', in Charles Tilly (ed.), *Historical Studies of Changing Fertility* (Princeton, Princeton University Press, 1978); Richard A. Easterlin and Eileen M. Crimmins, *The Fertility Revolution: A Supply-Demand Analysis* (Chicago, University of Chicago Press, 1985); and Bulatao and Lee (eds.), *Determinants*, i.
25. L. Henry, 'Some Data on Natural Fertility', *Eugenics Quarterly*, 8/1 (1961), 81–91.
26. United Nations, *Fertility Behaviour*.
27. M. Cain, 'Perspectives on Family and Fertility in Developing Countries', *Population Studies*, 36/2 (July 1982), 159–75.
28. See, for example, Samuel H. Preston, 'Introduction', and A. K. M. Alauddin Chowdhury, Atiqur Rahman Khan, and Lincoln C. Chen, 'Experience in Pakistan and Bangladesh', in Samuel H. Preston (ed.), *The Effects of Infant and Child Mortality on Fertility* (New York, Academic Press, 1978).

2 Women's Education and Fertility: The Direct Relationship

The evidence suggests seven major points of interest concerning the direct relationship between women's education and fertility:
- In the early stages of a country's development, as measured by income and literacy levels, and in settings with wide gender disparities in literacy, a small amount of education may increase fertility. Any negative effect education has on fertility is likely to be negligible;
- An inverse relationship is observed largely in countries with higher levels of development and more egalitarian settings;
- In most societies, there appears to be a threshold level of education beyond which marked differentials in fertility are generated; the highest thresholds exist in the least developed societies and those in which gender disparities in literacy levels are widest; only among more developed and egalitarian societies do the thresholds possibly drop to zero years of schooling. Correspondingly, the level of education at which fertility is highest falls systematically with improvements in income, literacy, and gender disparities in literacy;
- Differentials between the least and most educated women become progressively wider with improvements in income and literacy levels and the narrowing of gender disparities in literacy;
- The relationship between education and fertility is dynamic, changing its shape over time from curvilinear to inverse and from sharply inverse to moderately inverse;
- Even within countries, the shape of the relationship is not uniformly inverse, being more inverse in better developed and urban areas;
- The impact of women's education on fertility is usually stronger than that of men's education or household socio-economic characteristics.

What accounts for these different patterns, these variations in shape and thresholds, over time and place? The thesis to be advanced here is that such contextual factors as overall level of development and the extent to which the society is male-dominated can condition the effect that small amounts of education have on women's lives, including their reproductive behaviour. Hence, in highly gender-stratified or poorly developed settings, a small amount of education may be ineffectual in changing women's age at marriage, family-size preferences, or contraceptive behaviour. In more egalitarian and more developed settings, even small amounts of education may be sufficient to trigger changes in these fertility-inhibiting proximate determinants of fertility.

The expected inverse relationship of women's education to fertility is found only in certain settings. Its shape varies over time, level of development, region of the world and culture. Although the relationship of women's education to fertility is almost always inverse at the highest end of the educational scale—that is, women with some secondary or higher education have fewer children than do other women—few generalizations can be drawn about how modest exposure to formal education— particularly a lower primary education—affects women's fertility. To explain this, one must look at how education affects the situation of women in diverse cultures and settings in developing countries.

The Pattern for Individual Women

This chapter focuses on the relationship of education to fertility, analysed on the basis of studies of households and individuals rather than aggregate studies of developing countries as a whole. The latter tend to obscure variations that may be important to policy-makers (see Box 2.1). Most of the studies reviewed here were published in the 1980s and refer to the period since about 1970. The studies document for married women at the close of their reproductive years—generally 40 to 44 or 49 years—the relationship of their education to their fertility, that is, to the total number of children they bore.[1]

Shapes of relationships

The diagrams in Figure 2.1 illustrate a few of the statistical relationships found in the surveys reviewed. In addition to inverse—that is, negative—relationships between education and fertility, there are also positive relationships (in which fertility increases systematically—by 5 per cent or more—with education), no (or zero-effect) relationships, and a variety of curvilinear relationships.

Box 2.1.   *Relationship of female literacy and school enrolment to fertility indicators in developing countries as a whole*

For developing countries as a whole, data clearly indicate that the relationship between women's education and their fertility is inverse. The more literate or educated a country is, the lower its fertility level tends to be. Such findings have often formed the basis for statements on the universality of the effect of education on fertility. The danger is that aggregation may obscure considerable variations within countries. For individuals in many of the countries examined in Table 2.1, the relation of education to fertility is not as clearly inverse as it is on the global or even on the regional or state level. Hence, examining aggregate relationships between education and fertility may mislead policy-makers, who would be better informed by reviewing individual-level studies.

Table 2.1. *Relationship of female literacy and school enrolment to fertility-related indicators, for developing countries as a whole (Zero-order correlations)*

	Female literacy rate		Female enrolment ratio, 1989	
	1970	1990	Primary	Secondary
(Number of developing countries)	(100)	(100)	(100)	(100)
Crude birth rate	−0.6060*	−0.5939*	−0.6604*	−0.8030*
Total fertility rate	−0.6207*	−0.5815*	−0.5822*	−0.6990*
Age at marriage	0.5079*	0.5886*	0.5798*	0.6337*
Infant mortality rate	−0.5512*	−0.6780*	−0.7547*	−0.8174*
Couple protection rate	0.3759*	0.3553*	0.3573*	0.4975*

* Correlation is significant at the .001 level.

Notes: The couple protection rate is defined as the proportion of eligible couples (with the women aged 15–49) who use a non-terminal method of contraception or one of whom has been sterilized. The zero-order correlations above show the extent to which change in one variable is associated with change in another. The range is from zero (0), which indicates no association between the variables, to plus or minus 1.0, which indicates a perfect correlation. In a perfect correlation, an increase of 1 per cent in one variable is associated with a similar increase (or decrease) in the other. For example, the correlation of − 0.6060* in the 1970 column suggests that countries in which female literacy rates were high tended to have low crude birth rates, and vice versa. The negative sign indicates an inverse relationship—the higher the level of literacy, the lower the crude birth rate. The zero-order aggregate correlations between educational and fertility measures in these developing countries are strong and significantly negative at both dates.

Sources: The correlations have been computed by the author from data in United Nations, *The World's Women 1970–1990: Trends and Statistics* (New York, 1991); United Nations Children's Fund, *The State of the World's Children, 1992* (Oxford, Oxford University Press, 1992); United Nations Development Programme, *Human Development Report* (New York, UNDP, 1993); and United Nations Educational, Scientific and Cultural Organization, *Statistical Yearbook 1990* (Paris, UNESCO, 1991).

The usually expected inverse relationship (see Figure 2.1) is defined here as a pattern in which fertility falls by 5 per cent or more among women with both a moderate and a secondary-school education compared with uneducated women.

Curvilinear relationships are of several types, among them the following:

- The 'reversed-U' pattern, in which women with a small amount of education have peak fertility rates, higher—by 5 per cent or more—than those of uneducated women, but women with further amounts of education experience a uniform drop—by 5 per cent or more—in fertility. Highly educated women and uneducated women end up with similar fertility levels;
- The 'reversed-J' relationship, in which highly educated women end up with lower fertility than uneducated women. The 'reversed-J' and the less commonly observed 'reversed-U' shapes are similar in that, in both, the least and the best educated women report lower fertility levels than women with moderate levels of education;
- The '7-shaped relationship', in which primary-schooled and uneducated women have almost identical (less than 5 per cent difference) levels of fertility, followed by a more sustained decline among better educated women.

Clearly, differences between the most commonly observed shapes as described above hinge on the relative fertility of women with a small amount of education,

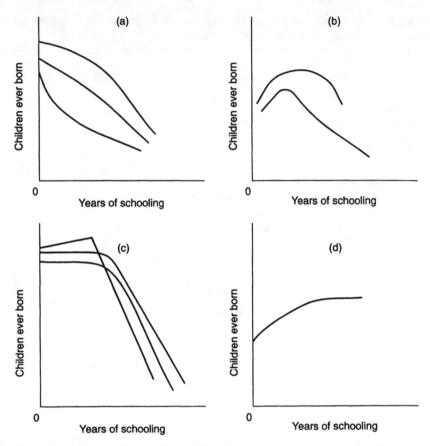

Fig. 2.1 *Illustrative patterns in the relationship between women's education and the number of children ever born: (a) Inverse relationships; (b) Curvilinear: Reversed-U and reversed-J relationships; (c) 7-shaped relationships; (d) Positive relationships*

usually those with primary schooling. This focus is justified for two reasons. First, any ambiguity in the relationship of women's education to fertility occurs largely as a result of the fertility of this group. Second, as literacy levels increase, increasing proportions of women in the developing world will have small amounts of education; their fertility behaviour will, therefore, have an important impact on overall fertility levels and trends.

Overall findings

Table 2.2 summarizes the patterns in the relationship of education to fertility in 59 developing countries listed in Appendix A. For countries represented more than once in Appendix A, only results from the most recent survey are included in Table 2.2.[2]

Table 2.2. *Patterns in the relationship of women's education to the total number of children ever born, by region, level of development, and gender disparity in literacy*

	Patterns in the relationship between years of schooling and total number of children ever born[a]				Total number of studies
	Inverse (negative)	Reversed U or reversed J	7	None/ positive	
A. Region[b]					
Sub-Saharan Africa	1	8	6	6	21
North Africa and the Middle East	5	1	2	0	8
East and South-East Asia	3	2	2	0	7
South Asia	4	1	0	0	5
Latin America and the Caribbean	13	1	3	1	18
B. Level of development					
1. Annual per capita income ($)					
500 or less	8	7	3	4	22
501–999	6	5	3	2	16
1000 or more	12	1	7	1	21
2. Overall female literacy rate (%)					
40 or less	8	7	2	5	22
41–80	9	5	8	1	23
81 or more	9	1	3	1	14
C. Gender disparity in literacy[c]					
250–700	8	6	3	5	22
701–850	3	5	7	1	16
851 or more	15	2	3	1	21
TOTALS	26	13	13	7	59

[a] Four patterns in the relationship of fertility to years of schooling are apparent: the inverse relationship is the usually expected one in which better educated women have progressively fewer children (by 5 per cent or more) than uneducated and moderately educated women do; the reversed-U or reversed-J relationship indicates that moderately educated women have more children (by 5 per cent or more) than uneducated women do, whereas better educated women have about as many (within 5 per cent) or fewer (by 5 per cent or more) than uneducated women do, respectively; the 7-shaped relationship indicates that moderately educated women have about as many children as uneducated women (within 5 per cent); and the positive relationship indicates that better educated women have progressively more children (by 5 per cent or more) than uneducated and moderately educated women do.

[b] Not all countries in a region are included, and those included are not necessarily representative of the region but are, rather, those countries for which the requisite data are available. Thus, the results are not necessarily representative of any particular region.

[c] The level of gender disparity in literacy is the number of literate females per 1000 literate males.

Notes: The studies selected for inclusion in this table appear in Appendix A, where they are marked with a dagger (†). For this table, the author examined sub-samples of the study populations of women in the age groups 40–44 or 40–49 years; the women were married or in union. Fertility is represented by the total number of children ever born to women in the sub-sample.

Sources: Of the 59 studies, 50 are based on World Fertility Survey (18) and Demographic and Health Survey (32) data, from United Nations, *Fertility Behaviour in the Context of Development: Evidence from the World Fertility Survey* (1987) or *Women's Education and Fertility Behaviour: Recent Evidence from the Demographic and Health Surveys* (1995), or other DHS reports. Sources are indicated in Appendix A.

The inverse relationship between women's education and fertility is less common than is often asserted.

- Of the 59 studies, fewer than half (26) find a straight inverse relationship between education and fertility;
- 13 studies find that women with a small amount of education bear more children than do either uneducated or more educated women (reversed-U or reversed-J shape);
- 13 studies find that uneducated women and those with a small amount of education have the same number of children, and women with more education have fewer;
- 7 studies find a positive or no relationship between women's education and fertility.

Such contextual factors as region; level of development, as indicated by per capita income and female literacy levels; and gender disparities in literacy, that is, the number of literate women per 1000 literate men, may condition the relationship of education to fertility. Although the inverse relationship is the most commonly observed pattern for all levels of income, literacy, and gender disparities in literacy, curvilinear and zero relationships predominate in the least developed settings and in settings with the widest gender disparities in literacy. Curvilinear and 7-shaped relationships predominate in more 'moderate' contexts, and straight inverse relationships predominate in the most developed and egalitarian contexts.

Region   Distinct variations are observed by region, which may well be related to the level of development. Studies in Latin America and the Caribbean, the most developed region under review, are the most likely to report inverse relationships:[3]

- Of the 18 Latin American and Caribbean studies, 13 report an inverse relationship;
- In contrast, only 1 of the 21 sub-Saharan African studies reports an inverse relationship.

Level of development   For all levels of income and literacy, the inverse relationship is the most commonly observed pattern. In the least developed settings, however, combinations of curvilinear and zero-effect relationships predominate.

In less developed societies—that is, societies with low per capita incomes and low literacy rates—the education-fertility relationship is least likely to be consistently inverse. In these settings, a small amount of education appears to lead to higher fertility or no change in fertility, and the typical relationship is reversed-U or 7-shaped.

- Studies in countries with per capita incomes of $999 (unless otherwise indicated, all dollar figures are US dollars) or below are more likely to exhibit curvilinear or irregular relationships than inverse relationships, whereas more than half (12 of 21) in countries with per capita incomes of $1000 or more showed inverse relationships;[4]
- Similarly, in the least literate societies, a small amount of education appears to

lead to higher fertility or no change in fertility[5] (the typical relationship is in the shape of a reversed U, reversed J, or 7). For example, 14 of the studies in settings where female literacy is low show a non-inverse relationship: 7 of these are reversed-U- or reversed-J-shaped, 2 are 7-shaped, and 5 are unrelated or positively related;

• In contrast, in highly literate settings (more than 80 per cent literate), an inverse relationship is observed in the majority of studies (9 of 14).

Gender disparities in literacy   Only in the most egalitarian settings (more than 850 literate women per 1000 literate men) is the inverse relationship the norm, observed in 15 of the 21 studies.

In short, there is the suggestion of a marked shift in the pattern of the relationship from non-inverse to inverse as income and literacy levels rise and as gender disparities in literacy narrow.

Differentials in fertility

Differences in the fertility of women with some secondary schooling—the highest level of education covered in this review—and women with no education are, in many cases, modest (Table 2.3).

• In only 23 of the 59 studies reported in Table 2.3 are there substantial differences of more than 40 per cent in the fertility of uneducated compared with the most educated women—i.e. women with some secondary education. In another 24, the differential is moderate (11–40 per cent);

• At the other extreme, in 12 of the 59 countries, the differential is marginal—10 per cent or less.

Differentials in fertility between the most and the least educated women tend to widen in more developed regions, in settings that are more developed and that have narrower gender disparities in literacy (Table 2.3).

Region   The variations observed by region may be related to level of development. In Latin America and the Caribbean, the most developed region under review, studies were more likely to report inverse relationships and wide differentials. Differentials were the narrowest in sub-Saharan Africa, and were more moderate in other regions.

• In 16 of 18 studies conducted in Latin America and the Caribbean, differentials between uneducated and secondary-schooled women exceed 40 per cent;

• In sub-Saharan Africa, the differentials in fertility between uneducated women and those with some secondary schooling never exceed 40 per cent. Moreover, 10 show differentials of 10 per cent or less.

Level of development   As the level of per capita income increases, differentials in fertility between the most and least educated women tend to widen.

• In 15 of 21 settings in high-income settings ($1000 or more), the fertility of the

Table 2.3.   *Differentials in the relationship of women's education to the total number of children ever born, by region, level of development, and gender disparity in literacy*

	Differences in fertility between uneducated and secondary-schooled women[a] (percentage differentials) NARROW ◄-----------------------► WIDE						Total number of studies
	10 or less	11–20	21–30	31–40	41–50	51 or more	
A. *Region*[b]							
Sub-Saharan Africa	10	5	4	2	0	0	21
North Africa and the Middle East	0	1	1	2	4	0	8
East and South-East Asia	0	2	1	1	1	2	7
South Asia	1	0	0	4	0	0	5
Latin America and the Caribbean	1	0	1	0	8	8	18
B. *Level of development*							
1. Annual per capita income ($)							
500 or less	8	3	4	5	1	1	22
501–999	3	3	2	2	3	3	16
1000 or more	1	2	1	2	9	6	21
2. Overall female literacy rate (%)							
40 or less	10	2	2	6	2	0	22
41–80	1	6	2	1	9	4	23
81 or more	1	0	3	2	2	6	14
C. *Gender disparity in literacy*[c]							
250–700	9	2	2	6	3	0	22
701–850	2	5	2	1	4	2	16
851 or more	1	1	3	2	6	8	21
TOTALS	12	8	7	9	13	10	59

[a] The term 'secondary-schooled women' here applies to women who have had some secondary education or completed or gone beyond secondary school—that is, women who have had more than six years of primary education.

[b] Not all countries in a region are included, and those included are not necessarily representative of the region but are, rather, those countries for which the requisite data are available. Thus, the results are not necessarily representative of any particular region.

[c] The level of gender disparity in literacy is the number of literate females per 1000 literate males.

Notes: The studies selected for inclusion in this table appear in Appendix A, where they are marked with a dagger (†). For this table, the author examined sub-samples of the study populations of women in the age groups 40–44 or 40–49 years; the women were married or in union. Fertility is represented by the total number of children ever born to women in the sub-sample.

Sources: Of the 59 studies, 50 are based on World Fertility Survey (18) and Demographic and Health Survey (32) data, from United Nations, *Fertility Behaviour in the Context of Development: Evidence from the World Fertility Survey* (1987) or *Women's Education and Fertility Behaviour: Recent Evidence from the Demographic and Health Surveys* (1995), or other DHS reports. Sources are indicated in Appendix A.

most educated women is more than 40 per cent below that of uneducated women.

Similarly, as literacy increases, the difference in fertility between uneducated women and the most educated women tends to widen:

- In 21 of 37 studies from countries in which female literacy rates are 41 per cent or more, differentials in fertility exceed 40 per cent;

- Differentials in fertility also exceed 40 per cent in 8 of the 14 countries in which female literacy rates are 81 per cent or more.

Gender disparity in literacy   Where disparities between genders in the level of literacy are wide, fertility differentials by education are marginal:
- In 9 of 22 studies in areas of great gender disparity, there are fertility differentials of 10 per cent or less;
- As settings become more egalitarian in terms of literacy, differentials widen: in 6 of the 16 moderately egalitarian settings and 14 of the 21 most egalitarian settings, the fertility of the most educated women is more than 40 per cent of that experienced by uneducated women.

Thresholds

One idea in explaining the process of demographic transition holds that improving economic and social conditions is unlikely to have much effect on high fertility until economic and social thresholds have been reached. Once those thresholds have been reached, fertility is likely to enter a decided decline.[6] The relationships of women's education to fertility found in many countries suggest, similarly, that a threshold level of education may be required before fertility declines are perceptible and sustained. Similarly, these educational thresholds may vary by level of development, region, or culture.

Education sets off changes in a variety of proximate determinants of fertility — some that enhance fertility and others that depress it. The actual number of children ever born to a woman is the net effect of these opposing forces. That uneducated women and women with small amounts of education have similar fertility levels in some settings does not necessarily mean that education has had no effect on fertility behaviour. A common finding is that modestly educated women may practise contraception for longer periods than uneducated women do; at the same time, following the birth of a child, they may experience significantly shorter periods in which they are unable to become pregnant as a result of shorter periods of breast-feeding and post-partum abstinence. The effect of increased contraception is fertility-inhibiting, whereas the effect of shorter periods of breast-feeding and post-partum abstinence is fertility-enhancing. The net result of these opposing effects is that modestly educated women continue to bear as many children as uneducated women. It is only after a threshold level of education is attained that the fertility-depressing effect exceeds the fertility-enhancing one and the net effect of women's education on fertility becomes uniformly inverse.

How much education, or what threshold level of education, would be required before modest (10 per cent) and substantial (20 per cent) fertility declines are attained?[7] Many studies in Table 2.2 show reversed-U and 7-shaped relationships. This suggests that a small amount of education may have no effect on reducing fertility. Table 2.4 shows the level of education by which 10 and 20 per cent declines in fertility are attained in the 59 studies reviewed.

Table 2.4. *Relationship of the duration of women's education to the total number of children ever born, by region, level of development, and gender disparity in literacy*

| | Fertility is highest at: | | | Educational level (years of schooling) by which: | | | | | | | | Total number of studies |
| | | | | A 10% fertility reduction is reached | | | | A 20% fertility reduction is reached | | | | |
	0 years	1–3 years	4–6 years	1–3	4–6	7+	Never	1–3	4–6	7+	Never	
A. Region [a]												
Sub-Saharan Africa	5	7	9	0	2	9	10	0	0	9	12	21
North Africa and the Middle East	5	2	1	2	4	2	0	1	0	7	0	8
East and South-East Asia	4	2	1	2	2	3	0	1	1	3	2	7
South Asia	4	1	0	0	2	2	1	0	0	4	1	5
Latin America and the Caribbean	16	1	1	12	5	0	1	0	13	4	1	18
B. Level of development												
1. Annual per capita income ($)												
500 or less	9	8	5	2	4	8	8	1	0	12	9	22
501–999	8	3	5	4	4	5	3	0	4	6	6	16
1000 or more	17	2	2	10	7	3	1	1	10	9	1	21
2. Overall female literacy rate (%)												
40 or less	10	4	8	1	4	7	10	0	0	11	11	22
41–80	13	7	3	8	7	7	1	2	7	10	4	23
81 or more	11	2	1	7	4	2	1	0	7	6	1	14
C. Gender disparity in literacy [b]												
250–700	10	4	8	1	5	7	9	0	0	12	10	22
701–850	7	7	2	3	5	6	2	2	1	9	4	16
851 or more	17	2	2	12	5	3	1	0	13	6	2	21
TOTALS	34	13	12	16	15	16	12	2	14	27	16	59

[a] Not all countries in a region are included, and those included are not necessarily representative of the region but are, rather, those countries for which the requisite data were available. Thus, the results are not necessarily representative of any particular region.

[b] The level of gender disparity in literacy is the number of literate females per 1000 literate males.

Notes: The studies selected for inclusion in this table appear in Appendix A, where they are marked with a dagger (†). For this table, the author examined sub-samples of the study populations of women in the age groups 40–4 or 40–9 years; the women were married or in union. Fertility is represented by the total number of children ever born to women in the sub-sample. Some appendix studies combine rates for women with 1–3 and 4–6 years of schooling; in such studies, rates are shown in the column marked 1–3.

Sources: Of the 59 studies, 50 are based on World Fertility Survey (18) and Demographic and Health Survey (32) data, from United Nations, *Fertility Behaviour in the Context of Development: Evidence from the World Fertility Survey* (1987) or *Women's Education and Fertility Behaviour: Recent Evidence from the Demographic and Health Surveys* (1995), or other DHS reports. Sources are indicated in Appendix A.

On the whole, the highest fertility is observed among uneducated women in more than half (34) of the 59 studies. Despite this, the results suggest the existence of thresholds, even in the attainment of a 10 per cent decline in fertility. In the majority of studies, a moderate (10 per cent) decline in fertility is observed once an upper primary education has been attained. In about half (27) of all countries, a 20 per cent decline is achieved only after at least seven years of schooling. (In 16 more, a differential of this proportion is never attained.)

Threshold levels of education also appear to vary by such contextual factors as region, level of development, and gender disparities in literacy.

Region Smaller amounts of education appear to be needed to set off perceptible changes in fertility in Latin America and the Caribbean than in other regions. For example, a 10 per cent decline in fertility occurs at 1–3 years of schooling in two out of three of the Latin American and Caribbean countries in this review. In contrast, for the majority of countries in North Africa and the Middle East and East and South-East Asia, a 10 per cent decline occurs among the majority with 1–3 years of schooling, or with 4–6 years of schooling. It occurs for the majority in South Asia with 4–6 or 7+ years of schooling and in sub-Saharan Africa only at 7 or more years of schooling or not at all. Also, although fertility declines of 20 per cent occur among women with 4–6 years of schooling in most Latin American and Caribbean countries, such declines take place only at 7 or more years, or not at all, in the majority of countries in every other region.

Level of development and gender disparities The threshold levels of education needed to achieve fertility declines of 10 per cent or 20 per cent appear to be higher in regions characterized by low levels of income and literacy and in less egalitarian settings (in terms of literacy). In poor, illiterate, and inegalitarian settings, it appears to take more education before a sustained decline in fertility occurs than in richer, more literate, and egalitarian settings.

- In the poorest countries, in almost three in four cases (16 of 22), a 10 per cent decline in fertility is attained only among secondary-schooled women or not at all;
- In contrast, in half the cases in high-income countries (10 of 21), women with 1–3 years of schooling attain a 10 per cent decline in fertility;
- The more literate the setting, the lower is the threshold of education. In low-literacy settings, a 10 per cent decline is achieved in the majority of countries either by the secondary-school level or not at all (17 of 22 studies); in moderately literate settings, thresholds have fallen somewhat, to 1–3 or 4–6 years for a 10 per cent decline and to secondary schooling for a 20 per cent decline; and in high-literacy settings, a 10 per cent decline is achieved in the majority at 1–3 years of schooling;
- The pattern by level of gender disparities in literacy is especially convincing. Among the most inegalitarian settings, in three in four cases (16 of 22), a 10 per

cent decline in fertility is attained either only among women with some
secondary schooling or not at all;
- In moderately egalitarian settings, a 10 per cent decline is attained by women
  with some primary schooling in half the cases (8 of 16);
- In the most egalitarian settings, a 10 per cent decline is attained by women with
  1–3 years of schooling in more than half the cases (12 of 21).

Implications

These results suggest a transition dependent upon development and gender equity in
the relationship of women's education to fertility. In the least developed and most
inegalitarian settings, women require a considerable amount of education before
fertility declines noticeably. As income and education levels improve, and as gender
disparities narrow, threshold levels fall. After a certain level of development, the
threshold drops to zero, and each incremental level of education has a sizeable
impact on fertility.

The finding that the level of education at which fertility is highest falls
systematically with improvements in income, female literacy, and gender disparities
suggests the conditioning effect of context on thresholds. High thresholds are seen
in such settings as sub-Saharan Africa and South Asia, suggesting the hypothesis
that the extent to which a setting is gender-stratified, rather like the level of overall
development, may condition the pace at which increments in education lead to lower
fertility. Where gender stratification is especially strong and gender disparities
especially wide, a considerable amount of education (middle or secondary, for
example) may be required before women are motivated or enabled to reduce fertility
or have a say in their reproductive behaviour. In other, more equal settings, even a
few years of education can have the effect of depressing fertility.

Changes over time

The shape of the relationship between women's education and fertility, as with the
level of development, appears to evolve systematically from positive, curvilinear, or
zero relationships to progressively more sharply inverse relationships, followed
finally by a weakening of the inverse relationship. At early points in time, there is a
strong likelihood of non-inverse relationships. Over time, straight inverse relationships become evident: the more educated women have fewer children. Presumably,
this occurs as fertility-depressing mechanisms, such as increased contraception, later
age at marriage, and the desire for smaller family size, gain importance in influencing the fertility of moderately and highly educated women.[8]

Table 2.5 presents data on the relationship between education and fertility from
20 countries for which comparable data are available at two points in time,
approximately 10 years apart. There are 7 such cases for Latin America and the
Caribbean, 7 for Africa, and 6 for Asia. For the most part, these cases are drawn
from the WFS and DHS results reported in Appendix A.

By and large, the experience of the 20 countries shown in Table 2.5 supports the proposition that the relationship between women's education and fertility changes over time[9] and, specifically, that it shifts from non-inverse to inverse.

- In 6 settings, the relationship remains non-inverse at both times;
- In 4 others, it remains inverse at both times;
- In the remaining 10 (4 in Latin America and the Caribbean, 3 in Asia, and 3 in North Africa), it shifts from non-inverse to inverse.

That not a single country among the 20 shifts from an inverse relationship back to a non-inverse one suggests that, once the relationship of education to fertility becomes truly inverse, there is little chance of this trend's reversing. In such settings, even a small amount of education will lead to a decline in fertility.

Another interesting feature of the pattern over time is that in more than half the cases (13 of 20), the differentials in fertility between uneducated women and those with some secondary schooling widen over time; in 6 cases, they remain unchanged; and in only 1 case does the differential narrow. As the 20 countries included are not representative, it is difficult to make statements about the hypothesis that, at late stages of the fertility transition, the relationship of education will narrow once again. It does, however, underscore the point that few countries have reached this point in the transition as of the 1990s.

Within-country differentials

Within countries, the impact of women's education on fertility also tends to be more consistently inverse in better developed regions or urban areas than in less developed or rural areas.[10] For example, a study in Nigeria reports a positive association between education and fertility in the lesser developed northern region and an inverse relationship (after primary schooling) in the more developed south.[11] Similarly, in Kenya, where the overall relationship tends to be curvilinear, the relationship tends to be inverse in less agricultural areas. In more agricultural areas, women with a small amount of education experience higher fertility than do uneducated women, followed by uniformly lower levels of fertility among women with further amounts of education (a reversed-U shape).[12] A non-inverse relationship is observed in rural areas and an inverse one in urban areas in, for example, China in 1958–61, India in 1972 and 1981, Pakistan in 1979–80 and 1991, Ghana in 1970, and Egypt in 1976.[13] In Nigeria, there is evidence of this pattern from several states: Bendel in 1985 and Ondo and Oyo states in 1986 and 1990, respectively.[14] This is true not only for studies reported in Appendices A and B but also for those in other countries, for example, Sierra Leone.[15]

In contrast, in certain poorly developed settings, there are non-inverse relationships in both rural and urban areas: Kenya in 1977, Pakistan in 1972, the Philippines in 1968, and the Sudan in 1973.[16] Finally, in some settings, an inverse relationship is observed in both rural and urban areas: in China by 1979–82 and in Mexico.[17] Evidence from Peru suggests that community-level influences can play an important role in conditioning the education-fertility relationship. There, the impact is sharply

Table 2.5. *Relationship of women's education to the total number of children ever born, and changes over time, in selected countries*

Country[a]	Date		Patterns in the relationship between years of schooling and total number of children ever born				Change in differential between secondary-schooled and uneducated women over time[b]		
	Earlier study	Later study	At earlier date		At later date		Widened	Same	Narrowed
			Non-inverse	Inverse	Non-inverse	Inverse			
Sub-Saharan Africa									
Ghana	1979/80	1988	✓	—	✓	—	✓	—	—
Kenya	1977/78	1989	✓	—	✓	—	✓	—	—
Senegal	1978	1986	✓	—	✓	—	—	✓	—
North Africa									
Egypt	1980	1988	✓	—	—	✓	✓	—	—
Morocco	1979/80	1987	✓	—	—	✓	—	—	✓
Sudan	1978/79	1989–90	✓	—	—	✓	✓	✓	—
Tunisia	1978	1988	—	✓	—	✓	—	✓	—
Asia									
Bangladesh	1975/76	1989	✓	—	✓	—	✓	—	—
India	1980	1989	✓	—	—	✓	✓	—	—
Indonesia	1975/76	1991	✓	—	✓	—	—	✓	—
Pakistan	1975	1990–1	✓	—	—	✓	✓	—	—
Sri Lanka	1975	1987	—	✓	—	✓	✓	—	—
Thailand	1975	1987	✓	—	—	✓	✓	—	—
Latin America and the Caribbean									
Colombia	1976	1986	✓	—	—	✓	✓	—	—
Dominican Republic	1975	1986	✓	—	—	✓	✓	—	—
Ecuador	1979	1987	—	✓	✓	—	—	✓	—
Haiti	1977	1989	✓	—	—	✓	✓	—	—
Mexico	1976	1987	✓	—	—	✓	✓	—	—
Peru	1977/78	1986	—	✓	—	✓	—	✓	—
Trinidad and Tobago	1977	1987	✓	—	—	✓	✓	—	—

[a] Not all countries in a region are included, and those included are not necessarily representative of the region but are, rather, those countries for which the requisite data are available. Thus, the results are not necessarily representative of any particular region.

[b] These columns show the changes in the differential in fertility (as indicated by the total number of children ever born) of 'secondary-schooled' women compared with women with no education. The term 'secondary-schooled women' here applies to women who have had some secondary education or completed or gone beyond secondary school—that is, women who have had more than six years of primary education.

Notes: The studies selected for inclusion in this table appear in Appendix A. For this table, the author examined sub-samples of the study populations of women in the age groups 40–44 or 40–49 years; the women were married or in union. Fertility is represented by the total number of children ever born to women in the sub-sample.

Sources: For all countries above, except India, the source of the earlier data is United Nations, *Fertility Behaviour in the Context of Development: Evidence from the World Fertility Survey* (1987). For India, the source of the earlier data is M. E. Khan and C. V. S. Prasad, *Family Planning Practices in India: Second All India Survey* (Baroda, Operations Research Group, 1983).

For all countries above, except Bangladesh, Haiti, India, Pakistan, and the Sudan, the source of the later data is United Nations, *Women's Education and Fertility Behaviour: Recent Evidence from the Demographic and Health Surveys* (1995). The sources for other countries are as follows: for Bangladesh, M. N. Huq and John Cleland, *Bangladesh Fertility Survey 1989 Main Report* (Dhaka, National Institute of Population Research and Training, 1989); in Haiti, M. Cayemittes et al., *1989 Haiti National Contraceptive Prevalence Survey* (Atlanta, Ga., US Department of Health and Human Services, Public Health Service, Centers for Disease Control, Center for Chronic Disease Prevention and Health Promotion, Division of Reproductive Health, 1991); for India, Operations Research Group, *Family Planning Practices in India: Third All India Survey* (Baroda, Operations Research Group, 1990); for Pakistan, National Institute of Population Studies *Pakistan Demographic and Health Survey 1990–1991* (Columbia, Md., Macro International Inc., 1992); and for the Sudan, Ministry of Economic and National Planning, Department of Statistics, *Sudan Demographic and Health Survey 1989–90* (Columbia, Md., Macro International Inc., 1991).

inverse in areas with a high level of community development and education and is more gradual in areas with low community development and education.[18] In contrast, a study in Goa, India, finds an inverse relationship regardless of the community's level of education.[19]

In short, the pattern observed earlier in the cross-country and over-time comparisons is repeated in comparisons within countries. The relationship of education to fertility tends to shift from curvilinear or non-inverse in rural and less developed regions of countries to increasingly inverse in urban and more developed regions. One hypothesis explaining this differential is that, in urban and more developed regions, educated women have both more reproductive choices and more autonomy and better access to services.

Net Impact of Education on Fertility Levels

This discussion has assumed that the relationship between the amount of education women have and the number of children they bear is genuine and not a result of confounding factors, such as household economic status. The discussion has also implicitly assumed that the education of the wife has a more powerful influence on fertility than does the education of her husband. The validity of these assumptions can be assessed by reviewing multivariate analyses in a variety of settings.

The available evidence suggests that some of the effect of women's education on fertility undoubtedly occurs through other factors, such as family income, husband's occupation, and husband's education. For example, about half of all women and their husbands are at the same educational level.[20] This kind of close association makes it difficult to extricate their individual effects. Nevertheless, consistent evidence from studies that control for socio-economic variables, summarized in Appendix B, suggests that women's education influences fertility more powerfully than does either husband's education[21] or household socio-economic charac-teristics.[22] In 15 countries covered by WFS, the wife's education emerged as the most decisive influence, even after controlling for residence, husband's education, husband's and wife's occupations, marriage duration, and age at marriage.[23] This was also true in every single region, except the Caribbean, when controlling for husband's education and socio-economic status.[24]

A comparison of WFS and DHS data from 15 countries finds that, after adjust-ments are made for residence and husband's education, the average differential between extreme categories of female education was reduced from -2.7 to -1.6 children in the 1970s (WFS) and from -2.3 to -1.1 children in the 1980s (DHS). Nonetheless, the net effect of women's education on fertility remained strong and significant.[25]

All these studies typically conclude that when controls for rural-urban residence and for husband's education and occupation are introduced, the effect of women's education on their fertility typically halves. The theoretical implication is that the economic advantages associated with higher levels of education (as represented by husband's education) cannot account in entirety for the ·link between women's schooling and child-bearing, that it is women's education which has a unique net effect on reproductive behaviour, independently of their husbands' education or economic status.

The majority of multivariate studies finds inverse relationships between women's education and fertility, rather than the more complicated patterns observed in Appendix A and Table 2.2. This occurs because the educational specification of years of schooling does not allow for a non-linear relationship. If education were measured by way of dummy variables which allow for as much gradation as the studies reported in Table 2.2, it is likely that non-uniformly inverse relationships would emerge more often. Indeed, a few studies reported in Appendix B have done so and are able to shed light on the effect of a small amount of education on fertility, net of controls for socio-economic and demographic characteristics. These studies confirm the relationships observed earlier, that although highly educated women usually experience lower levels of fertility than uneducated women, the effect of a small amount of education tends to be ambiguous—negligible or even positive—in many developing countries, including Kenya, Malawi, Nigeria, and Sierra Leone, and in Tamil Nadu, India.[26]

Most multivariate studies argue that women's education exerts a strong negative effect on fertility even after household economic status and husband's characteristics are controlled. These findings are consistent with the idea that it is women's situation, knowledge, and attitudes towards child-rearing and towards children rather than their socio-economic status which influences reproductive behaviour most strongly.

Notes

1. Although an attempt has been made to include as wide a range of studies as possible, the majority of these studies relies on the data generated in the World Fertility Surveys, published in United Nations, *Fertility Behaviour*, in the more recent Demographic and Health Surveys, published in the United Nations analysis of DHS data *Women's Education and Fertility Behaviour: Recent Evidence from the Demographic and Health Surveys* (New York, United Nations, 1995), and in various DHS final reports. See Appendices A and B for a complete list of sources.
2. Ibid.
3. The regional patterns shown in the table agree with those found in the 1987 United Nations study *Fertility Behaviour*, in which a reversed-U-shaped relationship or no relationship is evident in 10 of 12 African countries, 7 of 12 Asian countries, and 2 of 13 Latin American countries.
4. This finding is similar to that observed by S. H. Cochrane in *Fertility and Education: What Do We Really Know?* (Baltimore and London, The Johns Hopkins University Press, 1979).
5. This finding was also observed in Cochrane's review, *Fertility and Education,* and in the United Nations study *Fertility Behaviour.*
6. Further, thresholds are not necessarily fixed; they can vary by culture and time. See United Nations, *The Determinants and Consequences of Population Trends* (New York, United Nations, 1973).

7. John Knodel and Etienne van de Walle, for example, defined the onset of fertility decline over time as the point at which, similarly, fertility declined by an estimated 10 per cent; see 'Lessons from the Past: Policy Implications of Historical Fertility Studies', *Population and Development Review*, 5/2 (1979), 217–45.

8. There is some evidence in the literature that, among countries at the end of the fertility transition, the inverse relationship tends to narrow once again. The reason is that, in these settings, low-fertility norms become diffused throughout the society, regardless of education. Few developing countries are, however, at this late stage of the transition.

9. Evidence of a shift over time comes also from a study of successive cross-sections of women in Tamil Nadu, India. Here, the effect of five years of education, compared with no education, was a marginally higher fertility at the earlier time (1970) and a reduction by more than half a child 10 years later. See S. J. Jejeebhoy, 'Women's Status and Fertility: Successive Cross-sectional Evidence from Tamil Nadu, India, 1970–80', *Studies in Family Planning*, 22/4 (July–Aug. 1991), 217–30.

10. Cochrane, *Fertility and Education*; and J. Holian, 'The Effect of Female Education on Marital Fertility in Different Size Communities of Mexico', *Social Biology*, 31/3–4 (1984), 298–307.

11. A. A. Adewuyi, 'Education and Fertility: The Nigerian Case', *Ife Social Sciences Review*, 9/1–2 (1986), 29–45.

12. An-Magritt Jensen and A. A. Khasakhala, 'Women, Family Planning and Child Mortality: Case Study of Selected Areas in Kenya, Western and Coast Provinces', in Alhassan Manu (ed.), *Health and Environment in Developing Countries, Proceedings from an International Workshop* (Oslo, Centre for Development and the Environment, Oslo University, 1992).

13. For China, see W. Lavely *et al.*, 'The Rise in Female Education in China: National and Regional Patterns', *The China Quarterly*, 121 (March 1990), 61–93; for India, see A. Jain and M. Nag, 'Importance of Female Primary Education for Fertility Reduction in India', *Economic and Political Weekly*, 21/36 (6 Sept. 1986), 1602–8; for Pakistan in 1979–80, see Zeba Sathar *et al.*, 'Women's Status and Fertility Change in Pakistan', *Population and Development Review*, 14/3 (Sept. 1988), 415–32, and in 1991, see Z. A. Sathar, 'Women's Status and Fertility in Pakistan: The Most Recent Evidence' (New York, United Nations Population Division, 1992); for Ghana, see Smock, *Women's Education*; and for Egypt, see H. Abou-Gamrah, 'Fertility Levels and Differentials by Mother's Education in Some Countries of the ECWA Region', in *Determinants of Fertility in Some African and Asian Countries*, Research Monograph Series No. 10 (Cairo, Cairo Demographic Centre, 1982).

14. For Bendel, see C. E. E. Okojie, 'Women's Status and Fertility in Bendel State of Nigeria', Center Discussion Paper No. 597 (New Haven, Economic Growth Center, Yale University, Feb. 1990); for Ondo and Oyo, see M. M. Kritz and D. T. Gurak, 'Women's Economic Independence and Fertility Among the Yoruba', paper presented at the Demographic and Health Surveys World Conference, Washington, DC, Aug. 1991.

15. N. Birdsall and S. H. Cochrane, 'Education and Parental Decision Making: A Two-Generation Approach', in L. Anderson and D. M. Windham (eds.), *Education and Development* (Lexington, Mass., D. C. Heath, 1982).

16. For Kenya, Pakistan, and the Philippines, see Smock, *Women's Education*; for the Sudan, see Birdsall and Cochrane, 'Education and Parental Decision-Making'.

17. For Mexico, see Rosa Maria Cordova, 'Instituciones sociales y reproduccion' (Mexico,

Centro de Estudios Demograficos y de Desarrollo Urbano de El Colegio de Mexico, 1991); for China, see W. Lavely *et al.*, 'Rise in Female Education in China'.

18. M. Tienda, 'Community Characteristics, Women's Education and Fertility in Peru', *Studies in Family Planning*, 15/4 (July–Aug. 1984), 162–9.

19. T. K. Roy, G. Rama Rao, and Rajiva Prasad, 'Education, Fertility and Contraception Among Hindus and Roman Catholics in Goa', *Journal of Biosocial Science*, 23 (1991), 353–8.

20. The United Nations study of WFS data (*Fertility Behaviour*) finds, for example, a correlation coefficient of 0.57 between the number of years of schooling the woman and her husband have had.

21. United Nations, *Fertility Behaviour*; Cochrane, *Fertility and Education*; Cochrane, 'Effects of Education'; and G. Rodriguez and J. Cleland, 'Socio-economic Determinants of Marital Fertility in Twenty Countries: A Multivariate Analysis', *World Fertility Survey Conference, Record of Proceedings*, ii (London, World Fertility Survey, 1980); Cleland and Rodriguez, 'Effect of Parental Education'; and L. Zanamwe, 'The Relationship Between Fertility and Child Mortality in Zimbabwe', in *Proceedings of the African Population Conference, Dakar, Senegal*, 7–12 November 1988, ii (Liège, IUSSP, 1988).

22. United Nations, *Fertility Behaviour*; and R. A. LeVine *et al.*, 'Women's Schooling and Child Care in the Demographic Transition: A Mexican Case Study', *Population and Development Review*, 17/3 (Sept. 1991), 459–96.

23. United Nations, *Fertility Behaviour*; and M. B. Weinberger, 'The Relationship Between Women's Education and Fertility: Selected Findings from the World Fertility Surveys', *International Family Planning Perspectives*, 13/2 (June 1987), 35–46.

24. Cleland and Rodriguez, 'Effect of Parental Education'.

25. Rodriguez and Aravena, 'Socio-economic Factors'.

26. For Kenya, see R. Anker, 'Problems of Interpretation and Specification in Analysing Fertility Differentials: Illustrated with Kenyan Survey Data', in G. M. Farooq and G. B. Simmons (eds.), *Fertility in Developing Countries: An Economic Perspective on Research and Policy Issues* (Geneva, International Labour Office, 1985), and E. U. Emereuwaonu, 'Determinants of Fertility: A Regression Analysis of Kenya Data', *Genus*, 40/3–4 (July–Dec.), 77–96; for Malawi, see W. R. M. M'Mange and M. L. Srivastava, 'Socio Economic and Demographic Determinants of Family Size in Malawi: A Multivariate Analysis' (University of Malawi, Chancellor College, Demographic Unit, Oct. 1990); for Nigeria, see B. J. Feyisetan and O. Togunde, 'Fertility and Indices of Women's Status: A Study of Relationships in Nigeria', *Genus*, 44/1–2 (Jan.–June 1988), 229–46, and B. J. Feyisetan and A. Bankole, 'Mate Selection and Fertility in Urban Nigeria', *Journal of Comparative Family Studies*, 22/3 (Autumn 1991), 273–92; for Sierra Leone, see M. Bailey, 'Differential Fertility'; and for Tamil Nadu, see Jejeebhoy, 'Women's Status and Fertility'.

3 Education and Women's Autonomy

The literature supports the hypotheses that education enhances women's knowledge, decision-making power, confidence in interacting with the outside world, closeness to husband and children, and economic and social self-reliance. These effects of education are, however, by no means uniform across regions, cultures, or levels of development. Uneducated women often have relatively little autonomy, and highly educated women tend to have the most. What happens in between varies by culture and the extent of gender stratification. In other words, the norms of patriarchy play an important role in conditioning the impact of education on changes in women's autonomy. In settings that are highly stratified by gender, women may have little autonomy until they have attained relatively high levels of education, whereas in more egalitarian settings, the thresholds are lower. These findings bear out the conclusions of Chapter 2, which also suggest that, in many settings, the effect of education in reducing fertility is observed only after moderate levels of education have been attained.

Education can affect people's lives through several channels. It affects access to knowledge, information, and new ideas. It enhances overall efficiency, market opportunities, and social status. It also changes attitudes and behaviours, among other things, bringing about an openness to new ideas and experiences, an increasing independence from traditional authority, and a questioning of passivity and fatalism.[1] These effects apply generally to both sexes. However, young adult men are exposed to new ideas through their wider contacts with the world outside family and local community, as well as through formal schooling. In contrast, many women in the developing world have few contacts with the outside world; for them, formal schooling remains perhaps the primary channel for the transmission of new ideas.

Other effects of education are uniquely applicable to women. Education enables women to assume more autonomy or power in both traditional gender-stratified family settings and in more egalitarian ones. This enhanced autonomy takes the form of decision-making authority within the home, economic and social autonomy and self-reliance, emotional autonomy, the ability to forge close conjugal bonds, and physical autonomy in interacting with the outside world. These aspects of autonomy are acquired by men, in contrast, irrespective of their formal education and largely as a matter of course, simply by virtue of their gender.

Although education may trigger changes in women's autonomy in a number of ways, this chapter concentrates on the links that are most likely to have repercussions for fertility behaviour. In the vast literature linking women's education to fertility through a variety of intervening and proximate factors, most analyses overlook the role played by changes in women's autonomy. In contrast, the literature on mortality has long recognized the importance of women's autonomy as a link between mother's education and child survival. This link was first highlighted by J. C. Caldwell in a study of education as a factor in mortality decline in Nigeria. In this study, even after controlling for a host of demographic and socio-economic factors, including the socio-economic characteristics of husbands, Caldwell finds that women's education plays an important role in determining child survival.[2]

One of the few studies recognizing women's status as a link mediating the relationship between women's education and fertility argues that education is the key to transforming women's attitudes and values from traditional to more modern, and their behaviour from constrained to emancipated. Specifically, the study maintains that schooling increases a woman's knowledge and competence in all sectors of contemporary life; broadens her access to information via the mass media and written material; develops her intellectual capacities and exposes her to interpersonal competition and achievement; gives her an opportunity to pursue non-familial roles; raises her image of her potential and that of her children; and, simultaneously, imparts a sense of efficacy and trust in modern science and technology, which encourages a woman to control her fate and body. It also changes her outlook on the world as being controllable and raises her sense of self-worth. Moreover, it encourages her participation in an egalitarian nuclear family structure with greater conjugal affinity and more equal decision-making, in which her children are socialized to be more independent (and more demanding).[3]

The literature suggests five separate but interdependent elements of autonomy that are influenced by education and are especially important for fertility change:[4]

- Knowledge autonomy: education enhances women's knowledge of and exposure to the outside world;
- Decision-making autonomy: education strengthens women's say in family decisions and decisions concerning their own lives and well-being;
- Physical autonomy in interacting with the outside world: educated women face fewer constraints to physical mobility and have more self-confidence in dealing with the outside world and in extracting the most from available services;
- Emotional autonomy: education encourages a shift in loyalties from extended kin to the conjugal family and promotes greater bonding or intimacy between spouses and between parents and children and less self-denial among women; and
- Economic and social autonomy and self-reliance: education increases women's self-reliance in economic matters as well as self-reliance for social acceptance and status. In particular, education enhances women's economic independence and improves both access to and control over economic resources; it also enhances women's ability to rely on themselves, rather than on their children or husbands, to attain social status or acceptance.

The links of education to fertility through changes in these dimensions of women's autonomy and the intervening factors affecting fertility are listed in Table 1.3.

Enhanced Knowledge of, and Greater Exposure to, the Outside World

At the very least, schooling is expected to impart literacy, numeracy, and other cognitive skills. Greater amounts of education are expected to strengthen mastery over language and numbers and to promote a deeper understanding of several subjects. One study observes that the effect of education is significant for both numeracy and literacy, as measured by reading and writing and arithmetic tests.[5] However, the effect differs with the level of schooling. For literacy, a lower primary education (one to three years) has a weak though significant effect for men and, especially, for women, whereas completion of four years has a significantly greater effect. This finding suggests that four years of schooling may represent a threshold for literacy. In contrast, education has a linear, positive effect on numeracy for women. For males, education is less important than age for acquiring numeracy, suggesting that, for males, numeracy is absorbed also through learning by doing in daily work.

Aside from these cognitive outcomes, education has powerful indirect effects on values and outlooks which result not necessarily from the curriculum itself but from the act of attending school and interacting with teachers and peers.[6] These changes in values and outlooks include, for both women and men, a shift away from fatalism and superstition, brought about by the acquisition of greater reasoning powers and a reliance on scientific explanations for everyday phenomena (see Box 3.1). The changes also include a wider world view and greater sense of alternative lifestyles and opportunities rather than an outlook constrained by the narrow limits of the family compound or village. In addition, education moves women from a reliance on others for the acquisition of knowledge and new ideas to greater self-reliance and, correspondingly, to a greater questioning of traditional authority figures.[7]

The implications of these changes for reproductive behaviour vary. First, education provides women with knowledge about the treatment and prevention of illness, infant feeding, and the prevention of unwanted births. The most obvious change is the knowledge of the causes, prevention, and cure of disease, and children's nutritional requirements. This knowledge is expected to influence fertility through improved child survival (see Table 1.3, row 4). Studies in Ghana and Kenya find a systematic decline, with education, in the proportion of women attributing disease to supernatural causes.[8]

- In Ghana, for example, whereas more than half (52 per cent) of uneducated women attributed disease to supernatural causes, this proportion dropped to 31 per cent among women with primary school education and was even less for women with more education.

Educated women tend to be more aware of personal hygiene, household and courtyard sanitation and cleanliness, the health benefits of a more equitable distribution of food in the household, the need for rest during sickness, and the need for speedy treatment of illness and injuries.[9] The ability of better educated women to have healthy children is recognized by parents in Nigeria as an important reason why the educated can risk having fewer children.[10]

Box 3.1. *Diminishing reliance on the supernatural*

The reliance on superstition and the supernatural in traditional societies is strongest when dealing with such life-course events as birth, marriage, death, and the treatment of disease. In almost all traditional societies, the number and timing of births are considered to be governed largely by unknown forces. In a study of urban women in Burkina Faso, for example, only 14 per cent of women aged 30 and above had ever been to school, and women's lives were described as being regulated by the triad of culture, God, and biology: 'It's God who decides and God who gives. We don't understand about all that. God gives children, we don't know when.'[a]

Even the timing of sexual relations can be governed by the supernatural: in India, for example, sexual relations are prohibited on certain days of the moon in deference to the supernatural.[b] In most traditional settings, almost every disease is considered to be rooted in a supernatural cause or related to some superstition concerning behaviour which displeased the gods or some other supernatural force. Education tends to diminish this reliance on the supernatural by promoting rational explanations and, especially at more advanced levels, a scientific paradigm.

[a] F. van de Walle and N. Ouaidou, 'Status and Fertility among Urban Women in Burkina Faso', *International Family Planning Perspectives*, 11/2 (June 1985), 60–4.
[b] C. Chandrashekaran, 'Cultural Patterns in Relation to Family Planning in India', *Proceedings of the Third International Conference on Planned Parenthood* (Bombay, Family Planning Association of India, 1952).

Second, education exposes women to new ideas which may be incompatible with having many children and which can lead them, more generally, to question the old ways of life. Better educated women have more skills in expressing ideas and asking questions.[11] Better educated women are also more exposed to television and reading materials. In Mexico, for example, better educated women are more likely to read and more likely to watch educational programmes on television than uneducated women are; they are also more likely to keep up with current affairs and have a better sense of geography.[12] The interests of better educated women tend to extend beyond the home. In rural India, for example, educated adolescent girls are more likely to have non-domestic hobbies than uneducated girls are.[13]

Equally important in a traditional setting, educated women are respected for their knowledge, however grudgingly. Even older uneducated women, who, in many cultures, traditionally wield considerable power over the young, acknowledge the power of educated women's knowledge. In settings as diverse as sub-Saharan Africa and South Asia, the wisdom of the school is acknowledged as superior to the wisdom of the old.[14] For example, in focus-group discussions conducted in Sri Lanka, older women commented thus about young women: 'In education they have improved. In health they know better.' Older women accept the superior knowledge of young women: 'We say something is not good. They think it is good. When we think about it, they turn out to be right.'[15]

Educated women are also more knowledgeable about the range of options available to them to control fertility. They are better informed than uneducated women not only about available methods but also about the mechanics and potential side-effects of each method and about where each method can be obtained. The usual measure of contraceptive knowledge is awareness of at least one method. Educated women are more likely than uneducated women to know about more methods and to have correct knowledge of a particular method. Also, educated women are more likely to have been aware of contraception for a longer period than have uneducated women. For example, studies in urban Nigeria find a powerful association between women's education and the length of time since they first knew of family planning: the proportion who had been aware of contraception for ten years or longer increased from 4 per cent among uneducated women to 31 per cent among women with secondary schooling.[16]

Few authors have addressed the question of how much education is required before knowledge concerning disease causation or fertility control—or, more generally, knowledge of the larger world—is enhanced. It has been argued that, in contexts in which overall education levels are low or women's movement is curtailed, a small amount of education improves knowledge of more modern ways of life, in general, rather than of scientific explanations for everyday phenomena or of the outside world. Possibly, a small amount of education can enhance women's knowledge of good health behaviour—the importance of clean water, for example—even without enhancing knowledge of the scientific rationales underlying these changes in behaviour.[17]

- In Bangladesh, for example, there is little difference in the health-related knowledge of uneducated and primary-schooled women.[18] Women with a small amount of education tend to be more aware than are uneducated women of the importance of personal hygiene, boiling water and so on, but both groups are equally ignorant of the links of these changed behaviours to disease causation;[19]
- In Nigeria, only secondary-schooled women reveal an in-depth understanding of disease and prevention; lesser educated women are vague about many health issues and are unable to read what is written on their children's health cards. Yet, they are as likely as better educated women to have their children immunized, and young women with some education are no less likely than older, uneducated, but perhaps more experienced women to attribute sickness to witchcraft;[20]
- A study of Lebanese mothers finds that knowledge of nutritional needs improves substantially only among women with seven to nine years or more of education;[21]
- In rural India, one study observed that general knowledge levels of somewhat educated adolescents could not be distinguished from those of the uneducated.[22]

In short, education certainly enhances women's awareness of both new forms of behaviour and the rationale underlying these behaviours. Such consequences of education as knowledge of good health practices and contraceptive alternatives and the recognition that reproduction need not be left to fate are well documented. Moreover, they have obvious repercussions on the demand for children, influencing the desired family size, economic costs of children, and the time and opportunity costs of children (Table 1.3, rows 5, 10 and 11), as well as awareness of contraceptive methods and contraceptive use (rows 12 and D). Other consequences of education may be awareness of breast-milk substitutes and, more recently, the advantages of breast-milk over substitutes, and skepticism about the virtues of post-partum abstinence. These connections, though plausible and with obvious repercussions on the supply of children, are poorly documented in the literature.

How much education is required before there is awareness of new forms of behaviour, on the one hand, and the rationale underlying these changes, on the other, is less clear. The little evidence available hints that small amounts of education can immediately effect new forms of behaviour, whereas considerably larger amounts of education may be required before the rationale for them is understood.

Greater Decision-making Autonomy in the Home

Another possible consequence of education for women is greater decision-making autonomy within the home. It is usually hypothesized that, compared with uneducated young women who are rarely permitted to make a decision or voice an opinion, educated women are more confident of their ability to make decisions and more likely to insist on participating in family decisions. Such decisions range from those related to child care and feeding to those related to family expenditures and to contraception and family-size limitation. The enhanced decision-making which results from education (see the 'b's in column 3 of Table 1.3) is expected to influence fertility through a wide range of intervening pathways, from marital age (Table 1.3., row 1) and durations of breast-feeding and post-partum abstinence (rows 2 and 3) to child-health decisions (row 4) and to decisions concerning family size and contraception (rows 5, 10, 11, 12, 14, and D).

By and large, however, the evidence for this relationship is incomplete. Although the relationship does occur, it varies by cultural setting, the woman's age, and the kind of decision. Moreover, the degree of gender stratification in families appears to limit or condition the impact of education on women's decision-making authority. It likely conditions the extent to which age or stage of the life cycle confers decision-making autonomy on women, irrespective of education. It may also condition both the domains over which educated women make decisions and the amount of education necessary before women can make independent decisions.

Insight into the relationship between women's education and decision-making autonomy comes from qualitative studies and intensive village-level observations.

- Pioneering studies in gender-stratified settings as diverse as sub-Saharan Africa and South Asia find that educated women are more likely than uneducated women to challenge their mothers-in-law, and their mothers-in-law are much less likely to oppose such challenges;[23]

- Other studies in Africa and South Asia corroborate this pattern. In Sierra Leone and Zimbabwe, educated women have more leverage in bargaining within their families or with their husbands and have a greater say in spending household income than do uneducated women;[24]
- In the Sudan, educated women take greater control and responsibility for child-rearing themselves, unlike uneducated women whose children are more casually reared either by village members or by siblings;[25]
- In North India, village elders lament that young educated wives are insufficiently submissive to their mothers-in-law and are less likely to brook the kind of social restraints that the strict tradition requires.[26] An educated daughter-in-law has considerably more power than an uneducated women in her husband's home: she sets the standards for dress, for purchases, and for the education of children, and she is admired for the sophistication that accompanies her education;
- In South India, where gender relations are more egalitarian than in the north, when asked about whether they respond to their mother-in-law's demands, educated young women are much more likely than others to assert: 'In my house, it is my rule'.[27]

In gender-stratified settings, educated women do not so much assume a greater decision-making role as they are conceded greater decision-making power by their husbands and extended family elders.[28] Parents recognize that an educated daughter-in-law may resist decisions imposed on her by other family members and that an unhappy, educated daughter may have the power to draw their son's loyalty away from them, either emotionally or by insisting on setting up a separate household. Thus, shrewd in-laws may hedge their bets by conceding as many decisions to their daughter-in-law as is necessary for preserving the family unit.

The degree of gender stratification in families can, however, limit the domains over which educated women make decisions. Especially in highly gender-stratified settings, among the first domains of family life in which educated women make decisions, or, more likely, are conceded the authority to make decisions, are those considered more trivial by the larger family, although such decisions may have significant demographic repercussions.[29] A small amount of education might give women the freedom to make decisions in the domestic spheres most relevant to them, notably with regard to child health, internal food distribution, and other aspects of behaviour related to the conjugal family, and possibly with regard to sexual relations with their husbands.[30]

It takes the attainment of considerably more education, especially in highly gender-stratified societies, before women overcome these cultural constraints and are involved in decisions seen as major to the household, such as those relating to the household's honour or its economic survival (see Box 3.2). A small amount of education, however, would not necessarily change the traditional locus of major household decisions, such as large purchases, family marriage negotiations, or sexual controls on unmarried girls.[31] Even in Latin America, where women tend to be relatively educated, husbands continue to dominate in domestic decision-making.[32] In India, both educated and uneducated brides still know that their decision-making power is contingent on their proving themselves by bearing children, especially sons.[33]

Box 3.2. *Kinship structure and its effects on women's decision-making*

The extent to which the kinship structure conditions the relationship between education and decision-making is clear in a comparative study of migrant women from northern and southern India residing in a Delhi slum. The kinds of decisions included in this study are exclusively those required in the day-to-day running of the home, such as deciding on food expenditures, what to cook, and child treatment.

- Among North Indian women, who come from a highly gender-stratified kinship system, women with any education are considerably more involved in decision-making than are uneducated women. In contrast, among South Indian women whose kinship structure is less constraining, no such relationship can be discerned; women have autonomy in these everyday decisions irrespective of education.[a]

Another study in India, this one in rural Gujarat, also finds that better educated women are more likely to make independent decisions. This study examines a combination of four less and more important decisions, both day-to-day household decisions involving child health and daily purchases, and 'major' decisions entailing the clothing purchases for the children and the woman herself. In Gujarat, while illiterate women make independent decisions on an average of 1.4 issues, the number increases only moderately, to 1.6 and 1.7, among women with a primary and middle-school education, and then increases to 2.2 among women with a secondary or higher education. Furthermore, the proportion of women involved in all four decisions increased marginally from 18 per cent among uneducated women to 24 per cent and 26 per cent among primary- and middle-school-educated women and more sharply to 40 per cent among secondary-schooled women.[b] Women require some secondary education before they experience major gains in decision-making, especially when the range of decisions goes beyond those pertaining to everyday life.

[a] A. M. Basu, *Culture, the Status of Women, and Demographic Behaviour: Illustrated with the Case of India* (Oxford, Clarendon Press, 1992). This study did not control for age; such a control would presumably strengthen the positive relationship observed among northern women and might have shown a mild positive relationship even among southern women. To speculate, had the range of decisions included those perceived as more important by the larger family, such as decisions on major purchases or marriage negotiations, the relationships might have differed considerably. The relationship between education and decision-making might have been more positive for South Indian women than for North Indian women, for whom cultural constraints on these decisions are much more difficult to overcome via education.
[b] Calculated from Leela Visaria, 'Female Autonomy and Fertility Behaviour: An Exploration of Gujarat Data', in International Union for the Scientific Study of Population (IUSSP), *Proceedings of the International Population Conference, Montreal*, iv (Liège, IUSSP, 1993). Once again, differences would likely have been sharper had age been controlled.

Evidence from Bangladesh also indicates that a few years of schooling afford women a certain amount of decision-making in routine or short-term decisions. Much more education is required, however, for women to participate in longer term and more important ones. Educated women are certainly more likely to be involved in both routine decisions, such as going to a health clinic, and more important decisions, such as spending household resources. The pattern of the relationship of education to routine decision-making differs, however, from its relationship to participation in major decisions. For routine decisions, women's involvement in decision-making increases steadily with education: for example, among the least educated women, the decision about going to seek health care is made largely by the husband, whereas among even modestly better educated women, it is made mostly by the wife. In contrast, decisions on the disbursal of household income are not as easily relinquished by the husband; it takes considerably more education (than in the case of health-seeking) before women participate in household economic decisions.[34]

In recent years, demographic surveys have increasingly included questions on women's decision-making authority. Although many of these studies fail to control for age of the woman or stage of the life cycle—variables known to enhance decision-making authority independently of education—they offer, for the first time, empirical evidence of the link of education to women's decision-making autonomy.

• One study that effectively controls for stage of the life cycle was conducted in Cuernavaca and Tilzapotla, Mexico. This study focuses on the relationship of education to women's decision-making power among women with a young child, showing that better educated women were more likely than uneducated women to report that marital decisions were made jointly with their husbands. The percentage reporting joint decision-making increased from 67 per cent among women with one to five years of schooling to 79 per cent and 85 per cent among those with six and seven to nine years, respectively.[35]

Some studies that have not controlled for stage of the life cycle also find positive relationships between education and decision-making autonomy.

• In rural Bangladesh, for example, one study finds that the better educated a woman is, the more likely she is to participate in such everyday decisions as the purchase of medicine for sick children, children's education, visits to relatives, and the purchase of household necessities. An index derived from summing the number of decisions in which the woman participated suggests a systematic increase in decision-making authority with education: whereas uneducated women participated in an average of 1.1 decisions, the number increases to 1.6, 2.0, and 2.3 decisions among women with primary, middle, and secondary schooling.[36]

One indication that decisions are conceded selectively comes from a study of urban women in Karachi, Pakistan, which finds that better educated women were more likely to agree that women should have a say in important family-size decisions, regardless of their age. In contrast, however, it was only older women for whom education had a significant positive effect on whether they thought that women should be involved in family finances.[37] This finding supports Caldwell's view that, in gender-stratified cultures, even educated young women expect to be excluded from decisions pertaining to family finances.

In short, qualitative and quantitative evidence suggests that, although education improves women's decision-making autonomy, the degree of male dominance in families conditions the strength of the relationship. In gender-stratified contexts, important family decisions may remain out of the realm of even educated women. In extreme patriarchal settings, where the seclusion of women or their withdrawal from outside activities is a sign of prestige, better educated women may experience even less decision-making autonomy than do uneducated women.[38]

In more egalitarian structures, everyday decisions may be routine for all women, irrespective of education, whereas education may affect women's participation in more important decisions. Another feature affected by the degree of gender stratification is how much education is required before a woman can take control of decisions. In male-dominated settings, perhaps a primary-level education is sufficient for women to take charge of everyday issues perceived as unimportant to the larger household—what to eat, how to care for children, or how long to practice post-partum abstinence—which, nevertheless, have important implications for fertility and especially infant and child mortality. Much more than a primary education is required in such settings, however, before women's decision-making authority is expanded to include issues considered vital to the family's honour and economic survival—major purchases and investments; family prestige (such as marriage negotiations); whether to conform to traditional behavioural expectations—issues that would change women's traditional need for and reliance upon children for social and economic security. In contrast, in more egalitarian settings, a lower threshold of education may be necessary before women assume a voice in important decisions.

Greater Physical Autonomy in Interacting with the Outside World

Education is expected to enhance women's interaction with the outside world in two ways. The first applies in highly gender-stratified settings which restrict women's physical mobility; educated women in these settings are expected to have more freedom of movement than uneducated women have. The second applies more generally. Better educated women are expected to have more self-confidence in dealing with the outside world and in extracting more from available services than other women do. The influence of this greater interaction with the outside world on reproductive behaviour can operate in at least two ways. It can improve women's ability to interact and deal with health- and contraceptive-service providers and, thereby, influence child survival (Table 1.3, row 4), on the one hand, and contraceptive use (row D), on the other. Unfortunately, few studies specifically address the relationship between education and women's interaction with the outside world.

Physical mobility   The evidence for whether educated women face fewer restrictions on physical mobility comes entirely from South Asia and is mixed. A survey in Bangladesh shows that educated women are less likely than uneducated women to travel outside the village locality, and more likely to veil themselves in public and to require a male escort when out of the village. The effect of education on a mobility index constructed from these variables is inverse and significant, even after controlling for other variables, including age, marriage age, and socio-economic status.[39]

Evidence from Pakistan is mixed. In one study using DHS data, the proportion of women who are free to go to a hospital alone increases from 20 per cent among uneducated women to 32 per cent among those with primary education and 52 per cent among those with more education.[40] An earlier study, however, suggests that education increases physical mobility only among middle-school and better educated women and only in urban areas. That study shows that women with a primary-school education are actually more secluded and isolated from the outside world than uneducated women are, and more likely to practise purdah.[41] This 'sanskritization' effect reflects the greater ability of wealthier families than of poor ones to seclude their women.[42] However, that this effect persists even after age, husband's education, and household economic status are controlled suggests that women with a moderate amount of education prefer the prestige that goes with purdah to the autonomy that accompanies freedom of movement.[43]

Self-confidence   That educated women have more self-confidence in interacting with the outside world is well expressed by older, uneducated women in Sri Lanka, who report the difference between themselves and their educated daughters: '[Daughters] say, we know how to move in society unlike our mothers' and 'Those days we were shy to face society, even to talk. Now they are not.'[44]

Not only are better educated women more likely to know of available services and to make decisions regarding use of these services, they are also more likely to use these services appropriately, demand them as a right and not as a favour, and extract far more from them than uneducated women do. With greater education comes a greater responsiveness to new services, more self-confidence in interacting with officials and service providers, and a greater ability to demand what is due.[45] Hence, educated women tend to be taken more seriously both by their families and by such outsiders as service providers in settings as diverse as India, Indonesia, Mexico, and Sri Lanka.[46]

The most convincing evidence of better educated women's greater confidence in interactions with the outside world comes from their health-seeking behaviour. In every region where the issue has been studied—Africa, Asia, and Latin America—better educated women are considerably more likely than less educated women to use modern preventive and curative health services,[47] including prenatal and postnatal care, and to do so with greater timeliness, to demand a greater quality of care, and to continue treatment with greater persistence and accuracy.

• In rural Nigeria, 47 per cent of uneducated and poorly educated women who had delivered two years before the study had sought postnatal care; this percentage increased to 53 per cent for women with a primary education and 96 per cent for those with a secondary or higher education.[48]

In the case of child sickness, educated women are quicker to take appropriate action and are confident enough to explain symptoms to, and discuss treatment with, service providers. Evidence from rural South India, Punjab, and rural Nigeria suggests that educated women have more frequent and effective interactions with the health system than do less educated women.[49] They are more likely to seek follow-up if the child's health is not improving and to follow and persist with treatment. In contrast, less educated women are apprehensive about informing doctors and nurses that what they have prescribed is not working.

Surprisingly, no studies examine the relationship of education to service-seeking behaviour while controlling for socio-economic status, so it is difficult to judge whether the relationship reflects education's association with higher socio-economic status or, instead, reflects a true empowerment effect.

One would expect that the pattern of self-assertiveness observed concerning health would also occur in other areas of life—the school, the bank, the market-place, development programmes, and so forth. No data are available for educational differentials in these arenas, however.

There is little empirical work elaborating the relationship between education and women's interaction with the outside world. The little which is available focuses on the links of education to seclusion in South Asia and to the frequency and quality of educated women's interaction with the health system. Much of this information is drawn from qualitative and intensive village-level studies. What is available indeed suggests that better educated women have more freedom of movement and greater confidence in dealing with the outside world and in demanding the most from available services. These effects would surely have repercussions on such factors affecting fertility as child survival and contraceptive use (see Table 1.3). Again, however, the effect of education on enhancing women's interaction with the outside world is not necessarily straightforward. In the most patriarchal settings, apparently, women manifest freedom of movement only after they have attained a considerable amount of education. In South Asia, for example, the strong cultural tradition limiting women's autonomy, reinforced by strong seclusion practices for women, may remain a formidable barrier to the effectiveness of education in enabling women to interact with the world outside their homes.

Greater Emotional Autonomy:
Closer Emotional Bonds with Husband and Children

Increased female education implies several changes in family dynamics. These include a greater intimacy between spouses, an increased loyalty to the conjugal unit rather than to the larger extended-kin network, and a correspondingly greater child orientation. These changes constitute what has been termed 'emotional nucleation' of the family system.[50] The closer conjugal bonds which education promotes are expected to affect fertility in several ways (see Table 1.3). Increased intimacy with husbands may allow educated women to engage in freer discussion of contraception and family-size preferences; it may also result in a reluctance to adhere to traditional lengthy post-partum abstinence taboos or a reluctance to practise prolonged breast-feeding, with sexual relations discouraged during the period of breast-feeding. Also, the quest for intimacy within marriage may lengthen the search for a husband among educated women and, thereby, delay marriage among them (see Box 3.3).

Educated women are more likely to forge a close relationship with their husbands, implying greater social equality and emotional intimacy between spouses.[51] With the strengthening of the spousal link, women can become more independent of the extended family, emotionally and, in some cases, residentially. Close spousal ties are one reason why better educated women are somewhat more likely to reside in

---

Box 3.3.   *Relationship of education to closer marital bonds*

Insights into the links of education to closer husband–wife bonds come largely from qualitative and ethnographic studies. For example, in Turkey, husbands are said to prefer the advice of their educated wives to that of their largely uneducated mothers.[a] In Bangladesh, educated women are considerably more likely to express hopes for a close conjugal bond than uneducated women are.[b] In South India, educated women have warmer ties with their husbands than uneducated women do, even when they live in extended families.[c] Among Yoruba women in Nigeria, there tends to be an emotional distance between spouses, but conjugal relationships are observed to be much closer if the woman is educated.[d] Another study of Yoruba women in rural Nigeria points out that husband–wife closeness fostered by education encourages fathers to participate more fully in the rearing of children. Husbands of better educated women are more likely to contribute financially to, and participate more actively in, matters affecting their wives and children, particularly with regard to child health. Husbands are also more likely to pay heed to the arguments of educated wives than of uneducated ones.[e]

[a] J. C. Caldwell, 'The Mechanisms of Demographic Change in Historical Perspective', *Population Studies*, 35/1 (Mar. 1981), 5–27.
[b] S. Lindenbaum, M. Chakraborty, and M. Elias, *The Influence of Maternal Education on Infant and Child Mortality in Bangladesh*, Special Publication No. 23 (Dhaka, International Centre for Diarrhoeal Disease Research, 1985).
[c] J. C. Caldwell, P. H. Reddy, and P. Caldwell, 'The Causes of Demographic Change in Rural South India', *Population Studies*, 37 (1983), 343–61, and J. C. Caldwell, 'Cultural and Social Factors Influencing Mortality Levels in Developing Countries', *Annals*, 510 (July 1990), 44-59.
[d] Adekunbi Kehinde Omideyi, 'Women's Position, Conjugal Relationships and Fertility Behaviour among the Yoruba', *African Population Studies* 4 (Aug. 1990), 20–35, cited in M. M. Kritz and D. T. Gurak, 'Women's Economic Independence and Fertility Among the Yoruba', paper presented at the Demographic and Health Surveys World Conference, Washington, DC, Aug. 1991.
[e] I. O. Orubuloye, J. C. Caldwell, P. Caldwell, and C. H. Bledsoe, 'The Impact of Family and Budget Structure on Health Treatment in Nigeria', *Health Transition Review*, 1/2 (1991), 189–210.

nuclear families than uneducated women are. Even when they reside in extended families, educated women display a greater intimacy with their husbands than un-educated women do.[52]

In sub-Saharan Africa, closer husband–wife ties are fostered also by a shift towards monogamy, especially among better educated women. Better educated women are less likely to accept polygamous unions, as observed in parts of sub-Saharan Africa.[53] Even when educated women enter polygynous unions, they are able to maintain closer ties with their husbands than their uneducated co-wives are, as observed among the Mende of Sierra Leone, often to the material disadvantage of the uneducated women and their children.[54] Conjugal family orientation may also lead to a decline in child fostering, because educated women may be reluctant to abandon control over rearing and caring for their children and, unless they have no children themselves, they may be equally reluctant to assume responsibility for the children of others.[55]

Aside from ethnographic support, some empirical evidence exists that, compared with uneducated women, educated women have closer ties to their husbands. Compared with uneducated women, educated women are also more likely to have more egalitarian attitudes towards husband–wife relations.

- In Khartoum, the Sudan, a positive correlation (.49) was found between women's education and whether they accompanied their husbands to the theatre or to visit friends;[56]
- In Cuernavaca, Mexico, better educated women were systematically more likely to report egalitarian conjugal relationships than were less educated women;[57]
- In Bangkok, women's education was the most significant determinant of an index of 'attitudes to women's status' constructed from variables reflecting women's attitudes to equality in husband–wife relations;[58]
- In many settings, educated women are more likely than uneducated women both to have love marriages and to marry men who are closer to them in age. Both factors help to explain the closer emotional ties of educated women to their husbands.[59]

The literature also suggests that educated women are less likely to deny themselves, or have a greater sense of self-worth, than uneducated women do. Among Egyptian women, a strong relationship is found between education and the willingness of working women to spend money not just on their families but on themselves.[60] This may be an important aspect of autonomy as it relates to fertility, although there is little empirical evidence to support this link.

What little research is available suggests that education encourages greater intimacy between spouses and a greater loyalty to the conjugal unit than to the larger extended-kin network. This shift in loyalty can surely be expected to strengthen women's ability to challenge the authority of family elders in a variety of areas, ranging from labour-force participation to the use of earned income, from contraception to abstinence to choice of husband, and from child-rearing patterns to the timing and spacing of births.

Greater Economic and Social Autonomy and Self-reliance

Perhaps most important is the contribution of education to women's economic and social self-reliance. Educated women have greater control over material resources than do uneducated women. For example, they are more likely than uneducated women to express attitudes favourable to saving money for the future.[61] Their enhanced economic and social autonomy and self-reliance affect such intervening variables as marital age, child survival, family-size desires and its components, and contraceptive use (see the 'e's in column 3 of Table 1.3).

Self-reliance in old age   One indication of better educated women's greater economic self-reliance appears in statements concerning self-reliance in old age. Evidence from both India and Pakistan suggests that educated women, once they have crossed the middle-school threshold, intend to rely on their own resources in old age, either replacing or, more likely, complementing support from their sons. In rural Maharashtra, for example, even after economic status is controlled, educated women are more likely than others to expect to rely on their own income or savings for old age and, more immediately, for their children's education. This pattern exists among both younger and older age groups.[62] In Karachi, Pakistan, similarly, education is a powerful indicator of women's intention to support themselves in old age.[63]

Less evidence is available on the effect of education on enhancing women's self-reliance in securing themselves in their husbands' families, notably in gender-stratified settings. In South Asia, as elsewhere, educated women are considered with more respect by their in-laws than uneducated women are.[64] There is also ample anecdotal evidence from this region and from sub-Saharan Africa that educated women have more avenues than reproduction through which to secure their positions in their husbands' families.

Economic activity   The most commonly used indicator of women's control over resources is, however, their economic activity or extra-domestic participation in economic production. It is widely believed that education opens economic opportunities for women and increases their participation in the wage sector[65] and that such participation enhances women's control over material resources by giving them an independent source of income.[66] In turn, greater control over material resources may reduce educated women's reliance on children for material support and increase their ability to purchase health and contraceptive services (affecting child survival and contraceptive practice); it may also provide a motive for delaying marriage (Table 1.3).

The hypothesis that education enhances women's economic activity and, thereby, their control over resources has mixed support. In almost every setting, the most highly educated women are more likely to work for wages or income than are the least educated women, but the relationship at low and intermediate levels of education is often weak. In the more developed countries of the developing world and in settings where women have plentiful opportunities for formal-sector employment, women's education tends to be positively related to their labour-force participation, as expected.

Support for a positive relationship between women's education and work-force participation and wages comes from the more developed countries of Latin America and Asia.[67] The relationship between education and work-force participation is generally linear with two exceptions. First, the relationship can vary by type of activity. For example, in Mexico, women's work participation in middle-level occupations is strongly and positively related to education. Their participation in the agricultural sector, however, is strongly and inversely related to education. This strong inverse relationship is evident after controlling for age, marital status, number of children, and place of residence.[68] As a result of these mutually opposing effects, education is weakly related to whether a woman is engaged in any wage-earning activity. Second, in some cases, women with a small amount of education have lower labour-force participation rates or wage levels than uneducated women do.[69]

In other settings, however, the relationship of education to women's economic activity can be weak and even negative, at least until relatively high levels of education have been achieved. These relationships are found especially in highly gender-stratified settings—those in which the labour market is highly segmented by sex and age and those in which opportunities for formal-sector employment are limited. Except among women who have attained relatively high levels of education, work tends to be poverty-driven and, as a result of its interaction with the household's socio-economic status, the gross relationship of education to women's labour-force participation is rarely positive; the net relationship of education to work, however, may be positive. Generally, the positive relationship shows up when work is measured by participation in the formal sector, in non-agricultural occupations, or in regular as opposed to seasonal or part-time work.

In Pakistan, several studies find that work is most typically poverty-driven and is unrelated or even negatively related to education, except at the highest levels. Few women work out of choice, and most start working after having several children; economically, their household incomes are lower than those of non-working women, and the majority of them would give up work if their financial positions improved.[70] Similarly, a 1988 study of rural Bangladesh finds that education has a negligible but negative effect on women's labour-market participation as well as on their allocation of time to home and market production. A woman's time allocation is determined more by her husband's education than by her own education.[71] A 1991 study using county- rather than individual-level data reports a positive relationship between education and labour-force participation in urban areas of China, compared with no relationship in rural areas.[72] That the relationship is more uniformly positive in urban areas is also illustrated in a study in Karachi, where opportunities for formal-sector work are more widely available than in the rural areas of Pakistan. Here, education is significantly and positively related to whether women work in the formal sector. This finding holds for both younger women who are in the middle of their child-bearing years and older women who are nearing the close.[73] Education is also positively related to pre-nuptial employment.[74]

That moderately educated women do not necessarily command higher wages than uneducated women do is evident from a study in Indonesia, which examines the effect of education on the hourly wages of formally employed women and men, controlling for rural–urban residence and region. The results generally suggest that the more education both women and men have, the higher their earnings. The differences in returns between uneducated and primary-schooled women, however, are relatively inconsequential, whereas those between primary and better educated women are noteworthy.[75]

A few studies, mostly in patriarchal settings, suggest that a small amount of education—for example, primary schooling—has an ambiguous effect on women's labour-force participation, but that further amounts of schooling are usually associated with increased economic activity. This pattern has been observed in Indonesia, Pakistan, and Saudi Arabia.[76] Saudi Arabia represents a special case with regard to women's employment. In Saudi Arabia, the labour market is so segmented that the jobs available to women are those requiring a high level of education. As a result, the relationship of education to labour-force participation becomes positive only among college-educated women.[77] This evidence suggests the possibility that control over resources may be an important outcome of female education only after relatively high levels of education are attained.

Control over use of earnings   Economic activity does not, by itself, enhance women's control over material resources or power in the household. What is equally necessary for enhancing self-reliance is that working women have a say in how their earnings are used. In highly gender-stratified settings, working women, irrespective of education, are often expected to turn over their earnings to their husbands, mothers-in-law, or other senior members of the household, giving the women little opportunity to decide on their use. In these circumstances, work can hardly be expected to give educated women control over resources or economic self-reliance.

Evidence from a number of settings confirms a positive relationship between education and a control over earnings. One study in rural Bangladesh finds that education is strongly linked both to a woman's control over her own earnings and to those of her husband; the effect of education is significant even after controlling for age, marriage patterns, and husband's characteristics.[78] Similarly, qualitative evidence from Zimbabwe shows that educated women, especially those who are working, have more leverage in bargaining within their families. A teacher says, 'Because I also bring income which everybody, including the in-laws, enjoys, I am valued more, and nobody expects me to have more children.'[79]

Sometimes, educated women are in a better position to control family resources irrespective of their work status. It has been pointed out that access to, or the right to use, someone else's resources is a weak substitute for control over one's own environment; the former implies only the right to use or consume resources with the permission of those who hold the right to dispose of them.[80] In some cases, however, access to resources may influence control. For example, among Mende women in Sierra Leone, formal Western education is seen as a means of gaining greater control over household resources.[81] A study in Gujarat, India, suggests that better educated women score higher than less educated women on an income autonomy index which comprises six measures of control over resources (whether a woman works and whether she retains her earnings) and access to resources (including whether the husband provides cash to the wife, whether the wife keeps money herself, and whether she participates in economic decisions). Although both uneducated women and those with a primary-school education score 3.1, among women with middle and secondary schooling, the scores increase to 3.3 and 3.6, respectively.[82] Thus, in settings as diverse as Africa and South Asia, education enhances women's self-reliance, economic independence, and control over resources; this link presumably has repercussions on family-size preferences and contraception, on the one hand, and on delayed marriage, on the other.

The relationship of education to women's economic or social self-reliance, however, depends largely on the context. Cultural norms of both patriarchy and economic structure are important in determining the consequences of female education for women's self-reliance, labour-force participation, and control over resources. In highly gender-stratified settings, for example, it requires considerably more education before the expected positive association of education to women's labour-force participation appears than it does in more egalitarian settings. In many settings in which work is induced by poverty, it is the least educated women who are most likely to work; for better educated women who come from higher income households, it is a sign of prestige to withdraw from the labour-force. In work settings dominated by the informal sector, the relationship of education to economic activity tends to be far weaker than in settings in which there is a large formal sector. Whether work actually implies greater self-reliance or control over material resources is also dependent upon context; in highly stratified settings, moderately educated women may control neither the decision to work nor the resulting earnings.

Notes

1. A. Inkeles and D. Smith, *On Becoming Modern: Individual Change in Six Countries* (Cambridge, Mass., Harvard University Press, 1974); and Cochrane, *Fertility and Education*.

2. J. C. Caldwell, 'Education as a Factor in Mortality Decline: An Examination of Nigerian Data', *Population Studies*, 33/3 (1979), 395–413. Other scholars who have emphasized women's autonomy as a pathway relating women's education to child survival are H. Ware, J. Cleland, and J. K. van Ginneken. Each of these authors addresses changes in women's autonomy which, although specified as pathways affecting child health, are equally likely to have repercussions for fertility. See H. Ware, 'Effects of Maternal Education, Women's Roles and Child Care on Child Mortality', *Population and Development Review*, 10 (suppl.) (1984), 191–214; J. Cleland and J. K. van Ginneken, 'Maternal

Education and Child Survival in Developing Countries: The Search for Pathways of Influence', *Social Science and Medicine*, 27/12 (1988), 1357–68; Cleland, 'Maternal Education'; and J. C. Caldwell, 'Cultural and Social Factors Influencing Mortality Levels in Developing Countries', *Annals*, 510 (July 1990), 44–59.

3. Kasarda, Billy, and West, *Status Enhancement*.

4. Bulatao and Lee (eds.), *Determinants*, ii; Mason, *Status of Women*; Cochrane, *Fertility and Education* and 'Effects of Education'; Kasarda, Billy, and West, *Status Enhancement*; J. C. Caldwell, P. H. Reddy, and P. Caldwell, 'The Causes of Demographic Change in Rural South India: A Micro Approach', *Population and Development Review*, 8/4 (Dec. 1982), 689–727; and J. C. Caldwell, 'Education as a Factor'.

5. S. H. Cochrane and D. T. Jamison, 'Educational Attainment and Achievement in Rural Thailand', in A. Summers (ed.), *New Directions for Testing and Measurement: Productivity Assessment in Education*, No. 15 (San Francisco, Jossey-Bass, 1982).

6. J. C. Caldwell, 'Mass Education'.

7. Ibid.

8. G. B. Fosu, 'Disease Classification in Rural Ghana: Framework and Consequences for Health Behaviour', *Social Science and Medicine*, 15B (1981), 471–82; T. O. Eisemon, V. L. Patel, and S. O. Sena, 'Uses of Formal and Informal Knowledge in the Comprehension of Instructions for Oral Rehydration Therapy in Kenya', *Social Science and Medicine*, 25/11 (1987), 1225–34.

9. A. Bhuiya, K. Streatfield, and P. Meyer, 'Mothers' Hygienic Awareness, Behaviour and Knowledge of Major Childhood Diseases in Matlab, Bangladesh', in J. Caldwell *et al.* (eds.), *What We Know*, i; and S. Lindenbaum, M. Chakraborty, and M. Elias, *The Influence of Maternal Education on Infant and Child Mortality in Bangladesh*, Special Publication No. 23 (Dhaka, Bangladesh, International Centre for Diarrhoeal Disease Research, 1985).

10. P. Caldwell and J. C. Caldwell, 'The Function of Child-spacing in Traditional Societies and the Direction of Change', in H. J. Page and R. Lesthaeghe (eds.), *Child-spacing in Tropical Africa: Traditions and Change* (London, Academic Press, 1981).

11. Kritz and Gurak, 'Women's Status'.

12. LeVine *et al.*, 'Women's Schooling'.

13. C. Vlassoff, 'Unmarried Adolescent Females in Rural India: A Study of the Social Impact of Education', *Journal of Marriage and the Family*, 42/2 (May 1980), 427–36.

14. J. C. Caldwell, 'Education as a Factor'; J. C. Caldwell, Reddy, and P. Caldwell, 'Causes of Demographic Change'; J. C. Caldwell, P. H. Reddy, and P. Caldwell, 'Educational Transition in Rural India', *Population and Development Review*, 11/1 (Mar. 1985), 29–51; A. Tsui *et al.*, 'Young Women's Work and Family Formation: A District Study in Sri Lanka', paper prepared for the Annual Meeting of the Population Association of America, Toronto, 3–5 May 1990; and D. G. Mandelbaum, *Women's Seclusion and Men's Honor: Sex Roles in North India, Bangladesh and Pakistan* (Tucson, The University of Arizona Press, 1988).

15. Tsui *et al.*, 'Young Women's Work'.

16. G. A. Oni and J. McCarthy, 'Contraceptive Knowledge and Practices in Ilorin, Nigeria: 1983–88', *Studies in Family Planning*, 21/2 (Mar.–Apr. 1990), 104–9.

17. Cleland, 'Maternal Education'.

18. Cleland and van Ginneken, 'Maternal Education'.

19. S. Lindenbaum, 'Maternal Education and Health Care Processes in Bangladesh: The Health and Hygiene of the Middle Classes', in J. Caldwell *et al.* (eds.), *What We Know*;

Bhuiya, Streatfield, Meyer, 'Mothers' Hygienic Awareness'; and Cleland, 'Maternal Education'.

20. C. E. E. Okojie, 'Some Inter-relationships Between Maternal Education and Child Survival in Nigeria: Evidence from Household Surveys and Focus Group Discussions', in International Union for the Scientific Study of Population (IUSSP), *Proceedings of the International Population Conference, Montreal*, iv (Liège, IUSSP, 1993).

21. D. S. McLaren, 'The Home Environment of the Malnourished-Deprived Child', *Health Policy Education*, 2/91 (1982), quoted in Cleland and van Ginneken, 'Maternal Education'.

22. C. Vlassoff, 'Unmarried Adolescent Females in Rural India'.

23. J. C. Caldwell, 'Education as a Factor', and J. C. Caldwell, Reddy, and P. Caldwell, 'Causes of Demographic Change'.

24. Evidence from Sierra Leone is from C. Bledsoe, 'The Politics of Polygyny in Mende Education and Child Fosterage Transactions', in P. R. Sanday and R. G. Goodenough (eds.), *Beyond the Second Sex: New Directions in the Anthropology of Gender* (Philadelphia, University of Pennsylvania, 1990); evidence from Zimbabwe is from M. M. Mhloyi, 'Fertility Transition in Zimbabwe', paper presented at the Seminar on the Course of Fertility Transition in Sub-Saharan Africa, sponsored by the IUSSP Committee on Comparative Analysis of Fertility and the University of Zimbabwe, Harare, Zimbabwe, 19–22 Nov. 1991.

25. Mohamed El Awad Galal el Din, 'The Economic Value of Children in Rural Sudan', in J. C. Caldwell (ed.), *The Persistence of High Fertility: Population Prospects in the Third World*, pt. 2 (Canberra, Department of Demography, Australian National University, 1977), as reported in Caldwell, 'Social and Cultural Factors'.

26. D. G. Mandelbaum, *Human Fertility in India: Social Components and Policy Perspectives* (Berkeley, University of California Press, 1974), and *Women's Seclusion and Men's Honor*; L. Minturn, 'Changes in the Differential Treatment of Rajput Girls in Khalapur: 1955–1975', *Medical Anthropology*, 8/2 (1984), 127–32.

27. S. J. Jejeebhoy, 'Women in Rajasthan and Tamil Nadu: A Report of Intensive Village Level Studies' (1989).

28. J. C. Caldwell and P. McDonald, 'Influence of Maternal Education on Infant and Child Mortality: Levels and Causes', *Health Policy and Education*, 2 (1982), 251–67; and J. C. Caldwell, Reddy, and P. Caldwell, 'The Causes of Demographic Change'.

29. J. C. Caldwell, Reddy, and P. Caldwell, 'The Causes of Demographic Change'.

30. In rural South India, for example, even women with a small amount of education are more likely than uneducated women to insist on treatment for a sick child, on how and what to feed infants and children, and on whether to abstain from sexual relations with their husbands after giving birth. J. C. Caldwell, Reddy, and P. Caldwell, 'The Causes of Demographic Change'.

31. For South Asia, J. C. Caldwell, Reddy, and P. Caldwell, 'The Causes of Demographic Change'; for Latin America, LeVine *et al.*, 'Women's Schooling', and O. M. Acuna, 'La mujer en la familia y el valor de los hijos', in *Seminario Nacional de Demografia*, Direction General de Estadistica y Censos (San Jose, Departamento de Publicaciones, 1981), 112–29.

32. LeVine *et al.*, 'Women's Schooling'.

33. Mandelbaum, *Human Fertility in India*.

34. Deborah Balk, personal communication, 1993.

35. LeVine *et al.*, 'Women's Schooling'.

36. Deborah Balk, 'Individual and Community Aspects of Fertility and Women's Status in Rural Bangladesh', *Population Studies*, 48 (1994), 21–45; J. Cleland, 'Large Data-Sets and the Relationships Between "Women's Status" and Fertility in South Asia', paper presented at the Workshop on Female Education, Autonomy and Fertility Change in South Asia, New Delhi, Apr. 1993.
37. Z. A. Sathar and K. O. Mason, 'Why Female Education Affects Reproductive Behaviour in Urban Pakistan', revision of paper presented at the 1989 XXI General Conference of the IUSSP, New Delhi, India (1993); Z. A. Sathar, 'Women's Education and Autonomy as Factors in Fertility Change in Pakistan: Some Empirical Findings', paper presented at the Workshop on Female Education, Autonomy and Fertility Change in South Asia, New Delhi, Apr. 1993.
38. M. N. Srinivas, *Social Change in Modern India* (Bombay, Asia Publishing House, 1966).
39. Balk, 'Individual and Community Aspects'. In North India, a study by Mandelbaum, *Women's Seclusion*, finds that it requires a high school or college education before women become less stringent about their observance of purdah and have fewer restrictions imposed on their movement.
40. Sathar, 'Women's Education and Autonomy'.
41. N. M. Shah and E. Q. Bulatao, 'Purdah and Family Planning in Pakistan', *International Family Planning Perspectives*, 7/1 (Mar. 1981), 32–7.
42. Srinivas, *Social Change in Modern India*.
43. Shah and Bulatao, 'Purdah and Family Planning in Pakistan'. In urban areas, only middle-school and higher educated women become less secluded; in contrast, in rural areas where overall education levels are still low, this downturn in seclusion rates is not yet apparent.
44. Tsui *et al.*, 'Young Women's Work'.
45. J. C. Caldwell, 'Maternal Education as a Factor in Child Mortality', *World Health Forum*, 2/1 (1981), 75–8; Cleland and van Ginneken, 'Maternal Education'.
46. For India, see J. C. Caldwell, Reddy, and P. Caldwell, 'The Social Component of Mortality Decline: An Investigation in South India Employing Alternative Methodologies', *Population Studies*, 37 (1983), 185–205; for Indonesia, see K. Streatfield, M. Singarimbun, and I. Singarimbun, 'The Impact of Maternal Education on the Use of Child Immunisation and Other Health Services', *International Population Dynamics Program Research Note on Child Survival*, No. 8CS (Canberra, The Australian National University, 1986); for Mexico, see LeVine *et al.*, 'Women's Schooling'; for Sri Lanka, see Tsui *et al.*, 'Young Women's Work'.
47. For Africa, see C. Mbacke and E. van de Walle, 'Socioeconomic Factors and Access to Health Services as Determinants of Child Mortality', paper presented at the IUSSP Seminar on Mortality and Society in Sub Saharan Africa, Yaounde (1987), and for Nigeria, C. B. Okafor, 'Availability and Use of Services for Maternal and Child Health Care in Rural Nigeria', *International Journal of Gynaecology and Obstetrics*, 34/331 (1991), 331–46. For Asia, see J. S. Akin, C. C. Griffin, D. K. Guilkey, and B. M. Popkin, 'The Demand for Primary Health-Care Services in the Bicol Region of the Philippines', *Economic Development and Cultural Change*, 34 (1986), 755–82; E. L. Wong, B. M. Popkin, D. K. Guilkey, and J. S. Akin, 'Accessibility, Quality of Care and Prenatal Care Use in the Philippines', *Social Science and Medicine*, 24 (1987), 927–44; K. Streatfield, M. Singarimbun, and I. Diamond, 'Maternal Education and Child Immunization', *Demography*, 27/3 (Aug. 1990), 447–55; and Balk, 'Individual and Community Aspects'. For Latin America, see I. T. Elo, 'Utilization of Maternal Health-

care Services in Peru: The Role of Women's Education', *Health Transition Review*, 2/1 (1992), 44–69; R. Fernandez, 'Analysis of Information about Mother-Child Care Taken from Fertility Surveys in Latin America' (Voorberg, International Statistical Institute, 1984, unpub.); and R. S. Monteith *et al.*, 'Use of Maternal and Child Health Services and Immunization Coverage in Panama and Guatemala' *PAHO Bulletin*, 21 (1987), 1–15.

48. Okafor, 'Availability and Use of Services'.

49. For South India, see J. C. Caldwell, Reddy, and P. Caldwell, 'The Social Component of Mortality Decline'; and P. Krishnan, 'Mortality Decline in India, 1951–1961: Development vs Public Health Programme Hypothesis', *Social Science and Medicine*, 9 (1975), 475–79. For Punjab, see M. Das Gupta, 'Death Clustering, Mother's Education and the Determinants of Child Mortality in Rural Punjab, India', *Population Studies*, 44 (1990), 489–505. For rural Nigeria, see I. O. Orubuloye, J. C. Caldwell, P. Caldwell, and C. H. Bledsoe, 'The Impact of Family and Budget Structure on Health Treatment in Nigeria', *Health Transition Review*, 1/2 (1991), 189–210; and J. C. Caldwell, 'Education as a Factor'.

50. J. C. Caldwell, 'The Wealth Flows Theory of Fertility Decline', in J. C. Caldwell (ed.), *Theory of Fertility Decline*, and 'Toward a Restatement of Demographic Transition Theory', *Population and Development Review* 2/3–4 (1976). Elsewhere, Caldwell argues that the link of education to a strengthening of the conjugal bond is a necessary condition in the relationship of education to health decisions for children and is as important as the increased decision-making autonomy of educated women. See J. C. Caldwell, 'Cultural and Social Factors'.

51. J. C. Caldwell maintains that the educated woman is more likely to communicate with her husband, and her husband is less likely to reject such attempts. See 'Education as a Factor', and 'Maternal Education as a Factor in Child Mortality'.

52. J. C. Caldwell, Reddy, and P. Caldwell, 'The Causes of Demographic Change'; J. C. Caldwell, 'Cultural and Social Factors'.

53. P. Caldwell and J. C. Caldwell, 'Causes and Sequence in the Reduction of Postnatal Abstinence in Ibadan City, Nigeria', in Page and Lesthaege (eds.), *Child-Spacing in Tropical Africa*.

54. C. Bledsoe, 'The Politics of Polygyny in Mende Education and Child Fosterage Transactions', in B. D. Miller (ed.), *Sex and Gender Hierarchies* (Cambridge, Cambridge University Press, 1988).

55. Ibid.

56. Abdul-Aziz Farah and S. H. Preston, 'Child Mortality Differentials in Sudan', *Population and Development Review*, 8/2 (June 1982), 365–83.

57. LeVine *et al.*, 'Women's Schooling'.

58. This finding holds even after controlling for household economic status, woman's parents' education, occupation, attitudes to family relations, and whether the respondent had financial obligations to parents. See B. Limanonda, 'Analysis of Thai Marriage: Attitudes and Behaviour: A Case Study of Women in Bangkok Metropolis', Paper No. 56 (Bangkok, Institute of Population Studies, Chulalongkorn University, 1987).

59. Indeed, J. C. Caldwell suggests that the substantial age difference between spouses in regions as widespread as sub-Saharan Africa, North Africa, the Middle East, and South Asia was a powerful means of restricting the development of compassionate marital relationships. With the expansion of education has come a reduction in the age gap between spouses, a factor producing more compassionate marriages. J. C. Caldwell, 'Family Change and Demographic Change: The Reversal of the Veneration Flow', in

K. Srinivasan and S. Mukerji (eds.), *Dynamics of Population and Family Welfare* (Bombay, Himalaya Publishing House, 1987).

60. Lalla Nawar, Cynthia B. Lloyd, and Barbara Ibrahim, 'Women's Autonomy and Gender Roles in Egyptian Families' in Carla Makhlouf Obermeyer, *Gender, Family, and Population Policy: Views from the Middle East* (Cairo, The American University in Cairo, 1994).

61. Susan De Vos, *The Old-Age Security Value of Children in the Philippines and Taiwan*, Papers of the East–West Population Institute/60-G (Honolulu, East–West Center, 1984).

62. United Nations, *Women's Education and Fertility Behaviour: A Case-study of Rural Maharashtra, India* (New York, United Nations, 1993).

63. Sathar and Mason, 'Why Female Education Affects'.

64. Tsui *et al.*, 'Young Women's Work'; J. C. Caldwell, Reddy, and P. Caldwell, 'The Social Component of Mortality Decline'.

65. N. M. Birdsall and C. C. Griffin, 'Fertility and Poverty in Developing Countries', *Journal of Policy Modeling*, 10/1 (1988), 29–55; D. M. Blau, 'Investments in Child Nutrition and Women's Allocation of Time in Developing Countries', *Yale Economic Growth Centre Discussion Paper* (1981), 371.

66. Mason, *Status of Women*; M. Cain, S. R. Khanam, and S. Nahar, 'Class, Patriarchy and Women's Work in Bangladesh', *Population and Development Review*, 5/3 (1979).

67. For Argentina and Paraguay, see C. H. Wainerman, 'The Impact of Education on the Female Labour Force in Argentina and Paraguay', *Comparative Education Review* 24/2 (June 1980), S180–S195. For Mexico, see B. Garcia and O. de Oliveira, 'The Effects of Variation and Change in Female Economic Roles upon Fertility Change in Developing Countries', in International Union for the Scientific Study of Population (IUSSP), *Proceedings of the International Population Conference, New Delhi* (Liège, IUSSP, 1989), and 'Maternity and Work in Mexico in the Late Eighties', in M. Bronfman *et al.*, *Social Sectors and Reproduction in Mexico*, DHS Further Analysis Series No. 7 (Columbia, Md., and New York, Institute for Development Systems/Macro Systems Inc. and The Population Council, Apr. 1990). For Thailand, see T. P. Schultz, *Women and Development: Objectives, Frameworks, and Policy Interventions*, Policy, Planning and Research Working Papers: WPS 200 (Washington, DC, The World Bank, Population and Human Resources Department, 1989). For Indonesia, see D. Chernichovsky and O. A. Meesook, 'School Enrollment in Indonesia', World Bank Staff Working Papers No. 746 (Washington, DC, The World Bank, 1985). ·

68. Garcia and de Oliveira, 'Maternity and Work in Mexico in the Late Eighties'.

69. For Bolivia and Colombia, see Wainerman, 'The Impact of Education'; for Mexico, see Garcia and de Oliveira, 'Maternity and Work in Mexico in the Late Eighties'.

70. Zeba A. Sathar and Shahnaz Kazi, 'Women, Work and Reproduction in Karachi', *International Family Planning Perspectives*, 16/2 (June 1990), 66–9 and 80; Zeba Sathar *et al.*, 'Women's Status'.

71. S. R. Khandker, 'Determinants of Women's Time Allocation in Rural Bangladesh', *Economic Development and Cultural Change*, 37/1 (1988), 111–26.

72. R. E. Barrett *et al.*, 'Female Labor Force Participation in Urban and Rural China', *Rural Sociology*, 56/1 (Spring 1991), 1–21.

73. Sathar and Mason, 'Why Female Education Affects'.

74. Sathar, 'Women's Education and Autonomy'.

75. Chernichovsky and Meesook, 'School Enrollment in Indonesia'. For women, generally, moderate amounts of education do not enhance earning capacity, both in more developed

areas, such as Java, and in lesser developed ones, such as the outer islands. For men, this is not necessarily the case; in Java, even moderately educated men report higher earnings than do uneducated men.

76. For Indonesia, see Chernichovsky and Meesook, 'School Enrollment in Indonesia'. For Pakistan, see Sathar *et al.*, 'Women's Status', and Sathar and Kazi, 'Women, Work and Reproduction'. For Saudi Arabia, see S. A. Alsuwaigh, 'Women in Transition: The Case of Saudi Arabia', *Journal of Comparative Family Studies*, 20/1 (1989), 67–78.
77. Alsuwaigh, 'Women in Transition'.
78. Balk, 'Individual and Community Aspects'.
79. Mhloyi, 'Fertility Transition in Zimbabwe'.
80. Mason, *Status of Women*.
81. Bledsoe, 'The Politics of Polygyny in Mende Education'.
82. Calculated from Leela Visaria, 'Female Autonomy and Fertility Behaviour: An Exploration of Gujarat Data', in International Union for the Scientific Study of Population (IUSSP), *Proceedings of the International Population Conference, Montreal*, iv (Liège, IUSSP, 1993).

4 Education and Women's Age at Marriage

The positive relationship of education to marital age is one of the most pervasive findings in the literature. In many contexts, however, the effect of a small amount of education on postponing marriage is minimal. For the most part, the tendency for education to raise marriage age becomes universal only after a few years of primary education. This pattern persists irrespective of the country's overall levels of development and of gender disparity in literacy.

The reasons underlying the positive relationship of education to marital age include the greater say of educated women in marriage decisions, including whom and when to marry; the greater control over resources derived by educated women as a result of premarital employment; and, in many settings, the lessened marriageability of educated women at an early age. The impact of these factors may, however, be conditioned by the kinship structure. In highly gender-stratified cultures, the relationship of education to enhanced decision-making and premarital employment tends to be relatively weak; considerable amounts of schooling are required before women can resist traditional norms surrounding their marriages. In these settings, it is the more complicated marriage negotiations that have a prominent role in deferring age at marriage.

Education affects the supply of children or the number of children a couple has in at least four unintended ways, through the effects of education on age at marriage, breast-feeding, post-partum abstinence, and child mortality. Thus, education affects the supply of children as a result of changes in behaviour which were not deliberately undertaken to affect fertility. The most prominent of these effects is the result of delayed entry into marriage.[1] This chapter considers the evidence on the relationship between women's education and their age at marriage and on factors underlying this relationship.

Pattern of the Relationship

Marriage (or union) is important in fertility analysis because it defines, at least approximately, periods of exposure to sexual activity and child-bearing. Several measures of marriage are routinely used, such as age at marriage and proportions who ever marry. In this study, the focus is only on age at marriage or union.[2]

The positive relationship of education to age at marriage is widely documented. Positive relationships are regularly observed on the global level, as was seen in the zero-order correlations for 100 developing countries, presented in Table 2.1. More important, positive relationships are also observed at the individual level within countries. For example, WFS data from 38 developing countries reveal that the singulate mean age at marriage for the average woman with seven or more years of education was almost four years later than that for the average uneducated woman.[3]

Table 4.1 summarizes the relationship of education to age at marriage (usually first marriage) for 51 countries among the studies described in Appendix C.

Table 4.1. *Patterns in the relationship of women's education to age at marriage, by region, level of development, and gender disparity in literacy*

	Patterns in the relationship between years of schooling and age at marriage[a]			Total number of studies
	Positive	Reversed 7	None or curvilinear[b]	
A. Region[c]				
Sub-Saharan Africa	5	12	0	17
North Africa and the Middle East	3	3	0	6
East and South-East Asia	1	3	1	5
South Asia	0	4	1	5
Latin America and the Caribbean	8	8	2	18
B. Level of development				
1. Annual per capita income ($)				
500 or less	5	12	1	18
501–999	7	7	1	15
1000 or more	5	11	2	18
2. Overall female literacy rate (%)				
40 or less	6	11	1	18
41–80	7	12	0	19
81 or more	4	7	3	14
C. Gender disparity in literacy[d]				
250–700	6	11	1	18
701–850	4	8	0	12
851 or more	7	11	3	21
TOTALS	17	30	4	51

[a] Two distinct patterns in the relationship of marriage age to years of schooling are apparent: a positive relationship, which indicates that better educated women marry later (by 5 per cent or more) than uneducated women do; and a reversed-7 relationship, in which the difference between women with a small amount of education and uneducated women is negligible (less than 5 per cent), whereas substantial increases are recorded for women who are better educated.

[b] Includes one study each displaying a J- and a U-shaped relationship, and two displaying no relationship.

[c] Not all countries in a region are included, and those included are not necessarily representative of the region but are, rather, those countries for which the requisite data are available. Thus, the results are not necessarily representative of any particular region.

[d] The level of gender disparity in literacy is the number of literate females per 1000 literate males.

Notes: The studies selected for inclusion in this table appear in Appendix C, where they are marked with a dagger (†). The study populations were women of child-bearing age who were married or in union. Most studies reported the singulate mean age at marriage or the median age at marriage; a few reported percentages single at selected ages or the duration of marriage.

Sources: Of the 51 studies, 47 are based on World Fertility Survey (16) and Demographic and Health Survey (31) data, from United Nations, *Fertility Behaviour in the Context of Development: Evidence from the World Fertility Survey* (1987) or *Women's Education and Fertility Behaviour: Recent Evidence from the Demographic and Health Surveys* (1995), or other DHS and WFS reports. Sources are indicated in Appendix C.

Overall findings

The overall effect of education on marital age is positive, but this relationship is not necessarily linear or steep.

- Of the 51 studies, 17 display a clearly positive relationship between education and marital age: women with more education marry later; and
- 30 of the 51 studies show that a small amount of education produces a negligible change (less than 5 per cent) in the age at which women marry, although considerably more schooling produces substantial increases, termed a 'reversed-7-shaped' relationship (see Figure 4.1).

Although the reversed-7-shaped relationship is the most prevalent in all settings, there is some variation in this pattern by region, level of development (that is, per capita income and female literacy), and extent of gender disparities in literacy.

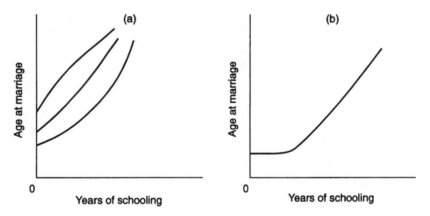

Fig. 4.1   *Illustrative patterns in the relationship between women's education and age at marriage: (a) Positive relationships; (b) Reversed-7 relationship*

Region   A straight positive relationship is most likely to be observed in Latin America and the Caribbean (8 of 18) and North Africa and the Middle East (3 of 6). In contrast, primary-schooled women marry no later than uneducated women in 12 of 17 studies in sub-Saharan Africa, 3 of 5 in East and South-East Asia, and 4 of 5 in South Asia.

Level of development   There is some, relatively weak, indication that, as per capita income levels increase, the positive effect of education on marital age becomes more evident. When the literacy context is considered, however, the pattern is unclear—in close to one third of countries in each setting, the positive effect of education on marital age is evident.

- In 12 of the 18 countries with per capita incomes of less than $500, reversed-7-shaped relationships between education and marital age are experienced;
- In higher-income countries, the reversed-7-shaped relationship is observed in 18 of 33 settings.

Gender disparities in literacy Similarly, the pattern by gender disparities in literacy suggests that a straight positive relationship occurs in one third of all settings, irrespective of level of disparity.

Differentials in marital age

Table 4.2 shows the distribution of percentage differentials in the age of marriage among women with no education compared with those with some secondary education (the highest level of education in these surveys).
- The percentage by which the age at marriage of women with some secondary education exceeds that of uneducated women is, for the majority, in the range of 11 per cent to 30 per cent.

Region Relatively wide differentials are observed in sub-Saharan Africa and in North Africa and the Middle East, where marital ages tend to be low, and in East and South-East Asia, where marital ages are relatively higher. In contrast, moderate differentials are observed in Latin America and the Caribbean, where marital ages tend to be highest. South Asia appears to be the exception, with low overall marital age and narrow differentials between extreme categories of schooling.

Level of development Differentials in marriage age tend to be wider among middle-income countries than either among low- or high-income countries. When differentials in marriage age are examined by overall female literacy rate, the widest differentials between extreme categories of education are experienced in the least literate settings (0–40 per cent):
- The size of the differential exceeds 30 per cent in 6 of the 18 studies in settings with low literacy rates, compared with only 5 of the 33 studies in settings with moderate and high literacy.

Gender disparities in literacy The size of the differential tends to narrow among more egalitarian settings.

Threshold educational levels producing increase in marital age

Table 4.3 shows the educational levels at which 10 per cent and 20 per cent increases in marital age are reached. In many cases, a primary education is ineffectual in delaying marriage and may even, in rare cases, act as a spur to early marriage. The effect of a small amount of education is thus ambiguous.

Table 4.2.   *Differentials in the relationship of women's education to age at marriage, by region, level of development, and gender disparity in literacy*

	Differences in marriage age between uneducated and secondary-schooled women[a] (percentage differentials) NARROW ◄------------------► WIDE					Total number of studies
	10 or less	11–20	21–30	31–40	41 or more	
A. Region[b]						
Sub-Saharan Africa	2	7	4	2	2	17
North Africa and the Middle East	0	2	1	2	1	6
East and South-East Asia	1	2	0	2	0	5
South Asia	1	2	2	0	0	5
Latin America and the Caribbean	3	5	8	2	0	18
B. Level of development						
1. Annual per capita income ($)						
500 or less	2	8	5	1	2	18
501–999	2	5	2	5	1	15
1000 or more	3	5	8	2	0	18
2. Overall female literacy rate (%)						
40 or less	1	5	6	3	3	18
41–80	3	8	6	2	0	19
81 or more	3	5	3	3	0	14
C. Gender disparity in literacy[c]						
250–700	1	5	6	3	3	18
701–850	3	7	2	0	0	12
851 or more	3	6	7	5	0	21
TOTALS	7	18	15	8	3	51

[a] The term 'secondary-schooled women' here applies to women who have had some secondary education or completed or gone beyond secondary school—that is, women who have had more than six years of primary education.
[b] Not all countries in a region are included, and those included are not necessarily representative of the region but are, rather, those countries for which the requisite data are available. Thus, the results are not necessarily representative of any particular region.
[c] The level of gender disparity in literacy is the number of literate females per 1000 literate males.

Notes: The studies selected for inclusion in this table appear in Appendix C, where they are marked with a dagger (†). The study populations were women of child-bearing age who were married or in union. Most studies reported the singulate mean age at marriage or the median age at marriage; a few reported percentages single at selected ages or the duration of marriage.

Sources: Of the 51 studies, 47 are based on World Fertility Survey (16) and Demographic and Health Survey (31) data, from United Nations, *Fertility Behaviour in the Context of Development: Evidence from the World Fertility Survey* (1987) or *Women's Education and Fertility Behaviour: Recent Evidence from the Demographic and Health Surveys*, or other DHS and WFS reports. Sources are indicated in Appendix C.

- In well over three-fifths of all studies reviewed, it takes more than a primary-school education before an increase in marital age of 10 per cent or more is attained. In almost all of the 51 studies, it takes more than a primary-school education before an increase of 20 per cent is attained.

Unlike the case of fertility, there is no consistent pattern either by region or by level of development in threshold levels. What is striking is that thresholds appear

Table 4.3. *Relationship of the duration of women's education to age at marriage, by region, level of development, and gender disparity in literacy*

	Educational level (years of schooling) by which:								Total number of studies
	A 10% increase in marital age is reached				A 20% increase in marital age is reached				
	1–3	4–6	7+	Never	1–3	4–6	7+	Never	
A. Region [a]									
Sub-Saharan Africa	5	3	8	1	0	1	11	5	17
North Africa and Middle East	1	3	2	0	0	2	2	2	6
East and South-East Asia	0	0	4	1	0	0	2	3	5
South Asia	0	1	3	1	0	0	3	2	5
Latin America and the Caribbean	1	5	10	2	0	0	13	5	18
B. Level of development									
1. Annual per capita income ($)									
500 or less	2	5	10	1	0	1	11	6	18
501–999	4	3	7	1	0	2	10	3	15
1000 or more	1	4	10	3	0	0	10	8	18
2. Overall female literacy rate (%)									
40 or less	5	5	7	1	0	3	11	4	18
41–80	1	4	13	1	0	0	12	7	19
81 or more	1	3	7	3	0	0	8	6	14
C. Gender disparity in literacy [b]									
250–700	5	5	7	1	0	3	11	4	18
701–850	1	3	7	1	0	0	5	7	12
851 or more	1	4	13	3	0	0	15	6	21
TOTALS	7	12	27	5	0	3	31	17	51

[a] Not all countries in a region are included, and those included are not necessarily representative of the region but are, rather, those countries for which the requisite data were available. Thus, the results are not strictly representative of any particular region.
[b] The level of gender disparity in literacy is the number of literate females per 1000 literate males.

Notes: The studies selected for inclusion in this table appear in Appendix C, where they are marked with a dagger (†). The study populations were women of child-bearing age who were married or in union. Most studies reported the singulate mean age at marriage or the median age at marriage; a few reported percentages single at selected ages or the duration of marriage. Some appendix studies combine rates for women with 1–3 and 4–6 years of schooling; for such studies, rates are shown in the column marked 1–3.

Sources: Of the 51 studies, 47 are based on World Fertility Survey (16) and Demographic and Health Survey (31) data, from United Nations, *Fertility Behaviour in the Context of Development: Evidence from the World Fertility Survey* (1987) or *Women's Education and Fertility Behaviour: Recent Evidence from the Demographic and Health Surveys* (1995), or other DHS and WFS reports. Sources are indicated in Appendix C.

to exist in low-literacy and low-income settings, in settings with wide gender disparities in literacy, and in regions in which overall age at marriage is low. Even moderate differentials of 10 per cent tend to be perceptible only among women with a secondary education.

Also striking is the finding that thresholds tend to be highest in the more developed and egalitarian settings. This is because of the trend for educational differentials to narrow once again among highly developed societies.

Differentials over time

Little can be said about the trend in the relationship over time, because the results of the few studies available are contradictory. Several studies suggest a widening of marriage age differentials over time. For example, the 1987 United Nations study on fertility behaviour observes that differentials were greater in younger cohorts than in older ones: women aged 20–29 experienced a 4.8-year spread between extreme educational categories (that is, between women with little or no education and those with secondary or more education), compared with a 3.5-year spread for women aged 40–49.[4] Corroborating this trend is evidence from two successive cross-sections (10 years apart) of women aged 35–44 in Tamil Nadu, India, which shows that each additional year of schooling reduced marital duration by 0.08 of a year (or about one month) in 1970, and by 0.39 of a year (about 4.5 months) a decade later.[5] Likewise, a study in the Philippines in 1983 and 1988 finds that the relationship of education to age at marriage became more positive over time among urban women under 35 and rural women over 35, although it remained unchanged for older urban women and younger rural women.[6]

Comparisons over time in 18 settings reported in Appendix C, however, suggest no clear pattern in educational differentials in marriage age over time.

- In nine countries (Colombia, Dominican Republic, Ecuador, Egypt, Kenya, Mexico, Peru, Senegal, and Sri Lanka), the difference in marriage age between women with secondary educations and uneducated women remained more or less constant at both points in time (within 5 per cent);
- In six other countries (Haiti, Indonesia, Morocco, the Sudan, Tunisia, and Thailand), the differential widened notably, and in three more countries (Ghana, Pakistan, and Trinidad and Tobago), it narrowed markedly.

This apparent failure of educational differentials to widen over time is corroborated by a comparison of the relationship of education to the mean age at first union of women married in the 20 years preceding the WFS versus the DHS in 15 countries. In each country studied, the differential observed in WFS surveys was virtually identical to that found in the DHS.[7] Similarly, a study that traced marriage cohorts over time in Karnataka, India, observes little change in the education-age at marriage relationship. In both the marriage cohorts of 1960 and 1979, age at marriage was unaffected by education up to ten years of schooling.[8]

In most studies, education exerts a consistent and powerful effect on women's marital age even after a host of other factors, such as economic status or characteristics of the husband, are controlled. Multivariate studies in diverse settings find that education is more consistently significant than many other factors, such as land owned by wife's parents at the time of her marriage, husband's education and occupation, childhood residence, premarital and post-marital work-force participation, income, economic status, and religion.

- For example, in rural Thailand, each additional year of school increases the age at marriage of northern Thai women by a significant 0.24 years, net of controls for husband's education, household economic status, rural–urban residence, and age;

- In Bangkok, even after economic status is controlled, the chances of marriage for women with secondary schooling or less are about 73 per cent higher than the chances among women with a bachelor's degree, while chances for women with even higher levels of education are about 13 per cent lower;
- In Bombay, India, even after controls for women's work status and household characteristics are applied, women who have completed secondary school marry on average three years later than those with less education;
- In sub-Saharan Africa, education accounts for 28 per cent of the variance in the proportion of women married at ages 15–19, after controlling for family social and economic characteristics (total explained variance: 46 per cent);
- Similarly, education is a significant determinant of marital age in Edo and Delta states of Nigeria, even after husband's education and occupation, ethnicity, community characteristics, and other attributes of women's status are controlled. Compared with uneducated women, women with primary, secondary, and tertiary schooling marry on average 0.67, 1.52 and 2.65 years later, respectively.[9]

Marriage does not always signify the initiation of sexual activity or of child-bearing. In many settings where premarital child-bearing is not uncommon, such as Africa, Latin America, and the Caribbean, the relationship of education to age at marriage may be less important than that of education to age at first union or, alternatively, first birth. Evidence on age at first birth by education in several African countries reveals a pattern similar to that observed elsewhere for age at marriage, with wide differentials between uneducated and secondary-schooled women.[10] In Guyana, there is a 3.5- to 4-year spread between the mean ages at first birth of uneducated women and women with a secondary-school education, at every age from 25 to 49.[11] A proportional hazards model suggests that young women with less than four years of education are significantly more likely than better educated women to experience an early first birth. This differential narrows among older women, however, suggesting the recency of education's effect on the timing of first births.

In summary, the recent evidence supports earlier findings that education is strongly related to the postponement of marriage[12]—more strongly than are socio-economic and other women's status variables. This review suggests, however, that the relationship of education to marital age is not necessarily linear. Only after a moderate amount of education has been reached does the positive relationship become universally observed.

How Education Delays Marriage

At least three hypothetical routes exist through which education can delay marriage.

- First, educated daughters have a greater say in their lives and, hence, may play a more active role in selecting husbands, thus resisting early, arranged marriages;

- Second, where education enhances premarital employment, it encourages women or their families—depending upon who benefits most from this employment—to postpone marriage in favour of work;
- The third hypothesis suggests a more passive or mechanical connection: educated women are less 'marriageable' at an early age, their marriages cost more, appropriate husbands are harder to find and, as a result, their marriages are delayed. At very advanced educational levels, women also remain in school well past the age at which many less educated women marry.

None of these hypotheses suggests that marriage is delayed with the specific intention of reducing fertility.

Educated daughters select their husbands

In many parts of the developing world, arranged marriages are the norm, and such arrangements usually involve young brides.[13] Education is one of the most powerful factors leading women to challenge or modify norms of arranged marriage. Educated women are expected to have an increasingly greater say in decisions about whom and when they will marry, and, hence, are better equipped to resist pressures for early marriage.[14] In relatively egalitarian cultures, the tendency is for better educated women increasingly to prefer 'love' marriages or to select their husbands entirely on their own. Even where marriages continue to be arranged, better educated women are more likely to veto unacceptable choices, and their families are more likely to accept this veto.[15] In both scenarios, the search for a husband is lengthened and the age of marriage delayed.

- A study conducted in nine major cities in Nigeria in 1987-1988 reports that the proportion of marriages initiated by the family was 33 per cent among uneducated women as opposed to 21 per cent and 13 per cent for women with a primary and secondary or higher education, respectively.[16] Moreover, the higher the age at marriage, the more likely the woman was to select her own spouse;
- Similarly, in Saudi Arabia, secondary-schooled young women were more likely to have participated in the selection of their husbands than were less educated women, and a growing number of totally unarranged marriages was reported among educated women.[17]

Most of the studies from South Asia attesting to educated women's greater role in selecting their husbands suggest that attitudinal modifications may come slowly. For example, education can affect the extent to which women are consulted in marriage negotiations even without disturbing strongly held traditional attitudes among educated women in favour of arranged marriage or dowry, as has been seen in studies in India and Pakistan.[18] In these settings, concern for preserving female modesty prohibits interaction between the sexes before marriage; the potential for individual selection of spouses is restricted even for educated women, who must continue to rely on their parents' involvement in marital decisions. Despite these constraints, better educated women are usually able to influence decisions concerning their marriages.

- A study of recent college graduates (aged 18 to 24) in a South Indian city, Bangalore, finds that the majority agreed that education had enabled them to have a say about prospective grooms and the timing of marriage (and, indeed, fewer than one-fifth were married);[19]
- In Bangladesh, too, secondary-schooled women were not only more likely to favour delayed age at marriage but also more successful in putting this preference into practice. Among secondary-schooled women, 89 per cent preferred to delay marriage beyond the age of 20 as compared with 41 per cent among secondary-school drop-outs, 17 per cent among those completing primary school, and 7 per cent among those with no schooling. That these attitudes are translated into behaviour is evident: more than 70 per cent of the less educated women and 62 per cent of the uneducated were already married, whereas only 30 per cent of the secondary-schooled girls were already married;[20]
- In Sri Lanka, education has tended to increase the proportion of love marriages, especially among the Sinhalese population and to a lesser extent among the Tamils and Moors; even so, most such marriages have parental approval, and many parents are known to pay for marriage costs and even dowries in such marriages.[21]

It appears, then, that even within the traditional framework of marriage selection, educated women can influence the timing of their marriages.

The more traditional the setting, however, the more education may be required before a woman's voice is heard. In a qualitative study of a village in rural Uttar Pradesh, North India, among Muslims and Hindus (Jats) alike, a woman's own educational status bore little relation to whether she was consulted in either the selection of her husband or the timing of her marriage. A Hindu woman with ten years of schooling explained, 'Neither was my opinion asked about this boy nor did anyone take any notice of any opinion of mine. If I had expressed my own wishes, my father would not have been able to stand the shock. . . . In this matter he considers it very bad for a girl to speak.' Only one woman with ten years of schooling voiced her opinion to her parents and delayed her marriage for a couple of years to further her education; even so, she was married at age 17 and not permitted to study further.[22]

In rural Karnataka, decisions on breast-feeding and even contraception are increasingly conceded to educated women; typically, however, marriage decisions are not as easily conceded.[23] In North India, the rare father who chooses to educate his daughter and delay her marriage can be the subject of ridicule and accused of 'sacrificing his daughter's chances to a mistaken whim intended to glorify his own name' if he cannot fulfil his duty to get his daughter married.[24] It seems reasonable to expect that education is more likely to facilitate individual choice in settings such as Africa, where the seclusion of women is relatively rare and there are relatively few restrictions on males and females mixing before marriage, than in Pakistan or India, where behaviour is strictly regulated.

In gender-stratified settings in which polygamous unions are common, decisions on marriage include not only whom and when to marry but also whether to enter a monogamous or polygamous union. Educated women in several sub-Saharan African contexts are less inclined to enter polygamous unions than are less educated women.[25] The quest for a monogamous marriage can also delay marital age.

- In Kenya, for example, 36 per cent of uneducated women aged 30 and above, compared with 22 per cent of those with some secondary education, were in polygamous marriages;
- In Togo, 38 per cent of uneducated women, compared with 50 per cent and 62 per cent, respectively, of those with a primary and secondary or higher education, were in monogamous unions;
- Qualitative evidence from Ghana suggests that educated women may be willing to forgo marriage rather than reside in a polygamous union.[26]

In more egalitarian cultures, such as those found in Latin America or South-East Asia, better educated women are expected to be less concerned with parental consent and more concerned with compatibility between spouses as a criterion for marriage than are less educated women. They are more likely to take an active role in the selection of their husbands and set higher standards of acceptability, in terms of educational and other socio-economic qualifications, for the men they are willing to marry. This greater focus on compatibility and minimum standards can easily prolong the search for a husband. In Thailand, the negative influence of education on the first marriage hazard rate has been attributed to the effect of education in raising the minimum standard considered acceptable for a match. Evidence from Singapore suggests that dating is more common among educated than among uneducated women. Not only do secondary-schooled unmarried women count more boys among their friends than less educated women do (48 per cent compared with 35 per cent) but they are also more likely to date and to identify a potential marriage partner from among their acquaintances (49 per cent compared with 31 per cent). Likewise, educated married women in Singapore are significantly more likely than uneducated women to have experienced a courtship with a man other than their eventual husbands (32 per cent versus 5 per cent). Undoubtedly, the focus of women on the qualities of an eligible mate and on personal compatibility both require an intensive and often time-consuming search and result in a delay of marriage.[27]

On the whole, then, for a variety of reasons, better educated women's greater decision-making role leads them to postpone marriage. The cultural context appears to condition this relationship, however. The more gender-stratified the culture, the weaker is the relationship of education to marital decision-making. In such cultures, correspondingly greater amounts of education may be required before women can participate in decisions about the timing of their marriages. Studies in countries as diverse as Bangladesh, India, Nepal, Nigeria, Pakistan, and Saudi Arabia have all offered support for this conditioning role of culture. Even in Sri Lanka, better educated women are systematically more likely to play the major role in selecting their husbands only among Sinhala women, whose kinship system is more egalitarian; among Tamil and Muslim women, whose kinship system is relatively male dominated, the impact of a small amount of education is far weaker.[28] In short, the more constrained women are by the kinship structure and gender traditions, the more education it takes before they are consulted in decisions on their marriages.

Education generates employment for unmarried women

Where education generates new employment opportunities for unmarried women, and where work outside the home is socially acceptable and available, women (or their parents) may defer early marriage in favour of participation in the labour-force. This effect of women's economic independence has been hypothesized as a leading motive for delayed marriage.[29] Both in gender-stratified settings, where families stand to gain from the employment of their educated daughters, and, especially, in more egalitarian settings, where the woman herself stands to gain, premarital employment is an important motive for delayed marriage (see Box 4.1).[30]

In India, the dependence of parents on educated girls who are employed is hypothesized to be one reason for delayed marriage.[31] In Sri Lanka, the economic advantages of educating daughters and delaying their marriages have led parents to make almost as extensive investments in the education of their daughters as in that of their sons. Although the marriage of daughters continues to be socially important, and arranged marriage remains the norm, parental priorities have shifted to education and employment opportunities for girls before marriage.[32] Suitable employment is often a major factor deciding the timing of marriage. An increasing number of educated women are reporting that they do not wish to marry until they have found suitable employment, not only because their earnings will be needed to help set up a household but also because their employability may never be

---

Box 4.1. *Premarital employment delays marriage age*

In gender-stratified cultures, in which the benefits of an unmarried woman's labour go to her natal family rather than herself and in which a woman's contributions to her natal family cease or diminish upon marriage, any increase in a daughter's earning capacity may motivate parents to postpone the daughter's marriage in favour of premarital employment.[a] Likewise, in more egalitarian settings, educated women may prefer to delay marriage until they have established a career or accumulated some savings. Educated women often postpone marriage in favour of work to repay their parents for the cost of their enhanced schooling, to help pay for their own marriage or dowry requirements, to help finance the education of younger siblings, or simply to contribute to the household's day-to-day expenses.

[a] K. O. Mason, *The Status of Women: A Review of Its Relationships to Fertility and Mortality* (New York, The Rockefeller Foundation, 1984) and 'The Impact of Women's Position on Demographic Change During the Course of Development: What Do We Know?', in Nora Federici, Karen Oppenheim Mason, and Solvi Sogner (eds.), *Women's Position and Demographic Change* (Oxford, Oxford University Press, 1993).

established unless they work before marriage. In fact, education and its economic potential are seen as a viable alternative to dowry in Sri Lanka, where, among unmarried men, more than three quarters preferred to marry an educated working woman to one who provided a dowry.[33]

In more egalitarian settings in which women have more direct control over their earnings, better educated women prefer to postpone marriage in favour of employment. Especially where marriage requires women to quit their jobs, educated women may be less willing to forgo earnings in favour of early marriage.[34] In Mexico, for example, better educated women deliberately maintained a longer courtship period, postponing marriage so that they could work and save enough money to establish a nuclear residence as soon after marriage as possible.[35] Educated women in the Territory of Hong Kong, perceiving premarital employment as a respite from responsibilities to both the natal family and her husband's family,[36] note the importance of savings: 'In contrast to the spontaneous and unplanned actions of older people, such as my mother . . . today we must plan! plan! plan! Plan when to marry. . . . Otherwise we wouldn't have enough money. . . . I'm postponing my marriage for at least five years.'[37]

In short, educated women appear to defer marriage in favour of increased premarital participation in the labour-force. There is more evidence of this pathway, however, in egalitarian cultures than in gender-stratified ones, where economic activity is less likely to be acceptable for women in general.

Education influences marriageability

In patriarchal cultures where marriages are arranged, educated women may be less marriageable at early ages than are uneducated women for at least four reasons. First, even in settings in which traditional attitudes and norms persist among the educated, the demand from educated men for literate wives has made female education an asset in arranging a good marriage[38] and, indeed, has been the major justification for delaying marriage beyond menarche.[39] To some extent, the mere fact of schooling may deter parents from postponing the search for a husband; the longer a young girl is kept in school, the longer she will remain out of the net of marriage negotiations.

Second, the pool of prospective grooms available to an educated woman is, by definition, smaller than that available to an uneducated daughter, because educated women require at least equally educated or well-qualified men. Because the pool of available better educated potential husbands is smaller, negotiations for the marriage of an educated daughter are, in all likelihood, far more time-consuming than those for an uneducated daughter. In both Sri Lanka and Kerala, parents of an educated daughter are reluctant to arrange her marriage to a man until he has a steady and acceptable job; parents of eligible grooms may also take a similar stance. It takes time for parents to judge the potential of a prospective son-in-law, and this may be one reason why marriages are delayed in settings in which parental decision-making is the key to marital age.[40]

Because a majority of men in the developing world have had at least some primary education, it is mainly women with a middle or secondary education who face a shrinking of the pool of eligible grooms. At the same time, a primary- school education may make a woman a more attractive marriage partner, at least in relatively egalitarian settings where women play strong economic roles in the family. For example, evidence from Thailand suggests that education has a curvilinear effect on determining the number of marriage offers a woman receives.[41] Women aged 26 and above who have completed a primary-school education have more marriage offers than either better or lesser educated women. Evidence of this kind supports the view that it is women with secondary and higher educations who are most affected by the shrinking pool of eligible potential husbands, whereas primary education has little effect and may even enhance this pool. This finding may explain why women with a small amount of education sometimes marry as early as, or earlier than, uneducated women.

Third, that better educated women must have equally or better qualified husbands has financial implications. Most evidence suggests that a better educated husband demands a larger economic contribution from his bride or her family.[42] It is argued that, in India, education has actually strengthened the dowry system[43] and that educated women routinely bring larger dowries than uneducated women bring.[44] In Karnataka, 70 per cent of the parents of lesser educated women paid a large dowry on the marriage of their daughters, whereas 86 per cent of the parents of better educated brides did so. In this region, a major apprehension about a daughter's schooling is the spiralling cost of marrying her to an equally educated male; the fear of such costs is often a deterrent for educating daughters beyond an affordable amount.[45]

A few studies suggest, however, that educated women can command lower dowries than uneducated women. A study of adolescent girls in Bangladesh who received stipends to complete their secondary education finds that education brought secondary-schooled women more attractive marriage offers and frequently allowed them to waive dowry altogether.[46]

Another study in Bangladesh highlights the point that a small amount of education does not necessarily raise marriage costs. One study shows marginal increases in both the incidence of dowry marriages and the amount of dowry paid among primary-schooled women, as compared with uneducated women, but significant increases among better educated women. Proportions of families who paid a dowry at marriage increased from 34 per cent among uneducated brides to 38 per cent among primary-schooled women and 50 per cent among better educated brides. The amount paid as dowry, similarly, remained constant among uneducated and primary-schooled women but increased fourfold among women with more than a primary education.[47] The weight of the evidence suggests the marriage of a woman with more than a small amount of education is more costly than that of less educated women. Often, the marriage has to be postponed until the prospective bride and her family can accumulate sufficient resources to meet the high dowry and marriage costs, as occurs in Sri Lanka.[48]

Fourth, in many settings, the autonomy that accompanies the education of women may itself be seen to lower their marriageability, resulting in a longer search for husbands for educated women and, thereby, a later age at marriage. Parents frequently fear that educated women who delay marriage are less certain of finding a suitable husband, a fear expressed in areas as diverse as South India and sub-Saharan Africa.[49] Parents often express the fear that girls who have been to school will revolt against tradition: against arranged marriages or polygamous marriages (as in Zaire)[50] and against the subservient behaviour expected of a dutiful wife (India).[51]

In some settings, though, education can hasten, rather than delay, the age at first union. This has been observed in parts of sub-Saharan Africa among schoolgirls who recognize the link of education to better wages and, hence, are motivated to further their educations. They are impeded by a lack of resources or the unwillingness of family members to invest in their schooling. Faced with such constraints, many girls in secondary and even some in primary schools who want to continue their schooling provide sexual favours in exchange for school-fee money from older men. In some cases, parents themselves obtain assistance for their daughter's education from men who help pay schooling expenses as a preliminary marriage payment. Although these arrangements may help schoolgirls to prolong their education, unintended pregnancies can frequently cut short further schooling.[52] Indeed, evidence from Mali suggests that parents often withdraw their daughters from schools because they fear that schooling encourages pregnancy.[53]

The hastening of marriage among secondary-schooled women appears to be the exception rather than the rule, however. By and large, and particularly in gender-stratified cultures, the evidence suggests that education is incompatible with early marriage for a number of reasons: the declining pool of eligible men, the lengthier negotiations involved in selecting a suitable husband, the financial burdens of marriage payments, and the possible reluctance of educated men and their families to accept an educated wife.

Notes

1. Bulatao and Lee (eds.), *Determinants*; Cochrane, 'Effects of Education'.
2. The proportions who ever marry tend to be of negligible importance in generating education differentials in fertility because there are few regions of the world in which, on average, more than 5 per cent of women remain single at the end of their reproductive years. Marital disruption, another commonly used measure, is not an important determinant either of fertility levels or of education differentials in fertility, in most developing countries. United Nations, *Fertility Behaviour*; Susheela Singh, John B. Casterline, and John Cleland, 'The Proximate Determinants of Fertility: Sub-national Variations', *Population Studies*, 39/1 (Mar. 1985), 113–35.
3. United Nations, *Fertility Behaviour*.
4. Ibid.
5. Jejeebhoy, 'Women's Status and Fertility'.
6. C. M. Raymundo *et al.*, 'Female Education and Fertility in the Philippines: Why the Two

Are Linked', paper presented at the International Population Conference (IUSSP), Montreal, 24 Aug.–1 Sept. 1993.

7. Rodriguez and Aravena, 'Socio-economic Factors'.

8. N. Hatti and R. Ohlsson, 'Impact of Education on Age at Marriage', *Demography India*, 14/2 (July–Dec. 1985), 159–73.

9. For findings from northern Thailand, see S. H. Cochrane and K. N. Nandwani, 'The Determinants of Fertility in 22 Villages of Northern Thailand', Discussion Paper No. 81-59 (Washington, DC, The World Bank, Population and Human Resources Division, 1981); from Bangkok, see Limanonda, 'Analysis of Thai Marriage'; from Bombay, India, see P. K. Bhargava and P. C. Saxena, 'Female Work Participation and Age at Marriage in an Urban Setting', in K. Srinivasan and S. Mukerji (eds.), *Dynamics of Population and Family Welfare* (Bombay, Himalaya Publishing House, 1985); from the Republic of Korea, see S. Kim and W. F. Stinner, 'Social Origins, Educational Attainment and the Timing of Marriage and First Birth among Korean Women', *Journal of Marriage and Family*, 42/3 (Aug. 1980), 671–9; from sub-Saharan Africa, see G. Kaufmann, R. Lesthaeghe, and D. Meekers, 'Marriage Patterns and Change in Sub-Saharan Africa', in *The Cultural Roots of African Fertility Regimes*, Proceedings of the Ife Conference, 25 Feb.–1 Mar. 1987; and from Edo and Delta states, Nigeria, see C. E. E. Okojie, 'The Relationship Between Women's Status, Proximate Determinants and Fertility in Nigeria', paper presented at the Seminar on Women and Demographic Change in Sub-Saharan Africa, sponsored by the IUSSP Committee on Gender and Population, Dakar, Senegal, 3–6 Mar. 1993. The Okojie study is of special significance because it suggests that the effect of education on age at marriage is strong even after other female-status factors, such as decision-making power and sex-role ideology, have been controlled and because its effect is stronger than any of these—even though some of the effect of education is, undoubtedly, captured by such variables as decision-making power and control over resources.

10. F. Eelens and L. Donne, 'The Proximate Determinants of Fertility in Sub-Saharan Africa', Interuniversity Programme in Demography (IPD) Working Paper, 1985-3 (Brussels, Vrije Universiteit, 1985), as quoted in T. P. Schultz, 'Returns to Women's Education', in King and Hill (eds.), *Women's Education*.

11. V. K. Rao and K. S. Murty, 'Covariates of Age at First Birth in Guyana: A Hazards Model Analysis', *Journal of Biosocial Science*, 19 (1987), 427–38.

12. Cochrane, 'Effects of Education'; Guy Standing, 'Women's Work Activity and Fertility', in Bulatao and Lee (eds.), *Determinants*, i; Peter C. Smith, 'The Impact of Age at Marriage and Proportions Marrying on Fertility', in Bulatao and Lee (eds.), *Determinants*, ii.

13. Mason, *Status of Women*.

14. Mason, 'Impact of Women's Position'.

15. Mason, *Status of Women*; Ruth B. Dixon, 'Women's Rights and Fertility.' *Reports on Population/Family Planning*, No. 17 (Jan. 1975).

16. Feyisetan and Bankole, 'Mate Selection'.

17. Alsuwaigh, 'Women in Transition'.

18. For India, see R. Kumari, 'Attitude of Girls Towards Marriage and a Planned Family', *Journal of Family Welfare*, 31/3 (Mar. 1985), 53–60; and C. Vlassoff, 'Unmarried Adolescent Females in Rural India'. For Pakistan, see J. Henry Korson, 'Modernization and Social Change in Pakistan', in *Pakistan in Transition*, edited by W. H. Wriggins (Islamabad, University of Islamabad Press, 1975), as reported in Smock, *Women's Education*.

19. R. L. Goldstein, 'Students in Saris: College Education in the Lives of Young Indian Women', *Journal of Asian and African Studies*, 5/3 (July 1970), 192–201.

20. L. G. Martin, D. R. Flanagan, and A. R. Klenicki, 'Evaluation of the Bangladesh Female Secondary Education Scholarship Program and Related Female Education and Employment Initiatives to Reduce Fertility' (Washington, DC, International Science and Technology Institute, Inc., 1985); and L. G. Martin, 'Female Education and Fertility in Bangladesh', *Asian and Pacific Population Forum*, 1/3 (May 1987), 1–7.

21. S. Jayaweera, 'Women and Education', in *Status of Women: Sri Lanka* (Colombo, University of Colombo, 1979); and J. Caldwell *et al.*, 'Is Marriage Delay a Multiphasic Response?'

22. P. Jeffery and R. Jeffery, 'North Indian Relationships: Jats and Sheikhs in Bijnor', paper presented at the Workshop on Female Education, Autonomy and Fertility Change in South Asia, New Delhi, Apr. 1993.

23. J. C. Caldwell, Reddy, and P. Caldwell, 'The Causes of Demographic Change'.

24. D. G. Mandelbaum, *Society in India: Continuity and Change*, 2 vols. (Berkeley, University of California Press, 1970), quoted in J. C. Caldwell, 'Mass Education'.

25. J. C. Caldwell and P. Caldwell, 'Cause and Sequence'; F. van de Walle and E. van de Walle, 'Woman's Autonomy and Fertility', in Federici, Mason, and Sogner (eds.) *Women's Position and Demographic Change*.

26. Evidence from Kenya is from Smock, *Women's Education*. Evidence from Togo is from A. J. Gage-Brandon and D. Meekers, 'The Changing Dynamics of Family Formation: Women's Status and Nuptiality in Togo', paper presented at the Seminar on Women and Demographic Change in Sub-Saharan Africa, sponsored by the IUSSP Committee on Gender and Population, Dakar, Senegal, 3–6 Mar. 1993. Evidence from Ghana is from Oppong and Abu, *Seven Roles of Women*.

27. There is evidence from both Singapore and Thailand in M. R. Montgomery, P. P. L. Cheung, and D. B. Sulak, 'Rates of Courtship and First Marriage in Thailand', *Population Studies*, 42 (1988), 375–88. The figures from Singapore concerning friendships and potential marriage partners among secondary-schooled women compared with less educated women are from M. R. Montgomery and P. P. L. Cheung, 'First Marriage and Assortative Mating in Singapore' (1991).

28. Jayaweera, 'Women and Education'.

29. J. Caldwell *et al.*, 'Is Marriage Delay a Multiphasic Response?'; Mason, 'Impact of Women's Position'; J. W. Salaff and A. K. Wong, 'Chinese Women at Work: Work Commitment and Fertility in the Asian Setting', in S. Kupinsky (ed.), *The Fertility of Working Women* (New York, Praeger Publishers, 1977).

30. Mason, *Status of Women* and 'The Impact of Women's Position'.

31. Jain and Nag, 'Importance of Female Primary Education'.

32. Caldwell *et al.*, 'Is Marriage Delay a Multiphasic Response?'.

33. S. Jayaweera, 'Women and Education'.

34. Smith, 'Impact of Age at Marriage'.

35. LeVine *et al.*, 'Women's Schooling'.

36. J. W. Salaff, *Working Daughters of Hong Kong: Filial Piety or Power in the Family?* (Cambridge, Cambridge University Press, 1981).

37. J. W. Salaff, 'The Status of Unmarried Hong Kong Women and the Social Factors Contributing to Their Delayed Marriage', *Population Studies*, 30/3 (1976), 391–412.

38. For Rajasthan, India, see L. Minturn, 'Changes'; for Karnataka, India, see J. C. Caldwell, Reddy, and P. Caldwell, 'Causes of Demographic Change'. See also C. Vlassoff,

'Against the Odds: The Changing Impact of Education on Female Autonomy and Fertility in an Indian Village', paper presented at the Workshop on Female Education, Autonomy and Fertility Change in South Asia, New Delhi, Apr. 1993.

39. Mhloyi, 'Fertility Transition in Zimbabwe'.
40. J. Caldwell *et al.*, 'Is Marriage Delay a Multiphasic Response?'.
41. Montgomery, Cheung, and Sulak, 'Rates of Courtship'.
42. Kasarda, Billy, and West (1986), *Status Enhancement*; Jain and Nag, 'Importance of Female Primary Education'.
43. K. M. Kapadia, *Marriage and Family in India* (Bombay, Oxford University Press, 1958).
44. For Bangalore, see Goldstein, 'Students in Saris'; for Rajastan, see Minturn, 'Changes'; and for Karnataka, see A. S. Seetharamu and M. D. Ushadevi, *Education in Rural Areas* (New Delhi, Ashish Publishing House, 1985).
45. J. C. Caldwell, Reddy, and P. Caldwell, 'Educational Transition in Rural India'.
46. L. G. Martin, D. R. Flanagan, and A. R. Klenicki, 'Evaluation of the Bangladesh Female Secondary Education Scholarship Program and Related Female Education and Employment Initiatives to Reduce Fertility' (Washington, DC, International Science and Technology Institute, Inc., 1985).
47. Sajeda Amin, 'The Correlates of Female Education and Fertility in Rural Bangladesh', paper presented at the Workshop on Female Education, Autonomy and Fertility Change in South Asia, New Delhi, Apr. 1993.
48. J. Caldwell *et al.*, 'Is Marriage Delay a Multiphasic Response?'
49. For India, see J. C. Caldwell, Reddy, and P. Caldwell, 'Educational Transition in Rural South India', and Jain and Nag, 'Importance of Female Primary Education'; for Mali, see F. van de Walle and E. van de Walle, 'Woman's Autonomy and Fertility'.
50. For evidence from the former Belgian Congo (now Zaire), see B. A. Yates, 'African Reactions to Education: The Congolese Case', *Comparative Education Review* 15 (1971), 158–71, as reported in J. C. Caldwell, 'Mass Education'.
51. Mandelbaum, *Human Fertility in India*, for evidence from India.
52. Bledsoe, 'School Fees'.
53. F. van de Walle and E. van de Walle, 'Woman's Autonomy and Fertility'.

5 Fertility-enhancing Effects of Education

The literature strongly supports the existence of an inverse effect of education on the duration of both breast-feeding and abstinence. Even a small amount of education leads to a decline in these durations, although there is evidence that the effect becomes stronger at higher levels of education. The inverse relationship of education to durations of breast-feeding and abstinence is influenced by several changes in the situation of women. These include the increased awareness among educated women of alternatives to prolonged breast-feeding and abstinence; greater decision-making power among educated women concerning such personal aspects of their lives; and increased husband–wife intimacy among educated women. Finally, in contexts in which opportunities for women's work outside the home are plentiful and where breast-milk substitutes are widely available and culturally acceptable, educated working women do seem to find breast-feeding incompatible with the demands of employment. They are, hence, more likely to breast-feed for shorter durations.

Several mechanisms have traditionally kept natural fertility relatively low in many regions of the developing world. The most obvious of these are prolonged breast-feeding and post-partum abstinence and their effects on extending the period of post-partum non-susceptibility. Education frequently erodes these practices, resulting in an increase in fertility. Other factors that may depress natural fertility are poor health, including reproductive health problems and exposure to sexually transmitted diseases, and poor nutrition, which also affects women's pace of child-bearing and risk of miscarriage. There is, however, relatively little information available on these fertility-reducing mechanisms, particularly on the relationship of education to them. This chapter focuses on breast-feeding and abstinence behaviours.

Breast-feeding: Pattern of the Relationship

Table 5.1 summarizes the relationship of education to the duration of breast-feeding for 54 studies reported in Appendix D.[1]

Overall findings

Education has an inverse relationship to the duration of breast-feeding, irrespective of region, level of development, or gender disparity in literacy. Women with more education breast-feed for shorter periods.

• In 41 of the 54 studies in Table 5.1, education has an inverse effect on the duration of breast-feeding;

Table 5.1.   *Patterns in the relationship of women's education to the duration of breast-feeding, by region, level of development, and gender disparity in literacy*

	Patterns in the relationship between years of schooling and duration of breast-feeding[a]		Total number of studies
	Inverse (negative)	7 or reversed J	
A. Region[b]			
Sub-Saharan Africa	11	8	19
North Africa and the Middle East	5	2	7
East and South-East Asia	6	0	6
South Asia	4	0	4
Latin America and the Caribbean	15	3	18
B. Level of development			
1. Annual per capita income ($)			
500 or less	11	7	18
501–999	12	4	16
1000 or more	18	2	20
2. Overall female literacy rate (%)			
40 or less	11	7	18
41–80	18	4	22
81 or more	12	2	14
C. Gender disparity in literacy[c]			
250–700	11	7	18
701–850	10	4	14
851 or more	20	2	22
TOTALS	41	13	54

[a] Two distinct patterns in the relationship of years of schooling to duration of breast-feeding are apparent: an inverse relationship, in which better educated women have shorter durations (by 5 per cent or more) of breast-feeding than uneducated women do; and a 7-shaped relationship, in which moderately educated women have about the same duration of breast-feeding as uneducated women do (within 5 per cent), but better educated women breast-feed for shorter durations. This column includes one case with a reversed-J-shaped relationship, in which breast-feeding durations of primary-schooled women exceed those of uneducated women by more than 5 per cent, but better educated women experience shorter durations of breast-feeding.

[b] Not all countries in a region are included, and those included are not necessarily representative of the region but are, rather, those countries for which the requisite data are available. Thus, the results are not necessarily representative of any particular region.

[c] The level of gender disparity in literacy is the number of literate females per 1000 literate males.

Notes: The studies selected for inclusion in this table appear in Appendix D, where they are marked with a dagger (†).

Sources: Of the 54 studies, 50 are based on World Fertility Survey (18) and Demographic and Health Survey (32) data, from United Nations, *Fertility Behaviour in the Context of Development: Evidence from the World Fertility Survey* (1987) or *Women's Education and Fertility Behaviour: Recent Evidence from the Demographic and Health Surveys* (1995), or other DHS and WFS reports. Sources are indicated in Appendix D.

- In another 12 studies, it has a 7-shaped relationship, in which the difference in breast-feeding durations of women with a small amount of education and uneducated women is negligible (less than 5 per cent), whereas substantial decreases are recorded for better educated women;

- In 1 study, a reversed-J-shaped relationship is observed, in which breast-feeding durations of primary-schooled women exceed those of uneducated women by more than 5 per cent, but durations of breast-feeding among better educated women are considerably lower.

Inverse relationships predominate in every region, from South Asia and sub-Saharan Africa, where prolonged breast-feeding is the norm, to Latin America and the Caribbean, North Africa and the Middle East, and East and South-East Asia, where it is not. Moreover, the inverse relationship holds irrespective of level of per capita income, female literacy, or gender disparity in literacy. These results suggest that, for the most part, even a small amount of education leads to marked declines in the duration of breast-feeding. This is a clear departure from the pattern of the relationship of education both to children ever born and to marital age, noted in Chapters 2 and 4, and underscores the importance of changes in breast-feeding in explaining the occasionally positive effect of small amounts of education on fertility.

Differentials

The size of the differential in the duration of breast-feeding between uneducated women and those who have secondary and higher educations averages between four and seven months. In percentage terms, however, the spread is quite wide and highly sensitive to contextual factors (see Table 5.2).

- A majority of studies shows wide differentials: 35 of 54 studies report differentials between the extremes of education of more than 20 per cent, whereas only 5 report differentials of 10 per cent or less;
- By region, differentials are narrowest in sub-Saharan Africa, where prolonged lactation is the norm;
- Differentials also widen systematically with rising levels of per capita income and female literacy and with narrowing gender disparities in literacy.

The widest differentials are suggested when studies are categorized by the country's level of per capita income: 18 of 20 studies in the high-income countries find differentials exceeding 20 per cent, compared with only 5 of 18 studies in low-income countries.

Differentials are narrower when studies are classified by female literacy levels.

- Half of all studies (9 of 18) in countries with low literacy levels report differentials exceeding 20 per cent; this proportion increases with literacy, to 86 per cent (12 of 14) of the studies in high literacy settings.

A similar pattern of differentials is evident when studies are classified by level of gender disparity in literacy. Almost half of all studies in countries with both wide (9 of 18) and moderate (8 of 14) gender disparities report differences exceeding 20 per cent compared with more than three-quarters of all studies in the most egalitarian settings (18 of 22).

In the large majority of studies, 44 of 54 (81 per cent), uneducated women experience the longest durations of breast-feeding (not shown in Table 5.1).

Table 5.2. *Differentials in the relationship of women's education to the duration of breast-feeding, by region, level of development, and gender disparity in literacy*

| | Differences in duration of breast-feeding between uneducated and secondary-schooled women[a] (percentage differentials) NARROW ◄------------------► WIDE | | | | | Total number of studies |
	10 or less	11–20	21–30	31–50	51 or more	
A. Region[b]						
Sub-Saharan Africa	4	8	4	3	0	19
North Africa and the Middle East	1	1	1	2	2	7
East and South-East Asia	0	0	1	4	1	6
South Asia	0	2	1	0	1	4
Latin America and the Caribbean	0	3	5	5	5	18
B. Level of development						
1. Annual per capita income ($)						
500 or less	4	9	4	0	1	18
501–999	1	3	4	7	1	16
1000 or more	0	2	4	7	7	20
2. Overall female literacy rate (%)						
40 or less	1	8	5	2	2	18
41–80	3	5	3	9	2	22
81 or more	1	1	4	3	5	14
C. Gender disparity in literacy[c]						
250–700	1	8	5	2	2	18
701–850	3	3	2	6	0	14
851 or more	1	3	5	6	7	22
TOTALS	5	14	12	14	9	54

[a] The term 'secondary-schooled women' here applies to women who have had some secondary education or completed or gone beyond secondary school—that is, women who have had more than six years of primary education.

[b] Not all countries in a region are included, and those included are not necessarily representative of the region but are, rather, those countries for which the requisite data are available. Thus, the results are not necessarily representative of any particular region.

[c] The level of gender disparity in literacy is the number of literate females per 1000 literate males.

Notes: The studies selected for inclusion in this table appear in Appendix D, where they are marked with a dagger (†).

Sources: Of the 54 studies, 50 are based on World Fertility Survey (18) and Demographic and Health Survey (32) data, from United Nations, *Fertility Behaviour in the Context of Development: Evidence from the World Fertility Survey* (1987) or *Women's Education and Fertility Behaviour: Recent Evidence from the Demographic and Health Surveys* (1995), or other DHS and WFS reports. Sources are indicated in Appendix D.

Thresholds

There is little evidence of thresholds; even a small amount of education usually leads to declines in breast-feeding durations (see Table 5.3).

Table 5.3 shows the level of education by which 10 per cent and 20 per cent declines in breast-feeding durations are attained by women with some education, compared with uneducated women. This information should provide a notion of

Table 5.3.   *Relationship of the duration of women's education to the duration of breast-feeding, by region, level of development, and gender disparity in literacy*

	Educational level (years of schooling) by which:								Total number of studies
	A 10% decline in breast-feeding is reached				A 20% decline in breast-feeding is reached				
	1–3 (1–6)	4–6	7+	Never	1–3 (1–6)	4–6	7+	Never	
A. Region [a]									
Sub-Saharan Africa	5	8	4	2	0	3	8	8	19
North Africa and the Middle East	4	2	0	1	2	2	1	2	7
East and South-East Asia	4	1	1	0	1	1	4	0	6
South Asia	3	1	0	0	1	0	2	1	4
Latin America and the Caribbean	7	6	5	0	1	7	8	2	18
B. Level of development									
1. Annual per capita income ($)									
500 or less	8	4	3	3	1	2	6	9	18
501–999	6	6	4	0	1	4	7	4	16
1000 or more	9	8	3	0	3	7	10	0	20
2. Overall female literacy rate (%)									
40 or less	9	7	1	1	2	3	7	6	18
41–80	9	4	8	1	2	6	8	6	22
81 or more	5	7	1	1	1	4	8	1	14
C. Gender disparity in literacy [b]									
250–700	9	7	1	1	2	3	7	6	18
701–850	5	3	5	1	1	3	5	5	14
851 or more	9	8	4	1	2	7	11	2	22
TOTAL	23	18	10	3	5	13	23	13	54

[a] Not all countries in a region are included, and those included are not necessarily representative of the region but are, rather, those countries for which the requisite data were available. Thus, the results are not necessarily representative of any particular region.

[b] The level of gender disparity in literacy is the number of literate females per 1000 literate males.

Notes: The studies selected for inclusion in this table appear in Appendix D, where they are marked with a dagger (†). Some appendix studies combine rates for women with 1–3 and 4–6 years of schooling; in such studies, rates are shown in the column marked 1–3.

Sources: Of the 54 studies, 50 are based on World Fertility Survey (18) and Demographic and Health Survey (32) data, from United Nations, *Fertility Behaviour in the Context of Development: Evidence from the World Fertility Survey* (1987) or *Women's Education and Fertility Behaviour: Recent Evidence from the Demographic and Health Surveys* (1995), or other DHS and WFS reports. Sources are indicated in Appendix D.

what threshold level of education is required before modest and substantial declines in breast-feeding durations are attained. The results suggest low overall thresholds.

• Of the 54 studies summarized, 23 show a 10 per cent decline in the duration of breast-feeding by one to three (or one to six) years of schooling, 18 by four to six years of schooling, and 10 by the secondary-school stage.

Most women with education to the lower or upper primary-school level thus experience a 10 per cent decline in the duration of breast-feeding, and this pattern persists irrespective of levels of income, female literacy, or gender disparities in literacy.

In the majority of cases, substantial (20 per cent) declines require an upper primary or, more often, a secondary education.[2]

As is the case for fertility and age at marriage, controlling for household economic status fails to eliminate the effect of education on durations of breast-feeding. For example, one study in an urban area of Nigeria finds that, even after controlling for such demographic and socio-economic factors as age, marital duration, contraception, work status, residence, religion, and husband's education, the risk of terminating breast-feeding among secondary-schooled women was 3.5 times higher than the risk among uneducated women, compared with a differential of 10 months in the unadjusted relationship.[3] Other multivariate studies in both rural and urban Nigeria confirm this finding.[4]

The evidence suggests that better educated women not only wean earlier than less educated women do but are less likely to practise exclusive breast-feeding. For example, in Bangladesh, even in cases where breast-feeding durations of educated women are not much shorter than those of uneducated women, their durations of post-partum amenorrhoea can be considerably shorter, because educated women are more likely to use liquid supplements.[5] Evidence from the Philippines (Cebu) suggests that each additional year of women's schooling reduces the probability of exclusive breast-feeding by 36 per cent, but of any breast-feeding by 5 per cent.[6] In Latin America, where overall durations of breast-feeding are short, education has little effect on the proportions of women who are breast-feeding but more powerful negative effects on the duration of breast-feeding and especially on the proportions who exclusively breast-feed for at least four months.[7]

Recent public focus on the advantages of breast-feeding seems not to have disturbed the essentially inverse relationship of women's education to durations of breast-feeding. In the Philippines, for example, a series of national demographic surveys conducted over the 1970s and 1980s has allowed researchers to track the influence of education on breast-feeding duration over time.[8] These studies find that, despite some evidence of a modest increase in the duration of breast-feeding (0.3 months) at each level of education over the 1973–83 decade,[9] the inverse relationship of education to the duration of breast-feeding remains strong over time, rural–urban residence, and cohorts.[10]

If the settings for which data are reported at more than one time in Appendix D are examined, several patterns can be discerned. None, however, challenges the constancy of the inverse effect of education on breast-feeding duration. In 13 of the

19 countries for which data are available at two points in time, approximately 10 years apart, the pattern was inverse at both times. Although overall durations of breast-feeding for all women have remained largely unchanged over time, the differential in the duration of breast-feeding between uneducated and secondary-schooled women has narrowed in the majority of settings (13 of 19), widened in 4 settings, and remained unchanged in 2. A narrowing of the relationship over time in the majority of studies was earlier noted in a study attributing the overall narrowing of differentials in the decade between the WFS and DHS surveys to the recent attention to breast-feeding having possibly led better educated women to breast-feed for longer durations than earlier.[11]

In short, the relationship of women's education to the duration of breast-feeding is inverse in the great majority of cases. There is little evidence of thresholds; even a small amount of education usually leads to declines in breast-feeding durations. For the most part, the inverse relationship is observed irrespective of region, level of development, or level of gender disparity in literacy. However, wider differentials are generated in regions with relatively short average durations of breast-feeding (Latin America, North Africa and the Middle East, and East and South-East Asia) than in regions with longer durations (sub-Saharan Africa and South Asia). The differentials are also wide in more developed and more egalitarian settings (in terms of gender disparities in literacy) as compared with less developed and more inegalitarian settings.

Abstinence: Pattern of the Relationship

There is much less evidence on the relationship of education to abstinence than to breast-feeding. What is available relates specifically to post-partum abstinence, although other kinds of abstinence practices also prevail—such as on special days[12] or terminal abstinence—and their observance is likely to be eroded by education. Traditionally, evidence on the relationship between female education and abstinence has been limited in geographic scope to the sub-Saharan African region and, particularly, to West Africa. With the results of the DHS, however, data have become available from other regions as well, as can be seen in Appendix E.

The focus on West Africa is appropriate. Although practised elsewhere, post-partum abstinence tends to be of relatively short duration in other regions compared with West Africa, where post-partum abstinence often exceeds one year and where the duration of abstinence can exceed the duration of amenorrhoea (Appendix E). In these cases, the duration of post-partum abstinence is a more important mechanism in determining natural fertility than is the duration of breast-feeding. There are wide regional variations in overall durations of post-partum abstinence, ranging from more than 10 months in certain countries of sub-Saharan Africa (Botswana, Ghana, Liberia, Nigeria, and Togo) to less than six months on average in the rest of Africa and in other regions.

Tables 5.4, 5.5, and 5.6 summarize the results of 31 studies drawn from the DHS

Table 5.4. *Patterns in the relationship of women's education to the duration of post-partum abstinence, by region, level of development, and gender disparity in literacy*

	Patterns in the relationship between years of of schooling and duration of post-partum abstinence[a]						Total number of studies
	Inverse (negative)	7	Reversed U or reversed J	U or J	Positive	None or irregular	
A. Region[b]							
Sub-Saharan Africa	4	0	3	3	1	2	13
North Africa and the Middle East	1	0	0	1	0	1	3
East and South-East Asia	1	1	0	0	0	0	2
South Asia	1	0	0	0	1	1	3
Latin America and the Caribbean	3	1	3	0	2	1	10
B. Level of development							
1. Annual per capita income ($)							
500 or less	4	0	1	2	1	4	12
501–999	5	0	3	1	1	0	10
1000 or more	1	2	2	1	2	1	9
2. Overall female literacy rate (%)							
40 or less	4	0	2	1	1	3	11
41–80	3	1	3	2	3	1	13
81 or more	3	1	1	1	0	1	7
C. Gender disparity in literacy[c]							
250–700	4	0	2	1	1	3	11
701–850	1	0	3	2	1	1	8
851 or more	5	2	1	1	2	1	12
TOTALS	10	2	6	4	4	5	31

[a] Several distinct patterns in the relationship of years of schooling to duration of post-partum abstinence are apparent: an inverse relationship, in which better educated women have shorter durations of abstinence (by 5 per cent or more) than uneducated women do; a U- or J-shaped relationship, in which moderately educated women experience shorter durations of abstinence (by 5 per cent or more) than uneducated and better educated women do; a reversed U or reversed J, in which moderately educated women experience longer durations of abstinence (by 5 per cent or more)than uneducated and better educated women do; a 7-shaped relationship, in which moderately educated women experience about the same duration of abstinence (within 5 per cent) as uneducated women do, but better educated women experience shorter durations; a positive relationship, in which better educated women experience longer durations of abstinence (by 5 per cent or more) than uneducated and moderately educated women do; and irregular or no relationships.

[b] Not all countries in a region are included, and those included are not necessarily representative of the region but are, rather, those countries for which the requisite data are available. Thus, the results are not necessarily representative of any particular region.

[c] The level of gender disparity in literacy is the number of literate females per 1000 literate males.

Notes: The studies selected for inclusion in this table appear in Appendix E, where they are marked with a dagger (†).

Sources: Of the 31 studies, 30 are based on Demographic and Health Survey data, from United Nations, *Women's Education and Fertility Behaviour: Recent Evidence from the Demographic and Health Surveys* (1995), or other DHS reports. Sources are indicated in Appendix E.

Table 5.5. *Differentials in the relationship of women's education to the duration of post-partum abstinence, by region, level of development, and gender disparity in literacy*

	Differences in duration of post-partum abstinence between uneducated and secondary-schooled women[a] (percentage differentials) NARROW ◄------------------► WIDE				Total number of studies
	10 or less	11–20	21–30	31 or more	
A. Region[b]					
Sub-Saharan Africa	7	2	0	4	13
North Africa and the Middle East	2	0	1	0	3
East and South-East Asia	0	0	1	1	2
South Asia	2	0	0	1	3
Latin America and the Caribbean	5	1	2	2	10
B. Level of development					
1. Annual per capita income ($)					
500 or less	7	2	0	3	12
501–999	4	0	2	4	10
1000 or more	5	1	2	1	9
2. Overall female literacy rate (%)					
40 or less	5	2	1	3	11
41–80	9	0	1	3	13
81 or more	2	1	2	2	7
C. Gender disparity in literacy[c]					
250–700	5	2	1	3	11
701–850	7	0	0	1	8
851 or more	4	1	3	4	12
TOTALS	16	3	4	8	31

[a] The term 'secondary-schooled women' here applies to women who have had some secondary education or completed or gone beyond secondary school—that is, women who have had more than six years of primary education.

[b] Not all countries in a region are included, and those included are not necessarily representative of the region but are, rather, those countries for which the requisite data are available. Thus, the results are not necessarily representative of any particular region.

[c] The level of gender disparity in literacy is the number of literate females per 1000 literate males.

Notes: The studies selected for inclusion in this table appear in Appendix E, where they are marked with a dagger (†).

Sources: Of the 31 studies, 30 are based on Demographic and Health Survey data, from United Nations, *Women's Education and Fertility Behaviour: Recent Evidence from the Demographic and Health Surveys* (1995), or other DHS reports. Sources are indicated in Appendix E.

and other surveys. The preponderance of DHS studies is a limitation, in so far as personal information on subjects such as abstinence is probably more reliably gathered from small in-depth and qualitative studies.

Overall findings

In general, there would seem to be a variety of patterns in the relationship of education to the duration of post-partum abstinence (Table 5.4). In the majority of

Table 5.6. *Relationship of the duration of women's education to the duration of post-partum abstinence, by region, level of development, and gender disparity in literacy*

	Educational level (years of schooling) by which:								Total number of studies
	A 10% decline in duration of post-partum abstinence is reached				A 20% decline in duration of post-partum abstinence is reached				
	1–3	4–6	7+	Never	1–3	4–6	7+	Never	
A. Region[a]									
Sub-Saharan Africa	5	5	1	2	3	4	3	3	13
North Africa and the Middle East	0	1	0	2	0	0	1	2	3
East and South-East Asia	1	1	0	0	0	2	0	0	2
South Asia	0	1	0	2	0	1	0	2	3
Latin America and the Caribbean	3	2	0	5	2	0	3	5	10
B. Level of development									
1. Annual per capita income ($)									
500 or less	4	4	1	3	3	5	1	3	12
501–999	4	3	0	3	1	1	4	4	10
1000 or more	1	3	0	5	1	1	2	5	9
2. Overall female literacy rate (%)									
40 or less	2	5	1	3	1	3	4	3	11
41–80	4	2	0	7	1	2	2	8	13
81 or more	3	3	0	1	3	2	1	1	7
C. Gender disparity in literacy[b]									
250–700	2	5	1	3	1	3	4	3	11
701–850	2	1	0	5	1	1	0	6	8
851 or more	5	4	0	3	3	3	3	3	12
TOTALS	9	10	1	11	5	7	7	12	31

[a] Not all countries in a region are included, and those included are not necessarily representative of the region but are, rather, those countries for which the requisite data were available. Thus, the results are not necessarily representative of any particular region.
[b] The level of gender disparity in literacy is the number of literate females per 1000 literate males.

Notes: The studies selected for inclusion in this table appear in Appendix E, where they are marked with a dagger (†).

Sources: Of the 31 studies, 30 are based on Demographic and Health Survey data, from United Nations, *Women's Education and Fertility Behaviour: Recent Evidence from the Demographic and Health Surveys* (1995), or other DHS reports. Sources are indicated in Appendix E. Some appendix studies combine rates for women with 1–3 and 4–6 years of schooling; in such studies, rates are shown in the column marked 1–3.

studies—18 of 31—highly educated women practise shorter durations of post-partum abstinence than do uneducated women; however, there is less consistency in the behaviour of moderately educated women. As a result, a uniform inverse relationship is observed in only about one-third of all studies (10 of 31). Several of these are studies in countries in which prolonged post-partum abstinence is the norm.

Other patterns include a U- or J-shaped relationship, in which the duration of abstinence declines among primary-schooled women and increases again thereafter (this pattern is observed in 4 countries, again mostly in sub-Saharan Africa). In 6 studies, a reversed-U- or reversed-J-shaped relationship is observed; in these, women with a small amount of education practise post-partum abstinence for longer durations than either uneducated or well-educated women (observed largely in sub-Saharan Africa and Latin America and the Caribbean). Other studies display 7-shaped relationships (2 studies), positive relationships (4), and irregular relationships (5).

Differentials

The differentials in the duration of post-partum abstinence between uneducated and highly educated women appear to be narrow: in half (16 of 31) the studies, differentials do not exceed 10 per cent (Table 5.5).

In those areas where post-partum abstinence is most prolonged, however, education generates the widest differentials. For example, in Ghana, Liberia, Nigeria, and Togo, where average durations exceed 10 months, secondary-schooled (7+ years of schooling) women practise post-partum abstinence for 60–80 per cent as long as uneducated women do. In contrast, levels of development and gender disparities in literacy have little conditioning effect on the relationship of women's education to the duration of post-partum abstinence.

Thresholds

Thresholds tend to be low, but this is largely the result of low thresholds in the sub-Saharan African region (see Table 5.6). A 10 per cent decline in abstinence durations is reached at the lower- or upper-primary level in two-thirds of all studies, and in more than three-quarters of all studies in sub-Saharan Africa (10 of 13), compared with half (9 of 18) in other regions.

Similarly, a 20 per cent decline is attained by the lower- or upper-primary-school level in about half of all studies in sub-Saharan Africa (7 of 13), compared with fewer than one in three in the remaining regions (5 of 18). Thresholds do not appear to vary systematically either by level of development or by gender disparities in literacy. A 10 per cent decline in the duration of abstinence is more likely to occur at the lower-primary stage in studies in low- and middle-income countries compared with those in high-income ones; however, thresholds tend to be lower in studies in high-literacy and more egalitarian settings compared with others.

Other evidence

Several smaller studies in West Africa corroborate the powerful influence of education on reducing durations of post-partum abstinence in this region. Better educated women are systematically less likely both to observe post-partum abstinence than are uneducated women and to observe it for shorter durations.[13] One study concludes that schooling reduces the duration of abstinence in virtually every region of Africa; the magnitude of the shifts, however, depends greatly upon contextual characteristics, such as religion and region.[14] In sub-Saharan Africa, for example, findings are mixed on the effect of a small amount of education on the duration of post-partum abstinence. Some studies report linear declines with increasing education. For example, in urban Nigeria, proportions of women who had children aged one to two years and who were abstaining at the time of the survey declined from 77 per cent among uneducated women to 51 per cent among secondary-schooled women.[15] At least three studies conducted in various parts of Nigeria observe a strong inverse relationship between women's education and the duration of post-partum abstinence.[16] Each of these studies shows substantial declines from the primary level onwards. For example, a study in Ilorin, Nigeria, finds that the duration of post-partum abstinence declines from 22 months among uneducated women to 16 months among primary-schooled women and to 13 months among secondary-schooled women.[17]

Other studies in sub-Saharan Africa, however, find evidence of irregular relationships of women's education to the duration of post-partum abstinence. For example, of the 11 DHS studies from sub-Saharan Africa reported in Appendix E, 6 report irregular relationships. In 3 of these, a small amount of education reduces post-partum abstinence durations considerably, but the durations of abstinence increase with further education; in the remaining 3, a positive or reversed-U-shaped relationship is evident.

Several studies in Nigeria have considered the effect of education on the duration of post-partum abstinence, excluding the effect of other demographic and socio-economic factors. They conclude that the net effect of education continues to be one of the strongest factors. After controlling for economic status and other factors, a hazard analysis conducted in Ilorin finds that, relative to illiterate mothers, the net odds that mothers with primary, secondary, and post-secondary education will terminate abstinence are 1.67, 2.42, and 3.27, respectively. A study of Yoruba women finds that, even after factors such as contraceptive use, the occupation of both wife and husband, marriage type, religion, and age are controlled, education (and family planning) are observed to be major determinants of the duration of post-partum abstinence; once education is controlled, marriage type, religion, and the occupation of husband or wife have little influence on the duration of post-partum abstinence. The difference between the least and the most educated women in this study averaged 6 months after adjustment and 12 months before. Differentials of similar magnitudes are observed in another study in Nigeria, which considers the effects of education net of other factors, including religion, age, and use of contraception, as well as work–family role incompatibility and husband–wife closeness. In this case, the difference between the least and the most educated women averaged 7 months after controls were introduced, compared with 12 months before. The only other variable that remained significant after controls were introduced was contraception: whereas contraceptors practised abstinence for 7 fewer months than non-contraceptors in the unadjusted relationship, the differential fell to 3.7 months in the adjusted one.[18]

The only exception is a study in Edo and Delta states, which finds that the net effect of education on the duration of post-partum abstinence is curvilinear: primary-schooled women abstain for somewhat longer periods than uneducated women do; secondary-schooled women abstain for about as long as uneducated women do; and only college-educated women abstain for significantly shorter periods.[19] Even so, the differential is less than two months.

The conclusions of all these studies, then, are that women's education—probably more than a small amount of education—exerts a unique influence on the duration of abstinence, which is not explained by economic status and husband's characteristics. They suggest the hypothesis that women's education affects such dimensions of autonomy as greater decision-making power and increased intimacy with husbands, which allow for the breakdown of strong abstinence taboos (see Box 5.1).

In part, long periods of breast-feeding and post-partum abstinence have been tolerated in sub-Saharan Africa because of polygyny and the availability of other wives.[20] There is evidence, however, that better educated women resist polygynous unions.[21] Even in Saudi Arabia, attitudes towards polygyny have changed considerably among young and educated women, which may have implications for abstinence (although this region is not known for long periods of post-partum abstinence).[22]

Prolonged post-partum abstinence is less likely to be observed in other regions, but the expected inverse effect of education is evident even in these regions (see Table 5.4 and Appendix E). In South Asia, periodic abstinence taboos on special

---

Box 5.1. *The erosion of abstinence taboos*

A study among Yoruba women in Nigeria finds that, even after controlling for age, marital duration, work status, husband's education, religion, contraceptive use, and migrant status, the proportion of women who have sexual relations during lactation increases from 40 per cent among uneducated women to 50 per cent among primary-schooled women and 64 per cent among those with more than a secondary education. Of all the determinants in this study, education is one of the most significant causes of the erosion of abstinence taboos; others are contraception and, more weakly, marital duration and husband's education. Even a primary-school education changes abstinence practices during lactation.

Source: B. J. Feyisetan, 'Postpartum Sexual Abstinence, Breastfeeding and Childspacing among Yoruba Women in Urban Nigeria', *Social Biology*, 37/1–2 (1990), 110–27.

days of the year are widespread and may have played a role in keeping fertility levels relatively low. In rural Karnataka, India, better educated women are considerably less likely than are uneducated women to continue to adhere to these traditional abstinence taboos.[23] Hence, a consideration solely of the post-partum period probably reveals only part of the variation in the duration of abstinence and its relationship to education.

In summary, the relationship of women's education to durations of abstinence is, for the most part, irregular, with only one in three studies indicating a uniformly inverse effect. Even small amounts of education lead to significant declines in the durations of abstinence in the majority of studies reported in West Africa, the only region in which post-partum abstinence is prolonged. In addition, qualitative evidence from Karnataka, South India, suggests that, even in areas where post-partum abstinence is brief, education depresses the observance of post-partum and other types of traditional abstinence taboos, including the practice among women with minimal amounts of schooling. In short, a traditional check on fertility has been relaxed among better educated women. Unless it is offset by increased contraception, this trend towards declining durations of abstinence among educated women would increase fertility.

Post-partum Non-susceptibility: Pattern of the Relationship

Other things being equal, educated women will have shorter durations of post-partum non-susceptibility and shorter natural birth intervals than will uneducated women. Even in regions such as the Arab world, where neither breast-feeding nor post-partum abstinence is traditionally prolonged, this difference is evident. For example, one study in Egypt finds that post-partum amenorrhoea declined from 11 months among uneducated women to about 9 months among primary-schooled women and 4 months among secondary-schooled women.[24] The relationship is especially strong in sub-Saharan Africa, where, one study of regional data suggests, breast-feeding and lactational amenorrhoea decline most sharply with low average levels of schooling.[25] A study in Lagos observes that the non-susceptible period falls from 20.9 months among uneducated women to 14.6 and 7.0 months among primary- and secondary-schooled women, respectively.[26]

The relationship of women's education to the duration of post-partum amenorrhoea is almost always inverse in every region and at every level of development (see Appendix E). Differentials between secondary-schooled and uneducated women are wide, and there is little evidence of thresholds in this relationship. A 10 per cent decline in the duration of post-partum amenorrhoea occurs at the primary stage in 20 of 22 settings for which data are available in Appendix E; declines of 20 per cent occur at the primary stage in 11. In short, even a small amount of education reduces the period of post-partum non-susceptibility, irrespective of region or level of literacy, thereby setting the stage for a positive relationship of education to fertility.

Fecundity: Pattern of the Relationship

Less is known about the relationship of education to fecundity in general than to post-partum non-susceptibility *per se*. There is an argument in favour of both a positive and a negative relationship between education and fecundity. When uneducated women marry in adolescence, it is possible that adolescent pregnancy itself results in complications leading to secondary sterility. In this case, lesser educated women are at greater risk of secondary sterility than are better educated women. Similarly, if better educated women are healthier and better nourished, they may be more able to conceive and carry a pregnancy to term than are uneducated women. On the other hand, because more educated women marry later, they may be more likely than less educated women to suffer primary sterility. Evidence on all these hypotheses is sparse.

- Some evidence from Pakistan suggests that rates of primary sterility increase marginally with education, from 3.9 per cent among uneducated women to 6.4 per cent among those with more than a primary-school education;[27]
- Other evidence from, for example, Nigeria and rural India, suggests that better educated women have systematically shorter first-birth intervals, implying higher levels of fecundability or ability to conceive among them.[28]

On balance, the evidence tentatively suggests that better educated women probably have higher levels of fecundity than uneducated women do.

How Education Enhances Fertility

The links of education to fertility-enhancing factors, such as reduced durations of breast-feeding and abstinence, are undoubtedly inadvertent in the sense that they do not involve deliberate attempts to enhance fertility. Even here, however, pathways from education to shorter durations of the non-susceptible period seem likely to operate through concomitant changes in the situation of women. Four major channels can be traced. All suggest that even small amounts of education encourage women to cut back on breast-feeding, thus providing a possible explanation for the uniformly inverse relationships observed earlier and the relative absence of thresholds.

First, the greater knowledge and exposure to new ideas that accompany education can introduce women to new ideas about infant-feeding practices and give them a greater awareness of breast-milk substitutes and how to use them. There is considerable anecdotal evidence that one of the new ideas to which education exposes women is the (mis)perception that the use of breast-milk substitutes is a more modern and prestigious practice than breast-feeding and, hence, more appropriate for the station of an educated woman.

Greater knowledge and exposure to new ideas can also raise questions regarding the rationality of traditional post-partum and other abstinence taboos. It is traditionally believed that intercourse during breast-feeding could result in semen contaminating the woman's milk, thereby endangering the life of the infant. Better educated women seem likely to regard these fears of the consequences of mixing breast-milk and semen as an old wives' tale and, therefore, to be more willing to have sexual relations during lactation.[29] Even where social propriety demands long birth intervals, educated women are more knowledgeable about ways, other than abstinence, of ensuring this.

Second, educated women seem less likely than uneducated women to permit interference in decisions regarding such issues as breast-feeding and abstinence durations. In many traditional kinship structures, the older generation often makes decisions about breast-feeding and abstinence practices. Decision-making in these areas, however, appears to be among the earliest concessions made to an educated daughter-in-law, as qualitative evidence from rural South India has shown.[30] The shift in the locus of decision-making enables women with even small amounts of education to deviate from traditional breast-feeding and post-partum abstinence practices.[31] This pattern is consistent with the finding that the relationship of women's education to the duration of breast-feeding is consistently inverse, with less evidence of thresholds than was found with respect to the variables discussed in earlier chapters.

Third, the strengthening of the conjugal bond that accompanies education may itself lead to a reluctance to adhere to long periods of post-partum abstinence. Abstinence is often tolerable because the patriarchal structure does not give primacy to emotional relationships of husband and wife or attach great importance to marital female sexuality. Education erodes these traditional forms of loyalty, with the consequence that husband–wife intimacy extends to their sexual lives. Hence, for example, studies in Nigeria observe that better educated women are systematically more likely to report that the major reason for premature resumption of post-partum sexual activity is sexual need.[32] In Sri Lanka, substantial education and an increasing trend toward love marriages emphasize the emotional relationship between spouses and their mutual sexual satisfaction; prolonged abstinence has become increasingly unpopular as a result.[33] In South Asia, where women typically return to their parental homes for prolonged periods at the time of delivery, if the strengthening of the conjugal bond among educated women leads them to curtail or discontinue this practice, the effect will be similar to a shortening or abandonment of abstinence taboos in other settings.

Finally, one explanation commonly given for less breast-feeding among educated women is the inconvenience when they work outside the home. This explanation is, however, uncertain and likely to be influenced by such contextual factors as the types of employment available to women outside the home, as well as the extent to which breast-milk substitutes have penetrated the market-place and the culture. Some studies have shown that employment has little effect on breast-feeding, especially once socio-economic status is controlled.[34] Others offer support for this hypothesis, however. In the Philippines, where many women work outside the home, and where infant formula is widely available and acceptable, one study finds that employment outside the home significantly reduced the chances of breast-feeding.[35]

Although few studies have explicitly attempted to identify the links of education to changes in breast-feeding or abstinence practices through these four pathways, considerable evidence suggests that, compared with uneducated women, even moderately educated women are more aware of alternatives to prolonged breast-feeding and abstinence, have greater decision-making power concerning personal aspects of their lives such as breast-feeding and abstinence practices, and experience greater intimacy with their husbands. In some but not all contexts, educated women find work outside the home incompatible with prolonged breast-feeding.

Notes

1. These 54 studies include 18 that use WFS data, reported in United Nations, *Fertility Behaviour;* 32 that use DHS data, reported in United Nations, *Women's Education and Fertility Behaviour: Recent Evidence from the Demographic and Health Surveys*, and in various DHS country reports; and 4 that use other surveys: for Belize, see Belize, Ministry of Health, *1991 Belize Family Health Survey: Final Report* (Atlanta, Ga., US Department of Health and Human Services, Public Health Service, Centers for Disease Control, Center for Chronic Disease Prevention and Health Promotion, Division of Reproductive Health, 1992); for Haiti, see M. Cayemittes *et al., 1989 Haiti National Contraceptive Prevalence Survey* (Atlanta, Ga., US Department of Health and Human Services, Public Health Service, Centers for Disease Control, Center for Chronic Disease Prevention and Health Promotion, Division of Reproductive Health, 1991); for Kuwait, see M. Al-Bustan and B. R. Kohli, 'Socio-economic and Demographic Factors Influencing Breast-feeding Among Kuwaiti Women', *Genus*, 44/1–2 (Jan.–June 1988), 265–77; and for India, see United Nations, *Women's Education and Fertility Behaviour: A Case-study of Rural Maharashtra, India.*
2. Aside from WFS, see also, for the Philippines, C. M. Mejia-Raymundo, 'Risk Factors of Breast-feeding Among Filipino Women', *Journal of Biosocial Science*, suppl. 9 (1985), 67–81.
3. Oni, 'Effects of Women's Education'.
4. R. Lesthaeghe, H. J. Page, and O. Adegbola, 'Child-spacing and Fertility in Lagos', in Page and Lesthaeghe (eds.) *Child-spacing in Tropical Africa*; B. J. Feyisetan, 'Postpartum Sexual Abstinence, Breastfeeding and Childspacing Among Yoruba Women in Urban Nigeria', *Social Biology,* 37/1–2 (1990), pp. 110–27; and Okojie, 'Women's Status, Proximate Determinants and Fertility'. Okojie's study controls not only for socio-economic and demographic factors but also for a range of community-level variables and female-status indicators such as decision-making, spousal age difference, and women's contribution to the household; her results show a significant net effect of education. So, also, the study by Lesthaeghe, Page, and Adegbola controls for such factors as religion, age, and use of contraception, as well as such indicators of autonomy as work–family role incompatibility and husband–wife closeness. As in Okojie's findings, education was the most powerful net determinant of breast-feeding durations. Without the controls, the differential between the least and most educated women was about 10 months; the introduction of these controls resulted in a moderate decline of differentials, to 7.7 months.

5. Martin, Flanagan, and Klenicki, 'Evaluation'.
6. The Cebu Study Team, 'Underlying and Proximate Determinants of Child Health: The Cebu Longitudinal Health and Nutrition Study', *American Journal of Epidemiology*, 133/2 (1991), 185–201.
7. See, for example, A. E. Sommerfelt *et al.*, *Maternal and Child Health in Bolivia: Report on the In-depth DHS Survey in Bolivia, 1989* (Columbia, Md., Institute for Resource Development/Macro Systems, Inc., 1991) for observations from Bolivia.
8. Mejia-Raymundo, 'Risk Factors'; D. K. Guilkey *et al.*, 'Changes in Breast-feeding in the Philippines, 1973–1983', *Social Science and Medicine*, 31/12 (1990), 1365–75; The Cebu Study Team, 'Determinants of Child Health'; and Raymundo *et al.*, 'Female Education'.
9. Guilkey *et al.*, 'Changes'.
10. Raymundo *et al.*, 'Female Education'.
11. Ravi K. Sharma *et al.*, 'A Comparative Analysis of Trends and Differentials in Breast-feeding: Findings from DHS Surveys', paper presented at the Annual Meeting of the Population Association of America, Toronto, May 1990.
12. C. Chandrashekaran, 'Cultural Patterns in Relation to Family Planning in India', *Proceedings of the Third International Conference on Planned Parenthood* (Bombay, India, Family Planning Association of India, 1952).
13. See, for example, Oni, 'Effects of Women's Education'; Lesthaeghe, Page, and Adegbola, 'Child-spacing and Fertility in Lagos'; and P. Caldwell and J. C. Caldwell, 'The Function of Child-spacing in Traditional Societies and the Direction of Change', in Page and Lesthaeghe (eds.), *Child-spacing in Tropical Africa*. For urban Nigeria, see J. C. Caldwell and P. Caldwell, 'Cause and Sequence'. For Kinshasa, see D. Shapiro and O. Tambashe, 'Women's Employment, Education and Contraceptive Behavior in Kinshasa', paper presented at the Seminar on the Course of Fertility Transition in Sub-Saharan Africa, sponsored by the IUSSP Committee on Comparative Analysis of Fertility and the University of Zimbabwe, Harare, Zimbabwe, 19–22 Nov. 1991.
14. R. Lesthaeghe *et al.*, 'Regional Variation in Components of Child-spacing: The Role of Women's Education', in R. J. Lesthaeghe (ed.), *Reproduction and Social Organisation in Sub-Saharan Africa* (Berkeley, University of California Press, 1989).
15. P. Caldwell and J. C. Caldwell, 'Function of Child-spacing'.
16. Ibid.; Oni, 'Effects of Women's Education'; and Lesthaeghe, Page, and Adegbola, 'Child-spacing and Fertility in Lagos'.
17. Oni, 'Effects of Women's Education'.
18. For the hazard analysis, see ibid.; for the study of Yoruba women, see J. C. Caldwell and P. Caldwell, 'Cause and Sequence'; and, for the study of net effects of education, see Lesthaeghe, Page, and Adegbola, 'Child-spacing and Fertility in Lagos'.
19. Okojie, 'Women's Status, Proximate Determinants and Fertility'.
20. Oppong and Abu, *Seven Roles of Women*.
21. For Cameroon, see Kritz and Gurak, 'Women's Status'; for Kenya, see Smock, *Women's Education*; and, for Nigeria, see J. C. Caldwell and P. Caldwell, 'Cause and Sequence'.
22. Alsuwaigh, 'Women in Transition'.
23. J. C. Caldwell, Reddy, and P. Caldwell, 'Causes of Demographic Change'.
24. S. Gadalla, J. McCarthy, and N. Kak, 'The Determinants of Fertility in Rural Egypt: A Study of Menoufia and Beni-suef Governorates', *Journal of Biosocial Science*, 19 (1987), 195–207.
25. R. Lesthaeghe, G. Verleye, and C. Jolly, 'Female Education and Factors Affecting

Fertility in Sub-Saharan Africa', IPD Working Paper 1992-2 (Brussels, c/o Centrum Voor Sociologie, 1992).

26. Lesthaeghe, Page, and Adegbola, 'Child-spacing and Fertility in Lagos'.
27. Z. A. Sathar, 'Does Female Education Affect Fertility Behaviour in Pakistan?', *The Pakistan Development Review*, 23/4 (1984), 573–90.
28. See, for example, A. A. Adewuyi and U. C. Isiugo-Abanihe, 'Regional Patterns and Correlates of Birth Interval Length in Nigeria', Research Note No. 107 (Canberra, Department of Demography, Research School of Social Sciences, Australian National University, 1990), for Nigeria; and United Nations, *Women's Education and Fertility Behaviour: A Case-study of Rural Maharashtra, India*, for rural India.
29. Feyisetan, 'Postpartum Sexual Abstinence'.
30. J. C. Caldwell, Reddy, and P. Caldwell, 'The Causes of Demographic Change'.
31. Ibid.
32. P. Caldwell and J. C. Caldwell, 'Function of Child-spacing'; and J. C. Caldwell and P. Caldwell, 'Cause and Sequence'.
33. J. Caldwell *et al.*, 'The Role of Traditional Fertility Regulation in Sri Lanka', *Studies in Family Planning*, 18/1 (Jan.–Feb. 1987), 1–21.
34. A. Jain and J. Bongaarts, 'Breastfeeding: Patterns, Correlates, and Fertility Effects', *Studies in Family Planning*, 12/3 (1981), 79–99.
35. Mejia-Raymundo, 'Risk Factors'.

6 Women's Education and Improved Infant and Child Survival

The inverse relationship of women's education to infant and child mortality is well established in all regions of the developing world. Even a small amount of education leads to improvements in child survival and well-being. Moreover, in most studies, a woman's education has a stronger net effect on child survival than does either the household's economic status or her husband's characteristics. The differentials between women with some secondary education and those with no education tend to be wider and threshold levels lower in higher income, higher literacy, and more egalitarian (in terms of literacy) settings. The literature speculates that the main reasons underlying the inverse relationship have to do with educated women's greater propensity to care for their children, to use modern health facilities, and to adopt modern health practices. This is not necessarily the result of their greater knowledge of disease causation; rather, it appears to result from their enhanced awareness of good health practices, their greater confidence about dealing with their environments, and their greater ability to make and implement independent decisions on children's well-being.

That better educated women have lower infant and child mortality is the most pervasive and consistently observed effect of women's education on any demographic factor. Indeed, the relationship is so predictable that it has been labelled 'boringly inverse'.[1] It is observed in all settings, across all major regions of the developing world, and across all levels of overall literacy and development. Not only is the relationship almost universally observed but also the documentation of factors connected with women's status that underlie this relationship is considerable, beginning with J. C. Caldwell's analysis in Nigeria.[2]

The relationship of infant and child mortality to fertility is also well established. Infant mortality leads to earlier cessation of breast-feeding and, consequently, a shorter period of post-partum infecundity. In addition, in some populations, there is a tendency to replace a dead child as soon as possible, resulting in a shorter birth interval than if the child had survived. Also, in high-mortality settings, there is a tendency to have more children than desired deliberately, as a hedge against child loss—an effect known as the insurance effect. A related finding is that couples who have experienced high rates of child survival are more likely to practise contraception than are couples who have experienced child mortality. Of all these effects, the effect through reduced breast-feeding and shorter subsequent birth intervals is the strongest and best documented in the literature.[3] Hence, infant or child mortality is included here as a supply-side intervening factor, although some of its effect may result from deliberate modifications of behaviour, notably from lower family size preferences and higher rates of contraception among couples.

These two effects—that of education on child mortality and that of child mortality on fertility—are strong. However, the overall effect of women's education on fertility through child mortality may be weaker than that observed through other intervening channels. This is so because the age at which child mortality has the strongest impact on fertility—infancy—is the age at which the link of women's education to child mortality is weakest. It has often been observed, for example, that such measures as the under-five mortality rate (U5MR or q5) are more sensitive to women's education than is q1 (mortality up to age 1) or neonatal mortality. This is not to say that the relationship is absent, however, but only that it is weaker at early childhood ages; and exceptions are observed in several settings.[4]

The theme of this chapter, the relationship of women's education to child mortality, has been more extensively explored than that of women's education to any other demographic factor.[5] Given the exhaustive treatment that the topic has received, this chapter offers a short overview of several recent analyses of the association of women's education to child mortality. Although both infant and child mortality relationships are considered, the effect of women's education on infant mortality is more salient in the relationship of women's education to fertility and, hence, more emphasis is placed on this relationship.

Pattern of the Relationship

Table 6.1 summarizes the relationship of women's education to early childhood mortality, that is, infant mortality or mortality up to age 2 (q2) in 34 studies, selected from those listed in Appendix F.

Overall findings on early childhood mortality

The inverse relationship of women's education to early childhood mortality is clear (Table 6.1).
  • Of the 34 studies included in Table 6.1, the relationship is uniformly inverse in 25, 7 shaped in 4, and irregular or curvilinear in 5.

The shape of the relationship of education to early childhood mortality varies little by region, levels of income, literacy, or gender disparities in literacy. Uniformly inverse relationships are slightly less prevalent in sub-Saharan Africa than in other regions, and in countries with low overall female literacy than in those with high literacy levels.

Differentials

Table 6.2 shows relatively wide differentials between uneducated women and women with some secondary education.
  • In 19 of 34 studies, women with seven or more years of schooling experience early childhood mortality levels which are at least 41 per cent below those

Table 6.1. *Patterns in the relationship of women's education to early childhood mortality, by region, level of development, and gender disparity in literacy*

	Patterns in the relationship between years of schooling and early childhood mortality rate[a]			Total number of studies
	Inverse (negative)	7	None or curvilinear	
A. Region[b]				
Sub-Saharan Africa	9	2	4	15
North Africa and the Middle East	3	0	0	3
East and South-East Asia	2	1	0	3
South Asia	3	0	0	3
Latin America and the Caribbean	8	1	1	10
B. Level of development				
1. Annual per capita income ($)				
500 or less	11	2	1	14
501–999	7	2	2	11
1000 or more	7	0	2	9
2. Overall female literacy rate (%)				
40 or less	11	1	3	15
41–80	6	2	1	9
81 or more	8	1	1	10
C. Gender disparity in literacy[c]				
250–700	11	1	3	15
701–850	4	1	1	6
851 or more	10	2	1	13
TOTALS	25	4	5	34

[a] Two distinct patterns in the relationship are apparent: an inverse relationship, in which better educated women experience progressively lower levels of early childhood mortality (5 per cent or more); and a 7-shaped relationship, in which moderately educated women experience about the same level of early childhood mortality as uneducated women (within 5 per cent), whereas better educated women have lower levels.
[b] Not all countries in a region are included, and those included are not necessarily representative of the region but are, rather, those countries for which the requisite data are available. Thus, the results are not necessarily representative of any particular region.
[c] The level of gender disparity in literacy is the number of literate females per 1000 literate males.

Notes: The studies selected for inclusion in this table appear in Appendix F, where they are marked with a dagger (†). The study populations were women of child-bearing age who were married or in union. Early childhood mortality refers to either infant mortality or mortality at ages 0–2.

Sources: Of the 34 studies, 26 are based on World Fertility Survey (5) and Demographic and Health Survey (21) data. Sources are indicated in Appendix F.

experienced by uneducated women; in 13 of these 19, women with seven or more years of schooling have about half the early childhood mortality levels of uneducated women.

Wide differentials have also been observed in a recent comparative analysis of 25 DHS countries, which finds that the overall average odds of dying before age two for the child of a woman with seven or more years of education are approximately 42.5 per cent of the odds for a child of an uneducated mother.[6]

In the magnitude of the differentials, however, disparities by region, income,

Table 6.2.   *Differentials in the relationship of women's education to early child-hood mortality, by region, level of development, and gender disparity in literacy*

	Differences in early childhood mortality rate between uneducated and secondary-schooled women[a] (percentage differentials) NARROW ◄------------------------► WIDE						Total number of studies
	10 or less	11–20	21–30	31–40	41–50	51 or more	
A. Region[b]							
Sub-Saharan Africa	4	2	2	0	5	2	15
North Africa and the Middle East	0	0	1	2	0	0	3
East and South-East Asia	0	0	0	0	0	3	3
South Asia	0	1	0	1	1	0	3
Latin America and the Caribbean	1	0	0	1	0	8	10
B. Level of development							
1. Annual per capita income ($)							
500 or less	2	2	3	1	3	3	14
501–999	1	0	0	3	3	4	11
1000 or more	2	1	0	0	0	6	9
2. Overall female literacy rate (%)							
40 or less	2	2	2	3	4	2	15
41–80	2	1	0	0	1	5	9
81 or more	1	0	1	1	1	6	10
C. Gender disparity in literacy[c]							
250–700	2	2	2	3	4	2	15
701–850	2	1	0	0	1	2	6
851 or more	1	0	1	1	1	9	13
TOTALS	5	3	3	4	6	13	34

[a] The term 'secondary-schooled women' here applies to women who have had some secondary education or completed or gone beyond secondary school—that is, women who have had more than six years of primary education.
[b] Not all countries in a region are included, and those included are not necessarily representative of the region but are, rather, those countries for which the requisite data are available. Thus, the results are not necessarily representative of any particular region.
[c] The level of gender disparity in literacy is the number of literate females per 1000 literate males.

Notes: The studies selected for inclusion in this table appear in Appendix F, where they are marked with a dagger (†). Early childhood mortality refers to either infant mortality or mortality at ages 0–2.

Sources: Of the 34 studies, 26 are based on World Fertility Survey (5) and Demographic and Health Survey (21) data. Other sources are indicated in Appendix F.

literacy, and levels of gender disparity in literacy are more obvious. Differentials in mortality between uneducated and secondary-schooled women tend to be stronger in Latin America and the Caribbean and in more developed settings, supporting conclusions from the WFS.[7]

• Women with some secondary schooling have experienced half the early child-hood mortality of uneducated women in 2 of 15 studies in sub-Saharan African settings, compared with 8 of 10 studies in Latin American and the Caribbean settings.

Similarly, differentials appear to widen as literacy and income increase:
- Differentials exceeding 50 per cent are observed in about one-fifth of the low-income settings, one-third of the middle-income settings, and two-thirds of the high-income ones;
- Differentials by literacy are equally evident: differentials exceeding 50 per cent are observed in only 2 of 15 studies in low-literacy settings, compared with more than half of the medium-literacy settings and three-fifths of the high-literacy settings;
- The pattern is especially distinct when studies are grouped by the level of gender disparity in literacy. Differentials exceeding 50 per cent are observed in only 2 of 15 studies in the most inegalitarian settings compared with one-third of moderately egalitarian settings and more than two-thirds of the settings in which gender disparities are narrowest.

Thresholds

Unlike the case of fertility, a threshold level of education is not necessary to precipitate declines in early childhood mortality (see Table 6.3).
- In 29 of 34 studies, even a primary education (lower or upper) affects early childhood mortality levels; in 22 studies, even a small amount of primary school leads to declines of 10 per cent or more in mortality.

Again, the regional and development contexts have a modest conditioning effect on this relationship. By and large, thresholds are somewhat higher in sub-Saharan Africa than in other regions. Thresholds fall as overall levels of per capita income and female literacy rise and as gender disparities in literacy narrow. This is especially evident for the level of education by which a 20 per cent decline in mortality is attained. For example, while a 20 per cent decline in early childhood mortality is attained by the early primary stage in one-third of all low-literacy settings, this proportion increases to more than two-fifths in the medium-literacy settings and three-fifths in the high-literacy settings.

Similarly, a decline of 20 per cent in early childhood mortality is attained by the early primary level in almost one-third of the low-income settings; this proportion increases to two-thirds of the high-income ones.

By level of gender disparity in literacy, a 20 per cent decline in early childhood mortality is attained by the early primary stage in one-third of the settings in which gender disparities are wide and moderate, compared with more than three-fifths of the settings in which gender disparities are progressively narrower.

Overall findings on child mortality

Tables 6.4, 6.5, and 6.6 show the relationship of education to child mortality (that is, mortality at ages 0 to 5 years) in 45 studies, selected from those listed in Appendix G. When overall under-five mortality is considered, the picture is generally similar to that of early childhood mortality. Although differentials are stronger, there is even

Table 6.3.   *Relationship of the duration of women's education to early childhood mortality, by region, level of development, and gender disparity in literacy*

	Educational level (years of schooling) by which:								Total number of studies
	A 10% decline in early childhood mortality is reached				A 20% decline in early childhood mortality is reached				
	1–3 (1–6)	4–6	7+	Never	1–3 (1–6)	4–6	7+	Never	
A. Region [a]									
Sub-Saharan Africa	7	4	2	2	5	4	4	2	15
North Africa and the Middle East	2	1	0	0	1	1	1	0	3
East and South-East Asia	2	1	0	0	2	0	1	0	3
South Asia	2	0	1	0	1	0	1	1	3
Latin America and the Caribbean	9	1	0	0	6	1	2	1	10
B. Level of development									
1. Annual per capita income ($)									
500 or less	8	3	3	0	4	4	5	1	14
501–999	6	4	0	1	5	2	3	1	11
1000 or more	8	0	0	1	6	0	1	2	9
2. Overall female literacy rate (%)									
40 or less	8	4	2	1	5	3	5	2	15
41–80	6	2	0	1	4	2	2	1	9
81 or more	8	1	1	0	6	1	2	1	10
C. Gender disparity in literacy [b]									
250–700	8	4	2	1	5	3	5	2	15
701–850	4	1	0	1	2	2	1	1	6
851 or more	10	2	1	0	8	1	3	1	13
TOTALS	22	7	3	2	15	6	9	4	34

[a] Not all countries in a region are included, and those included are not necessarily representative of the region but are, rather, those countries for which the requisite data are available. Thus, the results are not necessarily representative of any particular region.

[b] The level of gender disparity in literacy is the number of literate females per 1000 literate males.

Notes: The studies selected for inclusion in this table appear in Appendix F, where they are marked with a dagger (†). Early childhood mortality refers to either infant mortality or mortality at ages 0–2. Some appendix studies combine rates for women with 1–3 and 4–6 years of schooling; in such studies, rates are shown in the column marked 1–3.

Sources: Of the 34 studies, 26 are based on World Fertility Survey (5) and Demographic and Health Survey (21) data. Sources are indicated in Appendix F.

less evidence of thresholds. Other studies have also noted the absence of thresholds in the relationship of women's education to child mortality.[8] That few studies report thresholds suggests that it may not be the acquisition of knowledge, literacy, numeracy, or the formal curriculum *per se* that sets off these changes, but some more subtle change that education imparts in attitudes, exposure to the world, and ability to express problems.

Table 6.4. *Patterns in the relationship of women's education to child mortality, by region, level of development, and gender disparity in literacy*

	Patterns in the relationship between years of schooling and the child (under five years) mortality rate[a]			Total number of studies
	Inverse (negative)	7	None or curvilinear	
A. Region[b]				
Sub-Saharan Africa	11	4	1	16
North Africa and the Middle East	5	0	0	5
East and South-East Asia	5	1	0	6
South Asia	5	0	0	5
Latin America and the Caribbean	11	0	2	13
B. Level of development				
1. Annual per capita income ($)				
500 or less	14	2	1	17
501–999	11	1	1	13
1000 or more	12	2	1	15
2. Overall female literacy rate (%)				
40 or less	16	1	1	18
41–80	11	3	0	14
81 or more	10	1	2	13
C. Gender disparity in literacy[c]				
250–700	16	1	1	18
701–850	7	3	0	10
851 or more	14	1	2	17
TOTALS	37	5	3	45

[a] Two distinct patterns in the relationship are apparent: an inverse relationship, in which better educated women experience progressively lower levels of child mortality (5 per cent or more); and a 7-shaped relationship, in which moderately educated women experience about the same level of child mortality as uneducated women (within 5 per cent), whereas better educated women have lower levels.
[b] Not all countries in a region are included, and those included are not necessarily representative of the region but are, rather, those countries for which the requisite data are available. Thus, the results are not necessarily representative of any particular region.
[c] The level of gender disparity in literacy is the number of literate females per 1000 literate males.

Notes: The studies selected for inclusion in this table appear in Appendix G, where they are marked with a dagger (†). The study populations were women of child-bearing age who were married or in union.

Sources: Of the 45 studies, 43 are based on World Fertility Survey (23) and Demographic and Health Survey (20) data. Sources are indicated in Appendix G.

Other evidence

Two studies of WFS and other data from the 1970s conclude that each additional year of women's schooling results in a 7–9 per cent decline in infant and child mortality.[9] About a decade later, the effects continue to be strong: the relative risk of mortality at ages 1–23 months is roughly 2.5 times higher among the infants of uneducated women as among those of mothers with a secondary education, as found for a variety of DHS countries.[10] Studies using other data-sets have recorded similar magnitudes of effects.[11] Additionally, there is evidence that the effect of education may not diminish over time or with declines in overall mortality levels. A

Table 6.5.   *Differentials in the relationship of women's education to child mortality, by region, level of development, and gender disparity in literacy*

	Differences in child (under five years) mortality rate between uneducated and secondary-schooled women[a] (percentage differentials) NARROW ◄----------------► WIDE					Total number of studies
	10 or less[b]	21–30	31–40	41–50	51 or more	
A. Region[c]						
Sub-Saharan Africa	1	3	5	3	4	16
North Africa and the Middle East	0	0	1	2	2	5
East and South-East Asia	0	0	1	1	4	6
South Asia	0	0	0	3	2	5
Latin America and the Caribbean	1	1	1	0	10	13
B. Level of development						
1. Annual per capita income ($)						
500 or less	0	1	4	6	6	17
501–999	1	1	2	2	7	13
1000 or more	1	2	2	1	9	15
2. Overall female literacy rate (%)						
40 or less	1	0	4	6	7	18
41–80	0	3	2	2	7	14
81 or more	1	1	2	1	8	13
C. Gender disparity in literacy[d]						
250–700	1	0	4	6	7	18
701–850	0	3	2	2	3	10
851 or more	1	1	2	1	12	17
TOTALS	2	4	8	9	22	45

[a] The term 'secondary-schooled women' here applies to women who have had some secondary education or completed or gone beyond secondary school—that is, women who have had more than six years of primary education.
[b] No differentials in the range 10–20 per cent were observed.
[c] Not all countries in a region are included, and those included are not necessarily representative of the region but are, rather, those countries for which the requisite data are available. Thus, the results are not necessarily representative of any particular region.
[d] The level of gender disparity in literacy is the number of literate females per 1000 literate males.

Notes: The studies selected for inclusion in this table appear in Appendix G, where they are marked with a dagger (†).

Sources: Of the 45 studies, 43 are based on World Fertility Survey (23) and Demographic and Health Survey (20) data. Sources are indicated in Appendix G.

comparative analysis of data from 12 countries for which both WFS and DHS data are available suggests that, at both points in time, children of uneducated women were about 40 per cent more likely to die by age 5 than those born to women with a primary education.[12] Although the relative advantage in mortality for children of primary-educated women remained unchanged over the decade, the advantage enjoyed by the children of secondary-schooled women compared with those of primary-schooled women may have widened.

Although the relationship of women's education to child mortality is the focus of

Table 6.6.   *Relationship of the duration of women's education to child mortality, by region, level of development, and gender disparity in literacy*

| | Educational level (years of schooling) by which: | | | | | | | | Total number of studies |
| | A 10% decline in child mortality is reached | | | | A 20% decline in child mortality is reached | | | | |
	1–3 (1–6)	4–6	7+	Never	1–3 (1–6)	4–6	7+	Never	
A. Region[a]									
Sub-Saharan Africa	9	5	1	1	7	5	3	1	16
North Africa and the Middle East	5	0	0	0	5	0	0	0	5
East and South-East Asia	2	4	0	0	1	3	2	0	6
South Asia	5	0	0	0	4	0	1	0	5
Latin America and the Caribbean	11	1	1	0	9	0	3	1	13
B. Level of development									
1. Annual per capita income ($)									
500 or less	12	4	1	0	9	5	3	0	17
501–999	8	4	0	1	7	2	3	1	13
1000 or more	12	2	1	0	10	1	3	1	15
2. Overall female literacy rate (%)									
40 or less	14	3	0	1	13	3	1	1	18
41–80	9	4	1	0	6	3	5	0	14
81 or more	9	3	1	0	7	2	3	1	13
C. Gender disparity in literacy[b]									
250–700	14	3	0	1	13	3	1	1	18
701–850	6	3	1	0	3	2	5	0	10
851 or more	12	4	1	0	10	3	3	1	17
TOTALS	32	10	2	1	26	8	9	2	45

[a] Not all countries in a region are included, and those included are not necessarily representative of the region but are, rather, those countries for which the requisite data are available. Thus, the results are not necessarily representative of any particular region.

[b] The level of gender disparity in literacy is the number of literate females per 1000 literate males.

Notes: The studies selected for inclusion in this table appear in Appendix G, where they are marked with a dagger (†). Child mortality is mortality among children under five years of age Some appendix studies combine rates for women with 1–3 and 4–6 years of schooling; in such studies, rates are shown in the column marked 1–3.

Sources: Of the 45 studies, 43 are based on World Fertility Survey (23) and Demographic and Health Survey (20) data. Sources are indicated in Appendix G.

this chapter, men's education and the household's economic status also play an important role in determining child mortality. As in the case of fertility, however, a consistent finding is that the influence of women's education on child mortality is independent of, as opposed to merely reflecting, the effect of the household's economic status or the husband's characteristics.

• One study suggests that, of the reduction of approximately 9 per 1000 in infant and child mortality which results from each additional year of women's school-ing, approximately 6 per 1000 is the result of the woman's own education, and 3 per 1000 the result of the tendency of better educated women to be married to better educated husbands;[13]

- Another study based on WFS data concludes that the proportion of children dead (controlling for marital duration and age) is most powerfully influenced by women's education, even after controlling for household economic status, husband's education, and ethnicity.[14] Of the overall effect of a 7 per cent decline in child mortality for every additional year of schooling, 3.9 per cent, or more than half, persists when all other covariates are controlled.

Several multivariate studies provide evidence of the direct effect of women's education on child mortality.[15] About half of the overall effect of women's education on child mortality can, according to these studies, be attributed to the direct net effects of women's education, even after household economic status is controlled.

- A multivariate analysis of 25 DHS surveys finds that, even after controlling for such covariates of early childhood mortality (q2) as father's education, occu-pation, and region of residence, the overall average odds of dying by age two for a child born to a mother with seven or more years of education are 52 per cent of that of children of uneducated mothers (compared with gross odds of 42 per cent). In contrast, the gross effects of husband's education and occupation are substantially attenuated once women's education is controlled.[16]
- One study, in which hazard models of post-neonatal mortality (1–23 months) were estimated using data from 17 DHS countries, finds that the gross effect of women's education on child mortality is reduced by 30-50 per cent as a result of controls for economic status (measured by existence of piped water, latrine, and household possessions such as a radio or television, motorized transport, and non-dirt floor). Yet, at least half of the effect of women's education remains.[17] Similar conclusions are obtained from analyses of WFS and other data, using varying controls and methodologies.[18]

Such findings offer unequivocal support for the importance of women's education in lowering child mortality. The theoretical implication of these results is that the economic advantages associated with higher levels of women's education (as represented by husband's education or household economic status) cannot account in their entirety for the link between women's schooling and child mortality, that it is women's education which has a unique net effect on child mortality, quite independently of their husbands' education or economic status.

Some studies report a greater net influence of husband's or household characteristics than of wife's education on child mortality. For example, one study of 46 developing countries finds that, although women's education is a more important determinant of infant mortality than is the number of doctors and nurses, it is only three-fifths as important as income.[19] Likewise, a study in Sri Lanka shows that, although both husband's and wife's education were major determinants of child mortality, the husband's education remained a more powerful determinant than the wife's.[20]

Not only large-scale surveys but also smaller subnational investigations point to the relative importance of mother's education, as compared with the father's education or household factors, for child survival. These studies have been conducted in a variety of settings: in Africa, Nigeria and the Sudan; in Latin America, Colombia; in the Middle East, Kuwait and Jordan; and in Asia, Malaysia and rural Karnataka, India.[21]

The findings of this chapter also suggest that, although the level of education of individual women in a particular setting is related to child mortality, so, too, the contextual effect of schooling can be important in determining child mortality. As the context becomes more literate, more developed, and more egalitarian, the threshold levels of education necessary to precipitate declines in child mortality fall (Tables 6.3 and 6.6). In other words, a modest exposure to education tends to have less impact on child mortality in a context in which average levels of female education are low; it will have substantially more influence in settings in which female education levels are high. Clearly, the societal context conditions the link of female education to child mortality. What, then, are the features associated with women's education that are responsible for this effect?

How Women's Education Affects Child Survival

That the relationship of women's education to child survival operates, at least in part, through changes in the situation of women was brought into focus by J. C. Caldwell's analysis of Nigeria. He argues that women's education had a net effect on child survival that could not be explained by household economic characteristics; this net effect resulted from the following:

- A shift from fatalistic acceptance of sickness to a more active implementation of good health practices;
- An increased capability for dealing with the outside world, including the world of health-service providers; and
- A shift in the power structure of the family towards women as the major health decision-makers.[22]

Caldwell finds that educated women tend to be more familiar with the use of other institutions; they spend more time with doctors if a child is sick; they are more likely to report back the failure of treatment; and they exhibit greater freedom from other household members to act in case of child morbidity. In the 1980s, considerable evidence supporting these pathways was built up. The following sections place this evidence in the context of the framework adopted in Chapter 1.

Educated women are more knowledgeable about health

It is hardly unexpected that better educated women are more aware of good health practices and of ways to prevent, recognize, and treat illness than are other women. They are more aware of the importance of nutrition;[23] the dangers of unsafe water and contaminated foods; and the importance of personal hygiene, regular hand-washing, and sanitation.[24]

Educated women are also less fatalistic about illness, more skilled in interpreting symptoms in children, and more aware of modern, rather than traditional or indigenous, remedies for illness.[25] They are more likely to have accurate information on preventive therapies, such as oral rehydration therapy and immunization.[26] Educated women are more knowledgeable about the location of health facilities and more convinced of the value of seeking health care.[27] They are also more likely to take immediate action for sick children and more likely to report back the failure of treatment.[28] Educated women are also more likely to be attentive to developmental milestones of their children and to expect certain standards of intellectual and emotional development; thus, they are in a better position to take corrective action where these are retarded.[29]

All this does not necessarily imply, however, that education (at least small amounts of it) brings about a fundamental change in knowledge of disease causation.[30] It undoubtedly makes women more sensitive to modern health messages and gives them more faith in good health practices, even without a full understanding of the scientific roots of those practices. For example, in rural Bangladesh, better educated women are distinctly more likely to pay attention to personal hygiene and household cleanliness, and are less likely to use contaminated water than uneducated women are. They are not, however, necessarily more aware of the significance of these measures for health.[31] Other evidence from Bangladesh, however, suggests a strong link between women's education and awareness that regular hand-washing and boiled water have health benefits, as well as the association of education to the knowledge of the link between newborn tetanus and the use of unsterile instruments.[32] Even so, educated women, although more likely to attribute diarrhoea and dysentery to contaminated food or water, are no more likely than uneducated women to specify the presence of germs as the causal agent.[33] Evidence from Nigeria suggests that moderately educated women are about as likely as uneducated women to attribute certain diseases to witchcraft. They have decidedly more faith in modern medicine, however, as seen by their greater adherence to hospital deliveries, early registration, and reluctance to take traditional medicine during pregnancy.[34] In Kenya, women acquire a genuine understanding of the environmental causes of diarrhoea only after they reach secondary school. After four or more years of schooling, however, they correctly understand instructions for administering oral rehydration salts.[35]

Thus, small amounts of education probably have a greater effect on knowledge of good health behaviours than on an in-depth understanding of disease causation. Yet, even the superficial improvement in health knowledge that accompanies a small amount of education can have a profound effect on child mortality.

Educated women have a greater voice in family health decisions

Education also enhances the extent to which women make independent decisions relating to family health and the extent to which they are free to take action independently of other household members, including mothers-in-law, when their children are sick. In regions as diverse as West Africa and South Asia, educated women are more likely than uneducated women to decide early and with certainty that children are sick and need rest or treatment; they are correspondingly less likely to consult their husbands, mothers-in-law, or brothers-in-law about the diagnosis or treatment of children's illnesses.[36] Compared with uneducated women, educated women in rural India play an important decision-making role in child health and feeding decisions, even if not in other areas of family life.[37] In Karnataka, although it is almost always the mother who first detects child illness, illiterate women are uniformly less likely to take action or even to draw attention to the sickness, waiting instead for their mothers-in-law or husbands to take note and action. As a mother's education increases, she is more likely to be the chief decision-maker in actions regarding sick children. In fact, the need to safeguard the health of grandchildren was frequently cited in Karnataka as an important reason for acquiring an educated daughter-in-law.[38] That uneducated women lack the power to make health-care decisions is supported by qualitative data from North India on health decisions among illiterate women: of the 20 wives studied, 13 had no power to seek health care during sickness, nor did they feel confident about making treatment decisions.[39]

The link of women's education to decision-making concerning child health appears to be stronger in highly gender-stratified than in egalitarian cultures in which health decisions are more routinely made by women, irrespective of education. A comparison of North and South Indian women residing in a Delhi slum, for example, finds that South Indian women, who come from a more egalitarian kinship structure, are uniformly more likely to make child health decisions than are North Indian women.[40] Among North Indian women, education plays an important role in breaking with tradition. It thereby enhances women's ability to make decisions with respect to child health and to overcome traditional seclusion barriers to seeking health services (see Box 6.1). In contrast, in South India, where all women have greater decision-making authority, the educational differential in health decision-making is nil.

In highly male-dominated cultures, where the preference for sons is marked, educated women may make health-care decisions deleterious to the health of daughters. When this occurs, their enhanced decision-making ability may not translate into improved child survival. A study in Punjab, India, for example, finds that educated women discriminate against higher-order daughters (as compared with sons and eldest daughters) in health care and feeding practices, resulting in their higher mortality.[41] Similarly, in Bangladesh, with an increase in women's education, there is an unequal reduction in the risk of death for boys versus girls.

- A change in women's education from no schooling to one to five years of schooling results in a 45 per cent reduction of risk for boys, compared with 7 per cent for girls; and a change to six and more years reduces the risk of dying by 70 per cent for boys but only by 32 per cent for girls.[42]

In short, education enhances women's decision-making authority in the domain of

---

Box 6.1. *Women's autonomy in gender-stratified settings*

That even a small amount of education can change women's decision-making behaviour with regard to illness and health is seen in Pakistan, where the proportions who can go to the hospital alone are substantially greater among primary-schooled women (32 per cent) than among uneducated women (20 per cent), and greater still among secondary-schooled women (52 per cent). Even in a setting in which women are highly secluded, a small amount of education enables women to act autonomously in the domain of child health.

Source: Zeba A. Sathar, 'Women's Education and Autonomy as Factors in Fertility Change in Pakistan: Some Empirical Findings', paper presented at the Workshop on Female Education, Autonomy and Fertility Change in South Asia, New Delhi, Apr. 1993.

---

child health, and even a small amount of education enables women to participate more fully in the health care of their children. This effect of women's education on decision-making with respect to child health is probably stronger in gender-stratified structures, in which women are routinely excluded from these decisions, than in more egalitarian family systems, in which all women, irrespective of education, have some say in child health decisions.

Educated women have more confidence in obtaining services

Educated women are usually more confident in dealing with the outside world of service providers and health practitioners than are uneducated women. They are in a better position to locate appropriate facilities and make an informed choice about a facility or treatment. They are also more capable of demanding services, less likely to blame themselves if treatment does not help, and more likely to persist in obtaining accurate diagnosis and effective treatment.[43]

- In rural South India, for example, educated women spend considerably more time than uneducated women do with the doctor; they routinely seek medical assistance early and before attempting traditional methods of cure; they demand the attention of care providers; and they follow up on recommended treatments.[44]
- In contrast, uneducated women are often unable to elicit this kind of attention from care providers. For example, in rural Nigeria, uneducated women are often afraid to deliver in hospitals because nurses 'shout at women in labour', a fear not mentioned by the more self-confident, better educated women who were surveyed.[45]

Although education undoubtedly affects the extent to which women interact with service providers, the prevailing kinship structure conditions the extent of this interaction. For example, among both the more constrained North Indian women and the more egalitarian South Indian women, residing in a Delhi slum, the latter are significantly more likely than the former to have delivered in hospitals, whatever their level of education. Nevertheless, within each group, educated women are significantly more likely than uneducated women to have delivered in hospitals (15 per cent and 6 per cent among northern women; 48 per cent and 32 per cent among southern women).[46]

Educated women have closer bonds with their husbands and children

Along with enhanced decision-making, educated women often enjoy closer bonds with their husbands and children, a pattern that may have implications for health decisions. It has been argued that, where close bonds exist, disparities in food intake of males and females in India are reduced; in Africa, where close bonds exist, resources available for child health are increased.[47] In India, where, traditionally, women eat last and least, stronger husband–wife ties result in better distribution of food within the family; and it is better educated women who typically have these stronger ties.[48] Some researchers, however, are unable to find evidence that this more equal distribution of food is a major pathway between female education and child mortality.[49]

In sub-Saharan Africa, women traditionally maintain separate budgets and have considerable autonomy with regard to health decisions for themselves and their children. Their financial resources are constrained, however, because husbands do not necessarily participate in financing child care. There, a closer conjugal bond as well as any movement towards monogamy increases men's willingness to contribute to child health care. Notwithstanding these findings, the evidence in support of this pathway is weak.

Educated women exercise greater control over resources

Where education grants women greater economic independence, by granting control over either personal earnings or household resources, women are in a better position to improve child-feeding practices, because they can purchase food for their children. They can also take advantage of medical services. If they act on this ability, child survival will improve. Again, there is little direct evidence of this pathway between women's education and child survival. Some studies find that the income earned by mothers is more likely to be used to enhance child welfare than is the income earned by fathers; even with identical levels of income, a larger proportion is spent on children when the mother works than when she does not.[50] These findings suggest that economic independence gives women a greater say in the use of resources for child well-being.

Other evidence on the effect of women's employment on child survival, however, is cautionary. Although women who earn money may be in a better position to feed their children or purchase medical care for them, the increased time burden that paid work entails may leave children poorly supervised while their mothers work. This situation can increase the risks of infection and reduce chances of timely corrective action.[51] To the extent that educated, employed women can compensate for their time away from children by providing reliable substitute care for them, these women are likely to experience only the benefits of economic independence.

Links of Education to Health-care Utilization

The pathways discussed above are hypothesized to give better educated women the wherewithal to seek modern health services and to become responsive to new remedies, even if they do not necessarily understand the scientific rationale underlying disease.

The DHS and other recent studies provide an excellent opportunity to examine the links of education to health-care utilization in diverse settings. All of these studies show that the chances that a woman will have antenatal care, that births will be attended by trained medical personnel, that complete immunization of children will take place, and that sick children will receive timely and modern medical care are consistently affected by the mother's education.[52] The DHS data show that better educated women are more likely to take sick children to a medical facility than are less educated women: whereas between one-quarter and one-half of the uneducated women took a sick child to a medical facility, approximately three-quarters of mothers with secondary schooling did so. Another analysis of 17 DHS data-sets finds that, even after controls for economic and bio-demographic variables are applied, failure to use antenatal care was from 55 to 1300 per cent higher among uneducated than among secondary-schooled women.[53] Less spectacular but similar conclusions are drawn regarding the effect of women's education on the failure to use tetanus toxoid and child immunization.[54]

That women's education acts primarily through improved child-care practices is convincingly shown in an analysis of the determinants of child deaths in Punjab, India. Maximum likelihood estimates for models that include socio-economic, biological, and child-care controls (practice of rehydration, and antenatal and child immunization) show that women's education is not significantly related to child survivorship until the child-care variables are omitted from the equations.[55] This finding suggests that improved child-care practices of educated mothers is one major pathway through which education enhances child survival.

Another large data-set that demonstrates the net importance of women's education for child health comes from the Philippines. This study shows that each additional year of women's education increases the probability of preventive health-service utilization by about 4 per cent during any month in the child's first year of life; increases caloric intake by 7 per cent; reduces the probability of inadequate excreta disposal practices by about 9 per cent; and increases the probability of using soap by 2 per cent. On the negative side, an additional year of women's education is associated with a 36 per cent reduction in the duration of exclusive breast-feeding and a 5 per cent reduction in the practice of breast-feeding.[56] That the positives are more important than the negatives in determining child health is suggested by the fact that, on balance, a one-year increase in education results in a 5 per cent reduction in the incidence of diarrhoea, despite the diarrhoea-enhancing effect of reduced breast-feeding (especially in early infancy).

In the absence of good antenatal, preventive health care and contraceptive services, the erosion of prolonged breast-feeding and abstinence taboos can result in a curvilinear relationship between women's education and child morbidity, as measured by the prevalence of diarrhoea. Evidence from both Ghana and Liberia suggests that the incidence of diarrhoea can increase among the children of primary-schooled women compared with those of uneducated women; in Ghana, the prevalence of diarrhoea among the infants of primary-schooled women was 17 per cent higher than among those of uneducated women, even after demographic, socio-economic, and household-amenities variables were controlled.[57] Even so, this curvilinear effect was not translated into a similar effect on child mortality, largely because educated women are better equipped to seek appropriate health-care services.

Educational differentials in health-care utilization for children are evident in all settings, rural and urban, under both clean and unsanitary conditions, and regardless of access to health services.[58] Analyses of the relationship of women's education to child health-care utilization in several DHS settings, however, suggest that the educational advantage is especially strong in areas where services are not available; that, in the face of poor access, education puts women at an advantage in obtaining health services.[59] Supporting this conclusion, one study finds that women's education has a larger protective effect on child health in unsanitary communities with visible signs of excreta and in those located at considerable distance from a health-care facility than in other communities.[60] In another study, although child mortality was lowest in areas with both health-service facilities and women's wide access to education, it was education rather than the presence of health services that exerted a stronger influence.[61]

Other, more mechanical, links exist between education and child mortality. The most important of these is that educated women uniformly marry later and, hence, avoid child-bearing at high-risk ages, resulting in lower maternal and child mortality.[62] Similarly, to the extent that better educated women are more successful at spacing or limiting births through contraception, they are less likely to experience risky short birth intervals and high-parity births. Finally, to the extent that better educated women are themselves better nourished and less likely to experience low heights and weights, they have a better chance of delivering healthy babies.[63]

Notes

1. S. H. Cochrane, J. Leslie, and D. J. O'Hara, 'Parental Education and Child Health: Intracountry Evidence', *Health Policy and Education*, 2 (1982), 213–50.
2. See J. C. Caldwell, 'Education as a Factor'.
3. Preston, 'Introduction', and Chowdhury, Khan, and Chen, 'Experience in Pakistan and Bangladesh', in Preston (ed.), *Effects*.
4. For observations from Bolivia, Burundi, Colombia, and Mali, see G. T. Bicego and

T. Boerma, 'Maternal Education and Child Survival: A Comparative Analysis of DHS Data', paper presented at the Demographic and Health Surveys World Conference, Washington, DC, Aug. 1991; for observations from rural China, see N. O. Tsuya and M. K. Choe, 'Trends and Covariates of Infant and Child Mortality in Rural China: The Case of Jilin Province', paper presented at the Annual Meeting of the Population Association of America, Baltimore, 29 Mar.–1 Apr. 1989.

5. It has been explored in intensive studies in single settings (see, for example, J. C. Caldwell, Reddy, and P. Caldwell, 'The Social Component of Mortality Decline'; Das Gupta, 'Death Clustering'; and Lindenbaum, 'Maternal Education') and in multiple settings using large data-sets such as WFS and DHS: see Bicego and Boerma, 'Maternal Education'; J. Cleland, G. Bicego, and G. Fegan, 'Socioeconomic Inequalities in Childhood Mortality: The 1970s to the 1980s', *Health Transition Review*, 2/1 (1992); J. N. Hobcraft, 'Child Spacing and Child Mortality', in IRD/Macro International Inc., *Proceedings of the Demographic and Health Surveys World Conference, Washington, D.C., 1991*, ii (Columbia, Md., 1991); J. N. Hobcraft, J. W. McDonald, and S. O. Rutstein, 'Socio-economic Factors in Infant and Child Mortality: A Cross-national Comparison', *Population Studies*, 38 (1984), 193–223; and J. N. Hobcraft, J. W. McDonald, and S. O. Rutstein, 'Demographic Determinants of Infant and Early Child Mortality: A Comparative Analysis', *Population Studies*, 39 (1985), 363–85; and United Nations, *'Socio-economic Differentials*.

There are, in addition, excellent reviews of the relationship, many of which elucidate the female-status pathways through which education affects mortality. See Cochrane, Leslie, and O'Hara, 'Parental Education'; Cleland and van Ginneken, 'Maternal Education'; J. C. Caldwell, 'Cultural and Social Factors'; Cleland, 'Maternal Education'; and J. Hobcraft, 'Women's Education, Child Welfare and Child Survival', paper presented at the United Nations Expert Group Meeting on Population and Women, Gaborone, Botswana, 22–6 June 1992.

6. Hobcraft, 'Child Spacing and Child Mortality' and 'Women's Education'.

7. United Nations, *'Socio-economic Differentials*; Hobcraft, McDonald, and Rutstein, 'Socio-economic Factors'.

8. J. Ties Boerma, A. Sommerfelt, and Shea Rutstein, *Childhood Morbidity and Treatment Patterns*, Demographic and Health Surveys, Comparative Studies No. 4 (Columbia, Md., Institute for Resource Development, 1991); Hobcraft, 'Child Spacing and Child Mortality' and 'Women's Education'.

9. Cochrane, Leslie, and O'Hara, 'Parental Education'; United Nations, *Socio-Economic Differentials*.

10. Bicego and Boerma, 'Maternal Education'.

11. Schultz, *Women and Development* and 'Returns to Women's Education'; for Costa Rica, see M. R. Haines and R. C. Avery, 'Differentials in Infant and Child Mortality in Costa Rica, 1968–73', *Population Studies*, 36 (1982), 31–44; for the Sudan, see Farah and Preston, 'Child Mortality Differentials'.

12. Cleland, Bicego, and Fegan, 'Socioeconomic Inequalities'.

13. Cochrane, Leslie, and O'Hara, 'Parental Education'.

14. United Nations, *Socio-Economic Differentials*.

15. Hobcraft, McDonald, and Rutstein, 'Socio-economic Factors'; United Nations, *Socio-Economic Differentials*.

16. Hobcraft, 'Child Spacing and Child Mortality'.

17. Bicego and Boerma, 'Maternal Education'.

18. J. Hobcraft, 'Women's Education, Child Welfare, and Child Survival'; and Cochrane, Leslie, and O'Hara, 'Parental Education'.
19. A. T. Flegg, 'Inequality of Income, Illiteracy and Medical Care as Determinants of Infant Mortality in Underdeveloped Countries', *Population Studies,* 36/3 (1982), 441–58.
20. J. Trussell and C. Hammerslough, 'A Hazard-Model Analysis of the Covariates of Infant and Child Mortality in Sri Lanka', *Demography,* 20/1 (1983), 1–26.
21. In Africa, for Ibadan, Nigeria, see J. C. Caldwell, 'Education as a Factor'; for the Sudan, see Farah and Preston, 'Child Mortality Differentials'; in Latin America, for Colombia, see T. P. Schultz, 'Interpretations of the Relations Among Mortality, Economics of the Household and the Health Environment', in *Socioeconomic Determinants and Consequences of Mortality Differences* (Geneva, WHO, 1980), and C. E. Florenz and D. P. Hogan, 'Women's Status and Infant Mortality in Rural Colombia', *Social Biology,* 37/3–4 (1990), 188–203; in the Middle East, for Kuwait, see K. L. Kohli and M. Al-Omain, 'Levels and Trends of Foetal, Infant and Childhood Mortality, and Their Determinants: A Case Study of Kuwait', *Population Bulletin of ECWA,* 22/23 (1982), and, for rural Jordan, B. Edmonston, 'Community Variations in Infant and Child Mortality in Rural Jordan', *Journal of Developing Areas,* 71 (1983), 473–89; for Amman, Jordan, see B. Tekce and F. C. Shorter, 'Determinants of Child Mortality: A Study of Squatter Settlements in Jordan', *Population and Development Review,* 10 (Supplement) (1984), 257–80; and in Asia, for Malaysia, see DaVanzo, Butz, and Habicht, 'Biological and Behavioral Influences', and DaVanzo, 'Infant Mortality and Economic Development'; for rural Karnataka, India, see J. C. Caldwell, Reddy, and P. Caldwell, 'The Social Component of Mortality Decline'.
22. J. C. Caldwell, 'Education as a Factor'.
23. An-Magritt Jensen and Magdallen N. Juma, *Women, Childbearing and Nutrition: A Case Study from Bungoma, Kenya* (Oslo, Norwegian Institute for Urban and Regional Research, 1989).
24. For evidence from Mexico, see LeVine *et al.,* 'Women's Schooling'; from Bangladesh, see Lindenbaum, Chakraborty, and Elias, *Influence of Maternal Education,* and Bhuiya, Streatfield, and Meyer, 'Mothers' Hygienic Awareness'; from Ghana, see P. W. Stephens, *The Relationship Between the Level of Household Sanitation and Child Mortality: An Examination of Ghanaian Data,* African Demography Working Paper No. 10 (Philadelphia, Population Studies Center, University of Pennsylvania, 1984); from Kenya, see T. O. Eisemon, V. L. Patel, and S. O. Sena, 'Uses of Formal and Informal Knowledge in the Comprehension of Instructions for Oral Rehydration Therapy in Kenya', *Social Science and Medicine,* 25/11 (1987), 1225–34; and from India, see E. Goodburn, G. J. Ebrahim, and S. Senapati, 'Strategies Educated Mothers Use to Ensure the Health of Their Children', *Journal of Tropical Pediatrics,* 36/5 (Oct. 1990), 235–39.
25. For evidence from Ethiopia, see A. G. Yohannes and K. Streatfield, 'Utilisation of Health Facilities for Child Illness in Ethiopia 1983', *Child Survival Research Note* 19CS (Canberra, Australian National University, 1988); from Zaire, see A. Tsui, J. De Clerque, and N. Mangani, 'Maternal and Socio Demographic Correlates of Child Morbidity in Bas-Zaire: The Effects of Maternal Reporting', *Social Science and Medicine,* 26 (1988), 701–13; from Punjab, India, see Das Gupta, 'Death Clustering'; and from West Bengal, India, see Goodburn, Ebrahim, and Senapati, 'Strategies'.
26. J. Ties Boerma *et al., Immunisation: Levels, Trends and Differentials,* Demographic and Health Surveys Comparative Studies No. 4 (Columbia, Md., Institute for Resource Development, 1990). For India, see Goodburn, Ebrahim, and Senapati, 'Strategies'; for

Nigeria, see C. E. E. Okojie, 'Some Inter-relationships'; for Bangladesh, see A. Bhuiya, K. Streatfield, and A. M. Sarder, 'Mother's Education and Knowledge of Major Childhood Diseases in Matlab, Bangladesh', in International Union for the Scientific Study of Population (IUSSP), *Proceedings of the International Population Conference, Montreal,* iv (Liège, IUSSP, 1993); and Streatfield, Singarimbun, and Diamond, 'Maternal Education and Child Immunization'.

27. J. Caldwell, 'Education as a Factor'.
28. For Mexico, see LeVine *et al.*, 'Women's Schooling' and LeVine *et al.*, *Schooling and Maternal Behaviour in a Mexican City: The Effects on Fertility and Child Survival,* Fertility Determinants Research Notes No. 16 (New York, The Population Council, Feb. 1987); and for rural Karanataka, India, see J. C. Caldwell, Reddy, and P. Caldwell, 'The Social Component of Mortality Decline'.
29. For Mexico, see LeVine *et al.*, 'Women's Schooling'.
30. Cleland and van Ginneken, 'Maternal Education'; Lindenbaum, Chakraborty, and Elias, *Influence of Maternal Education.*
31. Lindenbaum, Chakraborty, and Elias, *Influence of Maternal Education.*
32. Bhuiya, Streatfield, and Meyer, 'Mothers' Hygienic Awareness'; Bhuiya, Streatfield, and Sarder, 'Mother's Education'.
33. Bhuiya, Streatfield, and Sarder, 'Mother's Education'.
34. Okojie, 'Some Inter-relationships'.
35. Eisemon, Patel, and Sena, 'Uses'.
36. J. C. Caldwell, 'Cultural and Social Factors' and 'Education as a Factor'; J. C. Caldwell, Reddy and P. Caldwell, 'Causes of Demographic Change' and 'The Social Component of Mortality Decline'.
37. J. C. Caldwell, Reddy, and P. Caldwell, 'The Causes of Demographic Change in Rural South India'; for rural Karnataka; Goodburn, Ebrahim, and Senapati, 'Strategies'.
38. J. C. Caldwell, Reddy, and P. Caldwell, 'The Causes of Demographic Change in Rural South India'.
39. M. E. Khan, S. K. Ghosh Dastidar, and R. Singh, 'Nutrition and Health Practices Among Rural Women: A Case Study of Uttar Pradesh, India', *Journal of Family Welfare*, 33/1 (Sept. 1986), 3–20; and M. E. Khan *et al.*, 'Inequalities Between Men and Women in Nutrition and Family Welfare Services: An In-Depth Inquiry in an Indian Village', *Social Action*, 38/4 (Oct.–Dec. 1988), 398–417.
40. Basu, 'Culture and the Status of Women' and *Culture, the Status of Women, and Demographic Behaviour* (Oxford, Clarendon Press, 1992).
41. M. Das Gupta, 'Selective Discrimination Against Female Children in Rural Punjab, India', *Population and Development Review*, 13/1 (Mar. 1987), 77–100.
42. A. Bhuiya and K. Streatfield, 'Mothers' Education and Survival of Female Children in a Rural Area of Bangladesh', *Population Studies*, 45 (1991), 253–64.
43. J. C. Caldwell, 'Education as a Factor'; Cleland and van Ginneken, 'Maternal Education'.
44. J. C. Caldwell, Reddy, and P. Caldwell, 'The Social Component of Mortality Decline'; also, in West Bengal, Goodburn, Ebrahim, and Senapati, 'Strategies'.
45. Okojie, 'Some Inter-relationships'.
46. Basu, *Culture, the Status of Women, and Demographic Behaviour.*
47. J. C. Caldwell, 'Cultural and Social Factors'.
48. J. C. Caldwell, Reddy, and P. Caldwell (1983), 'The Social Component of Mortality Decline'.
49. Cleland and van Ginneken, 'Maternal Education'.

50. For India, see J. P. Mencher, 'Women's Work and Poverty: Women's Contribution to Household Maintenance in South India', in D. Dwyer and J. Bruce (eds.), *A Home Divided: Women and Income in the Third World* (Stanford, Stanford University Press, 1988); for Panama, see K. Tucker and D. Sanjur, 'Maternal Employment and Child Nutrition in Panama', *Social Science and Medicine*, 26/6 (1988), 605–12.

51. Basu, *Culture, the Status of Women, and Demographic Behaviour*; and A. M. Basu and K. Basu, 'Women's Economic Roles and Child Survival: The Case of India', *Health Transition Review*, 1/1 (1991), 83–103.

52. Demographic and Health Surveys Program, *Women's Education: Findings from Demographic and Health Surveys*, prepared for the World Conference on Education for All, Bangkok, Thailand (Columbia, Md., Mar. 1990); Bicego and Boerma, 'Maternal Education', 17 DHS; for Bolivia, Sommerfelt *et al.*, *Maternal and Child Health in Bolivia*; for Peru, Elo, 'Utilization'; for Namibia, Demographic and Health Survey 1992, P. Katjiuanjo *et al.*, *Namibia Demographic and Health Survey 1992* (Columbia, Md.: Macro International Inc., 1993); for Zambia, K. Gaisie, A. R. Cross, and G. Nsemukila, *Zambia Demographic and Health Survey 1992* (Columbia, Md., Macro International Inc., 1993); for Egypt, see Egypt, National Population Council, *Egypt Demographic and Health Survey 1992: Preliminary Report* (Columbia, Md., Macro International Inc., Mar. 1993); and for rural Nigeria, Okojie, 'Some Inter-relationships'.

53. Bicego and Boerma, 'Maternal Education'.

54. Ibid. and Boerma *et al.*, *Immunisation*.

55. Das Gupta, 'Death Clustering'.

56. The Cebu Study Team, 'Determinants of Child Health'.

57. Eva Tagoe, 'Maternal Education and Infant/Child Morbidity in Ghana: The Case of Diarrhoea, Evidence from the Ghana D.H.S.', paper presented at the Seminar on Women and Demographic Change in Sub-Saharan Africa, sponsored by the IUSSP Committee on Gender and Population, Dakar, Senegal, 3–6 Mar. 1993; O. B. Ahmad, I. W. Eberstein, and D. F. Sly, 'Proximate Determinants of Child Mortality in Liberia', *Journal of Biosocial Science*, 23/3 (July 1991), 313–25.

58. J. Cleland and J. K. van Ginneken, 'Maternal Education and Child Survival in Developing Countries'.

59. Bicego and Boerma, 'Maternal Education'; Boerma *et al.*, *Immunisation*.

60. A. Barrera, 'The Role of Maternal Schooling and Its Interaction with Public Health Programmes in Child Health Production', *Journal of Development Economics*, 32 (1990), 69–91.

61. Orubuloye and Caldwell, 'Impact of Public Health Services'.

62. Hobcraft, 'Women's Education'.

63. In Bangladesh, educated mothers are less likely than uneducated mothers to be underweight or short and, as a result, bear heavier infants with greater survival chances. See A. K. Chowdhury, 'Education and Infant Survival in Rural Bangladesh', *Health Policy Education*, 2 (1982).

7 Women's Education, Family-Size Preferences, and the Structure of Demand

Five main points emerge regarding the relationship of women's education to their family-size preferences.

- Women's education has a moderate and consistently inverse effect on desired family size;
- By and large, a small amount of education does not markedly change family-size desires; an upper primary or secondary education is required to set off changes in demand;
- The strength of the relationship changes over time, although how it changes depends on the context: it becomes stronger over time in countries at early stages of the fertility transition and weaker in countries at later stages;
- Thresholds appear to fall in high-income countries as compared with low- and middle-income ones; however, the patterns by levels of female literacy and gender disparity in literacy tend to be irregular;
- After economic status and other covariates are controlled, about half of the gross effect of women's education on family-size desires remains. What is especially striking in several multivariate studies is the persistence of thresholds: the net effect of education is far more likely to be strong among women with secondary and higher educations than among those with primary schooling.

There is considerable evidence that education enhances women's economic and social self-reliance, so that educated women are less likely to want large numbers of children, or sons, to provide them economic support in old age or to legitimize their positions in their husbands' families. At the same time, the economic costs—and especially the time costs—of children are considerably higher among educated than among uneducated women.

There is also the possibility that educated women are more confident of the survival of the infants they bear and are, therefore, less likely to need to inflate family-size desires to ensure that some of their children survive. Evidence of this link, however, is relatively weak. The evidence seems to suggest that the relationship of education to these motives is conditioned largely by the cultural context. Where education gives women some degree of economic self-reliance and exposes them to the outside world, even moderately educated women turn away from children as a primary source of future support and a major avenue to social acceptance. In contrast, in gender-stratified settings where seclusion and economic dependency characterize the lot of women, even educated women continue to prefer sons and to want many children for purposes of legitimacy and security in their reproductive years and for risk insurance and security in their old age. In these settings, it takes considerably greater amounts of education before shifts in the perceived value and costs of children occur than in more egalitarian settings. In short, the cultural context conditions the ease with which educated women can afford to revise their reproductive goals.

The previous three chapters have documented the effects of women's education on fertility through variables related to the supply of children. This chapter turns to the question of how women's education affects the demand for children.

Surveys usually measure the demand for children in two ways, first, by asking respondents how many more children they want and, second, by asking them to state how many children they would want if it were possible to begin child-bearing all over again. For example, in the DHS, the question designed to elicit desired family size asks: 'If you could choose exactly the number of children to have in your whole life, how many would that be?' Both the WFS and DHS data indicate considerable regional variation in desired family size. The desired family size, when measured this way, is highest in sub-Saharan Africa (5–7 children), followed by West Asia and North Africa (3–6 children), and by East and South Asia and Latin America (3–4 children).[1]

The overall number of boys and girls desired is another important indicator of demand. As is well known, there is considerable heterogeneity from region to region in the extent to which sons are preferred. Evidence from the WFS on whether women wanted their next child to be male or female suggests that in only 15 out of 38 countries is a balanced average sex preference for the next child displayed.[2] Strong preferences for sons are evident in East Asia and South Asia. In South Asia, for example, more than 50 per cent of all women who desired additional children wanted their next child to be a boy, compared with less than 10 per cent who wanted a girl (except in Sri Lanka).[3] Son preference is evident but more moderate in sub-Saharan Africa, North Africa, and the Middle East, and least evident in Latin America and South-East Asia.

Education is hypothesized to reduce women's demand for children for several reasons (see Table 1.3). First and most important, because educated women are more likely to be economically and socially self-reliant than uneducated women, they are less likely to be dependent on children (or sons) for support in old age and in times of infirmity. Likewise, they are less likely to be dependent on children (or sons) to legitimize their position in the marital family. At the same time, educated women are expected to be less likely to depend on children (or sons) for the potential labour support they can provide in childhood. Second, largely as a result of their increased exposure to the outside world, their greater-decision making autonomy, and their greater control over resources, educated women are more likely than uneducated women to perceive children to be more costly, in terms of both time and money.

In addition to these effects, the demand for children is also affected by perceptions and experience of child loss. Educated women tend to want fewer children than uneducated women because they are more confident that the children they bear will survive and because they are less likely to need to replace dead children. However, as indicated in Chapters 1 and 6, these effects tend to be overshadowed by the mechanical effect of improved child survival on lengthening birth intervals.[4] As a result, this pathway is more appropriately considered one of the factors affecting the supply of children (see Table 1.3) and has been discussed at length in Chapter 6. Lower family-size preferences are, in turn, expected to enhance the motivation to control fertility, which will result in fewer births if obstacles to contraception are overcome.

Men as well as women undoubtedly have many motives for limiting the number of children. It is entirely possible that women and men have similar family-size preferences, as some scholars have observed,[5] but have different motives for this preferred number, as observed in a study of women and their husbands in rural India.[6] Although certain costs and values of children are likely to be important for both women and men, the motives underlying desired family size, such as support in old age and acceptance in the marital family, are likely to be especially strong for women, particularly those in highly gender-stratified societies where women experience extreme economic and social dependency. In addition, in many settings, women are more likely than men to bear the financial and, certainly, the time costs of raising children.

This chapter examines the pattern of the relationship of women's education to desired family size and looks at the effect of education on various motives underlying these preferences. The literature on the relationship of education to the demand for children and, particularly, to the motives underlying family-size preferences is generally much sparser than is the literature on education's relationship to supply-side factors. Hence, this chapter not only relies heavily on the few available studies but also speculates freely about the nature of the relationships.

Pattern of the Relationship

Cross-sectional surveys—that is, surveys of various respondents at one point in time—are clearly imperfect instruments for measuring the demand for children. Such surveys rely on current expressions and perceptions and current costs and values of children. Because this information is *ex post facto* for most women, it has to be assumed that current responses reflect the situation earlier in their child-bearing careers. To the extent, however, that respondents tend to rationalize their actual experiences, having additional children may well make women revise their desired family-size responses to favour higher fertility and, hence, inflate desired family size.[7]

Table 7.1 summarizes the findings of studies documenting for 53 countries the relationship of women's education to desired family size (referred to in demographic surveys as 'ideal' family size).[8] The studies are listed in Appendix H.

Overall findings

There is an overall inverse effect of women's education on desired family size (Table 7.1).

- In 32 of the 53 studies, women with more education desire fewer children than do women with less education;
- In more than one-third (19) of the studies, the relationship is 7- shaped (that is, there are insignificant or no declines in desired family size until after at least a lower primary education is attained).

Table 7.1. *Patterns in the relationship of women's education to desired family size, by region, level of development, and gender disparity in literacy*

	Patterns in the relationship between years of schooling and desired family size[a]			Total number of studies
	Inverse (negative)	7	Curvilinear	
A. Region[b]				
Sub-Saharan Africa	12	7	0	19
North Africa and the Middle East	6	0	0	6
East and South-East Asia	4	2	0	6
South Asia	0	4	1	5
Latin America and the Caribbean	10	6	1	17
B. Level of development				
1. Annual per capita income ($)				
500 or less	13	5	1	19
501–999	6	10	0	16
1000 or more	13	4	1	18
2. Overall female literacy rate (%)				
40 or less	11	7	1	19
41–80	12	8	0	20
81 or more	9	4	1	14
C. Gender disparity in literacy[c]				
250–700	11	7	1	19
701–850	9	5	0	14
851 or more	12	7	1	20
TOTALS	32	19	2	53

[a] Three distinct patterns in the relationship of years of schooling to desired family size are apparent: an inverse relationship, in which moderately educated women want progressively fewer children (5 per cent or more); a 7-shaped relationship, in which moderately educated women want about the same number of children as uneducated women do (within 5 per cent), but better educated women want fewer; and a reversed-J-shaped relationship, in which moderately educated women want more children than uneducated women do (more than 5 per cent), and better educated women want fewer.

[b] Not all countries in a region are included, and those included are not necessarily representative of the region but are, rather, those countries for which the requisite data are available. Thus, the results are not necessarily representative of any particular region.

[c] The level of gender disparity in literacy is the number of literate females per 1000 literate males.

Notes: The studies selected for inclusion in this table appear in Appendix H, where they are marked with a dagger (†). The study populations were women of child-bearing age who were married or in union.

Sources: Of the 53 studies, 51 are based on World Fertility Survey (19) and Demographic and Health Survey (32) data. Sources are indicated in Appendix H.

Region The shape of the relationship varies by region of the world.
- Straight inverse relationships occur in all of the North African and Middle East studies, two-thirds of the East and South-East Asian studies, and in three-fifths of the sub-Saharan African and Latin American and the Caribbean studies.
- In contrast, no studies in the South Asian region exhibit a straight inverse relationship.

Level of development and gender disparity in literacy There is no consistent pattern in the relationship of women's education to desired family size by per capita income levels. The shape of the relationship of education to desired family size varies only slightly by female literacy levels and the level of gender disparity in literacy.

- Inverse relationships are observed in about the same proportion in the poorest (13 of 19 studies) and wealthiest (13 of 18) settings, whereas they occur in less than two-fifths (6 of 16 studies) of the middle-income settings;
- About three out of five studies in every setting, irrespective of gender disparities, reveal a uniformly inverse relationship between women's education and desired family size.

Differentials

Table 7.2 shows the extent of the differences in desired family size among uneducated women and women with some secondary education.

- Education generates wide differentials in desired family size, ranging from 0.1 to 3.5 children between the most and the least educated women; women with some secondary schooling typically want about 20 per cent to 40 per cent fewer children than uneducated women want. (A comparison between Table 7.2 and Table 2.3 suggests that differentials in desired family size between uneducated and secondary-schooled women are somewhat narrower in the case of desired family size than in the case of children ever born.)
- The differentials in family-size desires between uneducated women and women with some secondary schooling are widest in sub-Saharan Africa, the region with the largest overall family-size desires. In sub-Saharan Africa, the desired family size tends to be approximately two children greater than the desired family size in other regions. In this region, secondary-schooled women typically (18 of 19 studies) want in excess of 20 per cent fewer children than uneducated women do. Differentials are also wide in North Africa and the Middle East, where, in 5 of 6 studies, secondary-schooled women want in excess of 20 per cent fewer children than uneducated women do. Differentials are somewhat narrower in Latin America and the Caribbean and in the two Asian regions;
- The differentials between the family-size desires of secondary-schooled women and uneducated women are wider among the poorest and richest countries than among middle-income ones;
- Similarly, the differentials in the desired family size of uneducated compared with secondary-schooled women are somewhat narrower in moderately literate settings than elsewhere: differentials of more than 30 per cent between uneducated and secondary-schooled women are observed in more than one in three studies in low- and high-literacy settings, compared with fewer than one-third in medium-literacy settings;
- The differentials in the desired family size of uneducated women compared with secondary-schooled women are narrower in the most egalitarian settings than they are elsewhere.

Table 7.2. *Differentials in the relationship of women's education to desired family size, by region, level of development, and gender disparity in literacy*

	Differences in desired family size between uneducated and secondary-schooled women[a] (percentage differentials) NARROW ◀------------------▶ WIDE				Total number of studies
	10 or less	11–20	21–30	31 or more	
A. Region[b]					
Sub-Saharan Africa	0	1	9	9	19
North Africa and the Middle East	0	1	2	3	6
East and South-East Asia	0	3	2	1	6
South Asia	1	1	3	0	5
Latin America and the Caribbean	2	6	4	5	17
B. Level of development					
1. Annual per capita income ($)					
500 or less	2	2	8	7	19
501–999	1	5	6	4	16
1000 or more	0	5	6	7	18
2. Overall female literacy rate (%)					
40 or less	1	1	10	7	19
41–80	1	7	6	6	20
81 or more	1	4	4	5	14
C. Gender disparity in literacy[c]					
250–700	1	1	10	7	19
701–850	1	4	4	5	14
851 or more	1	7	6	6	20
TOTALS	3	12	20	18	53

[a] The term 'secondary-schooled women' here applies to women who have had some secondary education or completed or gone beyond secondary school—that is, women who have had more than six years of primary education.
[b] Not all countries in a region are included, and those included are not necessarily representative of the region but are, rather, those countries for which the requisite data are available. Thus, the results are not necessarily representative of any particular region.
[c] The level of gender disparity in literacy is the number of literate females per 1000 literate males.

Notes: The studies selected for inclusion in this table appear in Appendix H, where they are marked with a dagger (†).

Sources: Of the 53 studies, 51 are based on World Fertility Survey (19) and Demographic and Health Survey (32) data. Sources are indicated in Appendix H.

Thresholds

Table 7.3 shows the educational levels at which substantial declines in desired family size take place.

- For the most part, a 10 per cent decline in desired family size occurs once an upper primary education has been attained; in the majority of cases, a 20 per cent decline occurs only after some secondary or higher education has been attained;
- Threshold levels of education before a 10 per cent decline in desired family size is attained tend to be lowest in North Africa and the Middle East, where a 10

Table 7.3.   *Relationship of the duration of women's education to desired family size, by region, level of development, and gender disparity in literacy*

	Educational level (years of schooling) by which:								Total number of studies
	A 10% decline in desired family size is reached				A 20% decline in desired family size is reached				
	1–3	4–6	7+	Never	1–3	4–6	7+	Never	
A. Region [a]									
Sub-Saharan Africa	6	10	3	0	0	6	12	1	19
North Africa and the Middle East	6	0	0	0	1	2	2	1	6
East and South-East Asia	1	2	3	0	0	1	2	3	6
South Asia	0	2	2	1	0	0	4	1	5
Latin America and the Caribbean	4	8	4	1	0	5	7	5	17
B. Level of development									
1. Annual per capita income ($)									
500 or less	5	9	4	1	0	5	11	3	19
501–999	5	5	5	1	0	4	6	6	16
1000 or more	7	8	3	0	1	5	10	2	18
2. Overall female literacy rate (%)									
40 or less	7	9	2	1	1	6	10	2	19
41–80	6	7	6	1	0	3	10	7	20
81 or more	4	6	4	0	0	5	7	2	14
C. Gender disparity in literacy [b]									
250–700	7	9	2	1	1	6	10	2	19
701–850	5	4	4	1	0	2	7	5	14
851 or more	5	9	6	0	0	6	10	4	20
TOTALS	17	22	12	2	1	14	27	11	53

[a] Not all countries in a region are included, and those included are not necessarily representative of the region but are, rather, those countries for which the requisite data are available. Thus, the results are not necessarily representative of any particular region.
[b] The level of gender disparity in literacy is the number of literate females per 1000 literate males.

Notes: The studies selected for inclusion in this table appear in Appendix H, where they are marked with a dagger (†). Some appendix studies combine rates for women with 1–3 and 4–6 years of schooling; in such studies, rates are shown in the column marked 1–3.

Sources: Of the 53 studies, 51 are based on World Fertility Survey (19) and Demographic and Health Survey (32) data. Sources are indicated in Appendix H.

per cent decline is attained at the lower primary stage in all 6 studies. In contrast, a 10 per cent decline is attained by the lower primary level in fewer than one-third of the studies in Latin America and the Caribbean (4 of 17) and sub-Saharan Africa (6 of 19); in these regions, declines of 10 per cent or more typically occur at the upper primary stage. Threshold levels are even higher in East and South-East Asia and, especially, in South Asia, typically occurring at stages beyond the lower primary level in 5 of the 6 studies in East and South-East Asia, and in all 5 studies in South Asia. In every region, a 20 per cent decline in desired family size typically occurs only after the secondary level is attained.

When countries are classified by per capita income levels, the trend becomes clearer: threshold levels are distinctly lower in high-income than in low- or middle-income countries. For example, a decline of 10 per cent or more in family-size desires occurs at the lower primary level in about one-third of all countries. It occurs at this level in one-quarter of the low-income countries, in almost one-third of the middle-income countries, and in almost two-fifths of the high-income countries.

The overall female literacy context has less of an effect on changing thresholds. A 10 per cent decline is attained at the lower primary level in about one-third of all studies conducted in all settings, irrespective of literacy level. For the majority of studies at each level of female literacy, 10 per cent declines occur only after the upper primary or higher level has been attained. Similar conclusions emerge when studies are classified by level of gender disparity in literacy, although here, thresholds are somewhat higher in the most egalitarian settings.

Other evidence

The existence of threshold levels of education before sustained declines in family-size preferences occur is substantiated by in-depth subnational studies. In Mexico, for example, in both an urban and a rural sample, women with six years of schooling could hardly be distinguished from less educated women in terms of desired family size (differentials of 0.3); substantial declines became obvious only among women with seven or more years of education.[9] Similarly, in Edo and Delta states of Nigeria, where overall desired family size is 6.8 children, primary-schooled women want negligibly fewer children than uneducated women do (about 0.3); it is only after women attain some secondary and, especially, tertiary education that desired family size falls substantially (by 0.6 and 1.0 children, respectively).[10] Similarly, in rural Maharashtra, India, the family-size desires of uneducated and primary-schooled women are virtually identical. A middle-school education reduces desired family size modestly. Only among secondary-schooled women are family-size desires significantly reduced.[11]

Changes over time in the relationship of women's education to desired family size appear to depend on contextual factors. Appendix H reports this relationship for 19 countries for which data at more than one time are available. Aside from suggesting a uniform decline over time in levels of desired family size, these data suggest that, for the most part, differentials in desired family size between uneducated women and women with some secondary education tend to remain the same over time or to widen rather than shrink. Exceptions are the more developed countries, such as Ecuador and Egypt, where a notable narrowing of differentials can be seen.[12] This narrowing of differentials occurs largely because of a substantially greater decline in desired family size among the least educated women than among other women (one child in each case).

In contrast, in settings at relatively early points in the fertility transition, where uneducated women continue to want large numbers of children—countries such as Ghana, Kenya, Pakistan, and the Sudan—differentials have either widened or remained the same over time. An example of widening differentials comes from Tamil Nadu, India. Here, a multivariate study at two successive points in the fertility transition finds that, at the earlier time, the net effect of education is weak (controlling for economic status, interspousal age difference, women's economic activity, decision-making power, and freedom of movement). Ten years later, education's impact on fertility desires becomes strong and significant.[13]

Studies in several settings have shown that women's education has a substantial net effect on family-size desires, controlling for household economic status and husband's characteristics (see Box 7.1).[14] In Nigeria, a logistic regression analysis of recent data on Yoruba and Hausa women examines future fertility intentions (desire for no more children) as a function of such covariates as women's education, age, residence, number of living children, pregnancy status, ethnicity, and whether the wife earns and controls income. The net odds ratios for education, although in the expected direction, are insignificant except among secondary-schooled women, suggesting once again the presence of thresholds. Moreover, secondary education has a stronger net effect on the demand for children among Hausa women, who come from a more gender-stratified culture, than among Yoruba women, who are generally much better educated and have more economic independence.[15] A study in Edo and Delta states of Nigeria also finds that a primary education has little net effect on desired family size after controlling for a host of economic and women's decision-making variables. It is only secondary and, especially, tertiary education

---

Box 7.1.   *The net effect of women's education on desired family size*

Women's education has an effect on desired family size even after controlling for the fact that educated women are younger, come from higher-income families, and marry better educated men than less educated women do. For example, the United Nations analysis of World Fertility Survey data from 37 countries breaks down the gross effect of wife's education on fertility desires into a direct, net effect and effects operating through family size, residence, husband's education, and husband's and wife's occupations. This analysis concludes that about half of the gross effect at each level of education can be attributed to the effect of the wife's education alone. The net effect is strongest in sub-Saharan Africa and weakest in Latin America. A strong net effect of women's education is observed, even though this analysis, like many others, controls for women's work or women's control over resources, which may capture some of the effects of education.

Source: United Nations, *Fertility Behaviour in the Context of Development: Evidence from the World Fertility Survey*, Population Studies No. 100 (New York, Department of International Economic and Social Affairs, United Nations, 1987).

that is associated with significant declines in family-size preferences.[16] Another study using DHS data from Oyo and Ondo states of Nigeria finds that, once such covariates as age, parity, residence, marital age, spousal communication, and control over economic resources are controlled, women's education has no effect on family-size preferences.[17] Several factors argued to be affected by education, however, including age, parity, spousal communication, and control over resources, were found to be significant, thereby implying that education has an indirect effect on fertility desires.

How Women's Education Reduces the Number of Children Wanted

The literature suggests that there are at least two major routes through which education can reduce the number of children women want. First, educated women are more self-reliant and less dependent on children for economic and social survival than uneducated women are. For example, they may be less likely to want many children for the economic and physical support children are expected to provide in their mothers' old age. They may also rely less on large numbers of children to legitimize their position in their husband's family. Second, the costs—both economic and time—associated with child-rearing are expected to be higher among better educated than among uneducated women.

A third route is through improved child-survival prospects. Educated women are more confident than poorly educated women that their children will survive and, hence, are less likely to need many children so that some survive; these effects, however, tend to be weaker than the other two described above. Moreover, child mortality experiences tend to be more powerfully related to the supply of children than to the demand for them.[18] Hence, the link of women's education to child mortality has been treated separately in Chapter 6 and is not reviewed in this chapter. Nevertheless, all of the motives described above lead educated women to want fewer children than uneducated women. How quickly this erosion occurs, however, depends on the extent to which the kinship structure allows educated women to assume non-traditional roles. Where the culture and its institutional mechanisms serve to limit women's economic autonomy relative to men's, the response to education may be sluggish.[19]

Educated women are more self-reliant

In traditional settings, women, like men, rely on children for child labour and for economic and residential support in old age (see Box 7.2). In contexts where women are barred from income-earning activities by norms of seclusion, or from controlling property, their reliance on children tends to be stronger than that of their husbands.[20] Unlike men, women also rely on children to legitimize their position in their husbands' families. Education is hypothesized to reduce women's reliance on children and, consequently, their need for large numbers of children.[21]

Box 7.2.   *The importance of old-age support*

Old-age support is one of the most pervasive motives underlying women's preference for large numbers of children in developing countries. A study in Zimbabwe documents this sentiment: 'The son of mine is my father. He will take care of me when I grow old.'[a] Although children are important to both parents, they are especially so for women, for several reasons. First, women are less likely to be able to fend for themselves economically, especially under conditions of purdah, where women are excluded from controlling property or other wealth, or where the labour market restricts the types of activities or locations in which women are employed.[b] A 1980 study finds that, among rural Indian land-owning families, women looked to their sons for old-age support, whereas rural men looked to their land.[c] Second, in many countries, other means of economic self-reliance, such as credit or state-sponsored support, are less available to women than to men. Third, given wide spousal age differences, it is more likely that women will be widowed than will men, meaning the loss of spousal support. In short, while men may rely on children (or sons, in some contexts), they have other means of economic survival; for women, children are more likely to be their only or major source of economic support.

[a] M. M. Mhloyi, 'Fertility Transition in Zimbabwe', paper presented at the Seminar on the Course of Fertility Transition in Sub-Saharan Africa, sponsored by the International Union for the Scientific Study of Population Committee on Comparative Analysis of Fertility and the University of Zimbabwe, Harare, Zimbabwe, 19–22 Nov. 1991.
[b] M. Cain, 'Perspectives on Family and Fertility in Developing Countries', *Population Studies*, 36/2 (July 1982), 159–75.
[c] Michael Vlassoff and Carol Vlassoff, 'Old Age Security and the Utility of Children in Rural India', *Population Studies* 34 (Nov. 1980), 487–99; K. O. Mason, *The Status of Women: A Review of Its Relationships to Fertility and Mortality* (New York, The Rockefeller Foundation, 1984).

As this section will show, however, the strength of this relationship varies from setting to setting. The extent to which education erodes women's reliance on children may well depend on the extent of gender stratification prevailing in a given setting: where educated women can control resources and have access to the outside world, education may be expected to erode maternal reliance on children more rapidly than in settings in which even educated women remain secluded and dependent.

Diminished need for old-age support   The general hypothesis is that education increases women's self-reliance for risk insurance and old-age economic and physical support, thereby diminishing their dependence on adult children's support. As women gain relative autonomy, control over family resources, and physical exposure to the outside world, their dependence on male family members and, consequently, their need for children for future support is expected to diminish.[22] The evidence for this effect is mixed. Highly educated women in all contexts appear to be less likely than uneducated women to express old-age support motives for large numbers of children. In some contexts, however, moderately educated women frequently express as strong old-age support motives for large numbers of children as uneducated women do.

That highly educated women expect to rely less on their children than uneducated women is evident from a variety of settings, including those in Latin America, South Asia, East and South-East Asia and sub-Saharan Africa.[23]

- In Cuernavaca, Mexico, for example, whereas 60 per cent of poorly educated women (with 1–5 years of schooling) expected economic support from their children, this proportion fell to 40 per cent among women with 7–9 years of education.[24] Similarly, schooling is inversely associated with expectations of living with a son or daughter in old age: while 39 and 38 per cent of poorly educated women expect to co-reside with a son or daughter, respectively, among women with 7–9 years of schooling, this proportion falls to 18 and 13 per cent respectively;
- In Karachi, Pakistan, where larger proportions of women express old-age motives for having large numbers of children, more than 90 per cent of uneducated women voiced this motive, compared with 61 per cent of women with 10 or more years of schooling;[25]
- Data from the Value of Children survey conducted in 1975 in the Philippines show stronger effects of education on women's expectations of old-age support from children. For example, 46 per cent of women with less than a primary-school education had strong expectations of support from children, compared with 23 per cent of women with a high school education, and 19 per cent of those with a college education.[26]

The effect of a few years of education on reducing women's need of children for old-age economic or residential support is less consistent and more context-specific. In highly gender-stratified societies, the old-age security motive for children appears to abate relatively little in response to changes in education *per se*, at least not until very high levels of education are attained, as seen in studies in sub-Saharan Africa and South Asia.[27]

- For example, in rural India (Maharashtra), neither a primary education nor, to a lesser extent, a middle-school education reduces women's expectations of old-age economic support from sons. It is only among secondary-schooled women that this effect is evident and, even so, secondary-schooled women had as strong expectations of co-residence with adult sons as uneducated women did;[28]
- In Karachi, Pakistan, similarly, old-age economic support motives are strongly voiced by more than 90 per cent of uneducated women as well as women with nine or fewer years of schooling; this percentage declines markedly only with 10 or more years of education.[29]

These examples suggest that, in less developed and gender-stratified cultures with relatively limited economic opportunities for women and strong seclusion norms, even moderately educated women must continue to rely on their sons. As a result, desired family size in these settings may not decrease until relatively high levels of education have been attained, a hypothesis consistent with the data shown in Table 7.3.

By comparison, in more developed or more egalitarian settings, even a few years of education are sufficient to reduce women's reliance on large numbers of children for future support. As a consequence, the threshold levels before a decline in desired family size is attained are correspondingly lower, which is again consistent with the data in Table 7.3.

- In Cuernavaca, Mexico, each incremental level of women's education affects women's old-age expectations of children. For example, whereas 38–39 per cent of the least educated women (with one to five years of schooling) expected to co-reside with a son or daughter, 18–19 per cent of women with six years of schooling expected to do so; expectations regarding old-age economic support, however, fall less markedly for women with six years of schooling (60 per cent compared with 56 per cent) followed by 40 per cent among women with seven to nine years of schooling.[30]

The other side of this equation is the effect of education on increasing women's economic self-reliance. Women's reliance on children for economic support in old age cannot be expected to diminish with education unless education can provide women with opportunities to gain economic self-reliance and control over resources. There is evidence from several countries of this effect. Especially strong effects are seen in more developed settings, those in which economic opportunities for educated women are relatively plentiful, and those in which women are not secluded.[31]

Even in highly gender-stratified settings, such as India and Pakistan, women's education is a powerful correlate of women's expectations of economic self-reliance in old age.[32] Threshold levels of education before self-reliance becomes apparent, however, are higher in these settings. For example, the evidence in rural India suggests that it is only women with more than a primary-school education who expect to be economically self-reliant. Expectations of increased economic self-reliance among educated women do not necessarily mean that educated women do not expect to rely on their sons or children, but simply that they have an additional source of support in case children do not live up to expectations. This kind of evidence supports the view that, in some settings, education may expand rather than change women's sources of old-age support. Educated women may be relatively less likely to acknowledge this motive for having large numbers of children. Yet children, albeit fewer and better educated, can continue to be desired for old-age residential and economic security even among educated women in these settings.[33]

Diminished need for security within husband's family   Aside from women's need of children for old-age support, education may also offer women greater self-reliance in securing their positions in their husbands' families in those cultures—ranging from sub-Saharan and North Africa to East and South Asia—in which fertility is an important means by which a woman can legitimize and secure her position in her marital family.[34] Unlike the old-age support motive for large numbers of children, this motive for children is felt exclusively by women. The rewards for having children range from prestige in the family to security in case of desertion, to simply better treatment in the household. In contrast, not having children is sufficient justification for desertion or for a husband to take a second wife and can result in social ostracism and an uncertain future.[35] In sub-Saharan Africa, where women have some control over economic resources but tend to have little autonomy within the home, it has been argued that having children as a means of legitimizing women's status may be a far more important motive for high fertility than is women's need of children for old-age support.[36]

Few studies have addressed the relationship of women's education to their need for many children to legitimize their positions in their marital families. The evidence tends to be based on small and qualitative studies and suggests that educated women may have other channels through which to secure their positions in the family. The reduced need for several children to legitimize their status in their husbands' families may be an important factor contributing to their lower desired family size.[37] For example, the available evidence suggests that educated women tend to be respected by the members of their husbands' families for their knowledge.[38] They are also valued for the income they bring into the household, especially if they are working in 'respectable' occupations.[39]

The greater intimacy with husbands that educated women enjoy may be yet another means by which educated women can gain security in their marital homes.[40] Even so, there is evidence that, both in countries where women tend to be highly dependent on men and in those where women have considerable economic independence, even educated women know that they have to prove themselves by bearing children or sons to secure their domestic positions.[41] At most, as one observer noted for North India, educated brides may be less compelled to prove themselves throughout the reproductive span by bearing additional children.[42]

Diminished need for child labour A third reason for educated women's reduced reliance on children, in general, is their diminished reliance on children's labour support during childhood. Educated women, like educated men, are less likely than the uneducated to accept the traditional sentiment that more hands mean more work, that children have one mouth but two hands, or that children plough back into the family economy twice as much as they consume. They are also more likely than the uneducated to give high priority to the education of their children, even at the expense of children's labour contributions to the family farm and housework.[43] School-going children are systematically less likely to help with housework or work on the family farm or business than other children,[44] and they enter the labour-force much later as well, thereby requiring longer periods of parental support. Because better educated women are more likely to have school-going children, they are less likely to derive labour support from children than are less educated women.

- Evidence from rural Maharashtra, India, indicates that both expected and actual labour support from sons declines significantly with women's education, even after controlling for husband's socio-economic position. Labour support from daughters in housework showed a more modest decline, however, largely because housework is not seen as competing with school time and because girls are not expected to take school as seriously as are their brothers. Not only does women's education affect whether children work or not, it also has a pronounced effect on the time contribution of working children: children of secondary-schooled women contribute no more than 60 per cent of the time contributed by the children of uneducated women.[45]

Finally, in highly gender-stratified settings, the existence of strong son preferences can condition the extent to which education reduces women's reliance on sons both as a means of old-age support (since, in these settings, daughters are unlikely to be able to offer much support once they are married) and as a means of legitimizing their positions in their marital families. As discussed in Chapter 3, in these settings, women must have a considerable amount of education before their mobility becomes less restricted and they have a say in matters relating to their own lives and gain some measure of economic independence. Thus constrained, even moderately educated women remain highly dependent on men and define their security largely in terms of surviving sons. As a result, son preference is, at best, weakly eroded by education. Evidence of how female education affects son preference is generally quite sparse from every region except South Asia.

- In India, for example, a national survey finds that all women, including those with some secondary education, overwhelmingly favour sons.[46] Only among those with secondary schooling do preferences become more balanced. While all women want at least one son, preferences for second or higher order sons are influenced by women's education: a quarter of uneducated and primary-school educated women are prepared to have three or more daughters in order to bear a second son, compared with 7 per cent of women who had completed secondary school who would do so. Again, this kind of evidence suggests that, in South Asia, it may require a secondary education for women's strong preferences for sons to diminish.

In sum, in most settings, education apparently makes women more economically self-reliant and, correspondingly, less likely to rely on children for old-age and other support. How much education is required for this effect to occur is, however, less clear. For the most part, a secondary education reduces women's need of children for old-age support in most settings. Even in low-income and gender-stratified settings, secondary-schooled women appear to have acquired, relative to uneducated women, greater self-reliance and independent control over resources that can supplement support from children in old age.

The effect of a moderate amount of education is more variable. The evidence suggests that, in low-income and male-dominated settings, old-age support motives for large numbers of children are strong among all but the most highly educated women. In more egalitarian and developed societies, in contrast, thresholds are lower, and even a small amount of education is sufficient to increase women's self-reliance and reduce their need for children. The implications for desired family size are evident: the threshold levels of education before desired family size falls are likely to be lower in more egalitarian or developed societies than in gender-stratified and less developed ones.

Educated women experience higher child-rearing costs

Even in traditional settings, parents recognize that child-rearing is costly.

- In Nigeria, for example, one in three women agreed that 'a man with ten children is a fool'; and three in four agreed that 'lots of children [mean] lots of misery'. Better educated women were systematically more likely to agree with these statements.[47]

Education not only leads to a greater consciousness of child costs but also is associated with increased costs of children as a consequence of the desire of better educated parents for better educated and higher quality, more expensive children. This preference involves both greater financial costs and greater time and opportunity costs. In most cultures, time and opportunity costs are borne by the mother. In contrast, the pattern of direct spending on child-rearing by mother versus father varies substantially by culture.

In many countries, a major economic cost of children is education. In some settings, marriage costs are also important. Although there are also costs of feeding, clothing, and sheltering children, these are less likely to be in the forefront of parents' calculations of the costs of children. The importance of schooling costs, both direct and indirect, has been recognized in both sociological and economic formulations of the fertility transition.[48] Educated parents are more willing to forsake numbers of children for the improved 'quality' of fewer of them.

- Educated parents are more likely to prefer private over public schools, have higher educational aspirations for their children, and more expensive standards of recreation, feeding, and other needs, thereby making their children much costlier than those of less educated parents.

In the absence of data on the direct and opportunity costs of schooling, the actual level of children's schooling serves as a reasonable proxy for these costs. This measure is imperfect in so far as better educated women provide higher quality, more expensive schooling to their children than uneducated women provide, something not captured by sheer numbers of years of schooling. Moreover, better educated women may expect schoolchildren to do less work than uneducated women expect, in which case actual differentials in child costs will be wider than observed. Even so, women's education is observed to be closely related to both whether children attend school and how much education they attain—a relationship that holds in every region of the developing world.[49]

Education also enhances women's educational aspirations for their children.

- In both Nigeria and Zimbabwe, educated women have more costly aspirations for their children. They frequently cite the costs of meeting these aspirations as a major disincentive for bearing large numbers of children;[50]
- In Mexico, mothers with more schooling express systematically higher occupational aspirations for their sons, although it is only the best educated

women who can be differentiated from other women in the case of daughters;[51]

- In Egypt, parental education is the most consistent factor predicting educational aspirations for children, even after socio-economic factors are controlled; it is an especially powerful determinant among rural women and is especially powerful for aspirations for daughters, but less so for sons because even uneducated women want educated sons;[52]

- In Pakistan, even a primary-school education changes women's aspirations for children's schooling markedly: while almost half of uneducated women considered religious education sufficient for their daughters, almost half of the primary-schooled women wanted their daughters to have at least some secondary education;[53]

- In India, secondary education involves considerable direct costs to parents. There, aspirations for at least a secondary education for sons increase from 47 per cent of uneducated women to 94 per cent of secondary-schooled women, and for daughters, from 28 per cent to 64 per cent, respectively. Aspirations are strongly influenced by women's education, even after household economic status is controlled;[54] and

- A multivariate analysis of the determinants of child schooling in northern Thailand finds that women's education has a significant effect, net of age, economic status, distance to schools, and paternal education. Moreover, when aspirations for child education and parental aptitude scores are added to the analysis, the direct effect of women's education disappears, thereby underscoring the importance of aspirations as the link between maternal education and children's schooling.[55]

Aside from schooling costs, in cultures in which the practice of dowry is widespread, marriage costs are a major expense of children, especially daughters. Most evidence suggests that better educated daughters must marry even better educated men, and well-educated men can extract larger dowries. In Bangladesh, dowry payments were found to increase uniformly with education.[56] In many parts of Bangladesh, India, and Pakistan, one major fear of parents about educating a daughter are the escalating marriage expenses likely to result from this, although contrasting evidence from some parts of Bangladesh suggests that education reduces marriage costs because educated women require smaller dowries.[57] Where educating a daughter implies higher marriage as well as educational costs, better educated parents are likely to face especially high child costs. This may exacerbate the child-cost differentials between the educated and the uneducated.

The economic costs of children are felt by both women and men, although who bears more of these expenses varies by culture. In sub-Saharan Africa, for example, child-rearing costs are distributed among the larger kinship structure and are not borne exclusively by the mother or father. High public investment in education and the prevalence of child-fostering in that region further reduce child costs, factors that may explain why child costs are not a major concern of either educated or uneducated women. The deteriorating economic situation in much of sub-Saharan Africa, along with growing educational aspirations for children and probably a limit to the willingness of better-off relatives to share child costs, has recently placed the economic burden of child-rearing more squarely on women. As a consequence, educated women are increasingly likely to cite costs as a major disincentive for having large numbers of children.[58]

In contrast, in South Asia and the Islamic societies of North Africa and the Middle East, where women are less likely to work, child costs may be more exclusively a male responsibility. Even so, the evidence suggests that, where women work, their earnings are more likely to be spent on the basic needs of their children than are the earnings of their husbands. A larger proportion of total family income appears to be spent on child-rearing in households where the wife is working, regardless of the level of total family income.[59]

The time and opportunity costs of children (see Table 1.3) are more specifically affected by women's (as opposed to parental) education. The higher the woman's education, the more she forgoes in wages and economic opportunities if she rears children as opposed to engaging in wage-earning employment. Given that the mother is the primary child-rearer, increases in women's earning potential provide an incentive to shift from non-market to market work, something likely to create an incompatibility with having large numbers of children.[60] The evidence for this link is quite mixed, however. This path may be relatively unimportant in less developed countries because child-care substitutes are often readily and cheaply available in these countries.[61] To the extent, however, that educated women are exposed to, and seek sources of, satisfaction and status outside the home and perceive large numbers of children to be incompatible with these alternative activities, children would become more costly to them than they would to lesser educated women.[62]

In addition to the greater opportunity costs of children that better educated women may experience in some settings are changes in women's perceptions of the amount of maternal time and attention needed by children. Such changes are likely to make caring for children more labour- and time-intensive for the mother.

- Convincing evidence of this comes from a recent study in Mexico in which schooling was found to lead women to reconceptualize child care as labour-intensive and requiring a great deal of maternal attention throughout the pre-school years. Educated women, for example, spent considerably more time than did less educated women responding to and communicating verbally with their children from infancy on. Unlike less educated women, who were more likely to delegate child-rearing to older siblings and other child-minders, educated women displayed a more time-, labour-, and energy-intensive style of child-rearing, requiring greater mother-child interaction; this was an important cost leading educated women to want fewer children.[63]

Other studies, including research in Malaysia and Ghana, support the idea of a changing notion of child-rearing among better educated women, who define the maternal role as requiring greater personal attention, deterring them from high fertility.[64] That child-rearing for educated mothers is more time-intensive than it is for lesser educated mothers is also evident from the observation that they spend more time on children's schoolwork, and that they pay more attention to children's hygiene and feeding.[65]

• In Ibadan, Nigeria, in 1973, women who were defined as demographic innovators (contraceptors with few children) were more likely both to be better educated than average and to emphasize their closeness to their children and the need for children to experience a good family life—both reflections of their readiness to devote more time to children.[66] Also, there is evidence that, in the more egalitarian marriages of educated women, intimacy and togetherness are highly valued, and the time-intensive child-rearing of many children is viewed as costing too much in lost conjugal leisure and togetherness.[67]

Education does appear to raise child-rearing costs in most settings. In comparison with the uneducated, educated women and their husbands tend to prefer few but more expensive children to many children of relatively poorer 'quality'. Second, the time and opportunity costs of children are more specifically affected by maternal (as opposed to parental) education. Although women's economic activity need not increase child costs in settings in which alternative child-minders are plentiful, evidence is increasing that the time costs of child-rearing are strongly felt by educated women and act as an important deterrent to high levels of desired fertility. Better educated women are exposed to new ideas on child-rearing, are more able to make and implement child-rearing decisions, and may have a greater control over resources to put these into effect.

Notes

1. United Nations, *Fertility Behaviour*; DHS reports.
2. The WFS data are from United Nations, *Fertility Behaviour*.
3. For a discussion of strong son preferences in East Asia, see Susan Greenhalgh, 'Sexual Stratification: The Other Side of Growth with Equity in East Asia', *Population and Development Review*, 11/2 (June 1985), 265–314. The data from South Asia are from United Nations, *Fertility Behaviour*.
4. Preston, 'Introduction', and Chowdhury, Khan, and Chen, 'Experience in Pakistan and Bangladesh', in Preston (ed.), *Effects*.
5. K. O. Mason and A. M. Taj, 'Difference Between Women's and Men's Reproductive Goals in Developing Countries', *Population and Development Review*, 14/4 (Dec. 1987), 611–38.
6. S. J. Jeejeebhoy and S. Kulkarni, 'Reproductive Motivation: A Comparison of Wives and Husbands in Maharashtra, India', *Studies in Family Planning*, 20/5 (Sept.–Oct. 1989), 264–72.
7. K. O. Mason, 'Norms Relating to the Desire for Children', in Bulatao and Lee (eds.), *Determinants,* i.
8. The 19 relying on WFS data are reported in United Nations, *Fertility Behaviour*; the 32 relying on DHS data are reported in United Nations, *Women's Education and Fertility Behaviour: Recent Evidence from the Demographic and Health Surveys*, and various DHS reports; the 2 relying on another survey are from Operations Research Group, *Family Planning Practices in India: Third All India Survey* (Baroda, Operations Research Group,

1990); and J. Bongaarts and R. Lightbourne, 'Wanted Fertility in Latin America: Trends and Differentials in Seven Countries', paper prepared for the Seminar on Fertility Transition in Latin America, sponsored by the IUSSP Committee on Comparative Analysis of Fertility and Family Planning in collaboration with CELADE and CENEP, Buenos Aires, 3–6 Apr. 1990.

9. LeVine *et al.*, 'Women's Schooling'.
10. Okojie, 'Women's Status, Proximate Determinants and Fertility'.
11. United Nations, *Women's Education and Fertility Behaviour: A Case-study of Rural Maharashtra, India.*
12. See also, for Colombia, the Dominican Republic, Ecuador, and Peru, M. B. Weinberger, C. Lloyd, and A. K. Blanc, 'Women's Education and Fertility: A Decade of Change in Four Latin American Countries', *International Family Planning Perspectives*, 15/1 (Mar. 1989), 4–14; for Colombia, Costa Rica, the Dominican Republic, Ecuador, Jamaica, Peru, and Trinidad and Tobago, see John Bongaarts and R. Lightbourne, 'Wanted Fertility in Latin America'.
13. Jejeebhoy, 'Women's Status and Fertility'.
14. For Brazil, see N. do Valle Silva *et al.*, 'The Determinants of the Demand for Children: Supply of Children and Costs of Fertility Regulation', *An Analysis of Reproductive Behaviour in Brazil*, DHS Further Analysis Series No. 6 (Columbia, Md., DHS, 1990). For Maharashtra, India, see United Nations *Women's Education and Fertility Behaviour: A Case-study of Rural Maharashtra, India.* For Nigeria, see Okojie, 'Women's Status, Proximate Determinants and Fertility'; Sathar and Kazi, 'Women, Work and Reproduction'; Kritz and Gurak, 'Women's Economic Independence'; and M. M. Kritz and Paulina Makinwa-Adebusoye, 'Women's Resource Control and Demand for Children in Africa', paper presented at the Seminar on Women and Demographic Change in Sub-Saharan Africa, sponsored by the IUSSP Committee on Gender and Population, Dakar, Senegal, 3–6 Mar. 1993.
15. Kritz and Makinwa-Adebusoye, 'Women's Resource Control'.
16. Okojie, 'Women's Status, Proximate Determinants and Fertility'.
17. Kritz and Gurak, 'Women's Economic Independence'.
18. Preston, 'Introduction', in Preston (ed.), *Effects.*
19. Mason, 'Impact of Women's Position'.
20. Cain, 'Perspectives on Family and Fertility'.
21. See, for example, De Vos, *Old-Age Security Value of Children.*
22. Cain, 'Perspectives on Family and Fertility'.
23. In Mexico, LeVine *et al.*, 'Women's Schooling'. In South Asia, for Pakistan, Sathar and Kazi, 'Women, Work and Reproduction'; for India, Operations Research Group, *Family Planning Practices in India.* In East and South-East Asia, De Vos, *Old-Age Security Value of Children.* In sub-Saharan Africa, for Nigeria, B. Akande, 'Some Socio-cultural Factors Influencing Fertility Behaviour: A Case Study of Yoruba Women', *Biology and Society*, 6/4 (Dec. 1989), 165–70.
24. LeVine *et al.*, 'Women's Schooling'.
25. Sathar and Kazi, 'Women, Work and Reproduction'.
26. De Vos, *Old-Age Security Value of Children.*
27. For Nigeria, see J. C. Caldwell, 'Fertility and the Household Economy in Nigeria' and 'The Economic Rationality of High Fertility: An Investigation Illustrated with Nigerian Survey Data', in Caldwell (ed.), *Theory of Fertility Decline*; and Akande, 'Some Socio-cultural Factors'; for Pakistan, see Sathar and Kazi, 'Women, Work and Reproduction',

and for India, see Operations Research Group, *Family Planning Practices in India*; see also United Nations, *Women's Education and Fertility Behaviour: A Case-study of Rural Maharashtra, India*.

28. United Nations, *Women's Education and Fertility Behaviour: A Case-study of Rural Maharashtra, India*.
29. Sathar and Kazi, 'Women, Work and Reproduction'.
30. LeVine *et al.*, 'Women's Schooling'.
31. For example, an analysis of data from a Value of Children survey in East Asia finds that education remained a strong and significant determinant of women's expectations of old-age support from children when other covariates, such as husband's occupation, family income, age, mass media exposure, and residence, were controlled: the odds of having no, versus some, support expectations were, on average, 2.29 times greater if a woman had completed one or more levels of education, for example, primary school compared with less than primary school. The net effect of education falls considerably, however, when the extent of women's economic self-reliance, measured by women's attitudes towards saving for the future, was included in the analysis. Then, the odds of having no, versus some, support expectations were 1.81 times greater at each level of education compared with the level below, suggesting that some of the effect of education operated through increased economic self-reliance. This finding suggests that expectations of economic self-reliance are an important pathway linking education to women's need of children for old-age support. See De Vos, *Old-Age Security Value of Children*.
32. Sathar and Mason, 'Why Female Education Affects'; United Nations, *Women's Education and Fertility Behaviour: A Case-study of Rural Maharashtra, India*.
33. P. Makinwa-Adebusoye, 'Changes in the Costs and Benefits of Children to Their Parents: The Changing Cost of Educating Children', paper presented at the Seminar on the Course of Fertility Transition in Sub-Saharan Africa, sponsored by the IUSSP Committee on Comparative Analysis of Fertility and the University of Zimbabwe, Harare, Zimbabwe, 19–22 Nov. 1991.
34. Ibid.; Akande, 'Some Socio-cultural Factors'; C. Oppong, 'Women's Roles, Opportunity Costs, and Fertility', in Bulatao and Lee (eds.), *Determinants*, i; Iravati Karve, *Kinship Organisation in India* (Bombay, Asia Publishing House, 1965); Dyson and Moore, 'On Kinship Structure'; Galal el Din, 'Economic Value of Children in Rural Sudan'; Mason, *Status of Women*; and Kasarda, Billy, and West, *Status Enhancement*.
35. R. N. Shain and V. H. Jennings, 'The Influence of Sex Roles on Fertility', in R. Shain and C. J. Pauerstein (eds.), *Fertility Control, Biologic and Behavioural Aspects* (Hagerstown, Md., Harper and Row, 1980).
36. Makinwa-Adebusoye, 'Changes'.
37. Oppong, 'Women's Roles'; and Kasarda, Billy, and West, *Status Enhancement*.
38. Tsui *et al.*, 'Young Women's Work'; J. C. Caldwell, Reddy, and P. Caldwell, 'Causes of Demographic Change'; and J. C. Caldwell, 'Mass Education'.
39. M. Mhloyi, 'Fertility Transition in Zimbabwe'.
40. J. C. Caldwell, Reddy, and P. Caldwell, 'Social Component of Mortality Decline'.
41. Galal el Din, 'Economic Value of Children in Rural Sudan'; Mandelbaum, *Human Fertility in India*.
42. Ibid.
43. J. C. Caldwell, Reddy, and P. Caldwell, 'Causes of Demographic Change' and 'Educational Transition in Rural India'; J. C. Caldwell, 'Education as a Factor'.
44. For Egypt, K. Faust *et al.*, 'Mass Education, Islamic Revival, and the Population

Problem in Egypt', *Journal of Comparative Family Studies*, 22/3 (1991), 329–41; for Mexico, LeVine *et al.*, 'Women's Schooling'; for India, J. C. Caldwell, Reddy, and P. Caldwell, 'Educational Transition in Rural India', and United Nations, *Women's Education and Fertility Behaviour: A Case-study of Rural Maharashtra, India*.

45. United Nations, *Women's Education and Fertility Behaviour: A Case-study of Rural Maharashtra, India*.
46. Operations Research Group, *Family Planning Practices in India*.
47. J. C. Caldwell, 'Fertility and the Household Economy in Nigeria'.
48. J. C. Caldwell, 'Mass Education', 'Toward a Restatement of Demographic Transition Theory', and 'The Wealth Flows Theory of Fertility Decline'; Schultz, 'Returns to Women's Education'.
49. Ines Bustillo, 'Latin America', in King and Hill (eds.), *Women's Education*; for Nicaragua, see B. Wolfe and J. Behrman, 'Who Is Schooled in Developing Countries? The Roles of Income, Parental Schooling, Sex, Residence and Family Size', *Economics of Education Review*, 3/3 (1984), 231–45; for Brazil, see N. Birdsall, 'Public Inputs and Child Schooling in Brazil', *Journal of Development Economics*, 18 (1985), 67–86; for Botswana, see D. Chernichovsky, 'Socioeconomic and Demographic Aspects of School Enrollment and Attendance in Rural Botswana', *Economic Development and Cultural Change*, 33/2 (Jan. 1985), 319–32; for North Africa and the Middle East, see N. El-Sanabary, 'Middle East and North Africa', in King and Hill (eds.), *Women's Education*; for Indonesia, Malaysia, and the Philippines, see J. B. G. Tilak, 'East Asia', in King and Hill (eds.), *Women's Education*; for Indonesia, see Chernichovsky and Meesook, 'School Enrollment in Indonesia'; for Pakistan, see Sathar *et al.*, 'Women's Status'; and for India, see United Nations, *Women's Education and Fertility Behaviour: A Case-study of Rural Maharashtra, India.*.
50. For Nigeria, see Makinwa-Adebusoye, 'Changes', and, for Zimbabwe, see Mhloyi, 'Fertility Transition in Zimbabwe'.
51. LeVine *et al.*, 'Women's Schooling'.
52. S. Cochrane, K. Mehra, and I. S. Osheba, 'The Educational Participation of Egyptian Children', in A. M. Hallouda, S. Farid, and S. H. Cochrane (eds.), *Egypt: Demographic Responses to Modernization* (Cairo, Central Agency for Public Mobilisation and Statistics, 1988).
53. N. M. Shah, 'Education: Level, Enrollment, Facilities and Attitudes', in Nasra Shah (ed.), *Pakistan Women* (Islamabad, Pakistani Institute of Development Economics, 1986).
54. United Nations, *Women's Education and Fertility Behaviour: A Case-Study of Rural Maharashtra, India*.
55. Cochrane and Jamison, 'Educational Attainment'.
56. Amin, 'Correlates of Female Education and Fertility'.
57. For evidence from India, Pakistan, and Bangladesh that parents fear higher marriage expenses because of education, see J. C. Caldwell, Reddy, and P. Caldwell, 'Causes of Marriage Change', and Amin, 'Correlates of Female Education and Fertility'. For evidence from Bangladesh that education reduces marriage costs, see Lindenbaum, 'Maternal Education', and Martin, 'Female Education'.
58. For evidence from Nigeria, see Makinwa-Adebusoye, 'Changes'; for evidence from Zimbabwe, see Mhloyi, 'Fertility Transition in Zimbabwe'.
59. For evidence from India, see Mencher, 'Women's Work'.
60. Schultz, *Women and Development*.
61. Mason, *Status of Women*; K. O. Mason and V. T. Palan, 'Female Employment and

Fertility in Peninsular Malaysia: The Maternal Role Incompatibility Hypothesis Reconsidered', *Demography*, 18/4 (Nov. 1981), 549–75; Sathar and Kazi, 'Women, Work and Reproduction'; and Oppong, 'Women's Roles'.

62. Caldwell, 'Mass Education'; Mason, *Status of Women*; and Kasarda, Billy, and West, *Status Enhancement*.

63. LeVine *et al.*, 'Women's Schooling'.

64. For Malaysia, see Mason and Palan, 'Female Employment and Fertility'; for Ghana, see Oppong and Abu, *Seven Roles of Women*.

65. For observations on spending time on children's schoolwork, see, for example, for North Africa and the Middle East, El-Sanabary, 'Middle East and North Africa', in King and Hill (eds.), *Women's Education*; for observations on paying more attention to children's hygiene, see, for example, Lindenbaum, 'Maternal Education', for Bangladesh.

66. J. C. Caldwell and P. Caldwell, 'The Achieved Small Family'.

67. Oppong, 'Women's Roles'.

8 Women's Education, Fertility Regulation, and Obstacles to Contraception

The relationship between women's education and the practice of contraception is direct and consistent, especially after a small amount of education is attained.

One reason for the relationship between education and contraceptive practice is that educated women face fewer obstacles relating to the practice of contraception than uneducated women face. Educated women have a more comprehensive knowledge of contraception, its mechanics and side-effects; they have more positive attitudes to the practice of deliberate fertility regulation; and they are less inhibited about discussing contraception and family size with their husbands.

That education is uniformly related to contraceptive use but not uniformly related to fertility itself brings into question the timing of contraception. Contraception is often undertaken after unwanted fertility has occurred rather than as a preventive measure. This may be one reason the relationship of education to excess fertility is so tenuous. Although women with moderate amounts of schooling are more likely than uneducated women to practise contraception, they may attain the decision-making authority to do so only after desired fertility levels have been exceeded. In contrast, better educated women may be more likely to have the authority and power to make decisions on reproductive and other matters from early in their married lives. Hence, they are both more likely to practise contraception and more likely to have initiated contraception as soon as desired family size was attained.

The difference between the supply of children and the demand for children determines the extent to which there is a potential demand for fertility regulation. In addition, several of the individual supply and demand variables listed in Table 1.3 are strongly associated with contraception. For example, in sub-Saharan Africa, the breakdown of traditional post-partum abstinence taboos is frequently replaced by increased contraception.[1] Women who have been married for a shorter time are systematically less likely to practise contraception than are those who have been married a long time. In addition, study after study has confirmed a positive association between child survival and contraceptive use.[2]

Aside from these factors, which collectively measure the motivation to practise contraception, whether fertility is actually regulated depends on several factors that constitute costs of contraception or obstacles to contraception.[3] These costs are both economic and non-economic. Most obvious are the direct money costs of acquiring contraceptives and services and the related time costs. Because such costs are considered relatively insensitive to education, they are largely ignored in this chapter. The other costs that constrain contraceptive use among motivated women are more subjective and more closely related to women's education and autonomy. These include ignorance of contraceptive methods, suspicion of contraception, poor access to family planning services or supplies, particularly good-quality services, and an absence of communication between spouses about contraception. Female education is expected to have a profound effect on some or all of these costs. For example, education makes information more accessible; it introduces new ways of life and, hence, changes attitudes towards contraception, as well as women's inclination to engage in new forms of behaviour. In addition, by fostering a strengthening of the conjugal unit, women's education breaks down barriers to communication between spouses about contraception. At the same time, it can enhance women's access to services by increasing their freedom of movement. Above all, the enhanced autonomy in domestic decision-making that women gain as a result of education leads them to act upon their lower family-size preferences even when doing so contradicts the preferences of family elders. The net effect of education through these variables, as well as via the motivation generated by the interplay of supply and demand factors, results in the positive relationship of education to contraceptive use and an inverse relationship to the extent of unmet need for contraception. The level of unmet need in a society is measured as the proportion of couples who want no more children and are fecund but are not practising contraception.

Contraceptive Practice

Female education is a key determinant of contraceptive use, as seen at both the macro level (Table 2.1) and the individual level. By virtue of their greater decision-making authority, more educated women are in a better position than less educated women to make reproductive and contraceptive decisions; their control over resources and their ability to operate in the outside world enable them to access services better; their spousal intimacy allows them to overcome shyness in making contraceptive decisions; and their wider knowledge of methods enables them to make more informed decisions with fewer chances of subsequent discontinuation or failure of contraception. In addition, educated women are less likely to experience child mortality and less likely to fear child loss than modestly educated women, which has been observed, in many settings, to motivate contraception.

Some of the many studies that find a positive relationship between female education and contraceptive use are listed in Appendix I. Because contraceptive use depends to a large extent on a woman's age, fertility, and duration of marriage, the education–contraception relationship should ideally be viewed with these factors controlled. Because net effects are unavailable, however, Appendix I also includes the results of studies that do not control for covarying factors. Because better educated women tend to be younger on average and, hence, married for shorter durations than other women, and because contraceptive use tends to rise with parity and, hence, with marriage duration, the effect of omitting a control for age or marriage duration is to provide a conservative estimate of the relationship. If anything, the net effects of education on contraceptive use should be stronger than the zero-order effects shown in the appendix. Table 8.1 summarizes information on the shape of the relationship of education to the proportions practising contraception for 54 countries selected from that appendix. [4]

Table 8.1. *Patterns in the relationship of women's education to contraceptive use, by region, level of development, and gender disparity in literacy*

	Patterns in the relationship between years of schooling and contraceptive use [a]			Total number of studies
	Positive	Reversed 7	None or other	
A. Region [b]				
Sub-Saharan Africa	4	15	1	20
North Africa and the Middle East	5	1	0	6
East and South-East Asia	3	2	1	6
South Asia	3	2	0	5
Latin America and the Caribbean	14	2	1	17
B. Level of development				
1. Annual per capita income ($)				
500 or less	7	11	2	20
501–999	9	6	1	16
1000 or more	13	5	0	18
2. Overall female literacy rate (%)				
40 or less	8	11	1	20
41–80	11	8	1	20
81 or more	10	3	1	14
C. Gender disparity in literacy [c]				
250–700	7	11	1	19
701–850	6	8	1	15
851 or more	16	3	1	20
TOTALS	29	22	3	54

[a] Two distinct patterns in the relationship of schooling to contraceptive use are apparent: a positive relationship, in which better educated women are progressively more likely (5 per cent or more) to practise contraception than are uneducated and moderately educated women; and a reversed-7-shaped relationship, in which the proportion of moderately educated women who practise contraception is about the same as that of uneducated women (within 5 per cent), whereas the proportion practising contraception among better educated women is considerably higher.

[b] Not all countries in a region are included, and those included are not necessarily representative of the region but are, rather, those countries for which the requisite data are available. Thus, the results are not necessarily representative of any particular region.

[c] The level of gender disparity in literacy is the number of literate females per 1000 literate males.

Notes: The studies selected for inclusion in this table appear in Appendix I, where they are marked with a dagger (†). The study populations were women who were married or in union. Contraceptive use is defined as the proportion of women or their husbands who were using a method of contraception or had been sterilized at the time of the survey.

Sources: Of the 54 studies, 49 are based on World Fertility Survey (18) and Demographic and Health Survey (31) data, from United Nations, *Fertility Behaviour in the Context of Development: Evidence from the World Fertility Survey* (1987) or *Women's Education and Fertility Behaviour: Recent Evidence from the Demographic and Health Surveys* (1995), or other DHS reports. Sources are indicated in Appendix I.

Overall findings

The positive relationship of women's education to contraceptive practice is less widespread than is often asserted.

- A uniformly positive relationship occurs in only slightly more than half of the studies reported (29 of 54);
- In another 40 per cent (22 of 54), the relationship is reversed-7-shaped, with moderate increases (under 5 per cent) up to the primary-school level followed by sharper increases at higher levels of schooling.

Region   Although the relationship is generally positive, its pattern varies by region.

- Straight positive relationships are observed in the large majority of studies from Latin America and the Caribbean (14 of 17) and North Africa and the Middle East (5 of 6), and in somewhat fewer in Asia (3 of 5 in South Asia and 3 of 6 in East and South-East Asia);
- In contrast, straight positive relationships are rarely observed in sub-Saharan Africa (4 of 20 studies), where the majority of studies (15 of 20) suggests a reversed-7-shaped relationship, in which moderate amounts of education affect contraceptive use negligibly but secondary and higher levels of education lead to substantial increases in contraceptive practice.

Level of development and gender disparity in literacy   The pattern of the relationship of education to the proportions practising contraception is also affected by overall levels of development and gender disparity.

- Positive relationships between female education and contraceptive prevalence increase steadily from about 2 in 5 in low-literacy settings (8 of 20) to almost 3 in 5 in medium-literacy settings (11 of 20) and to more than 2 in 3 (10 of 14) in the most literate settings;
- Per capita income levels condition the relationship of women's education to the proportions practising contraception in a more linear fashion than literacy levels do. The education–contraception relationship is positive in about one-third of the low-income settings (7 of 20), compared with more than half of the middle-income settings (9 of 16), and more than two-thirds of the high-income settings (13 of 18);
- One-third of the studies in settings in which wide gender disparities are observed reveal a straight positive relationship between education and the percentage of women practising contraception. This proportion increases to four-fifths (16 of 20) of studies in the most egalitarian settings.

Differentials

It is clear that secondary and better educated women are considerably more likely to practise contraception than uneducated women are, despite the variations seen in Table 8.1. Table 8.2 shows that most studies find relatively large differentials in contraceptive practice.

Table 8.2. *Differentials in the relationship of women's education to contraceptive use, by region, level of development, and gender disparity in literacy*

	Differences in percentage using contraception between uneducated and secondary-schooled women[a] NARROW ◄----------------► WIDE					Total number of studies
	10 or less	11–20	21–30	31–40	41 or more	
A. Region[b]						
Sub-Saharan Africa	4	8	5	3	0	20
North Africa and the Middle East	0	1	2	3	0	6
East and South-East Asia	1	2	2	1	0	6
South Asia	1	1	3	0	0	5
Latin America and the Caribbean	1	4	5	4	3	17
B. Level of development						
1. Annual per capita income ($)						
500 or less	5	8	5	2	0	20
501–999	2	4	5	4	1	16
1000 or more	0	4	7	5	2	18
2. Overall female literacy rate (%)						
40 or less	2	8	7	3	0	20
41–80	3	4	7	4	2	20
81 or more	2	4	3	4	1	14
C. Gender disparity in literacy[c]						
250–700	2	8	6	3	0	19
701–850	3	3	5	3	1	15
851 or more	2	5	6	5	2	20
TOTALS	7	16	17	11	3	54

[a] The term 'secondary-schooled women' here applies to women who have had some secondary education or completed or gone beyond secondary school—that is, women who have had more than six years of primary education.
 [b] Not all countries in a region are included, and those included are not necessarily representative of the region but are, rather, those countries for which the requisite data are available. Thus, the results are not necessarily representative of any particular region
 [c] The level of gender disparity in literacy is the number of literate females per 1000 literate males.

Notes: The studies selected for inclusion in this table appear in Appendix I, where they are marked with a dagger (†). Contraceptive use is defined as the proportion of women or their husbands who were using a method of contraception or had been sterilized at the time of the survey

Sources: Of the 54 studies, 49 are based on World Fertility Survey (18) and Demographic and Health Survey (31) data, from United Nations, *Fertility Behaviour in the Context of Development: Evidence from the World Fertility Survey* (1987) or *Women's Education and Fertility Behaviour: Recent Evidence from the Demographic and Health Surveys* (1995), or other DHS reports. Sources are indicated in Appendix I.

- In 31 of the 54 studies, the percentage of women with seven or more years of education who were practising contraception was more than 20 points greater than was the percentage of women with no education. In 14 of these 31 studies, the differential exceeded 30 points. This finding is consistent with earlier analyses of WFS data from 37 countries, which observed that, after controlling for age differences between various educational groups, the percentage of women with seven or more years of schooling who were practising contraception was about 24 points higher than was the percentage among women with no education.[5]

Region   There are variations in the differentials by region.
- Differentials in the proportions of uneducated and secondary-schooled women practising contraception are narrowest in sub-Saharan Africa. There, differentials exceeding 20 per cent are seen in fewer than half (8 of 20) of all settings;
- Differentials are widest in Latin America and the Caribbean and North Africa and the Middle East, exceeding 20 per cent in 12 of 17 and 5 of 6 settings, respectively.

Level of development   Other variations appear related to level of development. The magnitude of the differentials in contraceptive prevalence between uneducated women and women with some secondary schooling increases with increases in national per capita income levels.
- In low-income settings, differentials exceeding 20 per cent are observed in about one-third of all studies (7 of 20), compared with three-fifths of studies in middle-income settings (10 of 16), and more than three-quarters of studies in high-income settings (14 of 18).

Differentials are narrowest in low-literacy settings. They widen substantially in medium-literacy settings and narrow somewhat in high-literacy settings.
- Half (10 of 20) of the studies in low-literacy settings report differentials exceeding 20 per cent;
- In medium-literacy settings, 13 of 20 report differentials exceeding 20 per cent;
- In high-literacy settings, fewer than three-fifths—8 of 14—report differentials exceeding 20 per cent.

This tendency for differentials to widen and then narrow as settings become more literate has been observed by others.[6] The pattern suggests that, as the fertility transition gathers momentum, it is better educated women who first adopt contraception, hence, accounting for the widening differentials. As contraception becomes more widely practised, however, differentials begin to narrow as poorly educated women catch up with the better educated in their use of contraception.

Gender disparity in literacy   Furthermore, differentials widen as the setting becomes more egalitarian.
- Differentials exceeding 20 per cent are observed in fewer than half of all studies (9 of 19) in settings in which gender disparities are widest, compared with three-fifths (9 of 15) of studies in moderately egalitarian settings and almost two-thirds (13 of 20) in the most egalitarian settings.

In many settings where women have relied on traditional methods of contraception, differentials by education are wider if the use of only modern methods rather than all methods is considered. This occurs because, in these settings, traditional methods account for the overwhelming proportion of the methods used by uneducated women, whereas modern methods become progressively more common among better educated women.[7] In these settings, largely in sub-Saharan

Africa, the impact of education on effective contraception is probably much stronger than what is implied in Table 8.2.

Thresholds

Table 8.3 shows that thresholds at which contraceptive use increases by 10 per cent or more are generally low.

- A 10 per cent increase in the proportions practising contraception occurs at the lower-primary-school level in more than two-fifths of the cases; at the upper-primary level in another fifth of the cases; and at the secondary stage or not at all in the remaining cases.

Thresholds are strongly conditioned by region, levels of development, and gender disparities in literacy.

- A 10 per cent increase in contraception occurs by the lower-primary level in the majority of studies from Latin America and the Caribbean, and North Africa and the Middle East, and in half of all studies in East and South-East Asia and two-fifths of all studies in South Asia; it does not occur until the secondary level in sub-Saharan Africa;
- Likewise, although a 20 per cent increase in contraceptive practice does not occur until the secondary levels in almost half of all cases, the 20 per cent threshold ranges from the primary stage in North Africa and Latin America to the secondary stage in sub-Saharan Africa and South Asia.

Threshold levels fall dramatically as per capita income and female literacy levels rise and as gender disparities in literacy diminish.

- A 10 per cent increase in the proportions practising contraception usually occurs at the secondary-school level in the low-income settings, and at the lower-primary level in middle- and high-income countries;
- A decline in thresholds with rising income levels is also evident for the 20 per cent increase in contraception;
- The educational level at which a 10 per cent increase in contraceptive prevalence occurs also shifts, from the secondary stage in the least literate countries to the lower-primary level in the medium-literacy settings. Thresholds rise again in the most literate settings, where a 10 per cent increase in contraceptive use occurs most often at the upper-primary level.

As the context becomes more egalitarian, threshold levels necessary for a 10 per cent increase in contraception fall systematically.

- For example, in settings in which gender disparities are widest, one-third (6 of 19) of all studies suggests a 10 per cent increase in contraception by the lower primary stage; this proportion increases to two-fifths of studies in settings which are moderately egalitarian (6 of 15) and to half (10 of 20) of studies in the most egalitarian settings.

These findings suggest the importance of contextual factors in accounting for the magnitude of the effect of women's education—particularly modest amounts of schooling—on contraceptive practice.

Table 8.3.   *Relationship of the duration of women's education to contraceptive use, by region, level of development, and gender disparity in literacy*

	Educational level (years of schooling) by which:								Total number of studies
	A 10% increase in proportions using contraception is reached				A 20% increase in proportions using contraception is reached				
	1–3 (1–6)	4–6	7+	Never	1–3 (1–6)	4–6	7+	Never	
A. Region[a]									
Sub-Saharan Africa	2	3	13	2	0	0	13	7	20
North Africa and the Middle East	5	1	0	0	2	2	2	0	6
East and South-East Asia	3	1	1	1	0	1	2	3	6
South Asia	2	2	1	0	0	1	2	2	5
Latin America and the Caribbean	10	5	1	1	0	7	6	4	17
B. Level of development									
1. Annual per capita income ($)									
500 or less	4	3	11	2	0	1	11	8	20
501–999	8	2	4	2	1	5	5	5	16
1000 or more	10	7	1	0	1	5	9	3	18
2. Overall female literacy rate (%)									
40 or less	7	1	11	1	2	2	10	6	20
41–80	10	4	4	2	0	6	9	5	20
81 or more	5	7	1	1	0	3	6	5	14
C. Gender disparity in literacy[b]									
250–700	6	1	11	1	2	2	9	6	19
701–850	6	3	4	2	0	3	8	4	15
851 or more	10	8	1	1	0	6	8	6	20
TOTALS	22	12	16	4	2	11	25	16	54

[a] Not all countries in a region are included, and those included are not necessarily representative of the region but are, rather, those countries for which the requisite data are available. Thus, the results are not necessarily representative of any particular region.

[b] The level of gender disparity in literacy is the number of literate females per 1000 literate males.

Notes: The studies selected for inclusion in this table appear in Appendix I, where they are marked with a dagger (†). Some appendix studies combine rates for women with 1–3 and 4–6 years of schooling; in such studies, rates are shown in the column marked 1–3.

Sources: Of the 54 studies, 49 are based on World Fertility Survey (18) and Demographic and Health Survey (31) data, from United Nations, *Fertility Behaviour in the Context of Development: Evidence from the World Fertility Survey* (1987) or *Women's Education and Fertility Behaviour: Recent Evidence from the Demographic and Health Surveys* (1995), or other DHS reports. Sources are indicated in Appendix I.

Changes in contraceptive practice over time

Appendix I also sheds light on changes in the relationship of women's education to contraceptive prevalence over time in 21 countries for which data are available at two points in time.

- Although contraceptive prevalence rates have increased in almost all of these countries, educational differentials have stayed the same in 4, widened in 7, and narrowed in almost half (10).

Countries in which the differentials have widened are largely less developed; most are from sub-Saharan Africa. In the more developed settings and in Latin America and the Caribbean and North Africa and the Middle East, differentials between uneducated and secondary-schooled women have tended to narrow over time, suggesting that uneducated women are adopting contraception at a faster pace than other women are. This may arise from the emphasis of family planning programmes on the poorest and least literate segments of the populations.

- For example, a comparative analysis of WFS and DHS data from four Latin American and Caribbean countries—Colombia, the Dominican Republic, Ecuador, and Peru—finds that educational differentials in contraceptive use have decreased substantially in Colombia and the Dominican Republic, where contraceptive prevalence among uneducated women has recorded impressive increases. Educational differentials have decreased more modestly in Ecuador and Peru, where uneducated women have recorded correspondingly more modest increases in contraceptive use.[8]

The presence of family planning programme activities directed at the least educated and poorest sections of the population may also be responsible for the weak or erratic relationship of women's education to contraceptive use observed in a few of the studies listed in Appendix I (e.g. Bangladesh and Zimbabwe, along with Gujarat and Maharashtra, India).[9] Supporting this view is a study of two provinces in China, one with higher levels of education than the other. This study observes a convergence in fertility rates between the two provinces and attributes this convergence to an unusually powerful family planning programme focused on the less developed province.[10] In India, several cross-sectional studies observe negative associations between women's education and the use of sterilization, the method most vigorously promoted by the family planning programme, although a much sharper positive relationship of education to non-terminal method use is found.[11] A downturn in contraceptive use rates among better educated women is seen in both rural Bangladesh (at 10 or more years of education) and India.[12] Such patterns are probably the result of two factors: first, the levelling effects of a vigorous family planning programme that increased contraceptive use at the bottom end of the socio-economic spectrum; and, second, far shorter durations of marriage and, hence, less need for family planning among the best educated women, even after age is taken into account.

In sum, the relationship between women's education and contraceptive practice is direct and consistent, especially after a small amount of education is attained.

Thresholds are evident and appear to be higher in low-income than in high-income settings and in highly inegalitarian settings than in more egalitarian ones.

Causes of differences in contraceptive use

It is important to know whether it is women's education itself or some associated factor, notably economic status or urban residence, that causes differences in contraceptive use. For the most part, the results of the multivariate studies reported in Appendix I suggest that women's education plays a powerful direct role in determining contraceptive use, a much stronger role than either husband's characteristics or socio-economic status. Both wife's and husband's educations increase contraceptive use, but the wife's education typically has a stronger net effect.[13]

A United Nations analysis of 37 developing countries examines contraceptive use as a function of education, occupation, childhood place of residence, husband's education and occupation, as well as age at marriage and number of living children.

- When only the latter two demographic variables were controlled, the average proportion of currently married women practising contraception was 31 per cent higher for women with 10 or more years of schooling than for uneducated women;
- After socio-economic controls were applied, the average proportion of currently married women practising contraception was 16 per cent higher for women with 10 or more years of schooling than for uneducated women and remained significant in 32 countries.[14] This indicates that about half of the education–contraception relationship operates through women's education itself.

The net effect of education is strongest in Latin American countries and in the most developed countries. In Peru, for example, a woman's education remains a strong determinant of contraceptive use, even after controlling for her husband's education, work status, residence, whether additional children are desired, and number of surviving children.[15]

Other smaller scale studies corroborate the finding of a strong net effect of education on contraceptive use.

- In Kerala, women's education is a far stronger predictor of current contraceptive use than are husband's education, land ownership, or caste; only age has an equally strong effect;[16]
- In Matlab, Bangladesh, a study of the effects of gender preference on contraceptive use finds that, even after controlling for the number of boy and girl children, fertility, child mortality, age, the household head's level of education, and religion, women's schooling exerts a net positive and significant effect on contraceptive acceptance: each additional year of schooling increases the probability of practising contraception by 7 per cent. Other determinants significantly affecting contraceptive use include maternal age, measures of son preference, and child mortality experiences, but exclude the education level of the head of household.[17]

Multivariate studies provide additional support for the finding that development levels condition the effect of women's education on contraceptive practice, specifically, that the more developed the context, the stronger the education–contraception relationship.

- A multivariate analysis using DHS data for mostly Yoruba women from two states of Nigeria suggests that the net effect of women's education in explaining contraceptive use is considerably stronger in rural and urban Ondo State than in the less developed and rural Oyo State.[18]

Other studies in sub-Saharan Africa suggest the existence of threshold levels of education, after which education exerts a positive influence on contraceptive practice.

- A study in Kinshasa, Zaire, examines current contraceptive use as a function of women's education, employment status, husband's occupational status, migration status, and ethnic group, as well as such demographic factors as age, marital status, fertility, and whether additional children are desired. Weighted logistic regression analyses suggest little effect of a primary education on contraceptive use but a clear tendency for schooling beyond the primary level to be associated with a significantly greater likelihood of practising contraception. An even higher threshold level (secondary school) is required before a significant net effect of women's schooling on the use of modern methods is observed.[19]

Further support for the existence of threshold levels of education comes from a study in Nigeria's Edo and Delta states. This regression analysis measures 'ever use' and current use of contraception as a function of women's education, husband's education and occupation, community characteristics, ethnic group, and variables measuring women's decision-making and control over resources. The results suggest that women's education beyond primary school, but not at lower levels, is the single most powerful net predictor of contraceptive use. The only other significant variables are accessibility to a health centre, control over resources, and the extent to which household chores are shared by husband and wife.[20]

Thus, even when economic status and other household characteristics are controlled, the effect of women's education on proportions practising contraception is largely positive. Region and level of development do, however, condition the pattern of the relationship. Many studies in high-income settings find a linear positive relationship between education and contraceptive prevalence at all levels of education, whereas many in low-income settings, in settings in which gender disparities in literacy are pronounced, and in sub-Saharan Africa find a positive relationship only at the upper-primary or secondary level. This threshold effect is observed in both bivariate and multivariate estimates.

Women's Education, Unmet Need, and the Timing of Contraception

Not only are educated women more likely to practise contraception but they are also more likely to initiate contraceptive use as soon as a need for it is felt. Assuming that a need for contraception occurs when actual or potential family size equals or exceeds the desired number of children, educated women are far more likely than are uneducated women to take action to prevent unwanted pregnancies and are, therefore, much less likely to experience an unmet need for contraception.

Appendix J lists studies addressing the relationship of women's education to proportions of women expressing an unmet need for contraception. Drawn almost entirely from C. F. Westoff and L. H. Ochoa's 1991 analysis of DHS data,[21] Appendix J reports mean values of proportions expressing an unmet need for contraception separately for all women and for the uneducated, differentials between proportions expressing an unmet need for contraception among uneducated women and those with progressively higher levels of education, and the direction of the relationship.

Proportions of women with an unmet need for contraception range from 11 per cent in Thailand to 40 per cent in Togo. The effect of women's education on the level of unmet need is usually inverse, as expected.[22] Of the 25 countries listed in Appendix J, the relationship is clearly inverse in 13 settings, 7-shaped in another 3, and positive, curvilinear, or unrelated in 9. Inverse relationships are evident in most settings, except sub-Saharan Africa and the least developed countries. In sub-Saharan Africa, for example, the relationship tends to be positive or reversed-U- or reversed-J-shaped in 7 of 8 countries listed. In these same settings, educationally induced declines of 10 per cent in the level of unmet need are rarely reached until the secondary level.

Education is expected to affect not only whether contraception is practised but also the fertility level at which the practice is initiated. An indirect way of measuring this timing of contraception is through the level of unwanted fertility or the extent to which actual family size exceeds desired family size. Educated women are expected to initiate contraception closer to the time that desired family is attained, thereby reducing the chances of overshooting their preferences or experiencing excess or unwanted fertility.

The evidence, however, does not unambiguously support this hypothesis. An inverse relationship between education and unwanted fertility is found only in more developed settings, mostly in Latin America and the Caribbean.[23] In other settings, the pattern is more ambiguous—reversed-U-shaped or even positive.

- For example, in Asia and in North Africa and the Middle East, smaller proportions of uneducated and highly educated women compared with women with 1 to 6 years of schooling reported an unwanted birth in the WFS;[24]
- This pattern also extends to the DHS: a comparison of results from 26 countries suggests that, in 10 settings (mostly in North Africa and Asia), moderately educated women have more children than they desire, compared with uneducated and better educated women;[25]
- In sub-Saharan Africa, where, as a result of high desired family size, unwanted fertility levels are much lower than in any other region, the relationship of education to unwanted fertility is actually positive in 5 of the 10 countries analysed.[26]

Again, although educated women are systematically more likely to practise contraception and are less likely to experience unmet need, the effect of a small amount of education on reducing unwanted fertility is small or non-existent in all but the most developed settings. This finding is consistent with the hypothesis that, in some less developed settings, even motivated women with a small amount of education may not have the autonomy to limit family size until after some unwanted fertility has been experienced.

Evidence exists, however, that educated women systematically initiate contraception at earlier parities than uneducated women do. A United Nations study, comparing results of the DHS from 26 countries, finds an inverse relationship between education and the mean number of living children at first use of contraception in each of the 15 countries outside of sub-Saharan Africa.[27] These countries include those in which the relationship of education to proportions currently practising contraception was earlier found to be a reversed-7 shape.

- In Thailand, where lower-primary-schooled women were about as likely to practise contraception as uneducated women were, the mean number of surviving children at first use of contraception fell systematically from 3 children among uneducated women to 2.4 among women with 1–3 years of schooling to 1.9, 1.1, and 0.8 among women with 4–6, 7–9, and 10 or more years of schooling, respectively;
- In contrast, in sub-Saharan Africa, where the relationship of education to proportions practising contraception tended to be a reversed-7 shape, the relationship of education to the mean number of children at first use of contraception was, correspondingly, a 7 shape, with moderately educated women initiating contraception at about the same parity as uneducated women. Even so, secondary-schooled women initiated contraception more than one child earlier than uneducated and moderately educated women did.

Thus, the relationship of women's education to the level of unmet need mirrors its relationship to contraceptive prevalence. Just as the relationship of women's education to contraceptive prevalence tends to be largely positive, its effect on the level of unmet need tends to be negative. Exceptions are concentrated in sub-Saharan Africa and in the least developed settings, where the effect of education on contraceptive prevalence is less marked. In several of the least developed settings, education has been found to be unrelated or positively related to the level of unmet need, perhaps the result of genuinely lower desired family size combined with the high costs associated with obtaining contraception among educated women.

Finally, what little evidence is available suggests that the effect of education on parity at first use of contraception may be stronger than the effect of education on either contraceptive prevalence or the level of unmet need: contraception is initiated considerably earlier in the reproductive careers of educated than of uneducated women.

That unmet need for contraception declines with education in most parts of the developing world, except, currently, in sub-Saharan Africa, suggests that, once women are motivated to control family size, education enables them to overcome a range of social, psychological, and economic barriers to the use of contraception.

The next sections will examine the pathways through which education may break down these constraints to contraception.

How Women's Education Reduces the Obstacles to Contraception

Why does education reduce the obstacles to contraception that women face and increase the practice of contraception? Why is it that a small amount of education can have little effect on contraceptive practice and timing? The literature provides several hypotheses.

Educated women have greater knowledge of deliberate fertility control

First, and most direct, education may influence women's access to modern and comprehensive knowledge of contraception. Just as they are more likely to know about modern medicine, educated women are also more likely to know about contraception and about where to obtain family planning services. Thus, education is hypothesized to improve knowledge, in general, as well as the ability to absorb and comprehend technical information, to discount misinformation, and to seek out additional information.

Ample evidence exists of the link between education and contraceptive knowledge. Most studies of this relationship, however, measure awareness as the proportion of women who know about one or more methods of contraception, rather than a more discriminating measure, such as the number of methods known, or the proportions having in-depth knowledge of methods and how to obtain them. The use of measures of minimal knowledge is likely to generate the most conservative differentials by education, because knowledge of at least one method has become fairly universal across the developing world, even in countries in which contraceptive prevalence rates are low, as seen in Appendix K. Even with measures of minimal knowledge, the effect of education is uniformly positive in most of the studies summarized in Appendix K.[28]

Tables 8.4–8.6 summarize the results of 33 recent studies selected from those shown in Appendix K. These studies relate women's education to the proportions aware of at least one method of contraception.[29] The results suggest that the relationship of education to the proportions of women who know at least one method of contraception is generally positive.

 • The positive relationship is most likely to occur in sub-Saharan Africa, and in less developed and more inegalitarian settings, where contraceptive prevalence is relatively low. In other settings, where at least a superficial knowledge of contraception is widespread, education has less effect.

More stringent measures of contraceptive knowledge can include knowledge of proper use of contraception and its side-effects, knowledge of less widely known methods, the number of methods known, and knowledge of where to obtain methods. Unfortunately, there is a relative dearth of comparative data using these

Table 8.4. *Patterns in the relationship of women's education to contraceptive knowledge, by region, level of development, and gender disparity in literacy*

	Patterns in the relationship between years of schooling and knowledge of at least one modern contraceptive method[a]			Total number of studies
	Positive	Reversed 7	None	
A. Region[b]				
Sub-Saharan Africa	11	1	1	13
North Africa and the Middle East	1	0	3	4
East and South-East Asia	1	0	1	2
South Asia	1	1	1	3
Latin America and the Caribbean	6	2	3	11
B. Level of development				
1. Annual per capita income ($)				
500 or less	10	2	1	13
501–999	7	1	3	11
1000 or more	3	1	5	9
2. Overall female literacy rate (%)				
40 or less	9	1	2	12
41–80	8	2	3	13
81 or more	3	1	4	8
C. Gender disparity in literacy[c]				
250–700	9	1	2	12
701–850	5	2	1	8
851 or more	6	1	6	13
TOTALS	20	4	9	33

[a] Two distinct patterns in the relationship of years of schooling to contraceptive knowledge are apparent: a positive relationship, in which better educated women are progressively more likely (by 5 per cent or more) to know about one or more modern methods of contraception than are uneducated and moderately educated women; and a reversed-7-shaped relationship, in which the proportion of moderately educated women who know about one or more modern methods of contraception is about the same as that of uneducated women (within 5 per cent), whereas better educated women know about more methods.

[b] Not all countries in a region are included, and those included are not necessarily representative of the region but are, rather, those countries for which the requisite data are available. Thus, the results are not necessarily representative of any particular region.

[c] The level of gender disparity in literacy is the number of literate females per 1000 literate males.

Notes: The studies selected for inclusion in this table appear in Appendix K, where they are marked with a dagger (†). The study populations were women of child-bearing age who had ever been married or in union. Contraceptive knowledge is defined as the percentage aware of at least one method.

Sources: Of the 33 studies, 30 are based on Demographic and Health Surveys data, from United Nations, *Women's Education and Fertility Behaviour: Recent Evidence from the Demographic and Health Surveys* (1995), or other DHS reports. Sources are indicated in Appendix K.

measures. The available data suggest that the differentials may be wider when these measures are used than with the any-method measures. The reason is that educated women are both more likely to know about a fuller array of methods and more likely to have more comprehensive knowledge of the use and side-effects associated with each one. In India, for example, although knowledge of sterilization is universal and unaffected by education, far fewer women are aware of the intra-uterine device (IUD); the proportion who know about it climbs dramatically with increases in

Table 8.5.   *Differentials in the relationship of women's education to contraceptive knowledge, by region, level of development, and gender disparity in literacy*

	Differences in percentage knowing of one or more contraceptive methods between uneducated and secondary-schooled women[a] NARROW ◄----------------► WIDE					Total number of studies
	10 or less	11–20	21–30	31–40	41 or more	
A. Region[b]						
Sub-Saharan Africa	2	2	3	4	2	13
North Africa and the Middle East	3	0	0	0	1	4
East and South-East Asia	1	1	0	0	0	2
South Asia	2	0	1	0	0	3
Latin America and the Caribbean	5	1	1	1	3	11
B. Level of development						
1. Annual per capita income ($)						
500 or less	3	1	4	2	3	13
501–999	4	2	0	3	2	11
1000 or more	6	1	1	0	1	9
2. Overall female literacy rate (%)						
40 or less	3	0	3	3	3	12
41–80	5	4	0	1	3	13
81 or more	5	0	2	1	0	8
C. Gender disparity in literacy[c]						
250–700	3	0	3	3	3	12
701–850	3	2	0	1	2	8
851 or more	7	2	2	1	1	13
TOTALS	13	4	5	5	6	33

[a] The term 'secondary-schooled women' here applies to women who have had some secondary education or completed or gone beyond secondary school—that is, women who have had more than six years of primary education.
[b] Not all countries in a region are included, and those included are not necessarily representative of the region but are, rather, those countries for which the requisite data are available. Thus, the results are not necessarily representative of any particular region.
[c] The level of gender disparity in literacy is the number of literate females per 1000 literate males.

Notes: The studies selected for inclusion in this table appear in Appendix K, where they are marked with a dagger (†). Contraceptive knowledge is defined as knowledge of at least one modern method of contraception. This definition is least likely to generate educational differentials, since knowledge of at least one method is now almost universal. More stringent definitions (e.g. comprehensive knowledge or number of methods known) are more likely to reveal differences.

Sources: Of the 33 studies, 30 are based on Demographic and Health Surveys data, from United Nations, *Women's Education and Fertility Behaviour: Recent Evidence from the Demographic and Health Surveys* (1995), or other DHS reports. Sources are indicated in Appendix K.

education (even primary schooling increases knowledge by 31 per cent). In addition, women's education is strongly related to the proportions having correct information about a given method—from 43 per cent among uneducated women to 72 per cent among secondary-schooled women, in the case of tubectomy, and from 17 per cent to 71 per cent, in the case of the IUD.[30] Similarly, the average number of methods

Table 8.6. *Relationship of the duration of women's education to contraceptive knowledge, by region, level of development, and gender disparity in literacy*

	Educational level (years of schooling) by which:								Total number of studies
	A 10% increase in the percentage knowing one or more contraceptive methods is reached				A 20% increase in the percentage knowing one or more contraceptive methods is reached				
	1–3	4–6	7+	Never	1–3	4–6	7+	Never	
A. Region[a]									
Sub-Saharan Africa	9	2	0	2	3	3	3	4	13
North Africa and the Middle East	1	0	0	3	1	0	0	3	4
East and South-East Asia	1	0	0	1	0	0	0	2	2
South Asia	1	0	0	2	0	1	0	2	3
Latin America and the Caribbean	5	1	1	4	3	2	0	6	11
B. Level of development									
1. Annual per capita income ($)									
500 or less	9	1	1	2	3	3	3	4	13
501–999	5	2	0	4	3	2	0	6	11
1000 or more	3	0	0	6	1	1	0	7	9
2. Overall female literacy rate (%)									
40 or less	8	1	0	3	3	3	3	3	12
41–80	6	2	1	4	4	0	0	9	13
81 or more	3	0	0	5	0	3	0	5	8
C. Gender disparity in literacy[b]									
250–700	8	1	0	3	3	3	3	3	12
701–850	4	1	1	2	3	0	0	5	8
851 or more	5	1	0	7	1	3	0	9	13
TOTALS	17	3	1	12	7	6	3	17	33

[a] Not all countries in a region are included, and those included are not necessarily representative of the region but are, rather, those countries for which the requisite data are available. Thus, the results are not necessarily representative of any particular region.
[b] The level of gender disparity in literacy is the number of literate females per 1000 literate males.

Notes: The studies selected for inclusion in this table appear in Appendix K, where they are marked with a dagger (†). Some appendix studies combine rates for women with 1–3 and 4–6 years of schooling; in such studies, rates are shown in the column marked 1–3. Contraceptive knowledge is defined as knowledge of at least one modern method of contraception.

Sources: Of the 33 studies, 30 are based on Demographic and Health Surveys data, from United Nations, *Women's Education and Fertility Behaviour: Recent Evidence from the Demographic and Health Surveys* (1995), or other DHS reports. Sources are indicated in Appendix K.

known increases systematically with women's education. The best educated women often know of approximately two more methods than uneducated women know.[31]

Even in sub-Saharan African settings where women's education is, in general, positively related to knowledge of at least one method (Table 8.4), the differentials become wider when more stringent measures, such as knowledge of a modern method or knowledge of a source for a modern method are used.[32] Studies of Ilorin, urban Nigeria, show that women's education is markedly related to the duration since first knowledge of family planning.

- The proportion having knowledge about family planning for more than 10 years increased from 4 per cent and 8 per cent among uneducated and primary-schooled women to 15 per cent and 31 per cent among those having higher levels of education.[33]

Again, is it education itself or some other factor that causes differences in contraceptive knowledge? Several studies strongly suggest that women's education is a more powerful determinant of contraceptive knowledge than are her husband's characteristics or economic status.

- For example, a study in Brazil finds education a stronger determinant of a woman's knowledge of methods than region, urban–rural residence, education of husband, household income, ownership of consumer goods, media exposure, or age. Only the wife's religiosity plays a similarly central role, and this may itself be affected by her education.[34]

Several multivariate studies also attest to the independent effect of women's education.

- A study in Kerala, India, finds that, once age is controlled, women's education is a much stronger net predictor of knowledge of methods than are husband's education, household expenditure, land ownership, and caste;[35]
- A study in rural Maharashtra[36] and another in rural Tamil Nadu[37] also confirm the net importance of women's education, even though each analysis includes inappropriate controls that could undermine the net effect of education (e.g. women's work status, decision-making power, and freedom of movement);
- In Maharashtra, India, the net effect of women's education on methods known far exceeds that of mass media exposure, consumer goods owned, age, or work status.[38] The relationship is even more dramatic if knowledge of only non-terminal methods, which are less vigorously promoted by the family planning programme, are included;
- A multivariate analysis of Ghana, Kenya, Senegal, and northern Sudan, for which both WFS and DHS data are available (collected, respectively, in 1978-1980 and 1986-1989), finds that average levels of knowledge of modern contraceptive methods are strongly related to average female schooling levels.[39]

Educated women exert greater decision-making in areas related to contraception

The enhanced decision-making authority that often accompanies education extends into the field of reproduction. Through increased decision-making autonomy, better educated women are said to be more likely than uneducated women to approve of and engage in innovative behaviours, such as the use of contraception within marriage.[40] As a study in Ibadan, Nigeria, concludes, demographic innovators appear to be disproportionately drawn from among better educated women, so that women's education is of great importance in determining demographic changes.[41] Educated women are more likely to override the opinions of other family members and elders who oppose contraceptive use. Once in a position of potential excess demand, educated women's greater exposure to the modern world and their decision-making authority lead them to be less constrained by traditional opposition in their families and communities; they are equally unwilling to leave reproductive prospects to chance.

That educated women are more favourable to the use of contraception than are less educated women is evident from a variety of DHS reports and other surveys in Egypt, Pakistan, the Philippines, and northern Thailand (see Box 8.1).[42]

The little evidence that exists on the effect of education on women's contraceptive decision-making comes mainly from small investigations, most conducted in South Asia, or from extrapolations from more general evidence on the effect of education on women's decision-making (discussed in Chapter 3). One conclusion of Chapter 3 was that the more gender-stratified the culture, the more education is required before women have an active say in their own lives. It seems likely, then, that the

---

Box 8.1.   *Attitudes towards contraception*

By the 1980s, the relationship between education and favourable attitudes towards contraception was no longer of great interest because, in all but the least developed settings, the majority of women of reproductive age held almost uniformly favourable attitudes towards contraception. In most settings, even large proportions of uneducated women approve of contraception. Nevertheless, the effect of education on the proportions of women approving of contraception is almost universally positive, although differentials are often narrow. In Kenya, for example, 81 per cent of uneducated women approve of family planning, whereas 92 per cent of secondary-schooled women approve.[a]

Only in less developed, low-prevalence settings does education continue to generate strong differentials in the proportions approving of contraception. For example, in Liberia, 38 per cent of uneducated women approve of family planning as compared with 73 per cent of secondary-schooled women.[b]

More important for fertility outcomes than having favourable attitudes towards contraception *per se* is the ability of educated women to put their positive attitudes into practice. Compared with illiterate women, educated women are probably more likely to have the power which would allow them to go against the wishes of their husbands or mothers-in-law with respect to contraception.[c]

[a] Kenya, National Council for Population and Development, *Kenya Demographic and Health Survey 1989* (Columbia, Md., Macro Systems, inc., 1989).
[b] D. Chieh-Johnson *et al.*, *Liberia Demographic and Health Survey 1986* (Columbia, Md., Westinghouse, 1988).
[c] K. O. Mason, 'The Impact of Women's Position on Demographic Change During the Course of Development: What Do We Know?', in Nora Federici, Karen Oppenheim Mason, and Solvi Sogner (eds.), *Women's Position and Demographic Change* (Oxford, Oxford University Press, 1993).

extent of a society's gender stratification will condition the extent to which education gives women a say in contraceptive decisions. Even in the gender-stratified cultures of South Asia, there is evidence from urban areas of a positive relationship between women's education and contraceptive decision-making.

- A study in Karachi, Pakistan, finds that educated women are systematically more likely to think that they should be involved in decisions on family size, either on their own or jointly with their husbands. The proportion who felt this way increased from 63 per cent among uneducated women to 75 per cent among those with 1-9 years of schooling and 85 per cent with 10 or more years;[43]
- In Bangladesh, education is closely associated with women's decision-making authority on such matters as the schooling of children, visiting relatives, shopping, and seeking health care. A decision-making index created from these variables is, in turn, strongly related to contraception: compared with women who made decisions on all four issues, the odds of a woman scoring 1-3 using modern, reversible methods of contraception was 0.781, and for women who had no decision-making authority at all the relative odds were 0.45.[44]

Other studies in rural areas are less clear about whether a small amount of education can enhance decision-making concerning reproduction and whether it enhances decision-making relatively early in the reproductive career, in particular, before desired fertility levels have been exceeded. In rural South India, although the older generation has abdicated control of fertility decision-making to their educated daughters-in-law and sons, few educated young women would undergo sterilization without seeking the consent of the husband's parents. That contraceptive practice has increased among moderately educated women is attributed not so much to women's enhanced decision-making power *per se* but to the pro-contraception attitudes of their parents-in-law and to the effects of the official family planning programme, which strongly advocates contraception for young women.[45]

- A qualitative study in rural North India shows that neither Hindu (Jat) nor Muslim women decide to practise contraception by themselves, and educated women are no more likely than uneducated women to make this decision. Only one Jat woman had been sterilized without consulting her in-laws, and she was uneducated.[46]

Some evidence suggests that interventions enhancing women's control over resources can substitute for education in providing them with the decision-making authority or control over resources necessary for the adoption of contraception. A multivariate analysis in rural Bangladesh of the impact of women's participation in credit programmes on family planning behaviour suggests that the longer a woman participates in such a programme the more likely she is to practise contraception, even after controlling for age, socio-economic factors, access to services, and education. When participation in a credit scheme is included in the equation, the net effect of women's education is positive but not significant.[47]

In short, most women in developing countries have, by now, adopted favourable attitudes to contraception. Even so, educated women are more likely to approve of

it than are uneducated women. Educated women are also more likely to make independent decisions on the timing and method of contraception. In more traditional
settings, however, some evidence suggests that it takes more than a small amount of
education before women make contraceptive decisions entirely on their own, and
especially before women can assume these decisions at early stages in their
reproductive careers.

Educated women have closer conjugal relations and better spousal communication

Another important constraint to contraception is the absence of communication
between wife and husband on matters relating to sexuality and contraception. Considerable evidence exists that communication between husband and wife increases
contraceptive use and, thereby, lowers fertility.[48] Education is expected to enhance
this communication. As seen in Chapter 3, better educated women enjoy closer
intimacy with their husbands and are more likely to discuss with them various family
concerns, such as child welfare and financial matters. One manifestation of this
intimacy between spouses is a greater willingness to discuss such previously
forbidden subjects as sexual behaviour, contraception, and the number of children to
have, thus removing yet another barrier to contraception.

Again, in every region of the developing world, whatever little evidence exists—
however flawed and cursory in large-scale surveys—supports the hypothesis that
women's education enhances spousal communication on family planning.[49]
Educational differentials tend to be relatively narrow in settings in which close
conjugal relations are common.

- A study in Cuernavaca, Mexico, finds that the proportions of women who have
  discussed contraception with their husbands increased from 78 per cent among
  women with 1–5 years of schooling to more than 90 per cent among those with
  6 and more years.

In contrast, in gender-stratified settings characterized by less overall spousal
intimacy, education generates wider differentials in interspousal communication on
family planning.

- In Egypt, differentials are quite steep: while fewer than one in five women with
  a low level of education communicates with her husband, this proportion increases to one in two and four in five among those with a medium and high level
  of education, respectively;
- Similarly wide differentials are observed in India over the 1980s. Whereas
  overall levels of interspousal communication increased considerably between
  1980 and 1988 (from 35 per cent to 51 per cent), women's education generated
  strong differentials in the extent of interspousal communication at both points
  in time. At the earlier date, 25 per cent of uneducated women communicated
  with their husbands about contraception, compared with 49 per cent and 68 per
  cent of primary- and secondary-schooled women, respectively; at the later date,
  these percentages increased to 41 per cent, 59 per cent, and 78 per cent among

uneducated, primary- and secondary-schooled women, respectively. At neither time is there evidence of high thresholds. Another indicator of close spousal communication at both points in time is that better educated women are both much surer of their husbands' attitudes and much more likely to report favourable attitudes towards family planning among their husbands.[50]

Equally large are the differentials in Nigeria. A multivariate analysis using DHS data from Ondo and rural Oyo states examines spousal communication concerning family planning as a function of women's education, economic status (measured by amenities and house type), woman's control over resources, recent and cumulative fertility, and age at marriage. Education turns out to be one of the strongest predictors of spousal communication in each state and is generally more powerful than either economic status or marital age.[51]

Intimacy between spouses can encourage contraception for other reasons as well. For example, it has been argued that closer bonds between spouses can lead to a greater concern for the woman's health and well-being and for the health implications of frequent child-bearing; this concern can influence the likelihood and effectiveness of contraception.[52] Closer husband–wife links can also result in a shift away from traditional and less efficient contraceptive methods, because they detract from sexual pleasure, to more efficient ones.

- In Sri Lanka, for example, where abstinence and rhythm have traditionally been leading forms of contraception, educated women have shifted to the practice of more modern methods largely because abstinence and rhythm were perceived to inhibit husband–wife sexual relations and undermine notions of love in marriage.[53]

Educated women can ensure better access to contraceptive services

Other obstacles to contraceptive use among motivated women include constraints on their physical mobility, lack of interaction with service providers, and lack of access to, or control over, the economic resources necessary for travelling to the health centre or for acquiring contraceptive supplies. In settings in which women are secluded, education is hypothesized to grant women freedom of movement to seek health and contraceptive services, thereby enhancing contraceptive use.[54]

To the extent that education enables women to demand services, question service providers about alternative methods and potential side-effects, and seek follow-up for problems associated with contraception, educated women may be more likely to adopt a method that is ideally suited to them and less likely to discontinue it. No studies have been found, however, that provide direct evidence relevant to this hypothesis.

Notes
1. J. C. Caldwell and P. Caldwell, 'Cause and Sequence', and P. Caldwell and J. C. Caldwell, 'Function of Child-spacing'.

2. See, for example, Shea Rutstein and Vilma Medica, 'The Latin American Experience', in Preston (ed.), *Effects,* and Shireen J. Jejeeboy, 'The Shift from Natural to Controlled Fertility: A Cross-Sectional Analysis of Ten Indian States', *Studies in Family Planning,* 15/4 (July–Aug. 1984), 191–8.

3. Richard A. Easterlin, 'An Economic Framework for Fertility Analysis', *Studies in Family Planning,* 6 (Mar. 1975), 54–63 and 'Modernization and Fertility: A Critical Essay', in Bulatao and Lee (eds.), *Determinants.*

4. The 54 studies include 18 that use WFS data, reported in United Nations, *Fertility Behaviour;* 31 that use DHS data and various DHS country reports, from United Nations, *Women's Education and Fertility Behaviour: Recent Evidence from the Demographic and Health Surveys,* and 5 that use other surveys.

5. United Nations, *Fertility Behaviour;* Weinberger, 'Relationship'.

6. United Nations, *Fertility Behaviour;* Weinberger, 'Relationship'.

7. See, for example, Malawi, National Statistical Office, *Malawi Demographic and Health Survey 1992: First Report* (Columbia, Md., Macro International Inc., 1993); for Namibia, Katjiuanjo *et al., Namibia Demographic and Health Survey 1992;* for Zimbabwe, Mhloyi, 'Fertility Transition in Zimbabwe'; and for Ankole women in Uganda, J. P. M. Ntozi and J. B. Kabera, 'Family Planning in Rural Uganda: Knowledge and Use of Modern and Traditional Methods in Ankole', *Studies in Family Planning,* 22/2 (Mar.–Apr. 1991), 116–23.

8. Weinberger, Lloyd, and Blanc, 'Women's Education and Fertility'.

9. For example, rural Bangladesh, R. H. Chaudhury, 'The Influence of Female Education, Labour Force Participation and Age at Marriage on Fertility Behaviour in Bangladesh', *Social Biology,* 31/1–2 (1984), 59–74; Zimbabwe, Mhloyi, 'Fertility Transition in Zimbabwe'; Gujarat, India, Leela Visaria, 'Regional Variations in Female Autonomy and Fertility Behaviour in India', paper presented at the Workshop on Female Education, Autonomy and Fertility Change in South Asia, New Delhi, Apr. 1993; and Maharashtra, India, United Nations, *Women's Education and Fertility Behaviour: A Case-study of Rural Maharashtra, India.*

10. R. Freedman *et al.,* 'Education and Fertility in Two Chinese Provinces: 1967–1970 to 1979–1982', *Asia-Pacific Population Journal,* 3/1 (Mar. 1988), 3–30.

11. Operations Research Group, *Family Planning Practices in India;* K. C. Zachariah, 'The Anomaly of the Fertility Decline in India's Kerala State: A Field Investigation', World Bank Staff Working Papers No. 700 (Washington, DC, The World Bank, 1984).

12. For Bangladesh, see Chaudhury, 'Influence'; for Maharashtra, India, see, for example, United Nations, *Women's Education and Fertility Behaviour: A Case-study of Rural Maharashtra, India;* for Gujarat and Kerala, India, see Visaria, 'Regional Variations'; and for Goa, see Roy, Rao, and Prasad, 'Education, Fertility and Contraception'.

13. United Nations, *Fertility Behaviour.*

14. Ibid.

15. N. Mostajo, 'Actitudes de la mujer frente a la fecundidad y uso de methods anticonceptivos', *Auspiciado por la Oficina Nacional de Estadistica, Republica del Peru* (Santiago de Chile, Centro Latinoamericano de Demografia, 1981).

16. Zachariah, 'Anomaly of the Fertility Decline'.

17. M. Rahman *et al.,* 'Contraceptive Use in Matlab, Bangladesh: The Role of Gender Preference', *Studies in Family Planning,* 23/4 (July–Aug. 1992), 229–42.

18. Kritz and Gurak, 'Women's Economic Independence'.

19. Shapiro and Tambashe, 'Women's Employment'.

20. Okojie, 'Women's Status, Proximate Determinants and Fertility'.
21. C. F. Westoff and L. H. Ochoa, 'Unmet Need and the Demand for Family Planning', Demographic and Health Surveys Comparative Studies No. 5 (Columbia, Md., Institute for Resource Development, July 1991). Other sources of data were, for India, Operations Research Group, *Family Planning Practices in India*, and, for Mexico, Cordova's analysis of the DHS, in 'Instituciones sociales y reproduccion'.
22. C. Westoff and A. Pebley, 'Alternative Measures of Unmet Need for Family Planning in Developing Countries', *International Family Planning Perspectives*, 7/4 (1981), 126–36; C. Westoff and L. Moreno, 'The Demand for Family Planning: Estimates for Developing Countries', paper presented at the IUSSP Seminar of the Committee on the Comparative Analysis of Family Planning and Fertility, Tunisia, 26–30 June 1989; and Westoff and Ochoa, 'Unmet Need'.
23. United Nations, *Fertility Behaviour*; Bongaarts and Lightbourne, 'Wanted Fertility in Latin America'; Weinberger, Lloyd, and Blanc, 'Women's Education and Fertility'; and United Nations, *Women's Education and Fertility Behaviour: Recent Evidence from the Demographic and Health Surveys*.
24. United Nations, *Fertility Behaviour*.
25. United Nations, *Women's Education and Fertility Behaviour: Recent Evidence from the Demographic and Health Surveys*.
26. Ibid.
27. Ibid.
28. Cf. Cochrane's earlier findings in *Fertility and Education*.
29. Thirty of these studies are drawn from the DHS, reported in United Nations, *Women's Education and Fertility Behaviour: Recent Evidence from the Demographic and Health Surveys*, and various DHS reports.
30. Operations Research Group, *Family Planning Practices in India.*
31. For Kerala, see Zachariah, 'Anomaly of the Fertility Decline'; for Maharashtra, see United Nations, *Women's Education and Fertility Behaviour: A Case-study of Rural Maharashtra, India*
32. For Zambia, see, for example, Gaisie, Cross, and Nsemukila, *Zambia Demographic and Health Survey 1992.*
33. See, for example, Oni and McCarthy, 'Contraceptive Knowledge'.
34. do Valle Silva *et al.*, 'Determinants'.
35. Zachariah, 'Anomaly of the Fertility Decline'.
36. United Nations, *Women's Education and Fertility Behaviour: A Case-study of Rural Maharashtra, India.*
37. Jejeebhoy, 'Women's Status and Fertility'.
38. United Nations, *Women's Education and Fertility Behaviour: A Case-study of Rural Maharashtra, India.*
39. Lesthaeghe, Verleye, and Jolly, 'Female Education'. In this study, a lisrel analysis of 55 DHS regions finds a strong effect of female schooling on knowledge of modern contraception, even after controlling for the proportions of Muslims and for rural–urban residence, with the education effect being stronger than either of the other effects.
40. Dyson and Moore, 'On Kinship Structure'; Mason, *Status of Women.*
41. J. C. Caldwell and P. Caldwell, 'The Achieved Small Family'.
42. For Egypt, see A. M. Khalifa, 'The Influence of Wife's Education on Fertility in Rural Egypt', *Journal of Biosocial Science*, 8 (1976), 53–60; for Pakistan, see Sathar and Mason, 'Why Female Education Affects'; for the Philippines, see Raymundo *et al.*,

'Female Education'; and for northern Thailand, see Cochrane and Nandwani, 'Determinants of Fertility'.

43. Sathar and Kazi, 'Women, Work and Reproduction'.
44. J. Cleland, 'Large Data-Sets'.
45. J. C. Caldwell, Reddy, and Caldwell, 'Causes of Demographic Change'.
46. Jeffery and Jeffery, 'North Indian Relationships'.
47. S. R. Schuler, D. Meekers, and S. M. Hashemi, 'The Impact of Women's Participation in Credit Programs on Family Planning in Rural Bangladesh' (Mass. and Va., John Snow, Inc., JSI Research and Training Institute, not dated).
48. R. A. Bulatao, 'Reducing Fertility in Developing Countries: A Review of Determinants and Policy Levers', World Bank Staff Working Papers No. 680 (Washington, DC, The World Bank, 1984); L. J. Beckman, 'Communication, Power, and the Influence of Social Networks on Couple Decisions on Fertility', in Bulatao and Lee (eds.), *Determinants*.
49. See, for example, for Mexico, LeVine *et al.*, 'Women's Schooling'; for Egypt, Khalifa, 'Influence'; for Nigeria, Kritz and Gurak, 'Women's Economic Independence'; for India, Operations Research Group, *Family Planning Practices in India*.
50. M. E. Khan and C. V. S. Prasad, *Family Planning Practices in India: Second All India Survey* (Baroda, Operations Research Group, 1983); Operations Research Group, *Family Planning Practices in India*.
51. Kritz and Gurak, 'Women's Economic Independence'.
52. Mason, 'Impact of Women's Position'.
53. J. Caldwell *et al.*, 'Traditional Fertility Regulation in Sri Lanka'.
54. J. Cleland, 'Large Data-Sets'.

9 Women's Education and Fertility: The Relative Influence of Each Intervening Pathway

This chapter makes two points. First, the education–fertility relationship shifts from non-inverse to inverse as the setting becomes more developed or more egalitarian. Second, as the setting becomes more developed or more egalitarian, it takes less education to produce a pronounced reduction in fertility.

The reason underlying both these observations is that, in lesser developed and more gender-stratified settings, the most powerful effects of education are to reduce such traditional inhibitions on child supply as prolonged breast-feeding or post-partum abstinence rather than to delay marriage, reduce family-size desires, or increase contraception. Only in more developed and more egalitarian settings are the effects of education on the latter variables more powerful than their effects on the former, resulting in the more uniform inverse effect of education on fertility seen in these settings.

Previous chapters examined the relationship of women's education to each of a number of specific channels potentially affecting fertility. These channels included the dimensions of women's situation other than their education and factors influencing the natural supply of births, the demand for children, fertility-regulation behaviour, and obstacles to contraception. These chapters have underscored the finding that, in almost every setting of the developing world, schooling has a powerful and pervasive effect on reproductive behaviour. Earlier chapters have also observed that, although uneducated women have relatively little autonomy and relatively high fertility, and highly educated women have the most autonomy and the fewest children, what happens in between, especially at the lower end of the educational spectrum, varies from setting to setting, by culture and by the extent of gender stratification. Moreover, it is what happens at the lower end of the educational spectrum that determines the overall relationship of education to fertility.

This chapter attempts to synthesize the evidence concerning the pathways through which women's education affects fertility. It asks two questions. Which pathways are most important to the relationship of women's education to fertility under various cultural, regional, and developmental conditions? And how does the overall relationship of women's education to fertility vary under different cultural and developmental conditions?

Studies of the Education–Fertility Relationship

Surprisingly few studies attempt to estimate the relative contributions of various intervening pathways to the relationship of women's schooling and fertility. Those that do examine the links of women's education to fertility through the following:
- The proximate determinants, that is, delayed married, use of contraception, and prolonged breast-feeding;[1]
- Child supply, demand for children, and fertility-regulation factors;[2] and
- Such factors as women's work-force participation and husband's socio-economic characteristics.

Effects of proximate determinants

Table 9.1 summarizes the results of studies listed in Appendix L for 43 countries. The table illustrates the relative contributions of each proximate determinant to the percentage reduction in potential fertility at each of several levels of education using period rather than lifetime fertility measures.[3]

Regardless of setting, the fertility-inhibiting effects of contraception and delayed marriage rise fairly evenly with education, whereas the effect of lactational infecundability falls.
- Among uneducated women, fertility is kept below the biological maximum largely as a result of prolonged lactation, which has an effect, among these women, approaching twice that of either delayed marriage or increased contraception;
- Among women with some secondary schooling, the contributions of delayed marriage and contraception to reduced fertility far outweigh the effect of infecundability.

Region, development setting, and gender inequality (the gender disparity in literacy) also influence the relative strengths of the proximate determinants.
- In sub-Saharan Africa and South Asia, the most powerful pathway keeping fertility below maximum is lactational infecundability. Its contribution to fertility far outweighs the contributions of delayed marriage and contraception among both uneducated and moderately educated women. Even so, the relative contributions of delayed marriage and contraception increase steadily with education. Among secondary-schooled women, the effect of delayed marriage, in sub-Saharan Africa, and both delayed marriage and contraception in South Asia, play a dominant role in keeping fertility below maximum.
- In Latin America and the Caribbean, North Africa and the Middle East, and East and South-East Asia, lactational infecundability exerts a considerable effect on the fertility of the uneducated. It loses its predominance, however, among the very modestly educated. In all three regions, even among women with 1–3 years of schooling, the most important pathway keeping fertility below maximum is contraception. This trend continues among better educated women as well. In contrast, delayed marriage has a less regular effect on keeping fertility

Table 9.1. *Percentage contribution of each proximate determinant to the difference between potential and actual fertility, for various educational levels, by region, level of development, and gender disparity in literacy*

	Women's educational level (years of schooling)												Total number of studies
	No education			1–3 or 1–6 years			4–6 years			7+ years			
	Post-partum infecund-ability (%)	Delayed marriage (%)	Contra-ception (%)	Post-partum infecund-ability (%)	Delayed marriage (%)	Contra-ception (%)	Post-partum infecund-ability (%)	Delayed marriage (%)	Contra-ception (%)	Post-partum infecund-ability (%)	Delayed marriage (%)	Contra-ception (%)	
A. Region [a]													
Sub-Saharan Africa	66	24	10	57	31	12	50	36	15	34	44	22	(12)
North Africa and the Middle East	47	26	27	35	23	42	25	27	48	17	29	54	(6)
East and South-East Asia	34	33	33	33	26	41	27	30	43	16	38	46	(5)
South Asia	60	19	21	51	19	30	50	20	30	28	34	38	(3)
Latin America and the Caribbean	35	32	33	27	30	43	20	34	46	11	41	47	(17)
B. Level of development													
1. Annual per capita income ($)													
500 or less	63	24	14	52	26	21	47	30	23	29	41	30	(12)
501–999	53	26	22	44	27	29	35	32	33	24	38	38	(13)
1000 or more	32	33	35	26	30	44	19	34	47	11	42	47	(18)
2. Overall female literacy rate (%)													
40 or less	66	22	11	55	26	19	47	32	21	28	40	32	(13)
41–80	45	33	23	37	33	30	30	35	35	19	43	38	(16)
81 or more	32	30	38	26	27	47	21	30	49	13	40	48	(14)
C. Gender disparity in literacy [b]													
250–700	67	22	11	55	26	19	47	32	21	28	40	32	(13)
701–850	49	32	19	40	34	26	33	36	31	23	44	33	(11)
851 or more	33	30	38	27	26	47	21	30	49	13	39	48	(19)
TOTALS	47	28	26	39	28	33	32	32	36	20	40	40	(43)

[a] Not all countries in a region are included, and those included are not necessarily representative of the region but are, rather, those countries for which the requisite data are available. Thus, the results are not necessarily representative of any particular region.

[b] The level of gender disparity in literacy is the number of literate females per 1000 literate males.

Notes: The studies selected for inclusion in this table appear in Appendix L, where they are marked with a dagger (†). The methodology employed is described in the introduction to that appendix. Percentages are based on small totals and may not add to 100 per cent because of rounding.

Sources: Of the 43 studies, 42 are based on World Fertility Survey (16) or Demographic and Health Survey (26) data. Sources are shown in Appendix L.

below maximum among progressively better educated women, except among highly educated women. Similar results have also been observed in the United Nations study of several DHSs.[4]

Panels B and C of Table 9.1 corroborate these regional differences. First, in all settings, as women become better educated, delayed marriage and contraception become increasingly stronger in keeping fertility below its biological maximum. This pattern accounts for the fact that, almost without exception, well-educated women have considerably fewer children than uneducated women do. Second, the results suggest considerable differences in the relative contributions of each proximate determinant according to region, development level, and levels of gender inequality. In low-income, low-literacy, and inegalitarian settings, for example, fertility is kept below the biological maximum largely as a result of lactational infecundability. This effect predominates not only among uneducated women but also among women with modest educations (primary and middle school). Even so, while the major effect continues to be through infecundability among moderately educated women, the effects through delayed marriage and contraception increase systematically among better educated women. Only among secondary-schooled women, however, does the percentage contribution of infecundability drop to well below 50 per cent. Although both are important among secondary-schooled women, delayed marriage rather than contraception is primarily responsible for keeping fertility below maximum.

In contrast, in high-income, high-literacy, and more egalitarian settings, lactational infecundability loses its position of dominance at a lower level of education. Moreover, the most important pathway in these settings is increased contraception rather than delayed marriage.

In other words, in less developed and in inegalitarian settings, inadvertent pathways such as prolonged breast-feeding and delayed marriage—that is, pathways that are not specifically intended to reduce fertility—continue to dominate in the relationship of education to fertility even among the best educated. In contrast, in more developed and egalitarian settings, volitional factors—that is, factors directly related to reducing fertility and expressed here by contraception—are more important in keeping fertility below maximum, and their effect is pronounced among both modestly educated and well-educated women.

Effects of child supply, demand, and fertility-regulation factors

Studies reported in Appendix L use the Bongaarts proximate-determinants model.[5] Others use multivariate techniques with a wider range of intervening pathways.[6] Although studies have used different methodologies, and although studies reporting Bongaarts indices use period data whereas those employing a wider range of intervening pathways and multivariate techniques usually use lifetime data, their results are similar and complement the findings of previous chapters.

Several multivariate studies of the relationship of women's education to fertility have followed the modified path analysis technique presented schematically in

Table 1.3.[7] For example, a study of women in rural Maharashtra, India, breaks down educational differences in the fertility of women aged 30–44 into five intermediate variables: breast-feeding, abstinence duration, child mortality, age at marriage, and desired family size.[8] Although primary-schooled women had about as many births as uneducated women, middle-schooled women had fewer births, a difference attributed primarily to the effect of postponement of marriage among the latter group (−0.44 births), and secondarily to lower family-size desires (−0.12). At the same time, the fertility of middle-schooled women was estimated to be somewhat higher than what would otherwise have been the case because of their shorter birth intervals (0.14). The effects of secondary education were even stronger, resulting in a net reduction of one child: delayed marriage averted 0.91 births and lower desired family size averted 0.26 of a child, whereas reduced post-partum infecundability enhanced fertility by 0.25 of a child. Neither child mortality nor contraceptive costs turned out to be important channels accounting for fertility differentials among educational strata. A second decomposition that substituted contraception for family-size desires arrived at the same conclusion. The main implication of these findings was that the predominant effect of education in bringing about fertility decline was through delayed age at marriage rather than through the deliberate limitation of fertility after marriage. In this context, it is the more complicated marriage negotiations that educated women face—including larger dowries, the relatively small pool of eligible better educated men, as well as better educated women's ability to have a say in vetoing the decisions of their parents—that largely contribute to delayed marriage among women with middle-school and better educations.

Similar results have been obtained in other studies. For example, the effect of years of women's education on fertility through various supply, demand, and regulation cost factors in Sri Lanka and Colombia was analysed. This study attributes about half of the lower fertility of women with 10 years of schooling compared with uneducated women to increased marital age, and about a third to increased fertility control. Shorter periods of breast-feeding and lower levels of secondary sterility raised the fertility of the better educated women above the level it would otherwise have attained (by approximately 14 per cent).[9]

Other studies use such measures as whether women work as a proxy for volitional factors affecting fertility. One such study, conducted in Karachi, Pakistan, examines fertility as a function of marital age, attitude towards contraception, and such demand-side proxies as women's work status and general attitudes.[10] The results suggest that, although marital age plays the most important role in explaining why educated women have fewer children, demand for children proxies is not unimportant in this relationship. Compared with the bivariate coefficient of the effect of education on fertility, the introduction of controls for marital age and duration weakened the relationship considerably (from −0.132 to −0.076), suggesting that child-supply variables explain part, but not all, of the education–fertility relationship. The introduction of such child-demand proxies as formal-sector employment status and attitudes regarding women's role in family decisions also played an important though weaker role in determining the lower fertility of educated women. Other factors, such as women's attitudes to decisions on family size and the extent of approval of family planning, in contrast, played no more than a modest role in explaining the relationship of education to fertility.

A similar study of successive cross-sections of women in the Philippines in 1983 and 1988 finds that education had a strong, inverse relationship to cumulative and recent fertility throughout the 1980s.[11] As in the above-mentioned Karachi study, the educational differential in fertility could not be explained entirely by the consequences of schooling for age at marriage or other child-supply variables. Although the shorter marriage durations of well-educated women explained a significant portion of the education–fertility relationship, well-educated women were still estimated to have had lower fertility than less educated women, suggesting that child-supply variables were unable to explain the education–fertility relationship entirely. Again, as in Karachi, the costs of fertility regulation had little direct relationship to cumulative fertility, suggesting that it is not the costs of fertility regulation but rather the perceived costs of children and the resulting demand for children that are more important in explaining the relatively lower fertility of educated women.[12]

Few studies ask how the relative influence of the various pathways changes over the course of the fertility transition. One exception, a study of successive cross-sections of women in Tamil Nadu, India, confirms the growing influence of delayed marriage and contraception, and the declining influence of natural marital fertility, in explaining the relationship of education to fertility among women aged 35-44. At the earlier point in the transition (1970), the shift among females to the completion of primary school had a marginal positive effect on the number of children they bore (0.07). Two-thirds of the overall differential was attributed to natural fertility factors, 27 per cent to delayed marriage, and 11 per cent to increased contraception. The absence of the expected inverse relationship between women's education and fertility was explained by the unintended, fertility-enhancing effect which offset the negative effects of increased age at marriage and contraception. In contrast, 10 years later (1980), the overall effect of education on fertility had become inverse, and the principal underlying proximate pathways were delayed marriage and increased fertility control.[13]

Effects of women's work status and husband's characteristics

Multivariate analyses in a variety of settings suggest that the relationship between women's education and the number of children they bear is genuine. Although some of the effect of women's education on fertility undoubtedly occurs through other factors, such as family income, husband's occupation, and husband's education, the education of the wife has a more powerful influence on fertility than does the education of her husband or the economic status of the family.[14] For example, several studies examine the extent to which the education–fertility relationship persists even after controlling for such factors as rural–urban residence, husband's socioeconomic characteristics, and women's work-force participation. One such study examines the relationship of education to fertility using WFS data from 46 developing countries, after adjusting for husband's education, occupation and employment status, and wife's place of residence and age at marriage. Before adjustment, the wife's education was a significant determinant of reproductive behaviour in 36 of the 46 countries; after adjustment, in 21. Adjustment for these factors hardly reduced the net effect of education in sub-Saharan African countries, but reduced it by about one-third in Arab countries and by about one-half in Latin American and Asian countries (mostly in South-East Asia). In almost every country, moreover, the wife's education had a more decisive influence, after adjustment, than did the husband's characteristics.[15]

Also, a comparison of WFS and DHS data from 15 countries finds that, although the average difference between extreme categories of women's education was reduced from − 2.7 to − 1.6 children in the 1970s (WFS) and from − 2.3 to − 1.1 children in the 1980s (DHS) after adjustments were made for residence and husband's education, the net effect of women's education on fertility remained strong and significant.[16] All of these studies typically conclude that, when controls for rural–urban residence and for husband's education and occupation are introduced, the effect of women's education on fertility typically halves. The theoretical implication of these results is that the economic advantages associated with higher levels of women's education (as represented by husband's education or household economic status) cannot account in their entirety for the link between women's schooling and child-bearing. Women's education has a unique net effect on reproductive behaviour, quite independently of their husbands' education or economic status.

An important issue in the linkages of women's education, autonomy, and fertility behaviour is the extent to which it is the enhanced ability of educated women to control economic resources that leads to their lower fertility. In general, the enhanced ability to control economic resources affects a variety of intervening factors, as shown in Table 1.3. It may allow women to postpone marriage and it may provide them the resources to obtain timely medical care for sick children. Above all, it affects the demand for children, and notably it reduces the extent to which women rely on children for economic and social support, both in childhood and, especially, in the parents' old age. Moreover, educated women are more likely to be employed in remunerative activities, and these activities are less likely to be compatible with child-rearing; as a result of both these conditions, the costs of time devoted to child care are higher among educated women. Higher opportunity costs are expected to result in lower desired family size; they may also result in a postponement of marriage in some settings. By and large, studies seeking to explore these effects have measured the control of economic resources by women's current employment status or by whether they are engaged in remunerative work. The results of these studies must, however, be interpreted cautiously, because of difficulties in disentangling cause and effect and establishing causal ordering when current work status is related to fertility, which has occurred in the past. In particular, the problem of possible simultaneous relationships must be acknowledged.

The above-mentioned study using WFS data from 46 countries finds little support, however, for the argument that it is the enhanced ability of educated women to find remunerative employment which leads to their lower fertility. On the contrary, the study finds that the addition of a control for whether the wife was employed after marriage makes no difference to the effect of wife's education on fertility in any region.[17] This finding is significant. It suggests that female education does not necessarily affect reproductive behaviour through the economic consequences of a longer education, that is, by enhancing women's economic self-reliance, but through less tangible cognitive pathways.

Other studies attribute greater significance to economic opportunities for educated women as a factor mediating the relationship of women's education on fertility. For example, a recent analysis was made of DHS data from three Latin American countries at different stages in the fertility transition (Guatemala, early, with a total fertility rate of 5.6; Ecuador, middle, with a total fertility rate of 4.3; and Colombia, late, with a total fertility rate of 3.3). This multivariate analysis examines the effect of education on fertility net of husband's education and household characteristics, as well as such pathways as enhanced knowledge (as measured by mass-media exposure, knowledge of source of modern contraception and knowledge of the ovulatory cycle) and extent of control over resources (work before and after marriage), as well as contraceptive costs (proportions initiating contraception at a parity of 0 or 1), and marriage patterns (age at first union, type of union, premarital birth, or birth at ages under 18).[18] Results suggest the following:

- Except in Colombia (the low-fertility setting), a period of one to three years of education has little effect on reducing fertility in either the bivariate or the multivariate regression;
- The effect of education declines markedly when covariates are introduced; and
- Aside from economic status, important pathways through which education affects fertility are post-marital (but not premarital) work experience, the timing of the initiation of contraception, and marriage and first-birth patterns. In contrast, the knowledge of contraception or ovulation and mass-media exposure are relatively weak pathways. The size of the education coefficients is considerably weakened after controls are applied, suggesting once again that cognitive, economic, and attitudinal factors play a large role in the relationship of education to fertility. Even so, coefficients for education retain their statistical significance in the multivariate model, suggesting that the covariates included here only partially include the pathways mediating the relationship of education to fertility.

In urban Pakistan, also, there is evidence that formal-sector employment is an important factor in the relationship of education to fertility. One study concludes that, once such intervening factors as marital duration and age, formal-sector employment, attitudes of women, and family income are controlled, the originally strong relationship of education to fertility completely disappears.[19] This finding suggests, once again, that education may, in fact, operate also through these pathways in reducing fertility. Even so, marital duration and age, followed by the extent of formal-sector employment and, to a lesser extent, household income continue to be most important in explaining the lower fertility of educated women.

In short, then, few studies examine the extent to which the education–fertility relationship operates through differentials in women's autonomy. Of the various dimensions of autonomy discussed in Chapter 3, the channel studied most often is that of economic self-reliance and control over economic resources. Evidence of this link is, however, mixed. Some studies report no effect through women's work-force participation; others—mostly in more developed or urban settings—report some effect. What is almost always observed, however, is that women's education has an inverse effect on fertility independent of both their family income and their husbands' characteristics. Unfortunately, few studies, at present, would allow us to conclude that this unexplained effect operates through enhanced autonomy.

Implications

The studies reviewed here suggest that the ways in which women's education affects fertility are highly dependent upon context. In low-literacy, low-income, and gender-stratified settings, fertility is explained largely by child-supply factors. Here, especially among uneducated or modestly educated women, fertility is kept below its biological maximum largely as a result of prolonged breast-feeding and the resulting post-partum non-susceptibility. In these settings, however, breast-feeding diminishes at higher levels of schooling, suggesting the potential for a positive effect of education on fertility. It is not until a secondary education is attained in these settings that diminished breast-feeding is offset by delayed marriage and increased contraceptive use. Even so, the dominant pathway accounting for the low fertility of secondary-schooled women is delayed marriage; increased contraception plays a relatively modest role.

In contrast, in high-income, high-literacy and more egalitarian settings, the influence of post-partum non-susceptibility is muted for all women, irrespective of education. The educational level at which its effect is overpowered by other pathways becomes progressively lower as the setting becomes more developed and egalitarian. In addition, in these settings, contraception rather than delayed marriage is the more powerful fertility-inhibiting influence. The implication is that, in these settings, the conscious limitation of marital fertility plays the leading role in accounting for the lower fertility of progressively better educated women compared with uneducated women.

Less can be said about the contribution of other dimensions of women's autonomy in explaining the relationship between education and fertility. This is largely because little work has been done to distinguish the pathways in women's situation that would explain the relationship of education to fertility. What little is available has tended to examine the effect of women's workforce participation. The evidence is mixed concerning the hypothesis that some of the effect of education on fertility can be explained by the enhanced economic opportunities available to educated women.

For example, that hypothesis finds no support in a review of developing countries in the 1970s. Yet, more recent studies in more developed and urban settings find support for this pathway.

Notes

1. J. Bongaarts, 'A Framework for Analyzing the Proximate Determinants of Fertility', *Population and Development Review*, 4/1 (1978), 105–32, and 'The Fertility-Inhibiting Effects of the Intermediate Fertility Variables', *Studies in Family Planning*, 13/6–7 (1982), 179–89.
2. Easterlin and Crimmins, *Fertility Revolution*.
3. J. B. Casterline *et al.*, 'The Proximate Determinants of Fertility', *World Fertility Survey Comparative Studies Cross National Summaries*, No. 39 (Voorburg, Netherlands, International Statistical Institute, November 1984); United Nations, *Women's Education and Fertility Behaviour: Recent Evidence from the Demographic and Health Surveys*; and Oni, 'Effects of Women's Education' for Ilorin, Nigeria.
4. United Nations, *Women's Education and Fertility Behaviour: Recent Evidence from the Demographic and Health Surveys*.
5. Casterline *et al.*, 'Proximate Determinants'; United Nations, *Women's Education and Fertility Behaviour: Recent Evidence from the Demographic and Health Surveys*; Oni, 'Effects of Women's Education'. The Bongaarts model is described in Bongaarts, 'A Framework for Analyzing the Proximate Determinants of Fertility' and 'The Fertility-Inhibiting Effects of the Intermediate Fertility Variables'.
6. Easterlin and Crimmins, *Fertility Revolution*; United Nations, *Women's Education and Fertility Behaviour: A Case-study of Rural Maharashtra, India*; and Jejeebhoy, 'Women's Status and Fertility'.
7. Easterlin and Crimmins, *Fertility Revolution*.
8. United Nations, *Women's Education and Fertility Behaviour: A Case-study of Rural Maharashtra, India*.
9. Easterlin and Crimmins, *Fertility Revolution*.
10. Sathar and Mason, 'Why Female Education Affects'.
11. Raymundo *et al.*, 'Female Education'.
12. These studies have used somewhat similar techniques and measures in examining the relationship of women's education to fertility. Both studies (Sathar and Mason, 'Why Female Education Affects', and Raymundo *et al.*, 'Female Education') examine the relationship of women's education to fertility in a single equation that includes both women's education and the hypothesized intervening pathways. Both studies compare the bivariate effect of women's education on the number of children ever born to the effect after adding controls for supply, demand, and regulation/cost pathways.
13. Jejeebhoy, 'Women's Status and Fertility'. This study also employs the methodology used in Easterlin and Crimmins, *Fertility Revolution*.
14. United Nations, *Fertility Behaviour*; Cochrane, *Fertility and Education* and 'Effects of Education'; Rodriguez and Cleland, 'Socio-Economic Determinants'; Cleland and Rodriguez, 'Effect of Parental Education'; Zanamwe, 'Relationship'; and LeVine *et al.*, 'Women's Schooling'.
15. Cleland and Rodriguez, 'Effect of Parental Education'.

16. Rodriguez and Aravena, 'Socio-Economic Factors'.
17. Cleland and Rodriguez, 'Effect of Parental Education'.
18. T. Castro-Martin and F. Juarez, 'Women's Education and Fertility in Latin America: Exploring the Significance of Education for Women's Lives', paper presented at the International Population Conference (IUSSP), Montreal, 24 Aug.–1 Sept. 1993. This study uses ordinary least-squares regression with dummy variables for education levels.
19. Sathar and Mason, 'Why Female Education Affects'.

10 Summary and Conclusions

This review of literature has borne out the indisputable impact of education on women's lives. More specifically, this review has offered unambiguous, although qualified, support for the widely held belief that fertility reduction is one consequence of improvements in female education and consequent changes in women's autonomy. Support is unambiguous because in almost every known social setting, regardless of region, culture, or level of development, the best educated women bear fewer children than uneducated women do. Also, in almost every setting where it has been studied, the impact of female education on fertility is genuine; it cannot be explained by the fact that educated women marry better educated men or come from wealthier households.

Nevertheless, a modest amount of schooling does not necessarily reduce fertility in all contexts; in some contexts, education has no effect on fertility and, in others, it may even increase fertility. The thesis advanced here is that such contextual factors as the overall level of socio-economic development and the extent to which the society is male-dominated can condition the effect that small amounts of education have on women's lives, including their reproductive behaviour.

The evidence supports the suggestion that the situation of women in a society's traditional kinship structure conditions the variations in both the pace of educational expansion and the resulting changes in reproductive attitudes and behaviours.[1] For example, in highly literate and high-income countries and in settings in which there is more gender equality, straight inverse relationships are observed between education and fertility. In lesser developed and more gender-stratified settings, the overall relationship of women's education to fertility is not always linear and inverse. Although the impact of female education on fertility is stronger than that of either male education or household socio-economic characteristics in almost every setting, in less developed and highly gender-stratified settings, a small amount of education tends to increase fertility or has little effect on it. Further increases in education in these settings, however, are almost always associated with fertility declines. There appears to be a threshold level of education beyond which marked negative differentials in fertility are generated; the highest thresholds exist in the least developed societies. Only among more developed societies does the threshold often drop to the lowest level of schooling.

There also is evidence that this kind of non-linear relationship is not static. It changes, with time and the level of development, from curvilinear to inverse and from sharply inverse to moderately inverse.

Women's Education and Pathways to Fertility

The model developed in Table 1.3 traces the channels of influence between women's education and fertility, permitting an explanation of why education affects fertility differently in different settings. That model rests on the assumption that education affects fertility not directly but indirectly, through a variety of intervening variables. These variables, in turn, have a direct impact on fertility.

Fertility itself is the immediate outcome of three sets of factors:
- Those relating to the number of births a woman would have if no deliberate attempt were made to control fertility;
- A woman's demand for children or her family-size desires (and the motives underlying these); and
- The economic, time, and attitudinal costs of the means of fertility regulation.

These factors jointly determine whether and when women undertake deliberate fertility regulation.

Each of these immediate determinants of fertility is influenced by a number of factors relating to women's situation that are, in turn, affected by education: knowledge, decision-making power, freedom of movement and confidence in interacting with the outside world, emotional autonomy and closeness to husband and children, as well as economic and social autonomy and self-reliance.

The model also rests on the assumption that education can either increase or decrease fertility. It will increase fertility if the effects of shorter durations of both breast-feeding and post-partum sexual abstinence outweigh the effects of delayed marriage, smaller family-size desires, and increased contraception. Moreover, the balance between these opposing forces can shift from one educational level to another. Given the multiple pathways through which education affects fertility, it is hardly surprising that women with modest amounts of schooling may have as many children as uneducated women do.

Earlier chapters have described in detail the relationship of women's education to various intervening pathways affecting fertility; in particular, they have examined how education is related to other dimensions of women's autonomy, what patterns exist in the relationship of education to fertility, and how much education is required before sustained changes occur in the intervening pathways and, ultimately, in fertility.

In general, the literature supports the hypothesis that education enhances women's knowledge, decision-making power, confidence in interacting with the outside world, closeness to husband and children, and economic and social self-reliance. These effects of education are, however, by no means uniform across regions, cultures, or levels of development. In highly gender-stratified settings, the autonomy of women may be enhanced only after relatively high levels of education have been attained. In more egalitarian settings, thresholds are less regularly observed. These findings bear out other conclusions of this review suggesting that, in many settings, the familiar negative effect of education on fertility is observed only after moderate levels of education have been attained.

A look at the literature suggests little or no variation in the effect of a secondary education on fertility or its proximate determinants. In almost every setting, women with secondary schooling have fewer children than uneducated women do. Correspondingly, they marry later, breast-feed for shorter durations, are less likely to adhere to traditional abstinence taboos, and their children experience lower early childhood mortality; also, secondary-schooled women want fewer children and are more likely to practise contraception than are uneducated women.

Much more variable than the impact of secondary schooling on women's reproductive behaviour is the impact of a small amount of education on fertility. The impact of small amounts of education (lower or upper primary) on many of the proximate determinants of fertility and on women's autonomy also varies. For example, the literature suggests that, in highly gender-stratified settings, aspects of women's autonomy, such as their decision-making authority or social and economic self-reliance, remain modest until relatively high levels of education have been attained. A small amount of education does little more than grant women decision-making authority over domains considered unimportant to the family's honour or economic status. Such domains include the duration of breast-feeding or abstinence or child health care, which may have positive or negligible repercussions on fertility. In these gender-stratified settings, women must have considerable education before they have a say in the more important family decisions—whom and when to marry, how to utilize household resources, whether to work, and so on—which are more likely to have fertility-inhibiting consequences.

Nor are economic realities any different for modestly educated women as compared with uneducated women; consequently, modestly educated women are not necessarily more socially or economically self-reliant. Nor are they less dependent on children both for supporting them in old age and for legitimizing their positions in their husbands' homes. Although modestly educated women are aware of fertility regulation in general, better educated women are considerably more likely to have in-depth information on the range of available methods—and on how to use them correctly, on what their side-effects are, and on where they can be obtained. Similarly, well-educated women are considerably more likely to communicate with their husbands on family size and family planning than are uneducated or poorly educated women. Correspondingly, in those settings where women's freedom of movement is severely curtailed, it takes more than a few years of schooling for women to overcome these constraints and attain the physical autonomy necessary to get access to contraception.

In more egalitarian settings, in contrast, modestly educated women appear to have considerably more autonomy than uneducated women do. In these settings, for example, even women with a small amount of education are more likely than uneducated women to have access to economic opportunities and earnings. So also, modestly educated women are more likely to have control over household resources and have more of a say in household decisions than uneducated women are. In egalitarian settings, unlike gender-stratified settings, the behaviour of women irrespective of their level of education is less likely to be controlled by extended kin, and particularly the senior generation. Moderately educated women may also be more likely than uneducated women to have more labour-intensive child-rearing aspirations.[2] The combination of these forces may lead moderately educated women in these settings to settle for fewer children than uneducated women do.

Table 10.1 highlights the findings of earlier chapters concerning the existence of thresholds in intervening variables that affect fertility. The table presents the number of years of education required to generate a 10 per cent or greater change in each intervening pathway as observed in the modal number of studies reported in earlier chapters. The results suggest the following:

- It takes more years of schooling to generate changes in some pathways than others;
- For certain intervening variables, threshold levels of education tend to fall with a rise in the overall level of per capita income, female literacy, or gender disparity in literacy;
- At the same time, for several of the intervening variables, differentials between women with seven or more years of schooling and uneducated women widen as the context becomes more developed and egalitarian (not shown in Table 10.1).

With regard to thresholds, these findings support the thesis that, in more egalitarian and more developed settings, even small amounts of female education are sufficient to trigger changes both in women's autonomy and in the fertility-inhibiting proximate determinants of fertility. In contrast, in gender-stratified and less developed contexts, a few years of schooling are relatively ineffectual. But schooling produces a more profound change in the behaviour of those with seven or more years of schooling in more developed and egalitarian settings than in others.

The first four variables in Table 10.1 are the major factors affecting the supply of children. For three of these four variables—child mortality, the duration of breast-feeding, and, less consistently, the duration of post-partum abstinence—the threshold levels of women's education are low. In other words, it takes only a small amount of education to affect fertility via these variables. In almost every setting of the developing world, even schooling of a year or two is sufficient to generate improvements of 10 per cent or more in child mortality. This low threshold is consistent with the findings of Chapter 3, that even a few years of education enhance women's knowledge of good health practices. Schooling of between one and six years is sufficient to generate declines of 10 per cent or more in the duration of breast-feeding and the duration of post-partum abstinence. As indicated in Chapters 5 and 6, even a small amount of education enhances women's decision-making authority with regard to decisions on child health and durations of breast-feeding or abstinence (in settings of prolonged post-partum abstinence norms). Thus, a small amount of education may be sufficient to affect the supply of children (through improved child mortality to a decline in fertility; through reduced breast-feeding and abstinence durations to an increase in the pace of child-bearing), and these effects may exist at almost every level of income, literacy, and gender disparity in literacy. Even so, women with seven or more years of schooling tend, on average, to experience considerably lower infant mortality and shorter durations of breast-

Table 10.1. *Summary of relationship of women's education to intervening variables affecting fertility, by region, level of development, and gender disparity in literacy*

Summary of thresholds (years of schooling) by which a 10 per cent or greater change takes place in the intervening variable:

	Age at marriage	Duration of breast-feeding	Duration of post-partum abstinence	Early childhood mortality	Desired family size	Contraceptive use	Contraceptive knowledge
A. Region [a]							
Sub-Saharan Africa	7+	4–6	1–6	1–3	4–6	7+	1–3
North Africa and the Middle East	4–6, 7+	1–3	4–6, N	1–3	1–3	1–3	N
East and South-East Asia	7+	1–3	1–6	1–3	7+	1–3	N
South Asia	7+	1–3	4–6, N	1–3	4–6, 7+	1–3, 4–6	N
Latin America and the Caribbean	7+	1–3	1–6, N	1–3	4–6	1–3	1–3
B. Level of development							
1. Annual per capita income ($)							
500 or less	7+	1–3	1–6	1–3	4–6	7+	1–3
500–999	7+	1–3, 4–6	1–3	1–3	1–3, 4–6, 7+	1–3	1–3
1000 or more	7+	1–3	N	1–3	1–6	1–3	N
2. Overall female literacy rate (%)							
40 or less	7+	1–3, 4–6	4–6	1–3	4–6	7+	1–3
41–80	7+	1–3	1–6	1–3	4–6	1–3	1–3
81 or more	7+	4–6	1–6	1–3	4–6	4–6	N
C. Gender disparity in literacy [b]							
250–700	7+	1–3, 4–6	4–6	1–3	4–6	7+	1–3
701–850	7+	1–3	N	1–3	1–3	1–3	1–3
851 or more	7+	1–3	1–6	1–3	4–6	1–3	N
TOTALS	7+	1–3	1–6	1–3	4–6	1–3, 7+	1–3, N

[a] Not all countries in a region are included, and those included are not necessarily representative of the region but are, rather, those countries for which the requisite data are available. Thus, the results are not necessarily representative of any particular region.

[b] The level of gender disparity in literacy is the number of literate females per 1000 literate males.

Note: N=A 10 per cent change is not seen at levels 1–3, 4–6, or 7+ for the modal number of studies.

Sources: The years of education required to generate a 10 per cent change represent the level reported in the modal number of studies in Tables 4.3, 5.3, 5.6, 6.3, 7.3, 8.3, and 8.6.

feeding than uneducated women do in settings that are more developed and egalitarian than in other settings.

Another major variable affecting the supply of children is age at marriage. For this variable, the threshold level of women's education is consistently high. As Table 10.1 shows, it takes at least seven years of schooling before women's age at marriage rises, on average, by 10 per cent or more in most studies. Again, as with the other child-supply variables, thresholds are similar across all settings, and differentials now appear to be wider in the lesser developed and inegalitarian settings than in others. This result, too, is consistent with the evidence in Chapter 3 on the relationship of women's education to their decision-making autonomy and economic and social self-reliance. For example, in gender-stratified settings, it requires a considerable education before women participate in decisions considered critical to the family unit—and decisions pertaining to marriage remain important for family honour. As a result, moderately educated women in gender-stratified settings tend to have little say in deciding when and whom they marry; those with a secondary education exercise greater veto power in marriage choices.

Also, the enhanced economic self-reliance that accompanies a secondary education is shown to delay marriages in gender-stratified settings for two reasons: parental dependence on well-educated daughters who are employed and the difficulty parents face in finding a suitable match and acquiring the required dowry for educated daughters. In more developed and more egalitarian settings, where marital age tends to be high in general, the high threshold can be attributed partly to the delay in marriage that secondary-schooled women themselves impose in pursuit of a compatible spouse or of accumulated savings for the future and partly to the fact that uneducated women in these settings already marry at a relatively late age.

For desired family size and contraceptive practice, educational thresholds occur at an intermediate level in the modal number of studies. The threshold levels for these variables, unlike child-supply variables, tend to be sensitive to context.

- For example, in the least literate, poorest, and most inegalitarian settings, a 10 per cent or greater decline in desired family size is observed when women attain four to six years of schooling;
- In the most literate, high-income, and egalitarian settings, the decline in desired family size is observed at somewhat lower levels of schooling;
- Moreover, although the differential for the modal number of studies in the family-size desires of women with seven or more years of schooling and uneducated women is in the range of 21–30 per cent in less developed and inegalitarian settings, it is usually wider as the settings become more developed and egalitarian.

Even more striking is the variation in the effect of education on contraceptive practice. It takes as many as seven or more years of schooling to produce a 10 per cent increase in contraceptive use in the least literate, poorest, and most inegalitarian settings, whereas it takes only one to three years of schooling to produce this effect in the highest income and most egalitarian settings. Again, there is a consistent widening of differentials as the context becomes more developed and egalitarian.

Consistent with these patterns, thresholds are highest and differentials narrowest in studies in the two poorest regions of the developing world.

- In sub-Saharan Africa and South Asia, a 10 per cent increase in contraceptive use occurs only when women reach the secondary or upper-primary level of education, respectively—much higher thresholds than are found in other regions.

These patterns correspond with the evidence on the relationship of education to women's decision-making autonomy. That evidence suggests that the degree of gender stratification in families appears to condition both the domains over which educated women make decisions and the amount of education necessary before women can make independent decisions.

In sum, at low levels of development and in more gender-stratified settings, the main fertility-related effect of a few years of formal education is apparently to erode traditional checks on fertility and, thereby, to increase fertility. In contrast, at higher levels of development, the main effect of education is to decrease fertility by raising the age at marriage, reducing the desire for children, and increasing the practice of contraception. In more egalitarian settings, educational thresholds for both fertility-enhancing and fertility-inhibiting intervening variables occur at a lower level. Because the effects of the fertility-inhibiting intervening variables are stronger, education shows a uniformly inverse relationship to fertility in these settings.

What does all this mean in terms of the role of women's education in accounting for fertility differentials? Several authors have addressed this question. Some have argued that a small amount of education is more likely to change attitudes and aspirations than economic realities.[3] Along the same lines, others have argued that, at least in South Asia, modestly educated women initially attain autonomy over limited, non-economic aspects of their lives, such as in areas relating to child care, breast-feeding, and sexual abstinence, rather than over decisions considered vital for the family's honour or economic status.[4] Other things being equal, modest increases in women's autonomy are unlikely to change women's demand for children or, if they do, are unlikely to translate into deliberate fertility control. Because of this, the expected linear negative effect of education on fertility is unlikely to occur in these settings. Rather, education is likely to lead to shorter periods of post-partum non-susceptibility and, only at higher levels, delayed marriage and, to a lesser extent, contraception. The result is thus a curvilinear or moderately negative relationship of education to fertility.

When women become more secure economically and their decision-making authority becomes more comprehensive, the effects of education on fertility are important because they lower desired family size and increase contraceptive use. The conditions under which this occurs vary. They appear to be especially sensitive to the extent to which the traditional kinship system allows women to have economic and other forms of self-reliance. For this reason, several authors hypothesize that, although the relationship of women's education to family formation in sub-Saharan

Africa or Pakistan is similar to that in East and South-East Asia and Latin America, the amount of education required to effect a change in fertility in these lesser developed settings is likely to be higher.[5] These conclusions are consistent with the suggestion that the status of women in any given society affects the pace at which mass educational efforts will have an effect on fertility.[6] Where women can exercise autonomy over family decisions and economics, as in parts of South-East Asia and Latin America, for example, even a little education may have a dampening effect on fertility. Where the traditional kinship structure assigns less autonomy to women, as in South Asia and parts of sub-Saharan Africa, high levels of education may be necessary to affect family-size preferences and contraception.

It might be argued, therefore, that, in highly gender-stratified settings, the effect of primary schooling acts mainly to provide women with a limited autonomy. This autonomy results, on the one hand, in a loosening of traditional checks on fertility and, on the other hand, in improved early childhood survival, which prolongs birth intervals and reduces the natural pace of child-bearing.

Among better educated women, education tends to reduce fertility largely as a result of delayed marriage and contraception. It is only at higher levels of education that child-demand factors and contraception come into play. Now, the strength of delayed marriage and weaker motives for having large numbers of children serve to offset pro-fertility effects, such as reduced breast-feeding. They also explain why there is a more sharply inverse relationship between education and fertility.

The scenario suggested by the above sequence is consistent with the evidence on the relationship of women's education to other dimensions of women's autonomy. In highly stratified settings, such dimensions of the autonomy of women as their decision-making authority and social and economic self-reliance are not enhanced until relatively high levels of education have been attained. In such settings, poorly educated women tend to have little say in deciding on when and whom they marry; nor have the economic realities changed for moderately educated women in a way that would enhance their self-reliance and reduce their dependence on children (or sons) for obtaining old-age support and for legitimizing their positions in their husbands' homes and, hence, reducing the number of children they want.

In more egalitarian settings, even modestly educated women have a considerable say in important family decisions, as is evident in Latin America.[7] In more egalitarian settings, where even moderately educated women are likely to make important family decisions, a few years of education are sufficient to change economic realities for women and to enhance women's work-force participation and control over earnings. In such settings, declines in family-size desires and increases in contraception occur simultaneously with (or slightly earlier than) changes in fertility-enhancing factors, thereby resulting in the overall inverse effect of women's education on fertility.

The results of this review clearly suggest that the impact of women's education on their fertility is greatest when education offers women an expanded role in family decisions and control over, or access to, resources. Where women's role in family affairs is limited to deciding on her breast-feeding behaviour, or on the treatment of sick children, or even veto rights over prospective husbands, education is unlikely to have a strong impact on fertility. When the economic realities start to change, that is, when education provides women with decision-making authority in a broader realm and greater control over and access to family resources, fertility is likely to turn sharply downward.

The results of this review also suggest that, in most settings, the wife's education tends to have a stronger effect on fertility than does the husband's education. This finding is consistent with the idea that it is women's situation and autonomy, rather than their socio-economic status or the tendency of educated women to marry high-status men, that influence their reproductive behaviour most strongly.[8]

These findings point to the possibility that it is by enhancing aspects of their autonomy that women's education produces the familiar negative effect on the number of children they bear. Thus far, however, hard evidence on the links of education to fertility through various dimensions of women's autonomy is lacking. For example, the evidence on whether a wife's economic activity could explain the relationship between her schooling and her fertility is inconclusive.

Implications for Policy

Several policy conclusions emerge from this review. Above all, the results argue strongly for sustained investment in women's education, specifically for ensuring universal primary-school enrolment and, more important, attendance—a minimum of six or seven years—for girls. The advantages of educating women beyond five or six years are manifold—education enhances women's autonomy and their social and economic self-reliance, improves child survival and family health, and also leads to lower fertility, higher age at marriage, lower family-size desires, and fewer chances of unwanted fertility.

Nonetheless, the results of this study also suggest that education cannot be expected to reduce fertility in all settings. In particular, in the least literate and poorest settings and in highly gender-stratified settings, it appears that a few years of schooling can lead to negligible changes or even to modest increases in fertility. As women receive more than a few years of schooling, however, the impact on fertility of delayed age at marriage and increased contraception almost always counterbalances the fertility-enhancing effects of shorter durations of post-partum infecundability, which a modest amount of education produces.

These patterns raise at least four policy issues. First, the developing world has come a long way in ensuring almost universal primary-school enrolment for girls; it is now time to ensure universal primary-school attendance and universal primary-school completion among girls—a policy with enormous implications both for improving women's lives and for offsetting the inadvertent fertility-enhancing effects of modest amounts of education. Innovative and culturally sensitive strategies to expand the exposure of girls to education and to invest more in the schooling of girls are urgently needed.

Second, the evidence suggests that education enhances the autonomy of women, or empowers women, in many spheres—in terms of knowledge, decision-making, control over economic and other household resources, interaction with the outside world, and intimacy within the conjugal family. These aspects of autonomy not only enhance women's well-being but also bear on decisions relating to reproduction. However, the full impact of these changes is usually felt only among women who have crossed a certain threshold of education. Programmes and strategies designed to enhance the autonomy of, or to empower, poorly educated women are, therefore, as important for female well-being as are strategies to enhance their education. Programmes and strategies that provide women with opportunities to develop skills, gain access to and control over economic resources, and become agents of change for themselves and their families and communities may, at the same time, reduce the time lag between inadvertent fertility-enhancing trends and compensatory trends in contraception and nuptiality and, thereby, affect fertility.

Third, it should be accepted that overall development and exposure to new ideas inevitably lead to the abandonment of traditional behaviours. Hence, it should be expected that all societies will experience such changes at early points in their development, just as has occurred at early stages of education. The appropriate policy would be the initiation of measures to minimize the time lag between factors increasing fertility and the countervailing forces offsetting those factors. Greater investments in education could well be used to minimize this lag.

Fourth, the global increase in literacy and enrolment rates means that, although poorly educated women will constitute the majority of the female population in much of the developing world, the proportion of uneducated women will continue to decline. Some decline in fertility can be anticipated as a result of this change. In addition, however, rapid fertility decline will depend upon changes in the behaviour of less educated women. Poorly educated women in almost every setting have higher fertility and family-size preferences—as well as more unwanted fertility and a greater unmet need for contraception—than well-educated women. Education, and particularly more than five or six years of education, is essential for placing women at a relative advantage in obtaining access to high-quality health or contraceptive services. This is especially so in settings in which accessibility or quality of health and contraceptive services is limited. Reducing obstacles to service accessibility and quality may, thus, have a direct effect on improving contraceptive usage and overall health. Similarly, reducing obstacles to primary-school attendance of girls or increasing access to income-generation opportunities for women may well improve the use of education and other services by uneducated rural women, which may, itself, have implications for reproductive behaviour. What is required, then, is the establishment of programmes that help uneducated women overcome difficulties in gaining access to health and contraceptive services, as well as other educational, economic, and social services to which they are theoretically entitled but, in practice, frequently denied.

Research Needs

This review has pointed to a variety of explanations of how schooling influences reproductive behaviour. These explanations need to be empirically examined in diverse cultural and developmental settings. More measures of women's autonomy and gender-role attitudes need to be included in analyses of education and fertility in developing countries. A wide range of proximate and intervening variables, and perhaps more rigorously defined variables, need to be included in analyses of women's education and fertility. For example, little evidence has been amassed on the relationship of women's education to abortion and the consequences of this for women's health and fertility. Given the importance of education in influencing reproductive behaviour, an understanding of the full range of impacts that women's schooling may have on their status as well as their reproductive behaviour is an important task for future research.

This review has found that, whereas secondary-schooled women in almost every setting have fewer children than have uneducated women, the effect of modest amounts of education is highly variable and context-specific. Region, income, literacy levels, and the extent of gender stratification are all conditions influencing the effect of small amounts of schooling on reproductive behaviour. In these circumstances, an understanding of the thresholds for fertility and its immediate determinants will help illuminate the short- and long-term consequences of education. Equally important is research on why this conditioning effect of context on the education-fertility relationship exists. Why, for example, is a primary-schooled woman more autonomous in a high-income or more egalitarian setting than in a poor or less egalitarian setting? Is it that there is likely to be a greater range of income-generating opportunities in the former than in the latter setting or that, for example, women in the former setting are freer of parental controls?

Related to this is the need for distinguishing the relative strengths of the mechanisms through which education affects fertility. Earlier chapters have identified various dimensions of women's autonomy—knowledge, decision-making, physical autonomy in interacting with the outside world, greater intimacy between spouses, economic and social autonomy, and control over economic resources. How important is each in explaining the education-fertility relationship?

This review has been constrained by the lack of research on a number of critical aspects of education and their possible linkages to reproductive behaviour. The first is that, for the most part, studies have measured education in terms of the number of years of formal schooling a woman has attained; information on the type and content of education is generally non-existent. Yet, the influence of secular education on fertility may be altogether different from that of Koranic or Catholic education, and that of private education may be different from public. Similarly, the content of education, not just the number of years of schooling, may influence reproductive behaviour. In addition, the possible influence of adult education, as compared with formal schooling of children, on women's lives and on their fertility needs to be explored.

This review reiterates the widely held view that education is important for women's lives in many ways—within and outside the home, and with regard to their autonomy and their reproductive behaviour. It argues strongly not only for universal primary-school enrolment among females but also for universal completion of at least a primary education among them. The evidence suggests that, even in the poorest and most highly gender-stratified settings, more than five or six years of education would enable women to enhance their interaction with the outside world, their decision-making authority in the home, and their overall knowledge and exposure to the outside world. In many settings, a secondary education also enhances women's social and economic independence. These changes are critical in enhancing women's reproductive choices, changing reproductive behaviour, and reducing fertility. From a policy standpoint, the close association between female education and well-being, including enhanced autonomy, improved family health and child survival, greater reproductive choices, and lower fertility, are strong enough to warrant sustained government investment in female education.

Notes

1. Mason, 'Impact of Women's Position'; Cleland and Rodriguez, 'Effect of Parental Education'.
2. LeVine *et al.*, 'Women's Schooling'.
3. J. Cleland and C. Wilson, 'Demand Theories of the Fertility Transition: An Iconoclastic View', *Population Studies,* 41/1 (1987), 5–30.
4. J. C. Caldwell, Reddy, and P. Caldwell, 'The Causes of Demographic Change in Rural South India'.
5. Kritz and Gurak, 'Women's Status'; Sathar and Kazi, 'Women, Work and Reproduction'.
6. Mason, 'Impact of Women's Position'.
7. LeVine *et al.*, 'Women's Schooling'.
8. Cochrane, *Fertility and Education* and 'Effects of Education'; Cleland and Rodriguez, 'Effect of Parental Education'.

Appendices

Introduction

Information in the appendices is presented by major region of the developing world: sub-Saharan Africa, North Africa and the Middle East, East and South-East Asia, South Asia, and Latin America and the Caribbean. The countries included are not necessarily representative of the region; they have been included because pertinent studies are available. Because of the paucity of data in North Africa and the Middle East, for example, only studies in more developed countries are represented. A country is represented more than once in an appendix if data are available for more than one time in that country. National rather than subnational relationships are reported in most cases. For large countries, such as India and Nigeria, subnational relationships are also reported and, in some cases, a rural or urban relationship is shown.

For each country, information is provided on the author and reference date of the survey, sample type and size, and the education measure employed. In Appendices A and C–K, all but one of which show studies included in the text tables, two measures of development for the country overall are also provided: levels of per capita income and of female literacy. One measure of gender disparity is included, for literacy (literate females per 1000 literate males), approximately at the date of the survey. If data on per capita income or literacy rates were unavailable for the same year as the survey, they were drawn from the closest available series.

An attempt has been made to include as wide a range of studies as possible. Most of these studies, however, rely on the data generated in the World Fertility Survey (WFS) and the more recent Demographic and Health Survey (DHS). Data from the WFS have been published in United Nations, *Fertility Behaviour in the Context of Development: Evidence from the World Fertility Survey*. Data from the DHS have been published in various DHS final reports and United Nations, *Women's Education and Fertility Behaviour: Recent Evidence from Demographic and Health Surveys*.

So that data reported in the studies included in appendix tables are comparable, educational categories, presented in a variety of ways, have sometimes required regrouping. First, in several studies, data for women with 1–3 and 4–6 years of schooling have been combined; in such cases, data reported for women with 1–6 years of schooling are shown in the column headed '1–3', since it is assumed that the majority fall into this category. Second, in the majority of studies, rates are provided for women with 7 or more years of schooling; in some cases, however, rates have been provided separately for women with 7–9 and 10 or more years of school. In such cases, rates have been recalculated for all women with 7 or more years of schooling; at the same time, the reported data for women with 10 or more years of schooling are also provided.

Appendix A

Appendix A shows the mean number of children ever born to all women and to uneducated women, the percentage difference between the mean number of children ever born to uneducated women and to women at each progressively higher level of education reported, and the direction of the relationship of women's education to fertility. Unless otherwise specified, all the studies reported in Appendix A have an age or marital-duration control.

Appendix B

Appendix B reports the results of some multivariate studies that aim at showing the net effect of women's education, once socio-economic and other variables are controlled. All the studies reported in Appendix B have an age or marital-duration control. Studies are included that (a) consider education as a continuous variable and indicate the effect of a unit increase in years of education and (b) consider education as a dummy variable and examine the relative effects of attaining progressively higher levels of education. Other variables included in the analysis are also indicated, along with their significance levels.

Appendix C

Most of the studies listed in Appendix C report the singulate mean age at marriage or a mean or median age at marriage; a few report the percentages of women who were single at selected ages or the duration of marriage. From cross-tabular studies and those that use multiple classification analysis, Appendix C also reports the age at marriage for all women and for uneducated women and the percentage difference between the marital age of uneducated women and of women at each successively higher level of education. For multivariate studies, the beta coefficients for education and the level of statistical significance are provided.

Two distinct patterns are reported in the shape of the relationship: a positive relationship and a reversed-7 relationship, in which the difference between women with a small amount of education and uneducated women is negligible (less than 5 per cent), whereas substantial increases are recorded for women who are better educated. In addition, a few studies report irregular, zero, or reversed-U-shaped relationships (see list of abbreviations and definitions, n. 2, below, for definitions of these relationships).

Appendices D and E

Most of the studies that document the relationship of female education to such natural fertility factors as the duration of breast-feeding and the duration of post-partum abstinence and post-partum amenorrhoea present reported durations from women's recent reproductive histories and refer to behaviour up to approximately three, four, or five years before the surveys. Many studies present results in the form of medians or means; some use multivariate techniques. From cross-tabular studies and those using multiple classification analysis, Appendix D reports mean values of durations of breast-feeding, and Appendix E, mean durations of post-partum abstinence and amenorrhoea for all women and uneducated women and the percentage differences between the breast-feeding durations of uneducated women and those at successively higher levels of education. In addition, for multivariate studies, beta coefficients and levels of significance are indicated.

Appendices F and G

Appendices F and G summarize the results of a number of studies substantiating the relationship of women's education to infant and child mortality. Mean levels of mortality for the total population and among uneducated women are provided, along with differentials in mortality between uneducated women and those with successively higher levels of schooling. For multivariate studies, beta coefficients and levels of significance are noted.

Appendix H

Two basic patterns in the direction of the relationships of women's education to desired family size are distinguished: inverse and the 7-shaped relationship, in which the difference in desired family size between women with a small amount of education and those with none is negligible (under 5 per cent), whereas substantial differentials are recorded for better educated women. For cross-tabular studies, Appendix H reports mean values of desired family size for all women and for uneducated women, as well as differentials in family-size desires of uneducated women compared with those with successively higher levels of education. For studies using multivariate analyses, beta coefficients and levels of significance are noted.

Appendix I

Many studies find a positive relationship between women's education and contraceptive use. Because contraceptive use depends to a large extent on a woman's age and duration of marriage, the education–contraception relationship should ideally be viewed with these factors controlled. Because net effects are unavailable, however, Appendix I also includes the results of studies that do not control for covarying factors. Because better educated women tend to be younger on average and, hence, have been married for shorter durations than other women, and because contraceptive use tends to rise with parity and, hence, with marriage duration, the effect of omitting a control for age or marriage duration is to provide a conservative estimate of the relationship. If anything, the net effects of education on contraceptive use should be stronger than the zero-order effects shown in the appendix.

From household-level studies, Appendix I reports mean values of proportions using contraception for all women and for uneducated women, and differentials in proportions practising contraception between uneducated women and those with successively higher levels of education. For multivariate studies, beta coefficients and levels of significance are noted.

Appendix J

Appendix J, which summarizes the studies addressing the relationship of women's education to the proportions of women expressing an unmet need for contraception, is drawn almost entirely from C. Westoff and R. H. Ochoa's (1991) analysis of DHS data, except for estimates for India, based on a large national survey (Operations Research Group, 1990); for Ecuador, based on a national survey (Monteith *et al.*, 1992); and for Mexico, based on R. M. Cordova's analysis of the DHS (1991). Appendix J reports mean values of proportions expressing an unmet need for contraception separately for all women and for the uneducated, differentials between proportions using contraception among uneducated women and those with successively higher levels of education, and the direction of the relationship.

Appendix K

There is ample evidence of the link between education and contraceptive knowledge. Most studies that examine this relationship, however, measure awareness as the proportion of women who know about one or more methods of contraception, rather than a more discriminating measure, such as the number of methods known or proportions having in-depth knowledge of methods and how to obtain or use them. The use of measures of minimal knowledge is likely to generate the most conservative differentials by education, because knowledge of at least one method has become fairly universal across the developing world. This is so even in countries in which contraceptive prevalence rates are low, as indicated in Appendix K. Even with measures of minimal knowledge, the effect of education is uniformly positive in most of the studies summarized in Appendix K.

Appendix L

Appendix L presents the relative contributions of each proximate determinant to the percentage reduction in potential fertility for a large number of countries for which Bongaarts indices are available at each level of women's schooling. The Bongaarts model is described in J. Bongaarts, 'A Framework for Analyzing the Proximate Determinants of Fertility' (1978) and 'The Fertility-Inhibiting Effects of the Intermediate Fertility Variables' (1982).

Since the Bongaarts model has been used in all the studies reported in Appendix L, a word about this model is appropriate. Also described below is the procedure laid out by J. B. Casterline *et al.* ('The Proximate Determinants of Fertility' (1984)) to obtain the relative contributions of each proximate determinant to the percentage reduction in potential fertility.

The Bongaarts model is a multiplicative model that expresses the actual level of fertility (TFR) as a function of the fertility-reducing effects of the proximate determinants on a hypothetical biological maximum. In this model,

$$TFR = Cm \times Cc \times Ca \times Ci \times TF \qquad (1)$$

where Cm is the index of marriage, Cc the index of contraception, Ca the index of abortion (studied relatively infrequently due to the paucity of reliable data), and Ci the index of lactational infecundability. The total fecundity rate (TF) reflects a hypothetical maximum for each population subgroup, assuming that marriage occurs at puberty and that contraception, breast-feeding, and abortion do not occur. The indices used in the model have a theoretical range from 0.0 to 1.0, with a value of 1.0 indicating that the specified determinant has no fertility-inhibiting effect and a value of 0.0 indicating an absolute effect. Thus, for example, a value of Cc = 0.80 implies that contraception accounts for a 20 per cent reduction in fertility below its maximum potential.

The advantage of the Bongaarts model is that it allows the measurement of relative effects and, thus, the assessment of the relative contribution of each of the indices to fertility, or the percentage of overall reduction from the total fecundity rate to the observed TFR that is due to each intervening pathway. The methodology employed here, used by Casterline *et al.*, involves a simple decomposition of the difference between potential and observed fertility. Using a logarithmic transformation, Casterline *et al.* express the Bongaarts model as:

$$\ln(TF) - \ln(TFR) = - \{\ln(Ci) + \ln(Cc) + \ln(Cm)\} \qquad (2)$$

The contribution of each pathway to the reduction of fertility from TF to TFR is, for example, for Ci:

$$100 \times \ln(Ci)/\{\ln(Ci) + \ln(Cc) + \ln(Cm)\} \qquad (3)$$

The percentage contributions calculated thus add to 100, the relative size of each index directly reflecting its relative importance. The calculation of percentage contributions is a form of standardization; absolute fertility levels and the differences between TF and TFR do not enter in.

In Appendix L, the indices Cc, Ci, and Cm reported for various countries (United Nations (1995), Oni (1985), and Casterline *et al.* (1984)) have been converted, using the above methodology, into the percentage of overall reduction from the total fecundity rate to the observed TFR that is due to each intervening pathway. As in other appendices, information in Appendix L is provided by major region of the developing world; a country is represented more than once if data are available for more than one time. For each study, information is provided on the author, site, reference date, and the reported effect through each pathway.

Abbreviations and Definitions Used in Appendices

1. Under the columns headed 'Levels of', the abbreviations L, M, and H stand for 'Low', 'Medium', and 'High', defined as follows:

Per capita income: L = $500 or less; M = $501–999; H = $1000 +

Female literacy rate: L = 40% or less; M = 41–80%; H = 81% or more

The abbreviations N, M, W under the column headed 'Gender disparity in literacy' stand for 'Narrow', 'Medium', and 'Wide', defined as follows:

Number of literate women per 1000 literate men: N = 851 or more; M = 701–850; W = 250–700

United Nations sources were used to classify country levels of per capita income, female literacy rate, and gender disparity in literacy.

2. Under the column headed 'Direction of relationship', the following patterns are distinguished:

7	The difference between moderately educated (those with less than some secondary education) and uneducated women is less than 5 per cent, followed by declines (exceeding 5 per cent) among better educated women
Reversed 7	The difference between moderately educated (those with less than some secondary education) and uneducated women is less than 5 per cent, followed by increases of 5 per cent or more among better educated women
U	Moderately educated women (those with less than some secondary schooling) experience rates that are more than 5 per cent lower than rates for both uneducated and better educated women; uneducated women and women with secondary school education have virtually identical rates (within 5 per cent)
Reversed U	Moderately educated women (those with less than some secondary schooling) experience rates that are more than 5 per cent higher than rates for both uneducated and better educated women; uneducated women and women with secondary-school education have virtually identical rates (within 5 per cent)
J	Moderately educated women (those with less than some secondary schooling) experience rates that are more than 5

	per cent lower than rates for both uneducated and better educated women; secondary-schooled women have considerably lower rates (by more than 5 per cent) than both uneducated and moderately educated women
Reversed J	Moderately educated women (those with less than some secondary schooling) experience rates that are more than 5 per cent higher than rates for both uneducated and better educated women; secondary-schooled women have considerably lower rates (by more than 5 per cent) than the rates of both uneducated and moderately educated women
– (Negative/Inverse)	Better educated women experience progressively lower rates than uneducated and moderately educated women do (the difference between even moderately educated and uneducated women is more than 5 per cent)
+ (Positive)	Better educated women experience progressively higher rates than uneducated and moderately educated women do (by 5 per cent or more)
0	The difference between uneducated women and women with all levels of education is less than 5 per cent.
Irreg.[ular]	No clear pattern emerges.

3. The following abbreviations are used throughout appendices:

AAM	Age at marriage
BA	Bachelor of Arts degree
Ca	Index of abortion (Bongaarts index)
CAFN1	Changing African Family, Nigeria 1 (Project)
Cc	Index of contraception (Bongaarts index)
CEB	Children ever born
Ci	Index of lactational infecundability (Bongaarts index)
Cm	Index of marriage (Bongaarts index)
CM	Child mortality
CMW	Currently married women
CMWRA	Currently married women of reproductive age
comp.	Completed
CPR	Contraceptive prevalence rate
CSURV	Children surviving
CU	Current (contraceptive) user
DHS	Demographic and Health Survey
DV	Dummy variable
EMW	Ever married woman
EU	Ever use (contraception)
EWFS	Egyptian World Fertility Survey
F	Female
FP	Family planning
H	High (see n. 1 above)
hs	High school
IM	Infant mortality
IMR	Infant mortality rate

IP	Incomplete primary
L	Low (see n. 1 above)
log reg	Logistic regression
m.	Month(s)
M	Medium (see n. 1 above)
MCA	Multiple classification analysis
N	Narrow (see n. 1 above)
n/a	Not applicable/not ascertained
NFHS	National Family Health Survey
NNM	Neonatal mortality
NT	Non-terminal
OLS	Ordinary least squares
PNNM	Post-neonatal mortality
prim.	Primary school
q(1) and 1q0	Mortality at ages 0–1
q(2)	Mortality at ages 0–2
q5 and 5q0	Mortality at ages 0–5
R	Reference category
Read	Can read
sec.	Secondary school
sec.+	Secondary school and higher levels
SIG	Significant
SMAM	Singulate mean age at marriage
ter.	Tertiary
TSLS	Two-stage least squares
U5MR	Under 5 (years) mortality rate
W	Wide (see n. 1 above)
WFS	World Fertility Survey

Appendix A. *Studies addressing the relationship between women's education and children ever born*

Site and survey date	Levels of:			Sample		Education variable (years of schooling)	Mean number of children ever born to:		Percentage difference between uneducated and better educated women[a] by years of schooling				Direction of relationship[b]	Author (date)[c]
	Per capita income	Female literacy rate	Gender disparity in literacy	Type; universe (sex and age); size	Sub-sample characteristics		All women[d]	Uneducated women[e]	1–3	4–6	7+	10+		
A. Sub-Saharan Africa														
Benin[†] 1982	L	L	W	WFS:F15–49 4018	F40–49	0, 1–6, 7+	6.2	6.2	−[f]	−19	−23	n/a	−	United Nations (1987)
Botswana[†] 1988	H	M	M	DHS:F15–49 4368	F40–49	0, 1–3, 4–6, 7–9, 10+	5.6	5.9	−3	−5	−16	−39	7	United Nations (1995)
Burundi[†] 1987	L	L	W	DHS:F15–49 3970	F40–49	0, prim., sec.+	6.9	6.8	13	−[g]	−3	n/a	rev. U	Segamba et al. (1988)
Cameroon[†] 1978	M	L	W	WFS:F15–49 8219	F40–49	0, 1–3, 4–6, 7+	5.2	5.2	−2	−6	−31	n/a	7	United Nations (1987)
Cote d'Ivoire[†] 1980	M	L	W	WFS:F15–49 5764	F40–49	0, 1–6, 7+	6.8	6.8	−[f]	0	−[g]	n/a	0	United Nations (1987)
Ethiopia[†] 1982	L	L	W	F15–55; 35+ 734	F35–44	0–6, 7–12	6.2	6.2	−1	−[g]	1	n/a	0	Haile (1990)
Ghana[†] 1979–80	—	—	—	WFS:F15–49 6125	F40–49	0, 1–3, 4–6, 7+	6.4	6.4	0	9	−14	n/a	rev. J	United Nations (1987)
Ghana[†] 1988	L	M	M	DHS:F15–49 4488	F40–49	0, 1–3, 4–6, 7–9, 10+	6.9	7.1	6	−4	−17	−30	rev. J	United Nations (1995)
Kenya 1980s	—	—	—	F18–78 132	W. Kenya: agricultural	0, prim., sec.	5.6	5.5	11	−[g]	−24	n/a	rev. J	Jensen and Khasakhala (1992)
					Coast: non-agricultural		4.0	4.6	−39	−[g]	−78	n/a	−	
Kenya 1977–8				WFS:F15–49 8100	F40–49	0, 1–3, 4–6, 7+	7.7	7.6	11	3	3	n/a	+	United Nations (1987)
Kenya[†] 1988–9	L	M	M	DHS:F15–49 7150	F40–49	0, 1–3, 4–6, 7–9, 10+	7.5	7.4	9	7	−15	−43	rev. J	United Nations (1995)
Lesotho[†] 1977	M	M	M	WFS:F15–49 3603	F40–49	0, 1–3, 4–6, 7+	5.1	4.9	2	6	6	n/a	+	United Nations (1987)
Liberia[†] 1986	M	L	W	DHS:F15–49 5239	F40–49	0, prim., sec.+	6.4	6.3	−[f]	13	0	n/a	rev. U	Chieh-Johnson et al. (1988)
Malawi 1992	—	—	—	DHS:F15–49 4850	F40–49	0, 7+	3.5	4.2	−[g]	−[g]	−52	n/a	−	Malawi, National Statistical Office (1993)

Country/Year				Survey	Age	Education								Source
Mali† 1987	L	L	W	DHS: F15–49 3200	F40–49	0, prim.+	7.1	7.0	-[1]	8	-[9]	n/a	+	Traore et al. (1989)
Mali 1987		–	–	DHS:F15–49 3200	F40–49	0, prim.+	7.1	7.0	-[1]	6	-[9]	n/a	+	United Nations (1995)
Mauritania† 1981	L	L	W	WFS:F15–49 3504	F40–49	0, prim.+	5.9	5.9	2	-[1]	-[1]	n/a	0	United Nations (1987)
Namibia† 1992	H	M	M	DHS:F15–49 5421	F40–49	0, prim., comp. prim., sec.+	5.7	6.3	-3	-13	-35	n/a	7	Kaijuanjo et al. (1993)
Nigeria 1984/6		–	–	CMW, Yoruba Oyo state 1200 two rounds	CM Yoruba women, Oyo state	0, prim., sec.+	n/a n/a	3.4 3.5	-12 -11	-26 -17	-9 -11	n/a n/a	– –	Edigbola (1988)
Nigeria† 1990	L	L	W	DHS:F15–49 8781	F40–49	0, prim., comp. prim., sec.+	5.4	5.5	10	5	-21	n/a	rev. J	Federal Office of Statistics (1992)
Senegal 1978		–	–	WFS:F15–49 3985	F40–49	0, 1–3, 4–6, 7+	6.0	6.9	0	0	-[9]	n/a	0	United Nations (1987)
Senegal† 1986	M	L	W	DHS:F15–49 4415	F40–49	0, prim., sec.+	7.3	7.0	-[1]	7	-16	n/a	rev. J	Ndiaye et al. (1988)
Togo† 1988	L	L	W	DHS:F15–49 3360	F40–49	1–3, 4+	7.1	7.2	-[1]	3	-[1]	n/a	0	United Nations (1995)
Uganda† 1988–9	L	L	W	DHS:F15–49 4730	F40–49	0, prim., comp. prim., sec.+	7.5	7.6	-3	-4	-6	n/a	7	Kaijuka et al. (1989)
United Republic of Tanzania† 1991–2	L	H	N	DHS:F15–49 9238	F40–49	0, prim., comp. prim., sec.+	6.9	6.9	3	-6	-30	n/a	7	Ngallaba et al. (1993)
Zaire (West)† 1975–7	L	L	M	CMW 15–59 monogamous Rural Kinshasa 25812	CMW 45–54	0, prim., comp. prim., sec.+	5.7 6.5	5.76 6.74	24 6	10 4	-7 -7	n/a n/a	rev. J rev. J	Sala-Diakanda (1982)
Zambia† 1992	L	M	M	DHS:F15–49 7000	F40–49	0, prim., sec.+	7.7	7.8	0	-[9]	-14	n/a	7	Gaisie et al. (1993)
Zimbabwe† 1988–9	M	M	M	DHS:F15–49 4201	F40–49	0, 1–3, 4–6, 7–9, 10+	6.6	6.7	7	4	-22	-33	rev. J	United Nations (1995)

B. North Africa and the Middle East

Country/Year				Survey	Age	Education								Source
Egypt 1973		–		F15–49 rural and semi-urban 1234	F15–49 rural and semi-urban	0, prim., middle, high	4.6	5.2	-40	-[9]	-56	n/a	–	Khalifa (1976)

Appendix A. (cont.)

Site and survey date	Levels of:			Sample		Education variable (years of schooling)	Mean number of children ever born to:		Percentage difference between uneducated and better educated women[a] by years of schooling				Direction of relationship[b]	Author (date)[c]
	Per capita income	Female literacy rate	Gender disparity in literacy	Type; universe (sex and age); size	Sub-sample characteristics		All women[d]	Uneducated women[e]	1-3	4-6	7+	10+		
Egypt 1976	—	—	—	Census: Urban Rural n/a	F45-49	0, read/ prim.; middle, >mid.+	5.4 5.1	5.4 5.5	-17 -5	-34 -5	-46 -32	n/a n/a	— —	Abou-Gamrah (1982)
Egypt 1980	M	—	—	WFS:F15-49 8788	F40-49	0, 1-3, 4-6, 7+	6.3	6.8	6	-4	-46	n/a	rev. J	United Nations (1987)
Egypt[t] 1988-9	M	L	W	DHS:F15-49 8911	F40-49	0, 1-3, 4-6, 7-9, 10+	6.0	6.6	-5	-15	-34	-50	—	United Nations (1995)
Jordan[t] 1976	H	M	M	WFS:F15-49 3612	F40-49	0, 1-3, 4-6, 7+	8.5	8.9	1	-19	-30	n/a	7	United Nations (1987)
Kuwait[t] 1975	H	M	W	Census: n/a	F45-49	0, read/ prim. middle >middle	6.3	6.4	4	-17	-42	n/a	7	Abou-Gamrah (1982)
Morocco 1979-80	—	—	—	WFS:F15-49 5801	F40-49	0, 1-3, 4-6+	7.1	7.1	3	-11	n/a	n/a	7	United Nations (1987)
Morocco[t] 1987	M	L	W	DHS:F15-49 5982	F40-49	0, 1-3, 4-6, 7-9, 10+	7.1	7.2	-6	-19	-50	-56	—	United Nations (1995)
Sudan 1978-9	—	—	—	WFS:F15-49 3115	F40-49	0, 1-3, 4-6, 7+	6.0	6.1	13	-5	-36	n/a	rev. J	United Nations (1987)
Sudan 1989-90[t]	L	L	W	DHS:F15-49 5860	F40-49	0, prim., comp. prim., sec.+	7.3	7.4	-1[f]	-7	-35	n/a	—	Ministry of Economic and National Planning (1991)
Syrian Arab Rep.[t] 1978	H	L	W	WFS:F15-49 4487	F40-49	0, 1-3, 4-6, 7+	7.5	7.8	-19	-15	-49	n/a	—	United Nations (1987)
Tunisia 1978	—	—	—	WFS:F15-49 4123	F40-49	0, 1-3, 4-6, 7+	6.4	6.8	-13	-6	-47	n/a	—	United Nations (1987)
Tunisia[t] 1988	H	M	M	DHS:F15-49 4184	F40-49	0, 1-3, 4-6, 7-9, 10+	6.1	6.2	-23	-23	-49	-55	—	United Nations (1995)
United Arab Emirates[t] 1975	H	L	W	Census: n/a	F married 20+ years	0, literate, prim., sec.+	6.3	5.2	25	29	-14	-29	rev. J	Abou-Gamrah (1982)

Country / Year			Survey; N	Age group	Education								Source
Yemen 1979	—	—	WFS:F15–49; 2605	F40–49	0, 1–3, 4–6, 7+, sec.+	6.4	6.8	n/a	n/a	n/a	n/a	0	United Nations (1987)
C. East and South-East Asia													
China† 1982	L	M	F35–45; 65024	Total	0, prim., middle, sec., college	4.2	4.74	−20	−35	−51	−59	—	Zhao and Sun (1984)
				Rural		4.4	4.78	−17	−26	−38	−54	—	
				Urban 1/1000 survey		2.9	3.97	−21	−35	−46	−52	—	
Fiji† 1974	M	M	WFS:F15–49; 4298	F40–49	0, 1–3, 4–6, 7+	6.2	6.9	3	−12	−19	n/a	7	United Nations (1987)
Indonesia 1976	—	—	WFS:F15–49; 9155	F40–49	0, 1–3, 4–6, 7+	5.2	5.2	17	8	−13	n/a	rev. J	United Nations (1987)
Indonesia 1987	—	—	DHS:F15–49; 11884	F40–49	0, 1–3, 4–6, 7–9, 10+	5.5	5.2	12	12	−8	−17	rev. J	United Nations (1995)
Indonesia† 1991	M	N	DHS:F15–49; 22909	F40–49	0, prim., comp. prim., sec.+	4.9	4.8	8	12	−12	n/a	rev. J	Central Bureau of Statistics (1992)
Malaysia† 1974	H	M	WFS:F15–49; 6316	F40–49	0, 1–3, 4–6, 7+	6.1	6.3	−2	−6	−41	n/a	7	United Nations (1987)
Philippines† 1978	M	N	WFS:F15–49; 9268	F40–49	0, 1–3, 4–6, 7+	6.5	7.0	6	−1	−26	n/a	rev. J	United Nations (1987)
Philippines 1968	—	—	EMW45–54; 7000	Total	0, 1–4, 5–7, 8–12, >12	n/a	5.6	16	14	5	−20	rev. J	Smock (1981)
				Rural		n/a	5.4	19	20	−2	−26	rev. J	
				Urban		n/a	6.6	3	−8	−9	−24	7	
Rep. of Korea† 1974	H	N	WFS:F15–49; 5430	F40–49	0, 1–3, 4–6, 7+	5.4	6.0	−5	−13	−33	n/a	—	United Nations (1987)
Thailand 1975	—	—	WFS:F15–49; 3778	F40–49	0, 1–3, 4–6, 7+	6.1	6.4	3	2	−38	n/a	7	United Nations (1987)
Thailand† 1987	H	N	DHS:F15–49; 6775	F40–49	0, 1–3, 4–6, 7–9, 10+	4.7	5.6	−16	−21	−57	−59	—	United Nations (1995)
D. South Asia													
Bangladesh 1975–6	—	—	WFS:F15–49; 6513	F40–49	0, 1–3, 4–6, 7+	6.9	6.9	1	10	0	n/a	rev. J	United Nations (1987)
Bangladesh† 1989	L	W	F15–49; 11903	F40–49	0, 1–3, 4–6, 7–	6.9	6.9	5	−5	−8	n/a	rev. J	Huq and Cleland (1990)
India 1980	—	—	F15–44; 34831	F40–44	0, any	5.4	5.4	7	—⁹	—⁹	n/a	+	Khan and Prasad (1983)
India† 1989	L	W	F15–44; 44918	F40–44	0, prim., sec.+	5.1	5.5	−6	—⁹	−34	n/a	—	Operations Research Group (1990)

Appendix A. (cont.)

Site and survey date	Levels of: Per capita income	Female literacy rate	Gender disparity in literacy	Sample Type; universe (sex and age); size	Sub-sample characteristics	Education variable (years of schooling)	Mean number of children ever born to: All women[d]	Uneducated women[e]	Percentage difference between uneducated and better educated women[a] by years of schooling 1-3	4-6	7+	10+	Direction of relationship[b]	Author (date)[c]
India, Maharashtra 1992–3	–	–	–	NFHS: F15–49 4106	F40–49	0, prim. to middle, middle comp., sec.+	4.25	4.69	–14	–[g]	–36	–41	–	Population Research Centre, Gokhale Institute et al. (1994)
India, Tamil Nadu 1992	–	–	–	NFHS: F15–49 3948	F40–49	0, prim. to middle, middle comp., sec.+	4.21	4.45	–3	–[g]	–29	–40	7	Population Research Centre, Gandhigram Institute et al. (1994)
India, Uttar Pradesh 1992–3	–	–	–	NFHS: F15–49 11438	F40–49	0, prim. to middle, middle comp., sec.+	5.97	6.24	–14	–[g]	–35	–44	–	Population Research Centre, Lucknow University et al. (1994)
Nepal[t] 1976	L	L	W	WFS:F15–49 5940	F40–49	0, 1–3, 4–6, 7+	5.6	5.7	–[i]	–[f]	–32	n/a	–	United Nations (1987)
Pakistan 1975	–	–	–	WFS:F15–49 4996	F40–49	0, 1–3, 4–6, 7+	6.9	6.9	–16	–6	–26	n/a	irreg.	United Nations (1987)
Pakistan[t] 1991	L	L	W	DHS:F15–49 6611	F40–49	0, prim., comp. prim., sec.+	6.4	6.5	–6	–18	–34	n/a	–	National Institute of Population Studies (1992)
Sri Lanka 1975	–	–	–	WFS:F15–49 6812	F40–49	0, 1–3, 4–6, 7+	5.6	6.4	–6	–9	–31	n/a	–	United Nations (1987)
Sri Lanka[t] 1987	L	H	N	DHS:F15–49 5865	F40–49	0, 1–3, 4–6, 7–9, 10+	4.6	5.9	–5	–17	–39	–49	–	United Nations (1995)
E. Latin America and the Caribbean														
Belize[t] 1991	H	M	N	F15–44 2656	F40–44	0, prim., comp. prim., sec., sec.+	6.1	7.7	–8	–21	–46	–62	–	Ministry of Health (1992)
Bolivia[t] 1989	M	M	M	DHS:F15–49 7923	F40–49	0, 1–3, 4–6, 7–9, 10+	5.6	6.5	–3	–18	–47	–52	7	United Nations (1995)
Brazil[t] 1986	H	M	N	DHS:F15–44 5892	F40–44	0, 1–3, 4–6, 7–9, 10+	4.6	6.8	–18	–43	–64	–71	–	United Nations (1995)

Country/Year				Survey	Age	Categories								Reference
Colombia 1976	—	—	—	WFS:F15–49 5378	F40–49	0, 1–3, 4–6, 7+	6.4	7.0	–3	–16	–36	n/a	7	United Nations (1987)
Colombia† 1986	H	H	N	DHS:F15–49 5329	F40–49	C, 1–3, 4–6, 7–9, 10+	5.5	7.1	–13	–37	–57	–69	–	United Nations (1995)
Costa Rica† 1976	H	H	N	WFS:F15–49 3935	F40–49	C, 1–3, 4–6, 7+	6.4	8.7	–17	–31	–59	n/a	–	United Nations (1987)
Dominican Rep. 1975	—	—	—	WFS:F15–49 3115	F40–49	0, 1–3, 4–6, 7+	6.5	7.2	–4	–19	–40	n/a	7	United Nations (1987)
Dominican Rep.† 1986	M	M	N	DHS:F15–49 7649	F40–49	0, 1–3, 4–6, 7–9, 10+	6.2	7.5	–10	–20	–47	–51	–	United Nations (1995)
Ecuador 1979	—	—	—	WFS:F15–49 6797	F40–49	0, 1–3, 4–6, 7+	6.6	7.9	–6	–22	–52	n/a	–	United Nations (1987)
Ecuador† 1987	M	H	N	DHS:F15–49 4713	F40–49	0, 1–3, 4–6, 7–9, 10+	6.0	7.1	–10	–21	–51	–56	–	United Nations (1995)
Ecuador 1989	—	—	—	F15–49 7961	F40–44	0, 1–3, 4–6, sec., superior	5.1	7.0	–9	–27	–58	–63	–	Monteith et al. (1992)
El Salvador† 1985	M	M	N	DHS:F15–49 5207	F40–49	0, 1–3, 4–6, 7–9, 10+	6.1	7.4	–12	–35	–58	–61	–	United Nations (1995)
Guatemala† 1987	M	M	M	DHS:F15–44 5160	F40–44	0, 1–3, 4–6, 7–9, 10+	5.9	6.7	–15	–33	–54	–60	–	United Nations (1995)
Guyana† 1975	L	L	N	WFS:F15–49 4642	F40–49	0, 1–3, 4–6, 7–9, 10+	6.3	7.5	–13	–8	–23	n/a	–	United Nations (1987)
Haiti 1977	—	—	—	F15–49 3365	F40–49	0, 1–3, 4–6, 7+	5.8	5.8	3	–3	–40	n/a	7	United Nations (1987)
Haiti† 1989	L	L	M	F15–49 1996	F40–44	0, 1–3, 4–6, 7+	4.8	4.9	6	–12	–45	n/a	rev. J	Cayemittes et al. (1991)
Jamaica† 1975–6	H	H	N	WFS:F15–49 3096	F40–49	0, 1–3, 4–6, 7+	5.5	4.4	25	39	20	n/a	+	United Nations (1987)
Mexico 1976	—	—	—	WFS:F15–49 7310	F40–49	0, 1–3, 4–6, 7–9, 10+	6.7	7.4	–4	–14	–49	n/a	7	United Nations (1987)
Mexico† 1987	H	H	N	DHS:F15–49 9310	F40–49	0, 1–3, 4–6, 7–9, 10+	5.9	7.5	–13	–33	–60	–61	–	United Nations (1995)
Panama† 1975–6	H	H	N	WFS:F15–49 3701	F40–49	0, 1–3, 4–6, 7+	5.7	7.1	–1	–17	–44	n/a	7	United Nations (1987)
Paraguay† 1979	H	H	N	WFS:F15–49 4682	F40–49	0, 1–3, 4–6, 7+	6.0	7.4	–3	–27	–58	n/a	7	United Nations (1987)
Peru 1977–8	—	—	—	WFS:F15–49 5640	F40–49	0, 1–3, 4–6, 7–	6.4	7.4	–11	–22	–47	n/a	–	United Nations (1987)
Peru† 1986	H	M	N	DHS:F15–49 4999	F40–49	0, 1–3, 4–6, 7–9, 10+	6.0	7.6	–13	–29	–49	–54	–	United Nations (1995)

Appendix A. (cont.)

Site and survey date	Levels of: Per capita income	Female literacy rate	Gender disparity in literacy	Sample Type; universe (sex and age); size	Sub-sample characteristics	Education variable (years of schooling)	Mean number of children ever born to: All women[d]	Uneducated women[e]	Percentage difference between uneducated and better educated women[a] by years of schooling 1-3	4-6	7+	10+	Direction of relationship[b]	Author (date)[c]
Trinidad and Tobago 1977				WFS:F15-49 4359	F40-49	0, 1-3, 4-6, 7+	5.5	7.1	-3	-14	-30	n/a	7	United Nations (1987)
Trinidad and Tobago[t] 1987	H	H	N	DHS:F15-49 3806	F40-49	0, 1-3, 4-6, 7-9, 10+	4.3	6.2	-13	-23	-48	-55	–	United Nations (1995)
Venezuela[t] 1977	H	M	N	WFS:F15-49 4361	F40-49	0, 1-3, 4-6, 7+	6.1	7.9	-13	-33	-49	n/a	–	United Nations (1987)

a Refers to the difference between the rates for women with no education compared with women at each successively higher level of education (1-3 years, 4-6 years and so on).

b See Introduction to appendices for discussion of the various types of relationships.

c See Bibliography for full citation.

d Refers to all women in the sample or in the sub-sample, if there was one.

e Refers to women with no education in the sample or in the sub-sample, if there was one.

f Not reported; fewer than ten cases.

g Merged with next level; if data are given for classes 1-3 and 4-6 together, results are shown under the lower category, 1-3.

t Studies included in Tables 2.2, 2.3, and 2.4.

* Statistically significant.

Notes: See Introduction to appendices for list of abbreviations and technical notes on the appendix. For studies in which more than one set of numbers are provided, see column headed 'Sub-sample characteristics' for the sub-population to which the rates refer.

Appendix B. *Multivariate studies addressing the relationship between women's education and fertility*

Site and Survey Date	Sample Type; universe; size	Special characteristics; co-variates; other variables and significance(*): (methodology)	Dependent variable	Education variable	Coefficients	Direction of relationship[a]	Author (date)[b]
A. Sub-Saharan Africa							
Kenya 1974	CMW 1160	Age*, mortality*, husband's education, land control*, urban residence, work status (OLS)	CEB	0, illit. but some school; some prim.; comp. prim.; sec.+	R 0.1085 -0.1697 -0.4341* -1.0541*	rev. U	Anker (1985)
		Age*, mortality*, husband's education, land control*, urban residence, work status (OLS)	CEB	Years	-0.0592*		
Kenya 1984	CMW aged 15–44 monogamous 1st marriage; 4 estates in Nairobi 346	age*, marital age*, couple communication*, child mortality*, husband's income, modern reproductive attitudes, ruralism FP attitudes, media use (OLS)	CEB	Years	0.023	+	Emerewaonu (1984)
Malawi n/a	CMWRA: Total CMWRA: Rural CMWRA: Urban n/a	Age*, desired family size*, birth rate*, marital age*, using contraception*, town1*, husband's education*, husband's occupation* (OLS)	CEB	Years	0.04* 0.04* 0.02*	+ + +	M'Mange and Srivastava (1990)
Nigeria 1981–2	WFS: CMW in first marriage 6918	Work status*, type of marriage childhood residence*, current residence*, contraceptive use, region*, religion*, husband's education*, interspousal age difference*, duration of marriage* (OLS)	CEB	None/Koranic; prim. incomp. prim. comp. sec.+	R 0.0190 -0.1597* -0.4470*	7	Feyisetan and Togunde (1988)
Nigeria 1985	EMW 15–50 1814	Age*, husband's education & occupation*, community charac-teristics*, ethnicity*, age differ-ence between spouses*, marriage type*, sex role attitude, decision making*, division of household labour*, wife contributes to hh* (OLS)	CEB	0, prim. sec. ter.	R -0.834* -3.136* -3.879*	–	Okojie (1993)

Appendix B. (cont.)

Site and Survey Date	Sample	Special characteristics; co-variates; other variables and significance(*); (methodology)	Dependent variable	Education variable	Coefficients	Direction of relationship*	Author (date)[b]
	Type; universe; size						
Nigeria, Ondo State 1986	CMW 15–40: all 1787	Age*, age at marriage, no. marriages*, marriage type*, prior births*, wife shares expenses*	Births in last 5 yrs	Years	−0.05	–	Kritz and Gurak (1991, DHS)
	CMW 15–30	Age*, age at marriage*, no. marriages*, marriage type*, prior births*, wife shares expenses			0.01	0	
	CMW 31–40	Age*, age at marriage*, no. marriages, marriage type, prior births, wife shares expenses* (OLS)			−0.05	–	
Oyo State	CMW 15–40: all 366	Age*, age at marriage*, no. marriages, marriage type*, prior births*, work status, wife kept income before marriage (OLS)			−0.01	0	
1990	CMW 15–30	Age*, age at marriage, no. marriages, marriage type, prior births*, work status, wife kept income before marriage (OLS)			0.07*	+	
	CMW 31–40	Age*, age at marriage*, no. marriages*, marriage type*, prior births, work status, wife kept income before marriage (OLS)			−0.01	0	
Nigeria, Urban 1987–8	EMW 35–49 9664	Mate selection, ethnicity*, religion, duration of marriage* employment*, interspousal age difference*, contraception* (OLS)	CEB	0 prim. sec. +	R 0.11 −0.37*	?	Feyisetan and Bankole (1991)

Sierra Leone 1979	CMW 15–49 rural women 2000	Marital age, family income, desired family size*, marital duration*, childhood residence*, current residence*, tribe, religion, (OLS)	CEB	Years	0.055	0	Bailey (1986)
B. East and South-East Asia							
Philippines 1983	EMW 15–49 national probability samples 22112	Urban CMW, <35 (3054)	CEB	Years	−0.102*	–	Raymundo et al. (1993)
		Urban CMW, 35+ (2134)	CEB	Years	−0.167*	–	
		Rural CMW, <35 (2673)	CEB	Years	−0.126*	–	
		Rural CMW, 35+ (1825)	CEB	Years	−0.207*	–	
1988		Urban CMW, <35 (3385)	CEB	Years	−0.11*	–	
		Urban CMW, 35+ (2566)	CEB	Years	−0.172*	–	
		Rural CMW, <35 (3722)	CEB	Years	−0.106*	–	
		Rural CMW, 35+ (2753) (correlations)	CEB	Years	−0.21*		
1983	Urban, aged <35	Marital duration*, marital age, breast-feeding duration*, husband education*, family income, wife's work status*, FP methods known*, FP approval, age difference between spouses*	CEB	Years	−0.018*	–	
1983	Urban, aged 35+	Marital duration*, marital age*, breast-feeding duration*, husband education*, family income, wife's work status*, FP methods known, FP approval, age difference between spouses*	CEB	Years	−0.019	–	
1983	Rural, aged <35	Marital duration*, marital age, breast-feeding duration*, husband education*, family income, wife's work status*, FP methods known, FP approval, age difference between spouses	CEB	Years	−0.016	–	
1983	Rural, aged 35+	Marital duration*, marital age*, breast-feeding duration*, husband education*, family income, wife's work status*, FP methods known, FP approval*, age difference between spouses* (OLS)	CEB	Years	−0.035	–	

Appendix B. (cont.)

Site and Survey Date	Sample — Type; universe; size	Special characteristics; co-variates; other variables and significance(*): (methodology)	Dependent variable	Education variable	Coefficients	Direction of relationship*	Author (date)[b]
1988	Urban, aged <35	Marital duration*, marital age*, breast-feeding duration*, husband education*, family income, wife's work status, FP methods known, age difference between spouses	CEB	Years	-0.035	–	
1988	Urban, aged 35+	Marital duration*, marital age*, breast-feeding duration*, husband education*, family income, wife's work status, FP methods known, age difference between spouses	CEB	Years	-0.063*	–	
1988	Rural, aged <35	marital dur*, marital age, breastfeeding dur*, husband educ*, family income, wife's work status, FP methods known*, age difference between spouses	CEB	Years	-0.011	–	
1988	Rural, aged 35+	marital duration*, marital age*, breast-feeding duration*, husband education*, family income, wife's work status, FP methods known, age difference between spouses (OLS)	CEB	Years	-0.043*	–	
C. South Asia Bangladesh 1975	WFS:EMW <50 4143	Ever work, age at marriage* (OLS)	CEB	0 / 1-5 / 6-9 / sec.+	R / -0.01 / -0.28* / -0.44*	7	Chaudhury (1984)
	EMW <50: Rural 3176	Ever work, age at marriage* (OLS)	CEB	0 / 1-5 / 6-9 / sec.+	R / -0.04 / -0.24 / -0.04	irreg.	

Country, year	Sample	Variables (method)	Dependent variable	Education	R	Sign	Source
Bangladesh 1988	EMW <50: Urban 967	Ever work, age at marriage* (OLS)	CEB	0 1–5 6–9 sec. +	R −0.04 −0.42* −0.65*	−	Balk (1994)
	CMWRA 4799	Age*, age difference*, no. marriages*, marital age*, presence of in-laws, house size, land owned, landless*, husband is daily worker*, wife works*, indicators of mobility*, authority, attitudes, Muslim*, region* (TSLS regression)	Cumulative fertility	Years	−0.087*		
India, Tamil Nadu 1970	CMWRA aged 35–44 2135	Woman's work, family type age difference, modern goods owned (OLS)	CEB	Effect of 5-yr increase in education	0.0733	+	Jejeebhoy (1991)
1980	CMWRA aged 35–44 798				−0.5499	−	
India, Maharashtra 1983–4 Rural	CMW 15–44 1956	Media exposure, age*, modern goods owned, wife's work*	CEB	0, prim, mid., sec. +	−0.09*	−	United Nations (1993)
	CMW 15–44 1956	Media exposure, age*, modern goods owned, wife's work* through marital age, natural fertility, child mortality, contraceptive duration (OLS)	CEB	effect of shift: from 0 to prim. from prim. to mid. from mid. to sec.	−0.173 −0.463 −0.671	?	
Pakistan 1979–80	EMW under 50 Pop., labour force and migration survey 9596	Adjusted for household income, wife's occupation, age at marriage, rural–urban residence (MCA)	CEB last 5 years deviation from grand mean	Total: 0 1–8 9+	0.02 −0.02 −0.07	?	Sathar et al. (1988)
		Adjusted for size of farm, husband's education, spousal age difference, age, age at marriage (MCA)		Rural: 0 1–8 9+	0.00 0.00 −0.90	?	
		Adjusted for household income, husband's education, spousal age difference, age, age at marriage (MCA)		Urban: 0 1–8 9+	0.09 −0.07 −0.24	?	

Appendix B. (cont.)

Site and Survey Date	Sample Type; universe; size	Special characteristics; co-variates; other variables and significance(*): (methodology)	Dependent variable	Education variable	Coefficients	Direction of relationship[a]	Author (date)[b]
Pakistan, Karachi 1987	EMW 15–52: 1000 working women: 680 not working: 320	Total; duration of marriage*, marital age*, FP approval*, household income*, wife works*, makes family-size decisions*, makes financial decisions, self-support in old age* (OLS)	CEB	Years	−0.033*	−	Sathar and Mason (1993)
		Women married <20 years: duration of marriage*, marital age*, FP approval*, household income*, wife works*, makes family-size decisions, self-support in decisions*, makes financial decisions*, self-support in old age* (OLS)	CEB	Years	−0.012	0	
		Women married >20 years: duration of marriage, marital age*, FP approval, household income, wife works, makes family-size decisions, self-support in decisions, makes financial decisions, self-support in old age (OLS)	CEB	years	−0.060	−	
Pakistan 1987	EMW 15–52: 1000 Karachi	Adjusted for type of employment*, rural–urban residence (MCA)	CEB last 5 years (means)	0 1–9 10+	0.85 0.83 0.83	0	Sathar and Kazi (1990)
D. Latin America and the Caribbean Colombia 1986	DHS:F15–49 5329	Husband's education*, exposed to radio, knows contraception, knows ovulation*, urban residence*, owns refrigerator*, early contraceptor*, early age at first union, cohabiting, premarital	CEB	0 1–3 4–6 7–9 10+	R −0.41* −0.77* −0.63* −0.55*	−	Castro-Martin and Juarez (1993)

		birth*, early 1st birth*, worked before marriage, worked after marriage* (OLS)					
Ecuador 1987	DHS:F15—49 4713	Husband's education*, exposed to radio*, knows contraceptor*, knows ovulation, urban residence*, owns refrigerator*, early contraceptor*, early age at first union*, cohabiting, premarital birth*, early 1st birth*, worked before marriage, worked after marriage* (OLS)	CEB	0 1–3 4–6 7–9 10+	R −0.01 −0.44* −0.54* −0.50*	–	Castro-Martin and Juarez (1993)
Guatemala 1987	DHS:F15—44 5160	Husband's education*, exposed to radio, knows contraception, knows ovulation, urban residence*, owns refrigerator*, early contraceptor*, early age at first union*, cohabiting*, premarital birth*, early 1st birth*, worked before marriage*, worked after marriage* (OLS)	CEB	0 1–3 4–6 7–9 10+	R −0.15 −0.33* −0.23 0.03	–	Castro-Martin and Juarez (1993)
Paraguay 1979	F15–49; 830	Women married 5+ yrs; adjusted for: age at birth; place of work; occupation; number of children aged 6+; residence (MCA)	CEB in last 5 years	<3 3–5 6 7+	0.17 0.00 −0.11 −0.14	–	Schoemaker (1981)

ᵃ See Introduction to appendices for discussion of the various types of relationships.
ᵇ See Bibliography for full citation.
* Statistically significant at the 0.05 level or better.

Notes: See Introduction to appendices for list of abbreviations and technical notes on the appendix. For studies in which more than one set of numbers are provided, see columns headed 'Type; universe, size', and 'Special characteristics' for the sub-population to which the rates refer.

Appendix C. *Studies addressing the relationship between women's education and age at marriage*

Site and survey date	Levels of:			Sample		Dependent variable (method if means n/a)	Education variable (years of schooling)	Age of marriage among:		Percentage difference between uneducated and better educated women[e] by years of schooling				Direction of relationship[b]	Author (date)[c]
	Per capita income	Female literacy rate	Gender disparity in literacy	Type; universe (sex and age); size	Sub-sample characteristics			All women[d]	Unedu-cated women[d]	1–3	4–6	7+	10+		
A. Sub-Saharan Africa															
Benin[†] 1982	L	L	W	WFS:F15–49 4018	F15–49	SMAM	0, 1–3, 4–6, 7+	18.2	16.9	12	15	43	n/a	+	United Nations (1987)
Botswana[†] 1988	H	M	M	DHS:F15–49 4368	F25–49	Median AAM	0, prim., comp.	17.3	16.9	1	3	6	n/a	rev. ?	Lestede (1989)
Burundi[†] 1987	L	L	W	DHS:F15–49 3970	F15–49	Median AAM	0, 1–3, 4–6, 7–9, 10+	20.0	19.8	2	3	12	15	rev. ?	United Nations (1995)
Cameroon[†] 1978	M	L	W	WFS:F15–49 8219	F15–49	SMAM	0, 1–3, 4–6, 7+	17.5	15.4	14	12	44	n/a	+	United Nations (1987)
Cote d'Ivoire[†] 1980	M	L	W	WFS:F15–49 5764	F15–49	SMAM	0, 1–3, 4–6, 7+	17.8	17.1	4	8	27	n/a	rev. ?	United Nations (1987)
Ghana 1979–80	—	—	—	WFS:F15–49 6125	F15–49	SMAM	0, 1–3, 4–6, 7+	19.3	17.4	5	10	18	n/a	+	United Nations (1987)
Ghana[†] 1988	L	M	M	DHS:F15–49 4488	F15–49	Median AAM	0, 1–3, 4–6, 7–9, 10+	18.4	17.8	1	1	9	12	rev. ?	United Nations (1995)
Kenya 1977–8	—	—	—	WFS:F15–49 8100	F15–49	SMAM	0, 1–3, 4–6, 7+	19.9	17.2	9	13	25	n/a	+	United Nations (1987)
Kenya (Nairobi) 4 estates 1970s				F15–44 346 monogamous 1st marriage	F15–44	Mean AAM	0, 1–8, 9+ (form 1–6)	n/a	18.1	4	—'	15	15	rev. ?	Emereuwaonu (1984)
Kenya[†] 1988–9	L	M	M	DHS:F15–49 7150	F15–49	Median AAM	0, 1–3, 4–6, 7–9, 10+	18.8	17.0	2	6	20	31	rev. ?	United Nations (1995)
Lesotho[†] 1977	M	M	M	WFS:F15–49 3603	F15–49	SMAM	0, 1–3, 4–6, 7+	19.7	17.6	11	7	14	n/a	+	Cochrane and Farid (1989)

Country/Year				Source	F age	Method	Categories								Reference
Liberia[†] 1986	M	L	W	DHS:F15–49 5239	F15–49	Median AAM	0, 1–3, 4–6, 7–9 10+	17.8	16.9	4	11	23	28	rev. 7	United Nations (1995)
Mali[†] 1987	L	L	W	DHS:F15–49 3200	F15–49	Median AAM	0, 1–3, 4–6, 7–9 10+	15.7	15.7	–1	2	11	23	rev. 7	United Nations (1995)
Nigeria, Bendel State (Edo and Delta) 1985	—	—	—	F15–50 2146	F15–50	AAM	0, prim., sec., ter.	n/a	0.67	—'	+1.52	+2.65	—'	+(0.01)	Okojie (1993) (Relationship Between Women's Status)
Nigeria, 1981–2	—	—	—	WFS:F15–49 9727	F15–49	SMAM	0, 1–3, 4–6, 7+	18.3	16.2	–5	20	52	n/a	J	Cochrane and Farid (1989)
Nigeria, Oyo & Ondo 1986	—	—	—	DHS:F20–40 Yoruba Oyo: 366 Ondo: 1787	Oyo Ondo	AAM (OLS)	Years	n/a	n/a	n/a	n/a	n/a	n/a	b=0.59* b=0.39*	Kritz and Gurak (1991)
Nigeria[†] 1990	L	L	W	DHS:F15–49 8781	F20–49	AAM	0, prim., comp. prim., sec.+	17.1	15.7	13	19	27	n/a	+	Federal Office of Statistics (1992)
Senegal 1978	—	—	—	WFS:F15–49 3985	F15–49	SMAM	0, 1–3, 4–6, 7+	21.3	16.7	5	22	37	n/a	+	United Nations (1987)
Senegal[†] 1986	M	L	W	DHS:F15–49 4415	F15–49	Median AAM	0, 1–3, 4–6, 7–9, 10+	16.8	16.2	15	25	40	48	+	United Nations (1995)
Togo[†] 1988	L	L	W	DHS:F15–49 3360	F15–49	Median AAM	0, 1–3, 4–6, 7–9, 10+	18.6	17.8	4	10	25	31	rev. 7	United Nations (1995)
Uganda[†] 1988–9	L	L	W	DHS:F15–49 4730	F15–49	Median AAM	0, 1–3, 4–6, 7–9, 10+	17.4	16.6	2	7	19	36	rev. 7	United Nations (1995)
United Rep. of Tanzania[†] 1991–2	L	H	N	DHS:F15–49 9238	F15–49	AAM	0, prim., comp. prim., sec.+	17.9	16.7	4	19	38	n/a	rev. 7	Ngallaba et al. (1993)
Zambia[†] 1992	L	M	M	DHS:F15–49 7000	F25–49	Median AAM	0, prim., sec.+	17.4	16.7	1	—'	19	n/a	rev. 7	Gaisie et al. (1993)
Zimbabwe[†] 1988–9	M	M	M	DHS:F15–49 4201	F15–49	Median AAM	0, 1–3, 4–6, 7–9, 10+	19.1	17.2	3	6	18	30	rev. 7	United Nations (1995)

Appendix C. (cont.)

B. North Africa and the Middle East

Site and survey date	Levels of: Per capita income	Female literacy rate	Gender disparity in literacy	Sample: Type; universe (sex and age); size	Sub-sample characteristics	Dependent variable (method if means n/a)	Education variable (years of schooling)	Age of marriage among: All women[d]	Unedu-cated women[a]	\% difference 1-3	4-6	7+	10+	Direction of relationship[b]	Author (date)[c]
Egypt 1980	—	—	—	WFS:F15-49 8788	F15-49	Mean age, 1st union	0, prim., comp., prim., sec.+	18.0	17.3	4	12	31	n/a	rev. 7	Rodriguez and Aravena (1991)
1989	—	—	—	DHS:F15-49 8911	F20-49	Median age, 1st union	0, 1-3, 4-6, 7-9, 10+	19.0	17.6	4	9	32	n/a	rev. 7	United Nations (1995)
Egypt[t] 1988-9	M	L	W	DHS:F15-49 8911	F15-49	Median AAM	0, 1-3, 4-6, 7-9, 10+	19.5	17.4	2	14	32	39	rev. 7	United Nations (1995)
Jordan[t] 1976	H	M	M	WFS:F15-49 3612	F15-49	SMAM	0, 1-3, 4-6, 7+	21.6	19.2	-3	1	21	n/a	rev. 7	United Nations (1987)
Morocco 1979-80	—	—	—	WFS:F15-49 5801	F15-49	SMAM	0, 1-3, 4-6, 7+	21.3	20.3	16	24	28	n/a	+	United Nations (1987)
Morocco[t] 1987	M	L	W	DHS:F15-49 5982	F15-49	Median AAM	0, 1-3, 4-6, 7-9, 10+	19.8	18.7	17	25	40	40	+	United Nations (1995)
Sudan 1978-9	—	—	—	WFS:F15-49 3115	F15-49	SMAM	0, 1-3, 4-6, 7+	21.3	21.2	0	8	17	n/a	rev. 7	United Nations (1987)
Sudan[t] 1989-90	L	L	W	DHS:F15-49 5860	F25-49	AAM	0, prim., comp., prim., sec.+	17.8	16.2	9	24	46	n/a	+	Ministry of Economics and Natl. Planning (1991)
Syrian Arab Republic[t] 1978	H	L	W	WFS:F15-49 4487	F15-49	SMAM	0, 1-3, 4-6, 7+	22.1	20.5	-4	3	11	n/a	rev. 7	United Nations (1987)
Tunisia[t] 1988	H	M	M	DHS:F15-49 4184	F15-49	Median AAM	0, 1-3, 4-6, 7-9, 10+	22.1	20.6	9	11	19	19	+	United Nations (1995)
Tunisia 1978	—	—	—	WFS:F15-49 4123	F15-49	Mean age, 1st union	0, prim., comp., prim., sec.+	20.0	20.0	-3	-1	7	n/a	rev. 7	Rodriguez and Aravena (1991)
1988	—	—	—	DHS:F15-49 4184	F15-49			21.1	20.8	0	2	8	n/a	rev. 7	

C. East and South-East Asia

Country/Year			Sample	Definition	Measure	Education								Reference
Indonesia 1975	—	—	WFS:F15–49 9155	F15–49	AAM	0, prim., comp.	16.5	16.3	−3	2	23	n/a	rev. 7	Rodriguez and Aravena (1991)
1987	—	—	DHS:F15–49 11884	F20–49		prim., sec.+	17.7	17.2	−2	2	19	n/a	rev. 7	
Indonesia 1987	M	—	DHS:F15–49 11884	F15–49	Median AAM	0, 1–3, 4–6, 7–9, 10+	18.4	16.2	1	11	34	43	rev. 7	United Nations (1995)
Indonesia† 1991	M	N	DHS:F15–49 22909	F25–49	AAM	0, prim., comp., sec.+	17.7	16.3	5	7	33	n/a	+	Central Bureau of Statistics (1992)
Malaysia† 1974	H	M	WFS:F15–49 6316	F15–49	SMAM	0, 1–3, 4–6, 7+	23.1	21.9	−3	1	16	n/a	rev. 7	United Nations (1987)
Philippines† 1978	M	H	WFS:F15–49 9268	F15–49	SMAM	0, 1–3, 4–6, 7+	24.5	24.1	−10	−7	5	n/a	J	United Nations (1987)
Philippines 1983	—	—	CMW15–49		AAM (OLS)	Years								Raymundo et al. (1993)
			Urban 15–35 3054	F15–35	AAM (OLS)	Years	0.334*	n/a	n/a	n/a	n/a	n/a	+	
			Urban 35–49 2134	F35–49	AAM (OLS)	Years	0.331*	n/a	n/a	n/a	n/a	n/a	+	
			Rural 15–35 2673	F15–35	AAM (OLS)	Years	0.331*	n/a	n/a	n/a	n/a	n/a	+	
			Rural 35–49 1825	F35–49	AAM (OLS)	Years	0.344*	n/a	n/a	n/a	n/a	n/a	+	
1988	—	—	Urban 15–35 3383	F15–35	AAM (OLS)	Years	0.363*	n/a	n/a	n/a	n/a	n/a	+	
			Urban 35–49 2566	F35–49	AAM (OLS)	Years	0.306*	n/a	n/a	n/a	n/a	n/a	+	
			Rural 15–35 3722	F15–35	AAM (OLS)	Years	0.335*	n/a	n/a	n/a	n/a	n/a	+	
			Rural 35–49 2753	F35–49	AAM (OLS)	Years	0.401*	n/a	n/a	n/a	n/a	n/a	+	
Rep. of Korea† 1974	H	N	WFS:F15–49 5430	F15–49	SMAM	0, 1–3, 4–6, 7+	23.2	21.7	−2	4	12	n/a	rev. 7	United Nations (1987)
Rep. of Korea 1971	—	—	CMW 30–44 988	CMW 30–44 once married	AAM (OLS)	Years	0.46*	n/a	n/a	n/a	n/a	n/a	+	Kim and Stinner (1980)
Thailand 1978–9	—	—	EMW aged 26+ 1430	EMW aged 26+ 1034	AAM (logistic)	1–3, 4, 5+	n/a	R	−0.088	2.01*	n/a	n/a	rev. 7	Montgomery, Cheung, and Sulak (1988)

Appendix C. (cont.)

Site and survey date	Levels of: Per capita income	Female literacy rate	Gender disparity in literacy	Sample Type; universe (sex and age); size	Sub-sample characteristics	Dependent variable (method if means n/a)	Education variable (years of schooling)	Age of marriage among: All women[d]	Uneducated women[e]	Percentage difference between uneducated and better educated women[a] by years of schooling 1–3	4–6	7+	10+	Direction of relationship[b]	Author (date)[c]
Thailand (Bangkok) 1986	—	—	—	White-collar working ages 1004	White-collar working ages	Index of 1st marriage hazard rate	<BA, BA, >BA	1.73*, 1.00, 0.87*	n/a	n/a	n/a	n/a	n/a	—	Limanonda (1987)
Thailand (Rural North) 1977–8	—	—	—	F15–54 353	F15–54 303	AAM (OLS)	Years	0.24*	n/a	n/a	n/a	n/a	n/a	+	Cochrane and Nandwani (1981)
Thailand 1975	—	—	—	WFS:F15–49 3778	F15–49	Mean age at 1st union	0, prim., comp.	19.8	19.5	2	1	13	n/a	rev. 7	Rodriguez and Aravena (1991)
1987	—	—	—	DHS:F15–49 6775	F20–49		prim., sec. +	20.2	19.4	2	3	9	n/a	rev. 7	
Thailand[†] 1987	H	H	N	DHS:F15–49 6775	F15–49	Median AAM	0, 1–3, 4–6, 7–9, 10+	20.8	18.8	3	7	33	37	rev. 7	United Nations (1995)
D. South Asia Bangladesh[†] 1975–6	L	L	W	WFS:F15–49 6513	F15–49	SMAM	0, 1–3, 4–6, 7+	16.3	15.0	1	10	30	n/a	rev. 7	United Nations (1987)
Bangladesh, Rural 1985	—	—	—	F16–20 evaluation of school programme for secondary schooling 841	F16–20	% married	0, prim., incomplete sec., sec. +	n/a		n/a			n/a	—	Martin (1987)
India[†] 1981	L	L	W	Census Rural: 903928 Urban: 244573	CMW 15–49	AAM	0, prim., comp.; prim., sec. +	16.7, 17.6	16.5, 16.7	4, 4	7, 7	18, 19	n/a, n/a	rev. 7, rev. 7	India, Govt. of, Registrar General 1988 (Advance Report on Age)

Country, region, year			Sample	Women (age)	Measure	Education categories							Sig.	Source
India, Goa 1980s	—	—	CMW 30–49 Hindu: 654 Christian: 250	F30–49	AAM (MCA age adjusted)	0, 1–5, 6+	19.1	17.9	—'	—'	30	n/a	+	Roy, Rama Rao, and Prasad (1991)
India, Maharashtra 1983–4	—	—	CMW15–44 1956	F30–49	AAM (mean)	0, prim., middle, sec.+	20.6	19.2	—'	10	24	n/a	+	United Nations (1993)
				F30–44	AAM (mean)	0, prim., middle, sec.+	16.2	15.9	1	9	24	n/a	rev. 7	
					AAM (OLS)	Years				11			b=0.28*	
India, Maharashtra 1992–3	—	—	NFHS: F15–49 4106	F15–49	Median / AAM	0, prim. to middle, middle comp., sec.+	16.1	14.5	13	—'	40	48	+	Population Research Centre, Gokhale Institute et al. (1994)
India, Tamil Nadu 1992	—	—	NFHS: F15–49 3948	F15–49	Median / AAM	0, prim. to middle, middle comp., sec.+	18.1	16.8	8	—'	24	32	+	Population Research Centre, Gandhigram Institute et al. (1994)
India, Uttar Pradesh 1992–3	—	—	NFHS: F15–49 11438	F15–49	Median / AAM	0, prim. to middle, middle comp., sec.+	15.1	14.4	10	—'	32	42	+	Population Research Centre, Lucknow University et al. (1994)
Nepal† 1986	L	W	CMW 25–49, AAM<25 2642 Rural: 2481 Urban: 850	CMW 25–49 AAM<25	AAM	0, any	15.9	15.9	4	—'	—'	—'	0	Aryal (1991)
Pakistan 1975	—	—	WFS: F15–49 4996	F15–49	AAM	0, any	15.8	15.9	4	—'	—'	—'	0	United Nations (1987)
					AAM	0, any	16.4	16.1	7	—'	—'	—'	+	
					SMAM	0, 1–3, 4–6, 7+	19.8	18.9	1	6	36	n/a	rev. 7	
Pakistan 1979	—	—	F15–45+ Urban 6823	F15–45+	AAM	0, 1–8, 9+	n/a	19.5	12	—'	21	n/a	+	Sathar and Kiani (1986)
			Rural 10141			9+	n/a	19.8	7	—'	22	n/a	+	
Pakistan† 1991	L	W	DHS: F15–49 6611	F15–49	AAM	0, prim., comp. prim., sec.+	18.6	18.3	3	—'	23	n/a	rev. 7	National Institute of Population Studies (1992)
Sri Lanka 1971	—	—	Census 2346063	F15–49 677807	% married 15–19	0, 1–4, 5–9, O-level, A-level	n/a	n/a	n/a	n/a	n/a	n/a	–	Fernando (1977)

Appendix C. (cont.)

Site and survey date	Levels of:			Sample		Dependent variable (method if means n/a)	Education variable (years of schooling)	Age of marriage among:		Percentage difference between educated and better educated women[a] by years of schooling				Direction of relationship[b]	Author (date)[c]
	Per capita income	Female literacy rate	Gender disparity in literacy	Type; universe (sex and age); size	Sub-sample characteristics			All women[d]	Uneducated women[e]	1–3	4–6	7+	10+		
Sri Lanka 1975	—	—	—	WFS:F15–49 6812	F15–49	AAM	0, prim., comp.	20.3	18.5	2	5	19	n/a	rev. 7	Rodriguez and Aravena (1991)
1987				DHS:F15–49 5865	F20–49		prim., comp.	21.8	20.3	0	0	12	n/a	rev. 7	
Sri Lanka[†] 1987	L	H	N	DHS:F15–49 5865	F15–49	Median AAM	0, 1–3, 4–6, 7–9, 10+	22.9	21.0	0	1	14	20	rev. 7	United Nations (1995)
E. Latin America and the Caribbean															
Belize[†] 1991	H	M	N	F15–44 2656	F15–44	SMAM	0, prim., comp. prim., sec.+	21.2	18.0	8	17	25	n/a	+	Ministry of Health (1992)
Bolivia[†] 1989	M	M	M	DHS:F15–49 7923	F15–49	Median AAM	0, 1–3, 4–6, 7–9, 10+	20.6	20.0	–2	0	10	15	rev. 7	United Nations (1995)
Brazil[†] 1986	H	M	N	DHS:F15–44 5892	F15–44	Median AAM	0, 1–3, 4–6, 7–9, 10+	21.3	19.4	1	6	22	29	rev. 7	United Nations (1995)
Colombia 1976	—	—	—	WFS:F15–49 5378	F15–49	SMAM	0, 1–3, 4–6, 7+	22.1	19.5	4	8	27	n/a	rev. 7	United Nations (1987)
Colombia[†] 1986	H	H	N	DHS:F15–49 5329	F15–49	Median AAM	0, 1–3, 4–6, 7–9, 10+	21.2	18.4	7	12	29	43	+	United Nations (1995)
Costa Rica[†] 1976	H	H	N	WFS:F15–49 3935	F15–49	SMAM	0, 1–3, 4–6, 7+	22.7	24.2	–20	–8	–4	n/a	U	United Nations (1987)
Dominican Rep. 1975		H		WFS:F15–49 3115	F15–49	SMAM	0, 1–3, 4–6, 7+	20.5	18.0	–3	8	27	n/a	rev. 7	United Nations (1987)
Dominican Rep.[†] 1986	M	M	N	DHS:F15–49 7649	F15–49	Median AAM	0, 1–3, 4–6, 7–9, 10+	19.2	16.4	5	9	33	42	+	United Nations (1995)
Ecuador	—	—	—	WFS:F15–49	F15–49	SMAM	0, 1–3,	22.1	19.1	5	8	25	n/a	+	United Nations

Country, date				Sample	Pop.	Measure	Categories							rev.	Source
Ecuador† 1987	M	H	N	DHS:F15–49 4713	6797 F15–49	Median AAM	4–6, 7+ 0, 1–3, 4–6, 7–9, 10+	20.4	18.6	1	4	20	26	rev. 7	(1987) United Nations (1995)
Ecuador 1989	—	—	—	F15–49 7961	F15–49	Median age, 1st union	0, 1–3, 4–6, sec., superior	20.7	18.9	3	—	23	n/a	rev. 7	Monteith et al. (1992)
El Salvador† 1985	M	M	N	DHS:F15–49 5207	F15–49	Median AAM	0, 1–3, 4–6, 7–9, 10+	19.1	17.8	2	6	20	28	rev. 7	United Nations (1995)
Guatemala† 1987	M	M	M	DHS:F15–44 5160	F15–49	Median AAM	0, 1–3, 4–6, 7–9, 10+	18.8	17.7	5	12	20	34	+	United Nations (1995)
Guyana† 1975	L	H	N	WFS:F15–49 4642	F15–49	SMAM	0, 1–3, 4–6, 7+	20.0	17.7	8	6	14	n/a	+	United Nations (1987)
Haiti 1977	—	—	—	WFS:F15–49 3365	F15–49	SMAM	0, 1–3, 4–6, 7+	21.8	21.5	−3	−2	5	n/a	rev. 7	United Nations (1987)
Haiti† 1989	L	M	M	F15–49 1996	F15–49	SMAM	0, 1–3, 4–6, 7+	22.5	21.0	5	13	24	n/a	+	Cayemittes et al. (1991)
Jamaica† 1975–6	H	H	N	WFS:F15–49 3096	F15–49	SMAM	0–3, 4–6, 7+	19.2	18.3	—	−3	4	n/a	0	United Nations (1987)
Mexico 1976	—	—	—	WFS:F15–49 7310	F15–49	SMAM	0, 1–3, 4–6, 7+	21.7	17.4	11	25	27	n/a	+	United Nations (1987)
Mexico, urban 1983–5	—	—	—	F15–35 child 0–48 m., Cuernavaca and Tlizapotla 510	F15–35	Mean AAM / Age at 1st birth	<6, 6, 7–9 / 0, 1–5, 6, 7–9	n/a / n/a	17.8 / 18.3	— / 2	−1 / 3	3 / 9	n/a / n/a	0 / rev. 7	LeVine et al. (1991)
Mexico† 1987	H	H	N	DHS:F15–49 9310	F15–49	Median AAM	0, 1–3, 4–6, 7–9, 10+	20.3	17.2	6	15	32	40	+	United Nations (1995)
Panama† 1975–6	H	H	N	WFS:F15–49 3701	F15–49	SMAM	0, 1–3, 4–6, 7+	21.2	19.1	−3	6	21	n/a	rev. 7	United Nations (1987)
Paraguay† 1979	H	H	N	WFS:F15–49 4682	F15–49	SMAM	0, 1–3, 4–6, 7+	22.1	18.5	11	17	26	n/a	+	United Nations (1987)
Paraguay 1979	—	—	—	Women aged 25+, married at under 25 1892	F25–49 1st union <25	Mean age, 1st union	<3, 3–5, 6, 7+	18.6	17.7	—	9	14	n/a	+	Schoemaker (1981)
Peru 1977–8				WFS:F15–49 5640	F15–49	SMAM	0, 1–3, 4–6, 7+	23.2	21.0	−3	3	20	n/a	rev. 7	United Nations (1987)

Appendix C. (cont.)

Site and survey date	Levels of:			Sample		Dependent variable (method if means n/a)	Education variable (years of schooling)	Age of marriage among:		Percentage difference between uneducated and better educated women[a] by years of schooling				Direction of relationship[b]	Author (date)[c]
	Per capita income	Female literacy rate	Gender disparity in literacy	Type; universe (sex and age); size	Sub-sample characteristics			All women[d]	Uneducated women[e]	1–3	4–6	7+	10+		
Peru[†] 1986	H	M	N	DHS:F15–49 4999	F15–49	Median AAM	0, 1–3, 4–6, 7–9, 10+	21.0	18.7	0	6	25	33	rev. 7	United Nations (1995)
Puerto Rico 1982	—	—	—	F15–49 3175	F15–49	SMAM	<high sch.; high sch.; >high sch.	23.3	—[f]	—[f]	21	17	23	+	Warren (1987)
Trinidad and Tobago 1977	—	—	—	WFS:F15–49 4359	F15–49	SMAM	0, 1–3, 4–6, 7+	20.9	17.3	19	8	21	n/a	irreg.	United Nations (1987)
Trinidad and Tobago[†] 1987	H	H	N	DHS:F15–49 3806	F15–49	Median AAM	0, 1–3, 4–6, 7–9, 10+	19.7	17.9	–1	4	13	16	rev. 7	United Nations (1995)
Venezuela[†] 1977	H	M	N	WFS:F15–49 4361	F15–49	SMAM	0, 1–3, 4–6, 7+	21.8	19.0	1	7	21	n/a	rev. 7	United Nations (1987)

[a] Refers to the difference between the rates for women with no education compared with women at each successively higher level of education (1–3 years, 4–6 years, and so on).

[b] See Introduction to appendices for discussion of the various types of relationships.

[c] See Bibliography for full citation.

[d] Refers to all women in the sample or in the sub-sample, if there was one.

[e] Refers to women with no education in the sample or in the sub-sample, if there was one.

[f] Merged with next level; if data are given for classes 1–3 and 4–6 together, results are shown under the lower category, 1–3.

[†] Studies included in Tables 4.1, 4.2, and 4.3.

* Statistically significant.

Notes: See Introduction to appendices for list of abbreviations and technical notes on the appendix. For studies in which more than one set of numbers are provided, see column headed 'Sub-sample characteristics' for the sub-population to which the rates refer.

Appendix D. Studies addressing the relationship between women's education and the duration of breast-feeding

Site and survey date	Levels of:			Sample type; universe (sex and age); size; method if not mean or median	Education variable (years of schooling)	Duration of breast-feeding (months) among		Percentage difference between uneducated and better educated women[a] by years of schooling				Direction of relation-ship[b]	Author (date)[c]
	Per capita income	Female literacy rate	Gender disparity in literacy			All women[c]	Unedu-cated women[c]	1–3	4–6	7+	10+		
A. Sub-Saharan Africa													
Benin[†] 1982	L	L	W	WFS:births in last 48 m. 4018	0, 1–6, 7+	21.5	21.6	–18	—[i]	—[i]	n/a	–	United Nations (1987)
Botswana[†] 1988	H	M	M	DHS:births in last 36 m. 4368	0, 1–3, 4–6, 7–9, 10+	18.8	20.2	–8	5	–15	–22	–	United Nations (1995)
Burundi[†] 1987	L	L	W	DHS:births in last 36 m. 3970	0, 1–3, 4–6, 7–9, 10+	23.8	24.1	2	–11	–19	–18	7	United Nations (1995)
Cameroon[†] 1978	M	L	W	WFS:births in last 48 m. 8219	0, 1–3, 4–6, 7+	19.3	21.0	–9	–17	–30	n/a	–	United Nations (1987)
Côte d'Ivoire[†] 1980	M	L	W	WFS:births in last 48 m. 5764	0, 1–3, 4–6, 7+	19.5	20.4	–12	–28	–44	n/a	–	United Nations (1987)
Ghana 1979–80	—	—	—	WFS:births in last 48 m. 6125	0, 1–3, 4–6, 7+	19.3	21.3	–10	—[i]	–27	n/a	–	United Nations (1987)
Ghana[†] 1988	L	M	M	DHS:births in last 36 m. 4488	0, 1–3, 4–6, 7–9, 10+	20.2	22.7	–12	–11	–22	–25	–	United Nations (1995)
Kenya 1977–8	—	—	—	WFS:births in last 48 m. 8100	0, 1–3, 4–6, 7+	18.1	19.6	–11	–22	–36	n/a	–	United Nations (1987)
Kenya[†] 1988–9	L	M	M	DHS:births in last 36 m. 7150	0, 1–3, 4–6, 7–9, 10+	19.4	20.9	–7	–9	–10	–19	–	United Nations (1995)
Lesotho[†] 1977	M	M	M	WFS:births in last 48 m. 3603	0, 1–3, 4–6, 7+	21.3	24.0	–7	–8	–17	n/a	–	United Nations (1987)

Appendix D. (cont.)

Site and survey date	Levels of: Per capita income	Female literacy rate	Gender disparity in literacy	Sample type; universe (sex and age); size; method if not mean or median	Education variable (years of schooling)	Duration of breast-feeding (months) among: All women[d]	Uneducated women[e]	Percentage difference between uneducated and better educated women[a] by years of schooling: 1–3	4–6	7+	10+	Direction of relationship[b]	Author (date)[c]
Liberia[†] 1986	M	L	W	DHS:births in last 36 m. 5239	0, 1–3, 4–6, 7–9, 10+	17.0	18.7	–3	–14	–47	–55	7	United Nations (1995)
Mali[†] 1987	L	L	W	DHS:births in last 36 m. 3200	0, 1–3, 4–6, 7–9, 10+	21.5	21.6	11	–2	–19	–54	rev. J	United Nations (1995)
Mauritania[†] 1981	L	L	W	WFS:births in last 48 m. 3504	0, 1–3, 4–6, 7+	17.1	17.7	–3	–12	–11	n/a	7	United Nations (1987)
Namibia[†] 1992	H	M	M	DHS:births in last 5 yrs. 5421	0, prim., comp. prim., sec.+	17.3	19.7	–4	–14	–34	n/a	7	Katjiuanjo et al. (1993)
Nigeria, Lagos 1976	—	—	—	F25–49 1848 means adjusted by MCA	0, prim., sec.+	10.6 11.0	15.6 14.7	–33 –26	—' —'	–63 –52	n/a n/a	— —	Lesthaeghe, Page, and Adegbola (1981)
Nigeria, Ilorin 1983–4	—	—	—	CMW 15–35; 2 most recent births 913	0, prim., sec.+	16.3	21.4	–33	—'	–51	n/a	—	Oni (1985)
Nigeria, Urban 1987–8	—	—	—	EM Yoruba women 15–45 9 cities; 10340	0, prim., sec., sec.+	10.68	14.9	–21	–40	–52	n/a	—	Feyisetan (1990)
Nigeria, Edo and Delta 1985	—	—	—	MCA adjusted EMW 15–50; 2+ births, all alive at survey; 2146 (OLS)	0, prim., sec., ter.	10.68 —	13.5 R	–16 –1.04*	–28 —'	–36 –2.44*	n/a –3.99*	— —	Okojie (1993)
Nigeria[†] 1990	L	L	W	DHS:births in last 5 yrs. 8781	0, prim., comp. prim., sec.+	19.5	21.3	–8	–24	–29	n/a	—	Federal Office of Statistics (1992)

Senegal 1978	—	—	—	WFS:births in last 48 m. 3985	0, 1–6, 7+	20.0	21.1	-20	—'	—'	n/a	—	United Nations (1987)
Senegal[t] 1986	M	L	W	DHS:births in last 36 m. 4415	0, 1–3, 4–6, 7–9, 10+	18.8	19.4	-3	-17	-26	-30	7	United Nations (1995)
Togo[t] 1988	L	L	W	DHS:births in last 36 m. 3360	0, 1–3, 4–6, 7–9, 10+	22.6	24.2	-17	-21	-15	-26	—	United Nations (1995)
Uganda[t] 1988–9	L	L	W	DHS:births in last 36 m. 4730	0, 1–3, 4–6, 7–9, 10+	18.6	19.8	-12	-6	-15	-26	—	United Nations (1995)
United Rep. of Tanzania[t] 1991–2	L	H	N	DHS:births in last 5 yrs. 9238	0, prim., comp. prim., sec.+	21.2	21.8	0	-1	-9	n/a	7	Ngallaba et al. (1993)
Zambia[t] 1992	L	M	M	DHS:births in last 36 m. 7000	0, prim., sec.+	18.7	19.1	-2	—'	-6	n/a	7	Gaisie et al. (1993)
Zimbabwe 1984–5 1987–8	—	—	—	Rep Health Survey; DHS; births in last five yrs.; n/a	0, prim., comp. prim., sec.+	16.2 17.0	17.6 18.3	-6 -3	-30 -22	-29 -23	n/a n/a	— 7	Mhloyi (1991)
Zimbabwe[t] 1988–9	M	M	M	DHS:births in last 36 m. 4201	0, 1–3, 4–6, 7–9, 10+	17.7	19.1	-7	-12	-8	-10	—	United Nations (1995)
B. North Africa and the Middle East													
Egypt 1980	M	L	—	WFS:births in last 48 m. 8788	0, 1–3, 4–6, 7+	19.4	21.2	-8	-23	-52	n/a	—	United Nations (1987)
Egypt[t] 1988–9	M	L	W	DHS:births in last 36 m. 8911	0, 1–3, 4–6, 7–9, 10+	17.3	18.1	1	-12	-12	-4	7	United Nations (1995)
Jordan[t] 1976	H	M	M	WFS:births in last 48 m. 3612	0, 1–3, 4–6, 7+	12.3	13.9	-6	-24	-45	n/a	—	United Nations (1987)
Kuwait[t] 1985	H	M	N	KAP survey of breast-feeding 1553	0, prim., sec., diploma, univ.	6.4	13.2	-40	—'	-63	n/a	—	Al-Bustan and Kohli (1988)
Morocco 1979–80	—	—	—	WFS births in last 48 m. 5801	0, 1–6, 7+	16.2	16.7	-44	—'	—'	n/a	—	United Nations (1987)

Appendix D. (cont.)

Site and survey date	Levels of: Per capita income	Female literacy rate	Gender disparity in literacy	Sample type; universe (sex and age); size; method if not mean or median	Education variable (years of schooling)	Duration of breast-feeding (months) among: All women[d]	Uneducated women[e]	Percentage difference between uneducated and better educated women[a] by years of schooling: 1–3	4–6	7+	10+	Direction of relationship[b]	Author (date)[c]
Morocco[†] 1987	M	L	W	DHS:births in last 36 m. 5982	0, 1–3, 4–6, 7–9, 10+	14.4	15.4	−21	−40	−56	−66	−	United Nations (1995)
Sudan 1978–9	M	L		WFS:births in last 48 m. 3115	0, 1–3, 4–6, 7+	17.2	17.3	−7	−[f]	−[f]	n/a	−	United Nations (1987)
Sudan[†] 1989–90	L	L	W	DHS:births in last 36 m. 5860	0, prim., comp. prim., sec.+	19.5	20.0	−1	−9	−7	n/a	7	Ministry of Economic and Natl. Planning (1991)
Syrian Arab Republic[†] 1978	H	L	W	WFS:births in last 48 m. 4487	0, 1–6, 7+	12.8	12.9	−17	−[f]	−26	n/a	−	United Nations (1987)
Tunisia 1978				WFS:births in last 48 m. 4123	0, 1–3, 4–6, 7+	15.3	16.8	−48	−[f]	−60	n/a	−	United Nations (1987)
Tunisia[†] 1988	H	M	M	DHS:births in last 36 m. 4184	0, 1–3, 4–6, 7–9, 10+	15.5	18.2	−14	−33	−48	−53	−	United Nations (1995)
C. East and South-East Asia													
Fiji[†] 1974	M	M	M	WFS:births in last 48 m. 4298	0, 1–3, 4–6, 7+	11.1	13.0	−15	−9	−33	n/a	−	United Nations (1987)
Indonesia 1976	—	—	—	WFS:births in last 48 m. 9155	0, 1–3, 4–6, 7+	26.8	28.4	−5	−13	−52	n/a	−	United Nations (1987)
Indonesia[†] 1991	M	M	N	DHS:births in last 36 m. 22909	0, 1–3, 4–6, 7–9, 10+	25.1	28.1	−6	−8	−29	−36	−	United Nations (1995)
Malaysia[†] 1974	H	M	M	WFS:births in last 48 m. 6316	0, 1–3, 4–6, 7+	7.0	7.6	−25	−25	−50	n/a	−	United Nations (1987)

Country/Survey				Data / sample	Education categories							Corr.	Source
Malaysia 1974	—	—	—	WFS:births in last 48 m. (2+ live births); last interval >35m. breast-fed child survived 1876	0, prim., sec.+	8.1	8.8	-27	-'	-64	n/a	-	Othman (1985)
Philippines 1973	—	—	—	National Dem. Survey; CMW, last birth 3163	0 to prim., sec., college	12.0	10.1	-'	-'	-12	-24	-	Mejia-Raymundo (1985)
Philippines† 1978	M	H	N	WFS:births in last 48 m. 9268	0, 1–3, 4–6, 7+	15.5	18.9	-7	-22	-50	n/a	-	United Nations (1987)
Philippines	—	—	—	CMW; births in last 3 yrs 3573;	<4, 5–9, 10+	n/a	n/a	n/a	n/a	n/a	n/a	-	Guilkey et al. (1990)
1973 Natl. Demographic Survey	—	—	—	5396; simulation	Years	n/a	n/a	n/a	n/a	n/a	n/a	-0.356*	Raymundo et al. (1993)
1983 Natl. Demographic Survey	—	—	—	National Probability		n/a	n/a	n/a	n/a	n/a	n/a	-0.217*	
Philippines 1983 Natl. Demographic Survey	—	—	—	EMW 15–45; (CMW who breast-fed in last closed birth interval; 9686; 12426; correlation		n/a	n/a	n/a	n/a	n/a	n/a	-0.302*	
1988 Natl. Demographic Survey	—	—	—			n/a	n/a	n/a	n/a	n/a	n/a	-0.229*	
						n/a	n/a	n/a	n/a	n/a	n/a	-0.386*	
						n/a	n/a	n/a	n/a	n/a	n/a	-0.176*	
						n/a	n/a	n/a	n/a	n/a	n/a	-0.346*	
						n/a	n/a	n/a	n/a	n/a	n/a	-0.241*	
Rep. of Korea† 1974	H	H	N	WFS:births in last 48 m. 5430	0, 1–3, 4–6	17.5	21.0	-16	-14	-35	n/a	-	United Nations (1987)
Thailand 1975	—	—	—	WFS:births in last 48 m. 3778	0, 1–6, 7+	20.8	20.9	0	-'	-'	n/a	0	United Nations (1987)
Thailand† 1987	H	H	N	DHS:births in last 36 m. 6775	C, 1–3, 4–6, 7–9, 10+	16.6	18.6	-12	-2	-51	-60	-	United Nations (1995)
D. South Asia Bangladesh† 1975–6	L	L	W	WFS:births in last 48 m. 6513	0, 1–3, 4–6, 7+	33.8	34.4	-12	-'	-'	n/a	-	United Nations (1987)

Appendix D. (cont.)

Site and survey date	Levels of:			Sample type; universe (sex and age); size; method if not mean or median	Education variable (years of schooling)	Duration of breast-feeding (months) among		Percentage difference between uneducated and better educated women[a] by years of schooling				Direction of relationship[b]	Author (date)[c]
	Per capita income	Female literacy rate	Gender disparity in literacy			All women[d]	Uneducated women[e]	1–3	4–6	7+	10+		
India, Maharashtra 1983–4	—	—	—	F15–44, births in last 5 yrs.; (30–44) 1956	0, prim., middle, sec.+	20.3	20.8	−6	−13	−20	n/a	—	United Nations (1993)
India,[†] Maharashtra 1992–93	L	L	W	NFHS:F15–44, births in last 48m. 4106	0, prim. to middle, middle comp., sec.+	25.5	26.1	−13	—[f]	−23	−26	—	Population Research Centre, Gokhale Institute et al. (1994)
India, Tamil Nadu 1992	—	—	—	NFHS:F15–44, births in last 48m. 3948	0, prim. to middle, middle comp., sec.+	18.3	18.0	−8	—[f]	−30	−39	—	Population Research Centre, Gandhigram Institute et al. (1994)
India, Uttar Pradesh 1992–93	—	—	—	NFHS:F15–44, births in last 48m. 11438	0, prim. to middle, middle comp., sec.+	26.7	25.5	−4	—[f]	−10	−9	7	Population Research Centre, Lucknow University et al. (1994)
Pakistan 1975	—	—	—	WFS:births in last 48 m. 4996	0, 1–3, 4–6, 7+	22.4	22.0	−10	—[f]	—[f]	n/a	—	United Nations (1987)
Pakistan[†] 1991	L	L	W	DHS:births in last 5 yrs. 6611	0, prim., comp. prim., sec.+	13.5	18.0	−39	—[f]	−67	n/a	—	Sathar (1992)
Sri Lanka 1975	—	—	—	WFS:births in last 48 m. 6812	0, 1–3, 4–6, 7+	22.8	26.1	−5	−10	−29	n/a	—	United Nations (1987)
Sri Lanka[†] 1987	L	H	N	DHS:births in last 36 m. 5865	0, 1–3, 4–6, 7–9, 10+	22.6	27.0	−9	−15	−20	−27	—	United Nations (1995)
E. Latin America and the Caribbean													
Belize[†] 1991	H	M	N	Births in last 5 yrs.	0, prim., comp. prim.,	11.7	12.8	−9	—[f]	−20	n/a	—	Ministry of Health (1992)

2656

Country / Year				Source	n	Education categories								Reference
Bolivia 1989	M	M	M	DHS:births in last 36 m.	7923	sec.+ 0, 1–3, 4–6, 7–9, 10+	16.2	17.8	−2	−7	−26	−32	7	United Nations (1995)
Brazil 1986	H	M	N	DHS:births in last 36 m.	5892	0, 1–3, 4–6, 7–9, 10+	9.1	11.2	−5	−24	−36	−27	—	United Nations (1995)
Colombia 1976	—	—	—	WFS:births in last 48 m.	5378	0, 1–3, 4–6, 7+	10.3	11.9	−4	−30	−55	n/a	7	United Nations (1987)
Colombia 1986	H	H	N	DHS:births in last 36 m.	5329	0, 1–3, 4–6, 7–9, 10+	11.1	12.2	3	−12	−21	−22	7	United Nations (1995)
Costa Rica 1976	H	H	N	WFS:births in last 48 m.	3935	1–3, 4–6, 7+	6.1	n/a	8.1R	−43	−60	n/a	—	United Nations (1987)
Dominican Rep. 1975	—	—	—	WFS:births in last 48 m.	3115	0, 1–3, 4–6, 7+	9.7	12.2	−14	−30	−57	n/a	—	United Nations (1987)
Dominican Rep. 1986	M	M	N	DHS:births in last 36 m.	7649	0, 1–3, 4–6, 7–9, 10+	9.3	12.8	−11	−28	−41	−46	—	United Nations (1995)
Ecuador 1979	—	—	—	WFS:births in last 48 m.	6797	0, 1–3, 4–6, 7+	13.6	17.0	−15	−24	−48	n/a	—	United Nations (1987)
Ecuador 1987	M	H	N	DHS:births in last 36 m.	4713	0, 1–3, 4–6, 7–9, 10+	14.5	18.0	−12	−18	−34	−37	—	United Nations (1995)
Ecuador 1989	—	—	—	Births in last 24 m.	7961	0, 1–3, 4–6, sec., superior	15.4	20.7	−18	—	−38	n/a	—	Monteith et al. (1992)
El Salvador 1988	M	M	N	Births in last 36 m.	3579	0, 1–3, 4–6, 7–9, 10+	16.9	18.0	−5	−5	−18	−22	—	Castro et al. (1989)
Guatemala 1987	M	M	M	DHS:births in last 36 m.	5160	0, 1–3, 4–6, 7–9, 10+	20.6	22.9	−14	−20	−46	−54	—	United Nations (1995)
Guyana 1975	L	H	N	WFS:births in last 48 m.	4642	0, 1–3, 4–6, 7+	7.5	9.2	−16	—	−28	n/a	—	United Nations (1987)
Haiti 1977	—	—	—	WFS:births in last 48 m.	3365	0, 1–3, 4–6, 7+	17.4	19.0	−26	—	—	n/a	—	United Nations (1987)

Appendix D. (cont.)

Site and survey date	Levels of:			Sample type; universe (sex and age); size; method if not mean or median	Education variable (years of schooling)	Duration of breast-feeding (months) among		Percentage difference between uneducated and better educated women[a] by years of schooling				Direction of relationship[b]	Author (date)[c]
	Per capita income	Female literacy rate	Gender disparity in literacy			All women[d]	Uneducated women[e]	1–3	4–6	7+	10+		
Haiti[t] 1989	L	M	M	Births in last 24 m. 1996	0, 1–3, 4–6, 7+	18.2	18.6	1	–4	–19	n/a	?	Cayemittes et al. (1991)
Jamaica[t] 1975–6	H	H	N	WFS:births in last 48 m. 3096	4–6, 7+	9.0	—[l]	—[l]	4.6R	–30	n/a	–	United Nations (1987)
Mexico 1976	–	–	–	WFS:births in last 48 m. 7310	0, 1–3, 4–6, 7+	10.9	12.9	–16	–36	–71	n/a	–	United Nations (1987)
Mexico[t] 1987	H	H	N	DHS:births in last 36 m. 9310	0, 1–3, 4–6, 7–9, 10+	10.5	17.4	–28	–49	–62	–68	–	United Nations (1995)
Nicaragua 1977–8	–	–	–	Survey of EMW 15–45 and sibling data from sister 1281 reduced form	Years	–0.44*	n/a	n/a	n/a	n/a	n/a	–	Wolfe and Behrman (1982)
Panama[t] 1975–6	H	H	N	WFS:births in last 48 m. 3701	0–3, 4–6, 7+	8.5	n/a	13R	–29	–82	n/a	–	United Nations (1987)
Paraguay[t] 1979	H	H	N	WFS:births in last 48 m. 4682	0, 1–3, 4–6, 7+	12.2	15.7	–7	–27	–61	n/a	–	United Nations (1987)
Peru 1977–8	–	–	–	WFS:births in last 48 m. 5640	0, 1–3, 4–6, 7+	14.9	19.3	–14	–38	–64	n/a	–	United Nations (1987)
Peru[t] 1986	H	M	N	DHS:births in last 36 m. 4999	0, 1–3, 4–6, 7–9, 10+	16.6	21.0	–13	–15	–42	–46	–	United Nations (1995)
Puerto Rico 1982	–	–	–	Survey of fertility & FP;	<high sch., high sch.	3.0	n/a	n/a	n/a	n/a	n/a	–	Warren (1987?)

				Sample / women 15–49	comp., >high sch.							Source
Trinidad and Tobago 1977	H		N	3175 WFS:births in last 48 m. 4359	0–6, 7+	7.0	—'	10R	—'	–29	n/a	–	United Nations (1987)
Trinidad and Tobago† 1987	H	H	N	DHS:births in last 36 m. 3806	0–3, 4–6, 7–9, 10+	10.1	(3.2)	13.6R	–16	–30	–32	–	United Nations (1995)
Venezuela† 1977	H	M	N	WFS:births in last 48 m. 4361	0, 1–3, 4–6, 7+	8.4	11.6	–14	–42	–70	n/a	–	United Nations (1987)

* Refers to the difference between the rates for women with no education compared with women at each successively higher level of education (1–3 years, 4–6 years, and so on).

[b] See Introduction to appendices for discussion of the various types of relationships.

[c] See Bibliography for full citation.

[d] Refers to all women in the sample or in the sub-sample, if there was one.

* Refers to women with no education in the sample or in the sub-sample, if there was one.

† Merged with next level; if data are given for classes 1–3 and 4–6 together, results are shown under the lower category, 1–3.

† Studies included in Tables 5.1, 5.2, and 5.3.

* Statistically significant.

Notes: See Introduction to appendices for list of abbreviations and technical notes on the appendix. For studies in which more than one set of numbers are provided, see column headed 'Sample' for the sub-population to which the rates refer, and column headed 'Site and survey date' if different years. Current status data are data pertaining to births in the recent past (e.g. 36, 48, or 60 months).

Appendix E. Studies addressing the relationship between women's education and durations of post-partum abstinence and post-partum amenorrhoea

Site and survey date	Levels of:			Sample type; universe (sex and age); size	Dependent variable; (method if means n/a)	Education variable (years of schooling)	Durations of post-partum abstinence, amenorrhoea among		Percentage difference between uneducated and better educated women[a] by years of schooling				Direction of relationship[b]	Author (date)[c]
	Per capita income	Female literacy rate	Gender disparity in literacy				All women[d]	Uneducated women[e]	1–3	4–6	7+	10+		
A. Sub-Saharan Africa														
Botswana 1988	—	—	—	DHS:births in last five years 4368	Dur. of abstinence Dur. of amenorrhoea	0, prim., comp. prim., sec.+	12.7 11.6	11.6 12.6	22 0	6 −15	12 −20	n/a n/a	+ 7	Lestede et al. (1989)
Botswana[†] 1988	H	M	M	DHS:births in last 36 m. 4368	Dur. of abstinence	0, 1–3, 4–6, 7–9, 10+	12.7	11.6	22	23	9	10	rev. U	United Nations (1995)
Burundi 1987	—	—	—	DHS:births in last 36 m. 3970	Dur. of amenorrhoea	0, prim., sec.+	19.1	19.8	−14	−[i]	−51	n/a	−	Segamba et al. (1988)
Burundi[†] 1987	L	L	W	DHS:births in last 36 m. 3970	Dur. of abstinence	0, 1–3, 4–6, 7–9, 10+	3.5	3.6	−8	−25	−15	36	−	United Nations (1995)
Ghana 1988	—	—	—	DHS:births in last five years 4488	Dur. of amenorrhoea	0, prim., middle, sec.+	14.0	16.4	−15	−27	−45	n/a	−	Ghana Statistical Service (1989)
Ghana[†] 1988	L	M	M	DHS:births in last 36 m. 4488	Dur. of abstinence	0, 1–3, 4–6, 7–9, 10+	13.5	17.1	−25	−23	−42	−42	−	United Nations (1995)
Kenya 1988–9	—	—	—	DHS:births in last 36 m. 7150	Dur. of amenorrhoea	0, prim., comp. prim., sec.+	10.9	13.4	−18	−25	−37	n/a	−	Natl. Council for Population and Devel. (1989)

Country/Year			Sample/source	Measure	Categories								Reference
Kenya† 1988–9	L	M	DHS:births in last 36 m. 7150	Dur. of abstinence	0, 1–3, 4–6, 7–9, 10+	5.7	6.4	–8	–36	–5	–13	irreg.	United Nations (1995)
Liberia 1986	—	—	DHS:births in last 36 m. 5239	Dur. of amenorrhoea	0, prim., sec.+	11.2	12.4	–10	—'	–48	n/a	—	Chieh-Johnson et al. (1988)
Liberia† 1986	M	W	DHS:births in last 36 m. 5239	Dur. of abstinence	0, 1–3, 4–6, 7–9, 10+	13.2	14.1	9	–10	–37	–51	rev. J	United Nations (1995)
Mali 1987	—	—	DHS:births in last 36 m. 3200	Dur. of amenorrhoea	0, prim.+	15.3	15.6	–10	—'	—'	n/a	—	Traore et al. (1989)
Mali† 1987	L	W	DHS:births in last 36 m. 3200	Dur. of abstinence	0, 1–3, 4–6, 7–9, 10+	7.3	7.5	–5	–33	–7	–20	irreg.	United Nations (1995)
Namibia† 1992	H	M	DHS:births in last five years; 5421	Dur. of abstinence	0, prim., comp. prim., sec.+	6.0	4.2	102	86	24	n/a	+	Katjiuanjo et al. (1993)
				Dur. of amenorrhoea		8.3	12.4	–11	–34	–55	n/a	—	
Nigeria, Ibadan 1973	—	—	300 CAFN1	% currently abstaining (youngest child aged 1–2 years)	0, prim., sec.+	71.0	77.0	–10	—'	–34	n/a	—	Caldwell and Caldwell (1981)
Nigeria, Western State 1974–5	—	—	300 (Nigerian Family Study 2)	Dur. of abstinence	0, prim., sec.+	—	28.7	–22	—'	–63	n/a	—	Caldwell and Caldwell (1981)
				minus dur. of lactation		—	5.9	–61	—'	–92	n/a	—	
Nigeria, Lagos 1976	—	—	W25–49 1848	Dur. of amenorrhoea	0, prim., sec.	—	8.8	–43	—'	–68	n/a	—	Lesthaeghe, Page, and Adegbola (1981)
				Dur. of abstinence		13.6	19.2	–29	—'	–63	n/a	—	
Nigeria, Ibadan 1973	—	—	4763 CAFN	Dur. of amenorrhoea (unadjusted)	0, prim., sec.+	22.0	25.6	–24	—'	–48	n/a	—	Caldwell and Caldwell (1981)
				(MCA adjusted for occupation, marriage type, religion, FP use)		22.0	24.0	–15	—'	–27	n/a	—	Caldwell and Caldwell (1981)
Nigeria, Ilorin 1983–4	—	—	F15–35 913	Dur. of abstinence	0, prim., sec., sec.+	—	22.8	–29	—'	–44	n/a	—	Oni (1985)

Appendix E. (cont.)

Site and survey date	Levels of:			Sample type; universe (sex and age); size	Dependent variable; (method if means n/a)	Education variable (years of schooling)	Durations of post-partum abstinence, amenorrhoea among		Percentage difference between uneducated and better educated women[a] by years of schooling				Direction of relationship[b]	Author (date)[c]
	Per capita income	Female literacy rate	Gender disparity in literacy				All women[d]	Uneducated women[*]	1–3	4–6	7+	10+		
Nigeria, Urban 1987–8	—	—	—	EM Yoruba women 15–49; 9 cities 10340	% having sex during lactation adjusted for age, marital duration, husband's educ., work, religion, contraceptive status, migration status (MCA)	0, prim., sec., sec+	0.51	0.4	0.5	—[f]	0.6	—[f]	+	Feyisetan (1990)
Nigeria 1981–2	—	—	—	WFS: births in last 36 m. 9720 logistic regression	% with 1st birth interval >24 m. (logistic regression, odds ratio)	0, prim., sec.		1.0	0.69	—[f]	0.68	—[f]	–	Adewuyi and Isiugo-Abanihe (1990)
Nigeria Edo and Delta 1985	—	—	—	F15–50 2146	F15–50 Dur. of abstinence, controlling age, husband's educ., husband's occup.[*], community characteristics, ethnic group[*], sex role attitudes, decision-making, spousal age difference, contribution to household[*], polygamous union (OLS)	0, prim., sec., tertiary	n/a	R	0.67[*]	—[f]	-0.003	-0.99[*] rev. J		Okojie (1993)

Country/Year				Data	Variable	Category							rev.	Source
Nigeria[†] 1990	L	L	W	DHS:births in last five years; 8781	Dur. of abstinence / Dur. of amenorrhea	0, prim., comp. prim., sec.+	10.8 / 14.6	10.6 / 18.2	20 / −17	3 / −34	−20 / −57	n/a / n/a	rev. J / −	Federal Office of Statistics (1992)
Senegal 1986	−	−	−	DHS:births in last 36 m. 4415	Dur. of amenorrhea	0, prim., sec.+	16.2	17.2	−29	−'	−47	n/a	−	Ndiaye et al. (1988)
Senegal[†] 1986	M	L	W	DHS:births in last 36 m. 4415	Dur. of abstinence	0, 1–3, 4–6, 7–9, 10+	7.8	8.1	−5	−10	−31	−16	−	United Nations (1995)
Togo[†] 1988	L	L	W	DHS:births in last 36 m. 3360	Dur. of abstinence	0, 1–3, 4–6, 7–9, 10+	17.5	19.0	−14	−22	−33	−62	−	United Nations (1995)
Uganda 1988–9	−	−	−	DHS:births in last 36 m. 4730	Dur. of amenorrhea	0, prim., comp. prim., sec.+	12.7	14.8	−20	−25	−28	n/a	−	Kaijuka et al. (1989)
Uganda[†] 1988–9	L	L	W	DHS:births in last 36 m. 4730	Dur. of abstinence	0, 1–3, 4–6, 7–9, 10+	4.1	4.5	−22	−22	5	18	J	United Nations (1995)
United Republic of Tanzania[†] 1991–2	L	H	N	DHS:births in last five years; 9238	Dur. of abstinence / Dur. of amenorrhea	0, prim., comp. prim., sec.+	6.5 / 13.3	5.9 / 14.3	−20 / 6	25 / −15	22 / −54	n/a / n/a	J / rev. J	Ngallaba et al. (1993)
Zimbabwe[†] 1988–9	M	M	M	DHS:births in last 36 m. 4201	Dur. of abstinence	0, 1–3, 4–6, 7–9, 10+	5.3	5.2	−19	4	5	0	U	United Nations (1995)

B. North Africa and the Middle East

Country/Year				Data	Variable	Category							rev.	Source
Egypt 1983	−	−	−	EMW 15–49; Beni-Suef and Menoufia 8609	Dur. of amenorrhoea after last birth	0, prim., sec.+	11.6 / 9.2	11.0 / 10.0	−16 / −16	−' / −'	−65 / −42	n/a / n/a	− / −	Gadalla, McCarthy, and Kak (1987)
Egypt[†] 1988–9	M	L	W	DHS:births in last 36 m. 8911	Dur. of abstinence	0, 1–3, 4–6, 7–9, 10+	3.2	3.5	−9	−14	−24	−20	−	United Nations (1995)
Morocco 1987	M	L	W	DHS:births in last 36 m. 5982	Dur. of amenorrhoea	0, prim., sec.+	8.7	9.3	−31	−'	−51	n/a	−	Azelmat et al. (1989)
Sudan[†] 1989–90	L	L	W	DHS:births in last 36 m. 5860	Dur. of abstinence / Dur. of amenorrhoea	0, prim., comp. prim., sec.+	5.0 / 13.9	5.0 / 16.0	−2 / −19	2 / −27	2 / −39	n/a / n/a	0 / −	Ministry of Economic and Natl. Planning (1991)

Appendix E. (cont.)

Site and survey date	Levels of: Per capita income	Female literacy rate	Gender disparity in literacy	Sample type; universe (sex and age); size	Dependent variable; (method if means n/a)	Education variable (years of schooling)	Durations of post-partum abstinence, amenorrhoea among: All women[d]	Uneducated women[e]	Percentage difference between uneducated and better educated women[a] by years of schooling: 1–3	4–6	7+	10+	Direction of relationship[b]	Author (date)[c]
Tunisia[†] 1988	H	M	M	DHS:births in last 36 m. 4184	Dur. of abstinence	0, 1–3, 4–6, 7–9, 10+	1.8	1.7	–6	6	92	112	J	United Nations (1995)
C. East and South-East Asia														
Indonesia 1991	—	—	—	DHS:births in last five years 22909	Dur. of amenorrhoea	0, prim., comp. prim., sec.+	7.3	10.5	–11	–35	–52	n/a	—	Central Bureau of Statistics (1992)
Indonesia[†] 1987	M	M	N	DHS:births in last 36 m. 11884	Dur. of abstinence	0, 1–3, 4–6, 7–9, 10+	5.3	6.8	–15	–24	–41	–53	—	United Nations (1995)
Thailand 1987	—	—	—	DHS:births in last 36 m. 6775	Dur. of amenorrhoea	0, prim., sec., sec+	7.2	7.3	5	—[f]	–36	–32	rev. J	Chayovan et al. (1988)
Thailand[†] 1987	H	H	N	DHS:births in last 36 m. 6775	Dur. of abstinence	0, 1–3, 4–6, 7–9, 10+	3.5	4.4	2	–23	–23	–23	7	United Nations (1995)
D. South Asia														
India, Tamil Nadu, 1970, 1980	—	—	—	CMW 35–44 766 258 OLS	Natural birth interval	Years	–0.372* –0.149	— —	— —	— —	— —	— —	— —	Jejeebhoy (1991)
India,[†] Maharashtra 1983–4	L	L	W	CMW 35–44 1956	Dur. of amenorrhoea Dur. of abstinence First birth interval	0, prim., middle, sec.+	13.8 4.9 24.3	14.1 4.8 24.9	1 15 –6	–18 –6 –10	–33 12 –18	n/a n/a n/a	rev7 irreg. —	United Nations (1993)
Pakistan[†] 1991	L	L	W	DHS:births in last five years; 6611	Dur. of abstinence Dur. of amenorrhoea	0, prim to middle, sec.+	2.4 6.3	2.3 7.9	13 –43	—[f] –61	4 –61	n/a n/a	+ —	Nat. Institute of Population Studies (1992)

Country/Year				Source	Measure	Age groups								Reference
Sri Lanka 1987	—	—	—	DHS:births in last 36 m. 5865	Dur. of amenorrhoea	0, prim., sec., +	7.5	9.2	−13	—'	−17	−35	—	Ministry of Plan Implementation (1988)
Sri Lanka† 1987	L	H	N	DHS:births in last 36 m. 5865	Dur. of abstinence	0, 1–3, 4–6, 7–9, 10+	6.6	8.8	−7	−22	−35	−42	—	United Nations (1995)
E. Latin America and the Caribbean														
Bolivia† 1989	M	M	M	DHS:births in last 36 m. 7923	Dur. of abstinence	0, 1–3, 4–6, 7–9, 10+	6 1	6.0	5	8	−3	−3	rev. U	United Nations (1995)
Brazil† 1986	H	M	N	DHS:births in last 36 m. 5892	Dur. of abstinence	0, 1–3, 4–6, 7–9, 10+	2.9	1.7	71	82	96	106	+	United Nations (1995)
Colombia 1986	—	—	—	DHS:births in last five years 5329	Dur. of amenorrhoea	0, prim., sec.+	5.0	5.4	2	—'	−22	n/a	7	Heredia *et al.* (1988)
Colombia† 1986	H	H	N	DHS:births in last 36 m. 5329	Dur. of abstinence	0, 1–3, 4–6, 7–9, 10+	5.5	5.0	14	10	13	36	irreg.	United Nations (1995)
Dom. Republic† 1986	M	M	N	DHS:births in last 36 m. 7649	Dur. of abstinence	0, 1–3, 4–6, 7–9, 10+	4.9	4.3	12	12	19	23	+	United Nations (1995)
Ecuador 1987	—	—	—	DHS:births in last five years 4713	Dur. of amenorrhoea	0, prim., sec., +	8.4	11.5	−23	—'	−41	−41	—	Centro de Estudio de Poblacion (1988)
Ecuador† 1987	M	H	N	DHS:births in last 36 m. 4713	Dur. of abstinence	0, 1–3, 4–6, 7–9, 10+	5.3	6.8	−37	−12	−33	−34	—	United Nations (1995)
El Salvador† 1985	M	M	N	DHS:births in last 36 m. 5207	Dur. of abstinence	0, 1–3, 4–6, 7–9, 10+	8.8	10.0	−10	−16	−21	−20	—	United Nations (1995)
Guatemala† 1987	M	M	M	DHS:births in last 36 m. 5160	Dur. of abstinence	0, 1–3, 4–6, 7–9, 10+	6.8	6.6	6	12	−3	0	rev. U	United Nations (1995)
Mexico† 1987	H	H	N	DHS:births in last 36 m. 9310	Dur. of abstinence	0, 1–3, 4–6, 7–9, 10+	4.4	5.9	−20	−42	−26	−17	—	United Nations (1995)
Peru† 1986	H	M	N	DHS:births in last 36 m. 4999	Dur. of abstinence	0, 1–3, 4–6, 7–9, 10+	6.5	8.4	−2	−19	−49	−52	7	United Nations (1995)

Appendix E. (cont.)

Site and survey date	Levels of:			Sample type; universe (sex and age); size	Dependent variable; (method if means n/a)	Education variable (years of schooling)	Durations of post-partum abstinence, amenorrhoea among		Percentage difference between uneducated and better educated women[a] by years of schooling				Direction of relationship[b]	Author (date)[c]
	Per capita income	Female literacy rate	Gender disparity in literacy				All women[d]	Unedu-cated women[e]	1–3	4–6	7+	10+		
Trinidad and Tobago 1987	—	—	—	DHS:births in last five years; 3806	Dur. of amenorrhoea	0 to prim., comp. prim., sec., sec.+	3.5	4.6	—[f]	—[f]	-37	-42	—	Heath et al. (1988)
Trinidad and Tobago[†] 1987	H	H	N	DHS:births in last 36 m. 3806	Dur. of abstinence	0, 1–3, 4–6, 7–9, 10+	2.6	3.2	16	-19	19	-25	rev. J	United Nations (1995)

a Refers to the difference between the rates for women with no education compared with women at each successively higher level of education (1–3 years, 4–6 years, and so on).

b See Introduction to appendices for discussion of the various types of relationships.

c See Bibliography for full citation.

d Refers to all women in the sample.

e Refers to women with no education in the sample.

f Merged with next level; if data are given for classes 1–3 and 4–6 together, results are shown under the lower category, 1–3.

† Studies included in Tables 5.4, 5.5, and 5.6

* Statistically significant.

Notes: See Introduction to appendices for list of abbreviations and technical notes on the appendix. For studies in which more than one set of numbers are provided, see column headed 'Sample' for the sub-population to which the rates refer, and column headed 'Site and survey date' if different years.

Appendix F. *Studies addressing the relationship between women's education and the levels of infant or early childhood mortality*

Site and survey date	Levels of: Per capita income	Female literacy rate	Gender disparity in literacy	Sample type; universe (sex and age); size	Dependent variable; (method if means n/a)	Education variable (years of schooling)	Infant or early childhood mortality rate among All women[d]	Uneducated women[e]	Percentage difference between uneducated and better educated women[a] by years of schooling 1–3	4–6	7+	10+	Direction of relationship[b]	Author (date)[c]
A. Sub-Saharan Africa														
Benin[†] 1982	L	L	W	WFS:F15–49 4018	IMR	0, 1–3, 4–6, 7+	108	128	−28	−55	−71	n/a	–	Cochrane and Farid (1989)
Botswana[†] 1988	H	M	M	DHS:F15–49 4368	IMR	0, prim., comp. prim., sec. +	40	47	−26	−21	−20	n/a	–	Lestede et al. (1989)
Burundi[†] 1987	L	L	W	DHS:F15–49 3970	IMR	0, prim., sec.+	87	90	−9	−'	−64	n/a	–	Segamba et al. (1988)
Cameroon[†] 1978	M	L	W	WFS:F15–49 8219	IMR	0, 1–3, 4–6, 7–	105	116	−24	−29	−45	n/a	–	Cochrane and Farid (1989)
Côte d'Ivoire[†] 1980	M	L	W	WFS:F15–49 5764	IMR	0, 1–3, 4–6, 7–	113	132	15	−17	−46	n/a	rev. J	Cochrane and Farid (1989)
Ghana 1979–80	—	—	—	WFS:F15–49 6125	IMR	0, 1–3, 4–6, 7+	73	77	−20	−15	−10	n/a	–	Cochrane and Farid (1989)
Ghana[†] 1988	L	M	M	DHS:F15–49 4488	IMR	0, prim., middle, sec. +	81	88	−3	−21	−10	n/a	7	Ghana Statistical Service (1989)
Kenya[†] 1989	L	M	M	DHS:F15–49 7150	IMR	0, comp. prim., sec.+	59	72	−18	−31	−42	n/a	–	National Council, Pop. and Devel. (1989)
Liberia[†] 1986	M	L	W	DHS:F15–49 5239	IMR	0, prim., sec.+	153	164	23	−'	−9	n/a	rev. J	Chieh-Johnson et al. (1988)
Mali[†] 1987	L	L	W	DHS:F15–49 3200	IMR	0, prim.+	131	139	−47	−'	−47	n/a	–	Traore et al. (1989)
Mauritania[†] 1981	L	L	W	WFS:F15–49 3504	IMR	0, 1–3, 4–6, 7+	90	83	10	−32	−2	n/a	irreg.	Cochrane and Farid (1989)
Namibia[†] 1992	H	M	M	DHS:F15–49 5421	IMR	0, prim., comp. prim., sec.+	62	58	8	36	−2	n/a	rev. U	Katjiuanjo et al. (1993)
Nigeria, Ibadan 1973	—	—	—	Yoruba F15–59 6606	Proportion child deaths	0, prim., sec.+	n/a	n/a	n/a	n/a	n/a	n/a	n/a	Caldwell (1979)
				F35–39			0.173	0.216	−47	n/a	−55	n/a	–	
				F45–49			0.276	0.296	−16	n/a	−60	n/a	–	

Appendix F. (cont.)

Site and survey date	Levels of: Per capita income	Female literacy rate	Gender disparity in literacy	Sample type; universe (sex and age); size	Dependent variable; (method if means n/a)	Education variable (years of schooling)	Infant or early childhood mortality rate among: All women[d]	Uneducated women[e]	Percentage difference between uneducated and better educated women[a] by years of schooling: 1-3	4-6	7+	10+	Direction of relationship[b]	Author (date)[c]
Nigeria 1981-2	—	—	—	WFS:F15-49 9727	IMR	0, 1-3, 4-6, 7+	90	94	-1	4	-45	n/a	7	Cochrane and Farid (1989)
Nigeria, Ile-Ife 1981	—	—	—	Mothers of infants born in 1980-1 2111	Risk of infant death; (logistic regression)	0, prim., sec., post-sec. R	n/a	1.91*	—'	1.31	1.72*	R	R irreg.	Bankole (1989)
Nigeria, Edo and Delta 1985	—	—	—	F15-50 rural 1895	proportion surviving OLS	0, prim., ter.	n/a / n/a	R / R	0.01 / 0.03*	—' / —'	0.02 / 0.02	0.04* / 0.06	+ / +	Okojie ('Women's Status', 1993)
Nigeria[†] 1990	L	L	W	DHS:F15-49 8781	IMR	0, prim., comp. prim., sec., sec.+	91	96	2	-17	-16	-49	7	Federal Office of Statistics (1992)
Senegal 1978		L	W	WFS:F15-49 3985	IMR	0, 1-3, 4-6, 7+	112	121	-41	-22	-74	n/a	-	Cochrane and Farid (1989)
Senegal[†] 1986	M	L	W	DHS:F15-49 4415	IMR	0, prim., sec.+	91	96	-32	—'	-48	n/a	-	Ndiaye et al. (1988)
Uganda[†] 1988-9	L	L	W	DHS:F15-49 4730	IMR	0, prim., comp. prim., sec., sec.+	106	117	-11	-27	-28	-37	-	Kaijuka et al. (1989)
United Rep. of Tanzania[†] 1991-2	L	H	N	DHS:F15-49 9238	IMR	0, prim., comp. prim., sec., sec.+	99	103	-8	-4	-30	n/a	-	Ngallaba et al. (1993)
B. North Africa and the Middle East														
Egypt[†] 1980	M	L	W	WFS:F15-49 n/a	NNM PNNM 1q0	illiterate, read and write, prim., sec.+	n/a / n/a / n/a	65 / 75 / 140	-22 / 4 / -8	-35 / -35 / -35	-32 / -41 / -37	n/a / n/a / n/a	- / 7 / -	Nawar et al. (1986)
Morocco[†] 1987	M	L	W	DHS:F15-49 5982	IMR	0, prim.+	82	86	-37	—'	—'	n/a	-	Azelmat et al. (1989)

Setting				Sample	Measure	Education								Reference
Sudan 1973	—	—	—	Census 42586 F15–49	q(1)	0, 1–3, 4–6, 7+ Years	n/a	0.19	−30	−49	−63	n/a	—	Farah and Preston (1982)
					q(2)		n/a	0.20	−25	−46	−59	n/a	—	
					q(3)		n/a	0.21	−24	−43	−57	n/a	—	
Khartoum 1975				CMW 15–49 2213	CLS	Years	n/a	n/a	n/a	n/a	n/a	n/a	−0.0363*	
					Ratio of observed to expeced deaths	Years	n/a	n/a	n/a	n/a	n/a	n/a	−0.0362	
Sudan 1978	—	—	—	WFS:F15–49 3115	IMR	0, 1–3, 4–6, 7+ Years	79	80	10	5	−28	n/a	rev. J	Cochrane and Farid (1989)
Sudan, Southern 1985	—	—	—	CMW 15–34 5120	Child survival (logistic regression)	Years	n/a	n/a	n/a	n/a	n/a	n/a	+0.3086*	Roth and Kurup (1990)
Sudan† 1989–90	L	L	W	DHS:F15–49 5860	IMR	0, comp. prim., sec., sec. +	77	82	−15	−9	−25	−21	—	Ministry of Economic and Natl. Planning (1991)
C. East and South-East Asia														
China 1976–7†	L	M	M	F15–49 n/a	IMR	Illiterate, elem., junior, senior/+	r/a	52	−29	−56	−62	n/a	—	Cleland and van Ginneken (1988)
Indonesia† 1991	M	M	N	DHS:F15–49 22909	IMR	0, prim., comp. prim., sec., sec. +	74	89	−4	−16	−61	n/a	7	Central Bureau of Statistics (1992)
Malaysia 1976–7	—	—	—	EMW <50 3516	IM; (logistic regression)	Years	n/a	n/a	n/a	n/a	n/a	n/a	−1.00*	DaVanzo (1988)
Thailand† 1987	H	N	N	DHS:F15–49 6775	IMR	0, prim., sec., sec. +	38	54	−28	—'	−59	−64	—	Chayovan et al. (1988)
D. South Asia														
Bangladesh 1975–6				EMW <50 births 15 yrs. before survey, exposed to risk of mortality in infancy and between ages 1–5 13957	IMR	0, some	n/a	1.04*	0.96	—'	—'	—'	—'	Majumder (1988)

Appendix F. (cont.)

Site and survey date	Levels of:			Sample type; universe (sex and age); size	Dependent variable; (method if means n/a)	Education variable (years of schooling)	Infant or early childhood mortality rate among		Percentage difference between uneducated and better educated women[a] by years of schooling				Direction of relationship[b]	Author (date)[c]
	Per capita income	Female literacy rate	Gender disparity in literacy				All women[d]	Uneducated women[e]	1–3	4–6	7+	10+		
Bangladesh, Matlab 1984	L	L	W	Births in 1982 7913	Crude risk of dying 6–35 m. 6–35 m.; (hazard logit model coeff.)	0, 1–5, 6+	n/a n/a	0.028 0.369	—' —f	0.021 0.064	0.014 −0.433	—' —f	– –	Bhuiya and Streatfield (1991)
India[†] 1981				Census F15–49 Total, 137517 Rural, 93429 Urban, 44088	q(1) q(1) q(1)	0, literate to middle, middle to matric., matric. +	n/a n/a n/a	120 130 86	−5 −2 −5	—' —' —'	−32 −27 −20	−55 −39 7 −52	– – –	India, Government of, Registrar General, Census of India 1981 (1988)
India, Punjab (rural) 1984–7				EMW 15–59 exposed to risk of conception 1187	IM 0–11 m.	Years	n/a	n/a	n/a	n/a	n/a	n/a	−0.047*	Das Gupta (1990)
India, Maharashtra 1992–3				NFHS:F15–49 4106	IMR	0, prim. to middle, middle comp., sec. +	56	72	−45	—'	−55	−67	–	Population Research Centre, Gokhale Institute et al. (1994)
India, Tamil Nadu 1992				NFHS:F15–49 3948	IMR	0, prim. to middle, middle comp., sec. +	71	89	−31	—'	−54	−62	–	Population Research Centre, Gandhigram Institute et al. (1994)
India, Uttar Pradesh	–	–	–	NFHS:F15–49 11438	IMR	0, prim. to middle,	116	127	−43	—'	−49	−57	–	Population Research Centre,

Country/Year				Sample	Indicator	Education categories								Reference
1992-3						middle comp., sec.+ 0, some				—'	n/a		—	Lucknow University et al. (1994)
Pakistan† 1975	L	L	W	F15-49 4996	1q0	0, some	n/a	146	-18	—'	—'	n/a	—	Sathar (1984)
Sri Lanka† 1987	L	H	N	DHS:F15-49 5865	IMR	0, prim., sec., sec+	32	52	-35	-44	-49	-62	—	Ministry of Plan Implementation (1988)
E. Latin America and the Caribbean														
Argentina† (1966-71)	H	H	N	F15-49 n/a	q2	0, 1-3, 4-6, 7-9, 10+	58	96	-22	-39	-68	-73	—	Behm (1980)
Bolivia† 1989	M	M	M	DHS:F15-49 7923	IMR NNM PNNM	0, 1-5, 6-8, 9+	96 41 55	124 57 66	-13 -24 -3	—' —' —'	-57 -53 -48	-62 -66 -60	— — —	Sommerfelt et al. (1991)
Brazil 1970	H	M	N	F15-49	Proportion children died	0, 1-4, 5-9, 10+	22.4 16.3	30.1 23.2	-40 -38	—' —'	-58 -65	-69 -78	— —	Merrick (1985)
1976†				n/a										
Chile 1972	H	M		F15-49 n/a	IMR NNM PNNM	0, prim., sec.+	75 32 43	153 57 96	-48 -43 -51	—' —' —'	-81 -56 -81	— n/a n/a	— — —	Taucher (1989)
1978†	H		N		IMR NNM PNNM		41 20 21	99 40 58	-51 -55 -51 -58	—' —' —'	-71 -55 -81	n/a n/a n/a	— — —	
Colombia† 1986	H	H	N	DHS:F15-49 5329	IMR	0, prim., sec.+	39	60	-33	—'	-53	n/a	—	Heredia et al. (1988)
Cuba† 1966-71	M	H	N	F15-49 n/a	q2	0, 1-3, 4-6, 7+	41	46	-2	-26	-37	n/a	7	Behm (1980)
Dominican Rep.[1] 1986	M	M	N	DHS:F15-49 7649	IMR	0, prim., sec., sec.+	68	102	-25	—'	-57	-66	—	Consejo Nacional de Poblacion y Familia (1987)
Ecuador† 1987	M	H	N	DHS:F15-49 4713	IMR	0, prim., sec.+	65	106	-35	—f	-72	-79	—	Centro de Estudios de Poblacion (1988)
Mexico 1979	H	H	N	F15-49 n/a	IMR	0, prim., comp. prim.+	n/a	82	-22	—'	-32	n/a	—	Cordova (1991)
1984†	H	—	—	F15-45 263	IMR; (regression)	Years	n/a	72	-11	—'	-68	n/a	—	Wolfe and Behrman (1987)
Nicaragua 1977-8	—		—	n/a	IMR; (regression)		n/a	n/a	n/a	n/a	n/a	n/a	-1.1	
Trinidad and Tobago† 1987	H	H	N	DHS:F15-49 3806	IMR	0-prim., comp. prim., sec., sec.+	31	28	-12	—'	91	118	J	Heath et al. (1988)

Appendix F. (cont.)

[a] Refers to the difference between the rates for women with no education compared with women at each successively higher level of education (1–3 years, 4–6 years, and so on).

[b] See Introduction to appendices for discussion of the various types of relationships.

[c] See Bibliography for full citation.

[d] Refers to all women in the sample or in the sub-sample, if there was one.

[e] Refers to women with no education in the sample.

[f] Merged with next level; if data are given for classes 1–3 and 4–6 together, results are shown under the lower category, 1–3.

[†] Studies included in Tables 6.1, 6.2, and 6.3

[*] Statistically significant.

Notes: See Introduction to appendices for list of abbreviations and technical notes on the appendix. For studies in which more than one set of numbers are provided, see column headed 'Sample type' for the sub-population to which the rates refer, and column headed 'Site and survey date' if different years.

Appendix G. Studies addressing the relationship between women's education and the levels of child (under 5) mortality

Site and survey date	Levels of: Per capita income	Female literacy rate	Gender disparity in literacy	Sample type; universe (sex and age); size	Dependent variable (method if means n/a)	Education variable (years of schooling)	Child mortality rate among: All women[d]	Uneducated women[e]	Percentage difference between uneducated and better educated women[a] by years of schooling 1-3	4-6	7+	10+	Direction of relationship[b]	Author (date)[c]
A. Sub-Saharan Africa														
Benin[†] 1982	L	L	W	WFS:F15–49 4018	Mort. at ages 2–5	0, 1–3, 4–6, 7+	74	83	–6	–26	–64	n/a	–	Cochrane and Farid (1989)
Botswana[†] 1988	H	M	M	DHS:F15–49 4368	U5MR	0, prim., comp. prim., sec.+	56	64	–22	–11	–27	n/a	–	Lestede et al. (1989)
Burundi[†] 1987	L	L	W	DHS:F15–49 3970	U5MR	0, prim., sec.+	186	193	–20	–ʲ	–57	n/a	–	Segamba et al. (1988)
Cameroon[†] 1978	M	L	W	WFS:F15–49 8219	Mort. at ages 2–5	0, 1–3, 4–6, 7+	59	69	–32	–38	–48	n/a	–	Cochrane and Farid (1989)
Côte d'Ivoire[†] 1980	M	L	W	WFS:F15–49 5764	Mort. at ages 2–5	0, 1–3, 4–6, 7+	38	51	–51	–56	–39	n/a	–	Cochrane and Farid (1989)
Ghana 1979–80				WFS:F15–49 6125	Mort. at ages 2–5	0, 1–3, 4–6, 7+	34	43	–6	–68	–52	n/a	–	Cochrane and Farid (1989)
Ghana[†] 1988	L	M	M	DHS:F15–49 4488	U5MR	0, prim., middle, sec.+	154	175	–15	–26	–43	n/a	–	Ghana Statistical Service (1989)
Kenya[†] 1977–8				WFS:F15–49 8100	U5MR	0, 1–3, 4–6, 7+	162	181	–9	–29	–39	n/a	–	Hobcraft et al. (1984)
Kenya[†] 1989	L	M	M	DHS:F15–49 7150	U5MR	0, prim., comp. prim., sec.+	91	109	–12	–33	–41	n/a	–	Natl. Council, Pop. and Devel. (1989)
Lesotho[†] 1977	M	M	M	WFS:F15–49 3603	U5MR	0, 1–3, 4–6, 7+	190	224	–4	–17	–25	n/a	7	Hobcraft et al. (1984)
Liberia[†] 1986	M	L	W	DHS:F15–49 5239	U5MR	0, prim., sec.+	230	242	19	–ʲ	–7	n/a	rev. J	Chieh-Johnson et al. (1988)
Mali[†] 1987	L	L	W	DHS:F15–49 3200	U5MR	0, prim.+	279	290	–31	–ʲ	–31	n/a	–	Traore et al. (1989)
Mauritania[†] 1981	L	L	W	WFS:F15–49 3504	Mort. at ages 2–5	0, 1–3, 4–6, 7+	74	86	–26	–81	–79	n/a	–	Cochrane and Farid (1989)
Namibia[†] 1992	H	M	M	DHS:F15–49 5421	U5MR	0, prim., comp., prim., sec.+	92	97	0	2	–22	n/a	7	Katjiuanjo et al. (1993)

Appendix G. (cont.)

Site and survey date	Levels of: Per capita income	Female literacy rate	Gender disparity in literacy	Sample type; universe (sex and age); size	Dependent variable (method if means n/a)	Education variable (years of schooling)	Child mortality rate among: All women[d]	Uneducated women[e]	Percentage difference between uneducated and better educated women[a] by years of schooling 1-3	4-6	7+	10+	Direction of relationship[b]	Author (date)[c]
Nigeria[†] 1990	L	L	W	DHS:F15–49 8781	U5MR	0, prim., sec.+	191	210	−9	−34	−36	−63	−	Federal Office of Statistics (1992)
Nigeria 1981–2	−	−	−	WFS:F15–49 9727	Mort. at ages 2–5	0, 1–3, 4–6, 7+	48	50	−10	−15	−50	n/a	−	Cochrane and Farid (1989)
Senegal 1978	−	−	−	WFS:F15–49 3985	U5MR	0, 1–3, 4–6, 7+	287	296	−40	−62	−94	n/a	−	Hobcraft et al. (1984)
Senegal[†] 1986	M	L	W	DHS:F15–49 4415	U5MR	0, prim., sec.+	210	225	−38	−[1]	−68	n/a	−	Ndiaye et al. (1988)
Uganda[†] 1988–9	L	L	W	DHS:F15–49 4730	U5MR	0, prim., comp. prim., sec., sec.+	188	198	−1	−23	−36	−51	7	Kajuka et al. (1989)
United Rep. of Tanzania[†] 1991–2	L	H	N	DHS:F15–49 9238	U5MR	0, prim., comp. prim., sec.+	154	162	−4	−12	−38	n/a	7	Ngallaba et al. (1993)
B. North Africa and the Middle East														
Egypt[†] 1980	M	L	W	WFS:F15–49 8788	5q0	illiterate, read and write, prim., sec.+	n/a	250	−36	−51	−60	n/a	−	Nawar et al. (1986)
Jordan[†] 1976	H	M	M	WFS:F15–49 3612	U5MR	0, 1–3, 4–6, 7+	100	112	−26	−25	−40	n/a	−	Hobcraft et al. (1984)
Morocco[†] 1987	M	L	W	DHS:F15–49 5982	U5MR	none, prim.+	118	126	−48	−[1]	−[1]	n/a	−	Azelmat et al. (1989)
Syrian Arab Rep.[†] 1978	H	L	W	WFS:F15–49 4487	U5MR	0, 1–3, 4–6, 7+	95	104	−28	−28	−52	n/a	−	Hobcraft et al. (1984)
Sudan 1978–9				WFS:F15–49 3115	U5MR	0, 1–3, 4–6, 7+	140	146	−25	−[1]	−[1]	n/a	−	Hobcraft et al. (1984)
Sudan 1973				Census 42586 F15–49	q(5)	0, 1–3, 4–6, 7+	n/a	220	−23	−39	−51	n/a	−	Farah and Preston (1982)
Sudan[†] 1989–90	L	L	W	DHS:F15–49 5860	U5MR	0, prim., comp. prim., sec., sec.+	135	152	−28	−30	−43	−48	−	Ministry of Econ. and National Planning (1991)

Region / Country (year)			Sample	Measure	Education groups								Source
Sudan 1978	M	M	WFS:F15–49 3115	Mort. at ages 2–5	0, 1–3, 4–6, 7+	43	46	–48	–66	–83	n/a	–	Cochrane and Farid (1989)
C. East and South-East Asia													
China, Jilin Province 1985	M	M	Births 1962–85 to EMW15–60 5399	CM(1–4) (hazard model)	0, prim. +	n/a	0.65	0.61	–'	–'	n/a	–	Tsuya and Choe (1989)
Fiji† 1974	M	M	WFS:F15–49 4298	U5MR	0, 1–3, 4–6, 7+	59	70	–5	–14	–34	n/a	–	Hobcraft et al. (1984)
Indonesia 1975	M	M	WFS:F15–49 9155	U5MR	0, 1–3, 4–6, 7+	180	193	1	–26	–60	n/a	7	Hobcraft et al. (1984)
Indonesia† 1991	M	N	DHS:F15–49 22909	U5MR	0, prim., comp. prim., sec. +	107	131	–5	–22	–64	n/a	–	Central Bureau of Statistics (1992)
Malaysia† 1974	H	M	WFS:F15–49 6316	U5MR	0, 1–3, 4–6, 7+	61	67	–4	–16	–73	n/a	7	Hobcraft et al. (1984)
Philippines† 1978	M	N	WFS:F15–49 9268	U5MR	0, 1–3, 4–6, 7+	90	130	–9	–28	–59	n/a	–	Hobcraft et al. (1984)
Rep. of Korea† 1974	H	N	WFS:F15–49 5430	U5MR	0, 1–3, 4–6, 7+	83	107	–12	–31	–48	n/a	–	Hobcraft et al. (1984)
Thailand 1975	—	—	WFS:F15–49 3778	U5MR	0, 1–3, 4–6, 7+	116	145	–28	–24	–74	n/a	–	Hobcraft et al. (1984)
Thailand† 1987	H	N	DHS:F15–49 6775	U5MR	0, prim., sec. +	49	74	–34	–'	–72	n/a	–	Chayovan et al. (1988)
D. South Asia													
Bangladesh† 1975–6	L	W	WFS:F15–49 6513	U5MR	0, 1–3, 4–6, 7+	215	222	–11	–16	–45	n/a	–	Hobcraft et al. (1984)
Bangladesh 1975–6	—	—	WFS:F15–49; 6513 births 15 yrs. before survey 7246	Mort. at ages 2–5	0, some	n/a	1.15	0.87	n/a	n/a	n/a	–	Majumder (1988)
India† 1981	L	W	Census F15–49 Total, 137517	q(5)	0, literate to middle, middle to matric., matric. +	n/a	172	–34	–'	–60	–77	–	India, Govt. of, Registrar General, Census 1981 (1988)
			Rural, 93429	q(5)		n/a	185	–27	–'	–51	–64	–	
			Urban, 44088	q(5)		n/a	129	–33	–'	–57	–71	–	

Appendix G. (cont.)

Site and survey date	Levels of: Per capita income	Female literacy rate	Gender disparity in literacy	Sample type; universe (sex and age); size	Dependent variable (method if means n/a)	Education variable (years of schooling)	Child mortality rate among: All women[d]	Uneducated women[c]	Percentage difference between uneducated and better educated women[a] by years of schooling: 1-3	4-6	7+	10+	Direction of relationship[b]	Author (date)[e]
India, Tamil Nadu 1970	—	—	—	CMW 35-44 766	CM (OLS)	Years	-0.0590	n/a	n/a	n/a	n/a	n/a	−	Jejeebhoy (1991)
India, Tamil Nadu 1980				CMW 35-44 258			-0.0854	n/a	n/a	n/a	n/a	n/a	−	
India, Maharashtra 1983-4				CMW 15-44 1956	CMW 15-44 (OLS)	0, prim., middle, sec.+	9 / -0.0648*	11 / n/a	-46 / n/a	-55 / n/a	-55 / n/a	n/a / n/a	− / −	United Nations (1993)
India, Maharashtra 1992-3	—	—	—	NFHS:F15-49 4106	U5MR	0, prim.-mid., middle comp., sec., sec.+	76	99	-46	—'	-58	-67	−	Population Research Centre, Gokhale Institute et al. (1994)
India, Tamil Nadu 1992	—	—	—	NFHS:F15-49 3948	U5MR	0, prim.-mid., middle comp., sec., sec.+	95	122	-31	—'	-61	-68	−	Population Research Centre, Gandhigram Institute et al. (1994)
India, Uttar Pradesh 1992-3	—	—	—	NFHS:F15-49 11438	U5MR	0, prim.-mid., middle comp., sec., sec.+	162	178	-41	—'	-55	-64	−	Population Research Centre, Lucknow University et al. (1994)
Nepal[†] 1976	L	L	W	WFS:F15-49 5940	U5MR	0, 1-3, 4-6, 7+	259	261	-22	-40	-48	n/a	−	Hobcraft et al. (1984)
Pakistan[†] 1975	L	L	W	WFS:F15-49 4996	U5MR	0, 1-3, 4-6, 7+	202	208	-31	-34	-46	n/a	−	Hobcraft et al. (1984)
Sri Lanka 1975	—	—	—	WFS:F15-49 6812	U5MR	0, 1-3, 4-6, 7+	84	104	-7	-23	-47	n/a	−	Hobcraft et al. (1984)
Sri Lanka[†] 1987	L	H	N	DHS:F15-49 5865	U5MR	0, prim., sec., sec.+	42	71	-40	—'	-52	-64	−	Ministry of Plan Implementation (1988)
E. Latin America and the Caribbean														
Bolivia[†] 1989	M	M	M	DHS:F15-49 7923	U5MR	0, 1-5, 6-8, 9+	142	181	-11	—'	-59	-67	−	Sommerfelt et al. (1991)
Colombia 1976	—	—	—	WFS:F15-49 5378	U5MR	0, 1-3, 4-6, 7+	112	146	-13	-44	-66	n/a	−	Hobcraft et al. (1984)

Country/Year			Survey	N	Indicator	Education categories								Source
Colombia 1986	H	H	N	DHS:F15–49 5329	U5MR	0, prim., sec.+	52	82	−33	−ᶠ	−63	n/a	–	Heredia et al. (1988)
Costa Rica 1976	H	H	N	WFS:F15–49 3935	U5MR	0, 1–3, 4–6, 7+	95	157	−36	−46	−71	n/a	–	Hobcraft et al. (1984)
Dominican Rep. † 1975	M	M	N	WFS:F15–49 3115	U5MR	0, 1–3, 4–6, 7+	139	198	−29	−38	−59	n/a	–	Hobcraft et al. (1984)
Ecuador † 1987	M	H	N	DHS:F15–49 4713	U5MR	0, prim., sec., sec.+	90	160	−42	−ᶠ	−77	−83	–	Centro de Estudios de Poblacion (1988)
Guyana † 1975	L	H	N	WFS:F15–49 4642	U5MR	0, 1–3, 4–6, 7+	71	83	7	−4	−23	n/a	rev. J	Hobcraft et al. (1984)
Haiti † 1977	L	M	M	WFS:F15–49 3365	U5MR	0, 1–3, 4–6, 7+	214	226	−22	−9	−61	n/a	–	Hobcraft et al. (1984)
Jamaica † 1975–6	H	H	N	WFS:F15–49 3096	U5MR	0–3, 4–6, 7+	58	82	−5	−10	−38	n/a	–	Hobcraft et al. (1984)
Mexico † 1976	H	H	N	WFS:F15–49 7310	U5MR	0, 1–3, 4–6, 7+	114	153	−23	−43	−67	n/a	–	Hobcraft et al. (1984)
Panama 1975–6 †	H	H	N	WFS:F15–49 3701	U5MR	0, 1–3, 4–6, 7+	65	134	−33	−61	−68	n/a	–	Hobcraft et al. (1984)
Paraguay † 1979	H	H	N	WFS:F15–49 4682	U5MR	0, 1–3, 4–6, 7+	77	110	−20	−39	−71	n/a	–	Hobcraft et al. (1984)
Peru † 1977–8	H	M	N	WFS:F15–49 5640	U5MR	0, 1–3, 4–6, 7+	170	237	−28	−59	−77	n/a	–	Hobcraft et al. (1984)
Trinidad and Tobago 1977	–	–	–	WFS:F15–49 4359	U5MR	0, 1–3, 4–6, 7+	49	74	−9	−20	−42	n/a	–	Hobcraft et al. (1984)
Trinidad and Tobago 1987	H	H	N	DHS:F15–49 3806	U5MR	0–prim., comp. prim., sec., sec.+	34	33	−11	−ᶠ	65	87	J	Heath et al. (1988)
Venezuela † 1977	H	M	N	WFS:F15–49 4361	U5MR	0, 1–3, 4–6, 7+	61	79	−24	−24	−56	n/a	–	Hobcraft et al. (1984)

ᵃ Refers to the difference between the rates for women with no education compared with women at each successively higher level of education (1–3 years, 4–6 years, and so on).

ᵇ See Introduction to appendices for discussion of the various types of relationships.

ᶜ See Bibliography for full citation.

ᵈ Refers to all women in the sample or in the sub-sample, if there was one.

ᵉ Refers to women with no education in the sample or in the sub-sample, if there was one.

ᶠ Merged with next level; if data are given for classes 1–3 and 4–6 together, results are shown under the lower category, 1–3.

† Studies included in Table 6.4, 6.5, and 6.6

* Statistically significant.

Notes: See Introduction to appendices for list of abbreviations and technical notes on the appendix. For studies in which more than one set of numbers are provided, see column headed 'Sample type' for the sub-population to which the rates refer, and column headed 'Site and survey date' if different years.

Appendix H. Studies addressing the relationship between women's education and desired family size

Site and survey date	Levels of:			Sample type; universe (sex and age); size; (method if means n/a)	Education variable (years of schooling)	Mean number of children desired by:		Percentage difference between uneducated and better educated women[e] by years of schooling				Direction of relation-ship[b]	Author (date)[c]
	Per capita income	Female literacy rate	Gender disparity in literacy			All women[d]	Unedu-cated women[e]	1–3	4–6	7+	10+		
A. Sub-Saharan Africa													
Benin[†] 1982	L	L	W	WFS:F15–49 4018	0, 1–3, 4–6, 7+	7.4	7.7	–16	–27	–34	n/a	–	United Nations (1987)
Botswana[†] 1988	H	M	M	DHS:F15–49 4368	0, 1–3, 4–6, 7–9, 10+	5.4	6.0	–2	–10	–21	–33	7	United Nations (1995)
Burundi[†] 1987	L	L	W	DHS:F15–49 3970	0, 1–3, 4–6, 7–9, 10+	5.4	5.6	–9	–12	–27	–29	–	United Nations (1995)
Cameroon[†] 1978	M	L	W	WFS:F15–49 8219	0, 1–3, 4–6, 7+	8.1	8.1	4	1	–21	n/a	7	United Nations (1987)
Côte d'Ivoire[†] 1980	M	L	W	WFS:F15–49 5764	0, 1–3, 4–6, 7+	8.4	8.6	–4	–13	–27	n/a	7	United Nations (1987)
Ghana 1979–80				WFS:F15–49 6125	0, 1–3, 4–6, 7+	6.0	6.6	–12	–11	–21	n/a	–	United Nations (1987)
Ghana[†] 1988	L	M	M	DHS:F15–49 4488	0, 1–3, 4–6, 7–9, 10+	5.4	6.4	–16	–19	–28	–31	–	United Nations (1995)
Kenya 1977				WFS:F15–49 8100	0, 1–3, 4–6, 7+	7.2	7.6	–8	–9	–14	n/a	–	United Nations (1987)
Kenya[†] 1989	L	M	M	DHS:F15–49 7150	0, 1–3, 4–6, 7–9, 10+	4.7	5.4	–9	–13	–23	–30	–	United Nations (1995)
Lesotho[†] 1977	M	M	M	WFS:F15–49 3603	0, 1–3, 4–6, 7+	6.0	6.4	–2	–6	–11	n/a	7	United Nations (1987)
Liberia[†] 1986	M	L	W	DHS:F15–49 5239	0, 1–3, 4–6, 7–9, 10+	6.3	6.7	–13	–15	–29	–33	–	United Nations (1995)
Mali[†] 1987	L	L	W	DHS:F15–49 3200	0, 1–3, 4–6, 7–9, 10+	6.8	7.1	–9	–14	–34	–44	–	United Nations (1995)
Mauritania[†] 1981	L	L	W	WFS:F15–49 3504	0, 1–3, 4–6, 7+	8.7	9.0	–4	–21	–33	n/a	7	United Nations (1987)
Namibia[†] 1992	H	M	M	DHS:F15–49 5421	0, prim., comp. prim., sec.+	5.0	6.6	–15	–29	–39	n/a	–	Katjiuanjo et al. (1993)
Nigeria[†]	L	L	W	DHS:F15–49	0, prim.,	5.8	6.9	–9	–16	–29	n/a	–	Federal Office of

1990			8781									Statistics (1992)
Senegal 1976			WFS:F15-49 3985	comp. prim., sec.+	8.3	8.5	-2	-21	-41	n/a	7	United Nations (1987)
Senegal† 1986	M	W	DHS:F15-49 4415	0, 1-3, 4-6, 7+	7.0	7.2	-4	-26	-35	-36	7	United Nations (1995)
Togo† 1988	L	W	DHS:F15-49 3360	0, 1-3, 4-6, 7-9, 10+	5.6	6.0	-13	-25	-32	-35	–	United Nations (1995)
Uganda† 1988-9	L	W	DHS:F15-49 4730	0, 1-3, 4-6, 7-9, 10+	6.7	7.3	-8	-14	-22	-30	–	United Nations (1995)
United Rep. of Tanzania† 1991-2	L	N	DHS:F15-49 9238	0, prim., comp. prim., sec.+	6.1	7.3	-14	-27	-42	n/a	–	Ngallaba et al. (1993)
Zambia† 1991	L	M	DHS:F15-49 7000	0, prim., sec.+	5.8	6.8	-9	-'	-32	n/a	–	Gaisie et al. (1993)
Zimbabwe† 1988-9	M	M	DHS:F15-49 4201	0, 1-3, 4-6, 7-9, 10+	5.3	6.4	-3	-11	-32	-44	7	United Nations (1995)
B. North Africa and the Middle East												
Egypt† 1988-9	M	W	DHS:F15-49 8911	0, 1-3, 4-6, 7-9, 10+	2.9	3.1	-10	-10	-19	-19	–	United Nations (1995)
Egypt 1980			WFS:F15-49 8788	0, 1-3, 4-6, 7+	4.1	4.5	-13	-22	-42	n/a	–	United Nations (1987)
Egypt 1973			F15-49 1234	Low, medium, high	n/a	3.8	-22	-'	-29	n/a	–	Khalifa (1976)
Jordan† 1976	H	M	WFS:F15-49 3612	0, 1-3, 4-6, 7+	6.3	7.2	-12	-18	-35	n/a	–	United Nations (1987)
Morocco 1979-80			WFS:F15-49 5801	0, 1-3, 4-6, 7+	4.9	5.1	-22	-24	-33	n/a	–	United Nations (1987)
Morocco† 1987	M	W	DHS:F15-49 5982	0, 1-3, 4-6, 7-9, 10+	3.7	3.8	-13	-21	-28	-29	–	United Nations (1995)
Sudan, North 1978-9			WFS:F15-49 3115	0, 1-3, 4-6, 7+	6.3	6.5	-6	-17	-23	n/a	–	United Nations (1987)
Sudan† 1989-90	L	W	DHS:F15-49 5860	0, prim., comp. prim., sec.+	5.8	6.8	-16	-26	-32	n/a	–	Ministry of Econ. and Natl. Planning (1991)
Syrian Arab Rep.† 1978	H	W	WFS:F15-49 4487	0, 1-3, 4-6, 7+	6.1	7.0	-33	-33	-44	n/a	–	United Nations (1987)
Tunisia 1978			WFS:F15-49 4123	0, 1-3, 4-6, 7+	4.1	4.3	-7	-16	-26	n/a	–	United Nations (1987)
Tunisia† 1988	H	M	DHS:F15-49 4184	0, 1-3, 4-6, 7-9, 10+	3.5	3.8	-13	-16	-27	-29	–	United Nations (1995)

Appendix H. (cont.)

Site and survey date	Levels of: Per capita income	Levels of: Female literacy rate	Levels of: Gender disparity in literacy	Sample type; universe (sex and age); size; (method if means n/a)	Education variable (years of schooling)	Mean number of children desired by: All women[d]	Mean number of children desired by: Uneducated women[e]	Percentage difference between uneducated and better educated women[e] by years of schooling 1–3	4–6	7+	10+	Direction of relationship[b]	Author (date)[c]
C. East and South-East Asia													
Fiji[t] 1974	M	M	M	WFS:F15–49 4298	0, 1–3, 4–6, 7+	4.2	4.4	0	–2	–11	n/a	7	United Nations (1987)
Indonesia 1976	M	M	N	WFS:F15–49 9155	0, 1–3, 4–6, 7+	4.2	4.1	5	0	–2	n/a	rev. U	United Nations (1987)
Indonesia[t] 1987	M	M	N	DHS:F15–49 11884	0, 1–3, 4–6, 7–9, 10+	3.2	3.4	3	–9	–13	–15	7	United Nations (1995)
Malaysia[t] 1974	H	M	M	F15–49 6316	0, 1–3, 4–6, 7+	4.4	4.6	–7	–7	–15	n/a	–	United Nations (1987)
Philippines[t] 1978	M	H	N	WFS:F15–49 9268	0, 1–3, 4–6, 7+	4.4	5.4	–9	–15	–28	n/a	–	United Nations (1987)
Rep. of Korea[t] 1974	H	H	N	WFS:F15–49 5430	0, 1–3, 4–6, 7+	3.2	3.6	–5	–11	–22	n/a	–	United Nations (1987)
Thailand 1975				WFS:F15–49 3778	0, 1–3, 4–6, 7+	3.7	3.9	0	–5	–18	n/a	7	United Nations (1987)
Thailand 1977/8				CMW 15–54 fecund; total 353; rural, north, 171 (OLS)	Years	n/a	n/a	n/a	n/a	n/a	n/a	0(0.04)	Cochrane and Nandwani (1981)
Thailand[t] 1987	H	H	N	DHS:F15–49 6775	0, 1–3, 4–6, 7–9, 10+	2.8	3.5	–17	–20	–31	–31	–	United Nations (1995)
D. South Asia													
Bangladesh[t] 1975–6	L	L	W	WFS:F15–49 6513	0, 1–3, 4–6, 7+	4.1	4.1	–2	0	–2	n/a	0	United Nations (1987)
India[t] 1989	L	L	W	F15–44 44918	0, prim., sec.+	3.0	3.2	–4	–19	–25	n/a	7	Operations Research Group (1990)
India, Kerala 1980				EMW aged 15–49 2679	0, 1–4, 5–9, 10+	3.3	3.8	–11	–[f]	–28	–35	–	Zacharaiah (1984)

Location / date			Survey, sample	Years								Source
India, Tamil Nadu 1970			CMW 35–44 766		n/a	n/a	n/a	n/a	n/a	n/a	n/a	–0.0216	Jejeebhoy (1991)
India, Tamil Nadu 1980			258 (OLS)		n/a	n/a	n/a	n/a	n/a	n/a	n/a	–0.0648* (0.05)	
India, Maharashtra 1983			CMW 15–44 / CMW 15–29 / CMW 30–44 1956	None, prim., middle, sec.+	3.4 / 3.2 / 3.6	3.5 / 3.3 / 3.6	–3 / –3 / –3	–11 / –9 / –11	–20 / –15 / –19	n/a / n/a / n/a	7 / 7 / 7	United Nations (1993)
India, Maharashtra 1992–3			DHS:F15–49 4106	0, prim. to middle, middle comp., sec.+	2.5	2.8	–11	—[1]	–28	–32	—	Population Research Centre, Gokhale Institute *et al.* (1994)
India, Tamil Nadu 1992			DHS:F15–49 3948	0, prim. to middle, middle comp., sec.+	2.1	2.2	–5	—[1]	–12	–14	—	Population Research Centre, Gandhigram Institute *et al.* (1994)
India, Uttar Pradesh 1992–3			DHS:F15–49 11438	0, prim. to middle, middle comp., sec.+	3.4	3.6	–17	—[1]	–30	–33	—	Population Research Centre, Lucknow University *et al.* (1994)
Nepal† 1975	L	W	WFS:F15–49 5940	0, 1–3, 4–6, 7+	3.9	3.9	–4	–8	–21	n/a	7	United Nations (1987)
Pakistan 1975	L		WFS:F15–49 4996	0, 1–3, 4–6, 7+	4.2	4.2	–12	–14	–21	n/a	—	United Nations (1987)
Pakistan† 1990–1	L	W	DHS:F15–49 6611	0, prim., comp. prim., sec.+	4.1	4.3	–4	–16	–21	n/a	7	Natl. Institute of Population Studies (1992)
Sri Lanka 1975	L		WFS:F15–49 6812	0, 1–3, 4–6, 7+	3.8	4.2	–5	–7	–21	n/a	—	United Nations (1987)
Sri Lanka† 1987	H	N	DHS:F15–49 5865	0, 1–3, 4–6, 7–9, 10+	3.1	3.5	–3	–9	–20	–23	7	United Nations (1995)

E. Latin America and the Caribbean

Location / date			Survey, sample	Years								Source
Belize 1991	M	M	F15–44 2656	0–7, 8, 9+	2.9	3.1	—[1]	—[1]	–7	–10	—	Ministry of Health (1992)
Bolivia† 1989	M	M	DHS:F15–49 7923	0, 1–3, 4–6, 7–9, 10+	2.8	2.9	–3	–7	–6	–3	7	United Nations (1995)
Brazil† 1986	H	N	DHS:F15–49 5892	0, 1–3, 4–6, 7–9, 10+	3.0	3.4	–6	–15	–22	–24	—	United Nations (1995)

Appendix H. (cont.)

Site and survey date	Per capita income	Female literacy rate	Gender disparity in literacy	Sample type; universe (sex and age); size; (method if means n/a)	Education variable (years of schooling)	Mean number of children desired by: All women[d]	Uneducated women[e]	Percentage difference between uneducated and better educated women[a] by years of schooling: 1-3	4-6	7+	10+	Direction of relationship[b]	Author (date)[c]
Colombia 1976				WFS:F15-49 5378	0, 1-3, 4-6, 7+	4.1	4.7	-11	-19	-26	n/a	-	United Nations (1987)
Colombia[t] 1986	H	H	N	DHS:F15-49 5329	0, 1-3, 4-6, 7-9, 10+	3.0	3.7	-11	-22	-31	-32	-	United Nations (1995)
Costa Rica 1976				WFS:F15-49 3935	0, 1-3, 4-6, 7+	4.7	5.7	-2	-19	-35	n/a	7	United Nations (1987)
Costa Rica 1976	H	H	N	WFS:F15-49 3935	0, 1-6, 7+	3.0	3.3	-3[f]	-21	-[f]	n/a	7	Bongaarts and Lightbourne (1990)
Costa Rica 1985[t]				F15-49 n/a	0-6, 7+	2.7	3.0	-[f]	-23	-[f]	n/a	-	
Dominican Rep. 1975	M	M	N	WFS:F15-49 3115	0, 1-3, 4-6, 7+	4.6	4.8	2	-6	-15	n/a	7	United Nations (1987)
Dominican Rep.[t] 1986	M	M	N	DHS:F15-49 7649	0, 1-3, 4-6, 7-9, 10+	3.6	3.8	3	-8	-14	-16	7	United Nations (1995)
Ecuador 1979				WFS:F15-49 6797	0, 1-3, 4-6, 7+	4.1	4.7	-4	-15	-30	n/a	7	United Nations (1987)
Ecuador[t] 1987	M	H	N	DHS:F15-49 4713	0, 1-3, 4-6, 7-9, 10+	3.2	3.7	0	-11	-24	-24	7	United Nations (1995)
El Salvador[t] 1985	M	M	N	DHS:F15-49 5207	0, 1-3, 4-6, 7-9, 10+	3.9	4.9	-12	-31	-43	-43	-	United Nations (1995)
Guatemala[t] 1987	M	M	M	DHS:F15-49 5160	0, 1-3, 4-6, 7-9, 10+	4.2	4.9	-16	-33	-36	-39	-	United Nations (1995)
Guyana[t] 1975	L	H	N	WFS:F15-49 4642	0, 1-3, 4-6, 7+	4.6	5.0	-8	-2	-10	n/a	-	United Nations (1987)
Haiti[t] 1977	L	M	M	WFS:F15-49 3365	0, 1-3, 4-6, 7+	3.5	3.6	-6	-11	-11	n/a	-	United Nations (1987)
Jamaica[t] 1975-6	H	H	N	WFS:F15-49 3096	0, 1-3, 4-6, 7+	4.0	4.9	-5	-12	-20	n/a	-	United Nations (1987)
Mexico 1976	H	H	N	WFS:F15-49 7310	0, 1-3, 4-6, 7+	4.5	5.0	-4	-14	-32	n/a	7	United Nations (1987)
Mexico[t] 1976	H	H	N	DHS:F15-49	0, 1-3, 4-6, 7+	3.3	4.5	-18	-29	-40	-44	-	United Nations (1987)

Country and year	Type	Site and survey date	93·0	Education (7–9, 10+)								Source
Mexico 1983 / 1987		Cuernavaca Tilzapotla age 15–35, 1–9 yrs. of educ., ch. <4	510	1–5, 6, 7–9 / 0, 1–5, 6, 7–9	r/a, r/a	—′ / 3.7	3.6R / –3	–8 / –8	–25 / –24	n/a / n/a	— / 7	LeVine et al. (1991)
Panama[†] 1975–6	H H N	WFS:F15–49 3701		0, 1–3, 4–6, 7+	4.2	4.6	4	–4	–17	n/a	7	United Nations (1987)
Paraguay[†] 1979	H H N	WFS:F15–49 4682		0, 1–3, 4–6, 7+	5.1	5.9	–2	–15	–31	n/a	7	United Nations (1987)
Peru 1977		WFS:F15–49 55640		0, 1–3, 4–6, 7+	3.8	4.1	–5	–10	–17	n/a	—	United Nations (1987)
Peru[†] 1986	H M N	DHS:F15–49 4999		0, 1–3, 4–6, 7–9, 10+	2.9	3.2	3	–13	–20	–22	7	United Nations (1995)
Peru 1969 / 1977/8		F15–49 1734 / 2759		0, prim., comp. prim., sec.+	5.1 / 4.0	5.6 / 4.3	–9 / –8	–22 / –18	–33 / –26	n/a / n/a	— / —	Mostajo (1981)
Trinidad and Tobago 1977		WFS:F15–49 4359		0, 1–3, 4–6, 7+	3.8	4.0	13	0	–7	n/a	rev. J	United Nations (1987)
Trinidad and Tobago[†] 1987	H H N	DHS:F15–49 3806		0, 1–3, 4–6, 7–9, 10+	3.1	3.5	11	–6	–18	–20	rev. J	United Nations (1995)
Venezuela[†] 1977	H M N	WFS:F15–49 4361		0, 1–3, 4–6, 7+	4.2	4.9	–6	–16	–27	n/a	—	United Nations (1987)

[a] Refers to the difference between the rates for women with no education compared with women at each successively higher level of education (1–3, 4–6 years, and so on).

[b] See Introduction to appendices for discussion of the various types of relationships.

[c] See Bibliography for full citation.

[d] Refers to all women in the sample or in the sub-sample, if there was one.

[e] Refers to women with no education in the sample or in the sub-sample, if there was one.

[f] Merged with next level; if data are given for classes 1–3 and 4–6 together, results are shown under the lower category, 1–3.

[†] Studies included in Table 7.1, 7.2, and 7.3

[*] Statistically significant.

Notes: See Introduction to appendices for list of abbreviations and technical notes on the appendix. For studies in which more than one set of numbers are provided, see column headed 'Sample type' for the sub-population to which the rates refer, and column headed 'Site and survey date' if different years.

Appendix I. *Studies addressing the relationship between women's education and the practice of contraception, including sterilization*

Site and survey date	Levels of: Per capita income	Female literacy rate	Gender disparity in literacy	Sample type; universe (sex and age); size	Dependent variable (method if means n/a)	Education variable (years of schooling)	Practice of contraception (%) among: All women[d]	Uneducated women[e]	Percentage difference between uneducated and better educated women[a] by years of schooling: 1–3	4–6	7+	10+	Direction of relationship[b]	Author (date)[c]
Sub-Saharan Africa														
Benin[†] 1982	L	L	W	WFS:F15–49 4018	% CU	0, 1–3, 4–6, 7+	9.0	8.0	7	4	11	n/a	+	United Nations (1987)
Botswana[†] 1988	H	M	M	DHS:CMW 15–49 4368	% CU	0, 1–3, 4–6, 7–9, 10+	33.0	20.3	13	9	24	33	+	United Nations (1995)
Burundi[†] 1987	L	L	W	DHS:CMW 15–49 3970	% CU	0, 1–3, 4–6, 7–9, 10+	8.7	7.7	2	5	19	21	rev. 7	United Nations (1995)
Cameroon[†] 1978	M	L	W	WFS:F15–49 8219	% CU	0, 1–3, 4–6, 7+	2.0	0.0	3	5	17	n/a	rev. 7	United Nations (1987)
Côte d'Ivoire[†] 1980	M	L	W	WFS:F15–49 5764	% CU	0, 1–3, 4–6, 7+	3.0	2.0	2	4	15	n/a	rev. 7	United Nations (1987)
Ghana 1979–80				WFS:F15–49 6125	% CU	0, 1–3, 4–6, 7+	10.0	5.0	7	6	12	n/a	+	United Nations (1987)
Ghana[†] 1988	L	M	M	DHS:CMW 15–49 4488	% CU	0, 1–3, 4–6, 7–9, 10+	12.9	8.5	1	5	10	12	rev. 7	United Nations (1995)
Kenya 1977–8				WFS:F15–49 8100	% CU	0, 1–3, 4–6, 7+	7.0	4.0	1	5	11	n/a	rev. 7	United Nations (1987)
Kenya[†] 1989	L	M	M	DHS:CMW 15–49 7150	% CU	0, 1–3, 4–6, 7–9, 10+	26.9	18.3	4	9	17	26	rev. 7	United Nations (1995)
Lesotho[†] 1977	M	M	M	WFS:F15–49 3603	% CU	0, 1–3, 4–6, 7+	5.0	2.0	2	3	5	n/a	rev. 7	United Nations (1987)
Liberia[†] 1986	M	L	W	DHS:CMW 15–49 5239	% CU	0, 1–3, 4–6, 7–9, 10+	6.4	2.8	0	8	24	28	rev. 7	United Nations (1995)
Mali[†] 1987	L	L	W	DHS:CMW 15–49 3200	% CU	0, 1–3, 4–6, 7–9, 10+	4.7	2.8	4	4	31	50	rev. 7	United Nations (1995)

Country / Year			Sample	Measure	Education categories	(1)	(2)	(3)	(4)	(5)	(6)	(7)	Source
Mauritania† 1981	L	W	WFS:F15–49 3504	% CU	0, prim., comp. prim., sec.+	1.0	0.0	1	4	2	n/a	0	United Nations (1987)
Mauritius 1991	H		F15–44 3508	% CU	0–prim., comp. prim., sec.+	75.3	–'	–'	–4	–4	n/a	0	Ministry of Health (1993)
Namibia† 1992	M	M	DHS:F15–49 5421	% CU	0, prim., comp. prim., sec.+	28.9	16.8	2	13	31	n/a	rev. 7	Ministry of Health and Social Services (1992)
Nigeria 1981–2			WFS:F15–49 Standardized 9727	% CU mod. all	0, 1–3, 4–6, 7+	0.0	0.0	1	1	4	n/a	0	Cochrane and Farid (1989)
						4.0	3.0	4	4	10	n/a	rev. 7	
Nigeria, Ilorin 1983			CMW 15–35	% EU	0, prim., sec., sec.+	19.2	1.9	16	–'	37	58	+	Oni and McCarthy (1990)
1983			CMW 15–35 913	% CU		6.3	0.8	4	–'	12	22	rev. 7	
1988			CMW 15–35	% EU		30.3	9.7	14	–'	32	56	+	
1988			CMW 15–35 818	% CU		17.7	4.5	11	–'	19	35	+	
Nigeria, Edo and Delta States (Bendel) 1985			EMW 15–50 2146	% EU	0, prim., sec., ter.		0.18*	R	n/a	0.62*	1.34*	+	Okojie, 'Women's Status' (1993)
				% CU (probit estimates)[a]			0.01	R	n/a	0.57*	1.04*	+	
Nigeria, Ondo 1986			DHS CMW 15–40	% CU (OLS)	Years	0.64*	n/a	n/a	n/a	n/a	n/a	+	Kritz and Gurak (1991)
			<31			0.61*	n/a	n/a	n/a	n/a	n/a	+	
			>30 1787			0.72*	n/a	n/a	n/a	n/a	n/a	+	
Nigeria, Oyo 1990			CMW 15–40	% CU (OLS)	Years	0.11	n/a	n/a	n/a	n/a	n/a	+	
			<31			–0.10	n/a	n/a	n/a	n/a	n/a	–	
			>30 366			0.52	n/a	n/a	n/a	n/a	n/a	+	
Nigeria† 1990	L	W	DHS:F15–49 8781	% CU	0, prim., comp. prim., sec., sec.+	6.0	2.0	2	7	20	26	rev. 7	Federal Office of Statistics (1992)
Senegal 1978	M		WFS:F15–49 3985	% CU	0, 1–3, 4–6, 7–9, 10+	4.0	3.0	2	5	17	n/a	rev. 7	United Nations (1987)
Senegal† 1986	L	W	DHS:CMW 15–49 4415	% CU	0, 1–3, 4–6, 7–9, 10+	11.3	9.8	–2	9	23	31	rev. 7	United Nations (1995)
Togo† 1988	L	W	DHS:CMW 15–49 3360	% CU	0, 1–3, 4–6, 7–9, 10+	33.9	33.6	1	–4	9	15	rev. 7	United Nations (1995)

Appendix I. (cont.)

Site and survey date	Levels of: Per capita income	Female literacy rate	Gender disparity in literacy	Sample type; universe (sex and age); size	Dependent variable (method if means n/a)	Education variable (years of schooling)	Practice of contraception (%) among: All women[d]	Uneducated women[e]	% diff. 1-3	4-6	7+	10+	Direction of relationship[b]	Author (date)[c]
Uganda, Ankole 1984				EMW 15-49 683	% EU trad. % EU mod.	0, 1-4, 5+	34.0 8.5	34.1 9.9	-1 0	2 6	n/a n/a	n/a n/a	0 rev. 7	Ntozi and Kabera (1991)
Uganda[†] 1988-9	L	L	W	DHS:CMW 15-49 4730	% CU	0, 1-3, 4-6, 7-9, 10+	4.9	1.9	3	4	12	22	rev. 7	United Nations (1995)
United Rep. of Tanzania[†] 1991-2	L	H	N	DHS:F15-49 9238	% CU	0, prim., comp. prim., sec.+	10.4	3.7	9	11	39	n/a	+	Ngallaba et al. (1993)
Zaire, Kinshasa[†] 1990	L	L	M	F13-49: (working women)	% EU % CU	0, prim., sec., univ.	78.0 44.0	57.0 26.0	14 10	-' -'	28 26	34 29	+ +	Shapiro and Tambashe (1991)
				over-sampled ages 35+ 2400	% CU (weighted log. reg.)	0, prim., sec. (1-4), sec. (5-6), univ., other sch.		-0.04*	R	1.31*	2.52*	2.05*	+	
Zambia[†] 1992	L	M	M	DHS:F15-49 7000	% CU: all Mod Trad	0, prim., sec., sec.+	15.2 8.9 6.3	8.0 2.7 5.3	4 4 1	-' -' -'	30 21 1	51 47 4	rev. 7 rev. 7 U	Gaisie et al. (1993)
Zimbabwe[†] 1988-9	M	M	M	DHS:CMW 15-49 4201	% CU	0, 1-3, 4-6, 7-9, 10+	43.1	32.3	4	10	20	29	rev. 7	United Nations (1995)
B. North Africa and the Middle East														
Egypt 1973				CMW 15-49 rural and semi-urban 1234	% EU	Low, medium, high	35.0	28.3	26	-'	43	n/a	+	Khalifa (1976)
Egypt 1980				WFS:F15-49 8788	% CU	0, 1-3, 4-6, 7+	24.0	17.0	8	15	36	n/a	+	United Nations (1987)

Country, year			F15–49	% CU Mod	0, prim. or less, sec.+								Gadalla et al. (1987)
Egypt, rural 1983	M		F15–49 Menoufia 3412 Beni-Suef 6276	% CU Mod	0, prim. or less, sec.+	24.6	21.6	13	—'	12	n/a	+	Gadalla et al. (1987)
						8.4	7.5	8	—'	22	n/a	+	
Egypt† 1988–9	L	W	DHS:CMW 15–49 8911	% CU	0, 1–3, 4–6, 7–9, 10+	37.9	27.6	12	23	25	27	+	United Nations (1995)
Jordan† 1976	H	M	WFS:F15–49 3612	% CU	0, 1–3, 4–6, 7+	25.0	10.0	18	26	38	n/a	+	United Nations (1987)
Morocco 1979–80	M		WFS:F15–49 5801	% CU	0, 1–3, 4–6, 7+	20.0	16.0	21	37	40	n/a	+	United Nations (1987)
Morocco† 1987	L	W	DHS:CMW 15–49 5982	% CU	0, 1–3, 4–6, 7–9, 10+	35.9	30.8	21	29	35	38	+	United Nations (1995)
Sudan 1978–9	L		WFS:F15–49 3115	% CU	0, 1–3, 4–6, 7+	5.0	2.0	9	10	33	n/a	+	United Nations (1987)
Sudan† 1989–90	L	W	DHS:F15–49 5860	% CU Mod	0, prim., comp. prim., sec, sec.+	8.7	3.2	10	8	19	23	+	Ministry of Economic and Natl. Planning (1991)
Syrian Arab Rep.† 1978	H	W	WFS:F15–49 4487	% CU	0, 1–3, 4–6, 7+	20.0	9.0	28	28	37	n/a	+	United Nations (1987)
Tunisia 1978	H		WFS:F15–49 4123	% CU	0, 1–3, 4–6, 7+	31.0	25.0	21	25	37	n/a	+	United Nations (1987)
Tunisia† 1988	M	M	DHS:CMW 15–49 4184	% CU	0, 1–3, 4–6, 7–9, 10+	49.8	42.3	1	19	24	26	rev. 7	United Nations (1995)
C. East and South-East Asia													
Fiji† 1974	M	M	WFS:F15–49 4298	% CU	0, 1–3, 4–6, 7+	41.0	46.0	1	–7	–7	n/a	irreg.	United Nations (1987)
Indonesia 1976	M	M	WFS:F15–49 9155	% CU	0, 1–3, 4–6, 7+	26.0	22.0	8	11	21	n/a	+	United Nations (1987)
Indonesia† 1987	M	N	DHS:CMW 15–49 11884	% CU	0, 1–3, 4–6, 7–9, 10+	47.7	32.8	12	17	30	34	+	United Nations (1995)
Malaysia† 1974	H	M	WFS:F15–49 6316	% CU	0, 1–3, 4–6, 7+	33.0	22.0	10	17	26	n/a	+	United Nations (1987)
Philippines† 1978	M	N	F15–49 9268	% CU	0, 1–3, 4–6, 7+	36.0	11.0	11	23	37	n/a	+	United Nations (1987)
Rep. of Korea† 1974	H	N	WFS:F15–49 5430	% CU	0, 1–3, 4–6, 7–	35.0	28.0	2	7	13	n/a	rev. 7	United Nations (1987)

Appendix I. (cont.)

Site and survey date	Levels of: Per capita income	Female literacy rate	Gender disparity in literacy	Sample type; universe (sex and age); size	Dependent variable (method if means n/a)	Education variable (years of schooling)	Practice of contraception (%) among: All women[d]	Uneducated women[e]	% diff. 1-3	4-6	7+	10+	Direction of relationship[b]	Author (date)[c]
Thailand 1975	H	H	N	WFS:F15-49 3778	% CU	0, 1-3, 4-6, 7+	33.0	28.0	4	6	14	n/a	rev. 7	United Nations (1987)
Thailand[†] 1988				DHS:CMW 15-49 6775	% CU	0, 1-3, 4-6, 7-9, 10+	65.4	55.6	3	11	11	11	rev. 7	United Nations (1995)
D. South Asia														
Bangladesh 1975-6				WFS:F15-49 6513	% CU	0, 1-3, 4-6, 7+	8.0	6.0	5	7	24	n/a	+	United Nations (1987)
Bangladesh 1975				EMW15-49 Rural: 3667 Urban: 1117 Total: 4794	% CU	0, 1-5, 6-9, sec.+	8.6 / 23.5 / 12.0	6.8 / 15.4 / 8.3	7 / 7 / 8	13 / 29 / 25	7 / 33 / 34	n/a / n/a / n/a	rev. U / + / +	Chaudhury (1984)
Bangladesh[†] 1989	L	L	W	BFS:F15-49 n/a	% CU	0, prim., comp. prim., sec.+	30.8	28.0	5	11	21	n/a	+	Huq and Cleland (1990)
India, Goa 1980s				CMW 30-49 Hindus Christians indiv. and community educ. level 904	% CU	0, 1-5, 6+	53.0 / 31.0	48.0 / 30.0	16 / 3	—' / —'	11 / 2	n/a / n/a	+ / 0	Roy, Rama Rao, and Prasad (1991)
India 1970 1980 1988	L	L		F15-44 1970: 26060 1980: 34831 1988: 44918	% CU	0, prim., sec., sec.+	28.0 / 36.0 / 46.0	10.0 / 28.0 / 37.0	11 / 19 / 17	—' / —' / —'	29 / 28 / 23	46 / 36 / 28	+ / + / +	Operations Research Group (1990)
India[†] 1992-3	L	L	W	NFHS:CMW 13-49 89777	%CU	0, prim., comp. prim., middle, sec.+	40.6	33.9	18	15	28	31	+	Kanitkar et al. (1994)
India, Gujarat 1989				CMW 15-49 Bharuch Panchmahals	% CU CPR	0, prim., sec.+	56.5 / 38.2	58.2 / 36.0	-2 / 18	—' / —'	-3 / 10	-3 / 12	irreg. / +	Visaria (1993)

Region / year	Code	Code 2	Survey / N	Index	Controlling autonomy indices								Source
			Kheda Rajkot 12710	% CU		53.8 / 58.2	50.4 / 51.9	2 / 13	–' / –'	9 / 12	11 / 14	rev. 7 / +	
			Ernakulam Palghat Malapuram 3133	% EU	0, prim., sec, sec. comp.+	68.4 / 43.5 / 34.6	57.1 / 32.0 / 21.0	19 / 12 / 10	–' / –' / –'	11 / 17 / 20	10 / 18 / 22	+ / + / +	
Kerala 1991													United Nations (1993)
India, Maharashtra 1983–4			CMW 15–44; 1956	% EU	0, prim., middle, sec.+	62.9	59.9	5	23	10	n/a	+	Population Research Centre, Gokhale Institute et al. (1994)
India, Maharashtra 1992–3			DHS:CMW 15–49 4106	% CU	0, prim. to middle, middle comp., sec, sec.+	53.7	54.1	–1	–'	–1	4	0	Population Research Centre, Gandhigram Institute et al. (1994)
India, Tamil Nadu 1992			DHS:CMW 15–49 3948	% CU	0, prim. to middle, middle comp., sec, sec.+	49.8	47.5	4	–'	5	5	rev. 7	
India, Uttar Pradesh 1992–3			DHS:CMW 15–49 11438	% CU	0, prim. to middle, middle comp., sec, sec.+	19.3	15.5	13	–'	21	25	+	Population Research Centre, Lucknow University et al. (1994)
Nepal[†] 1976	L	W	WFS:F15–49 5940	% CU	0, 1–3, 4–6, 7+	2.0	2.0	4	9	16	n/a	rev. 7	United Nations (1987)
Pakistan 1975	L		WFS:F15–49 4996	% CU	0, 1–3, 4–6, 7+	5.0	4.0	7	6	18	n/a	+	United Nations (1987)
Pakistan[†] 1991	L	W	DHS:F15–49 6611	% CU	0, prim., comp. prim., sec.+	11.8	7.8	10	22	30	n/a	+	National Institute of Population Studies (1992)
Sri Lanka 1975	L		WFS:F15–49 6812	% CU	0, 1–3, 4–6, 7+	32.0	19.0	7	14	23	n/a	+	United Nations (1987)
Sri Lanka[†] 1987	H	N	DHS:CMW 15–49 5865	% CU	0, 1–3, 4–6, 7–9, 10+	61.7	53.9	8	11	8	7	+	United Nations (1995)
E. Latin America and the Caribbean													
Belize 1991	M		F15–44 2656	% CU	0–7, 8, 9+	46.7	38.0	–'	–'	17	18	+	Ministry of Health (1992)
Bolivia[†] 1989	M	M	DHS:CMW 15–49 7923	% CU	0, 1–3, 4–6, 7–9, 10+	30.2	11.5	11	20	38	41	+	United Nations (1995)

Appendix I. (cont.)

Site and survey date	Levels of: Per capita income	Levels of: Female literacy rate	Levels of: Gender disparity in literacy	Sample type; universe (sex and age); size	Dependent variable (method if means n/a)	Education variable (years of schooling)	Practice of contraception (%) among: All women[d]	Practice of contraception (%) among: Uneducated women[e]	Percentage difference between uneducated and better educated women[a] by years of schooling 1–3	4–6	7+	10+	Direction of relationship[b]	Author (date)[c]
Brazil[†] 1986	H	M	N	DHS:CMW 15–49 5892	% CU	0, 1–3, 4–6, 7–9, 10+	66.2	47.3	12	24	27	26	+	United Nations (1995)
Colombia 1976	H	H	N	WFS:F15–49 5378	% CU	0, 1–3, 4–6, 7+	43.0	23.0	11	28	42	n/a	+	United Nations (1987)
Colombia[†] 1986	H		N	DHS:CMW 15–49 5329	% CU	0, 1–3, 4–6, 7–9, 10+	64.7	52.7	8	12	20	20	+	United Nations (1995)
Costa Rica[†] 1976	H	H	N	WFS:F15–49 3935	% CU	0, 1–3, 4–6, 7+	64.0	56.0	5	10	12	n/a	+	United Nations (1987)
Dominican Rep. 1975	H	H	N	WFS:F15–49 3115	% CU	0, 1–3, 4–6, 7+	32.0	17.0	9	20	33	n/a	+	United Nations (1987)
Dominican Rep.[†] 1986	M	M	N	DHS:CMW 15–49 7649	% CU	0, 1–3, 4–6, 7–9, 10+	49.8	37.7	9	14	16	19	+	United Nations (1995)
Ecuador 1979	M	H		WFS:F15–49 6797	% CU	0, 1–3, 4–6, 7+	34.0	10.0	9	27	45	n/a	+	United Nations (1987)
Ecuador[†] 1987	M		N	DHS:CMW 15–49 4713	% CU	0, 1–3, 4–6, 7–9, 10+	44.3	18.4	18	25	38	43	+	United Nations (1995)
Ecuador 1989				F15–49 7961	% CU	0, 1–3, 4–6, sec., superior	52.9	22.5	26	—[f]	39	n/a	+	Monteith et al. (1992)
El Salvador 1987				DHS:CMW 15–49 5207	% CU	0, 1–3, 4–6, 7–9, 10+	47.3	36.7	5	18	14	27	+	United Nations (1995)
El Salvador[†] 1988	M	M	N	F15–44 3579	% CU	0, 1–3, 4–6, 7–9, 10+	47.1	33.6	10	17	28	31	+	Castro et al. (1989)
Guatemala[†] 1987	M	M	M	DHS:CMW 15–49 5160	% CU	0, 1–3, 4–6, 7–9, 10+	23.2	10.1	14	32	50	50	+	United Nations (1995)

Country/Year				Survey	Measure	Education								Source
Guyana† 1975	L	H	N	WFS:F15–49 4642	% CU	0, 1–3, 4–6, 7+	31.0	30.0	2	0	3	n/a	0	United Nations (1987)
Haiti 1977	L	M		WFS:F15–49 3365	% CU	0, 1–3, 4–6, 7+	19.0	13.0	15	23	26	n/a	+	United Nations (1987)
Haiti† 1989	M			F15–49 1996	% CU	0, 1–3, 4–6, 7+	10.2	8.2	2	4	11	n/a	rev. 7	Cayemittes et al. (1991)
Jamaica† 1975–6	H	H	N	WFS:F15–49 3096	% CU	0, 1–3, 4–6, 7+	38.0	17.0	10	14	24	n/a	+	United Nations (1987)
Mexico 1976	H			WFS:F15–49 7310	% CU	0, 1–3, 4–6, 7+	30.0	13.0	10	25	43	n/a	+	United Nations (1987)
Mexico† 1987	H	H	N	DHS:CMW 15–49 9310	% CU	0, 1–3, 4–6, 7–9, 10+	52.7	24.6	19	33	45	45	+	United Nations (1995)
Panama† 1975–6	H	H	N	WFS:F15–49 3701	% CU	0, 1–3, 4–6, 7+	54.0	37.0	5	17	25	n/a	+	United Nations (1987)
Paraguay† 1979	H	H	N	WFS:F15–49 4682	% CU	0, 1–3, 4–6, 7+	36.0	21.0	4	18	33	n/a	rev. 7	United Nations (1987)
Peru 1977–8	H			WFS:F15–49 5640	% CU	0, 1–3, 4–6, 7+	31.0	11.0	14	32	43	n/a	+	United Nations (1987)
Peru† 1986	H	M	N	DHS:CMW 15–49 4999	% CU	0, 1–3, 4–6, 7–9, 10+	45.7	19	14	27	45	48	+	United Nations (1995)
Puerto Rico 1982				F15–49 3175	% CU	<high school, high school, >high school	70.4	—	—	—	-1	0	0	Warren (1987)
Trinidad and Tobago 1977				WFS:F15–49 4359	% CU	0, 1–3, 4–6, 7+	52.0	38.0	8	7	15	n/a	+	United Nations (1987)
Trinidad and Tobago† 1987	H			DHS:CMW 15–49 3806	% CU	0, 1–3, 4–6, 7–9, 10+	52.7	31.4	11	18	24	26	+	United Nations (1995)
Venezuela† 1977	H	M	N	WFS:F15–49 4361	% CU	0, 1–3, 4–6, 7–	49.0	29.0	10	24	31	n/a	+	United Nations (1987)

Appendix I. (cont.)

^a Refers to the difference between the rates for women with no education compared with women at each successively higher level of education (1–3 years, 4–6 years, and so on).

^b See Introduction to appendices for discussion of the various types of relationships.

^c See Bibliography for full citation.

^d Refers to all women in the sample or in the sub-sample, if there was one.

^e Refers to women with no education in the sample or in the sub-sample, if there was one.

^f Merged with next level; if data are given for classes 1–3 and 4–6 together, results are shown under the lower category, 1–3.

^g Probit regression analysis is a statistical technique that, like logistic regression analysis, is used rather than ordinary least-squares analysis when a dependent variable is dichotomous.

† Studies included in Tables 8.1, 8.2, and 8.3.

* Statistically significant.

Mod Refers to modern method users and excludes users of such traditional methods as abstinence, rhythm, and coitus interruptus.

Trad Refers to traditional method users, that is those practising abstinence, rhythm or coitus interruptus.

BFS Bangladesh Fertility Survey.

Notes: See Introduction to appendices for list of abbreviations and technical notes on the appendix. For studies in which more than one set of numbers are provided, see column headed 'Sample type' for the sub-population to which the rates refer, and column headed 'Site and survey date' if different years.

Appendix J. *Studies addressing the relationship between women's education and the unmet need for contraception*

Site and survey date	Levels of:			Sample type; universe (sex and age); size	Education variable (years of schooling)	% of women with unmet need for contraception among:		Percentage difference between uneducated and better educated women[a] by years of schooling				Direction of relationship[b]	Author (date)[c]
	Per capita income	Female literacy rate	Gender disparity in literacy			All women[d]	Uneducated women[e]	Primary	Secondary and higher	Secondary	Higher		
A. Sub-Saharan Africa													
Botswana 1988	H	M	M	DHS:F15–49 1708	0, prim., sec.+	26.9	31.3	–4	–13	n/a	n/a	7	Westoff and Ochoa (1991)
Burundi 1987	L	L	W	DHS:F15–49 2669	0, prim., sec.+	25.1	23.4	10	13	n/a	n/a	+	Westoff and Ochoa (1991)
Ghana 1988	L	M	M	DHS:F15–49 3156	0, prim., sec.+	35.2	32.3	7	–5	n/a	n/a	rev. J	Westoff and Ochoa (1991)
Kenya 1989	L	M	W	DHS:F15–49 4765	0, prim., sec.+	38.0	36.5	4	–4	n/a	n/a	0	Westoff and Ochoa (1991)
Liberia 1986	M	L	W	DHS:F15–49 3529	0, prim., sec.+	32.8	29.8	11	15	n/a	n/a	+	Westoff and Ochoa (1991)
Mali 1987	L	L	W	DHS:F15–49 2948	0, prim., sec.+	22.9	21.8	8	7	n/a	n/a	+	Westoff and Ochoa (1991)
Togo 1988	L	L	W	DHS:F15–49 2454	0, prim., sec.+	40.1	36.9	14	2	n/a	n/a	rev. U	Westoff and Ochoa (1991)
Uganda 1988–9	L	L	W	DHS:F15–49 3180	0, prim., sec.+	27.2	24.4	5	11	n/a	n/a	+	Westoff and Ochoa (1991)
B. North Africa and the Middle East													
Egypt 1989	M	L	W	DHS:F15–49 8221	0, prim., sec., sec.+	25.2	29.3	–6	–13	–11	–16	–	Westoff and Ochoa (1991)
Morocco 1987	M	L	W	DHS:F15–49 5447	0, prim., sec., sec.+	22.1	23.7	–8	–14	–12	–15	–	Westoff and Ochoa (1991)
Tunisia 1988	H	M	M	DHS:F15–49 4012	0, prim., sec., sec.+	19.7	23.2	–6	–13	–13	–13	–	Westoff and Ochoa (1991)
C. East and South-East Asia													
Indonesia 1987	M	M	N	DHS:F15–49 907	0, prim., sec., sec.+	16.0	16.1	1	–4	–3	–4	0	Westoff and Ochoa (1991)
Thailand 1987	H	H	N	DHS:F15–49 6236	0, prim., sec., sec.+	11.1	14.5	–3.40	–8	–6	–8	7	Westoff and Ochoa (1991)
D. South Asia													
India 1988–9	L	L	W	F15–44 44918	0, prim., sec., sec.+	18.3	21.5	–5	–10	–10	–11	–	Operations Research Group (1990)

Appendix J. (cont.)

Site and survey date	Levels of:			Sample type; universe (sex and age); size	Education variable (years of schooling)	% of women with unmet need for contraception among:		Percentage difference between uneducated and better educated women[a] by years of schooling				Direction of relationship[b]	Author (date)[c]
	Per capita income	Female literacy rate	Gender disparity in literacy			All women[d]	Uneducated women[e]	Primary	Secondary and higher	Secondary	Higher		
Sri Lanka 1987	L	H	N	DHS:F15–49 5442	0, prim., sec., sec.+	12.3	15.2	-3	-3	-3	-4	0	Westoff and Ochoa (1991)
E. Latin America and the Caribbean													
Bolivia 1989	M	M	M	DHS:F15–49 4941	0, prim., sec., sec.+	35.7	45.1	-5	-28	-21	-33	-	Westoff and Ochoa (1991)
Brazil 1986	H	M	N	DHS:F15–44 3471	0, prim., sec., sec.+	12.8	29.6	-17	-25	-24	-26	-	Westoff and Ochoa (1991)
Colombia 1986	H	H	N	DHS:F15–49 2850	0, prim., sec., sec.+	13.5	22.0	-7	-16	-13	-19	-	Westoff and Ochoa (1991)
Dominican Rep., 1986	M	M	N	DHS:F15–49 4133	0, prim., sec., sec.+	19.4	29.6	-10	-17	-12	-21	-	Westoff and Ochoa (1991)
Ecuador 1987	M	H	N	DHS:F15–49 2957	0, prim., sec., sec.+	24.2	36.6	-9	-25	-19	-29	-	Westoff and Ochoa (1991)
Ecuador 1989	M	H	N	F15–49 7961	0, prim., sec., sec.+	24.6	42.0	-13	-29	-23	-32	-	Monteith et al. (1992)
El Salvador 1988	M	M	N	DHS:F15–49 3164	0, prim., sec., sec.+	26.0	31.7	-6	-18	-13	-22	-	Westoff and Ochoa (1991)
Guatemala 1987	M	M	M	DHS:F15–44 3377	0, prim., sec., sec.+	29.4	34.5	-7	-24	-24	-25	-	Westoff and Ochoa (1991)
Mexico 1988	H	H	N	DHS:F15–44 9310	0, prim., comp. prim., sec., sec.+	24.1	42.8	-15	-31	-28	-36	-	Cordova (1991)
Peru 1986	H	M	N	DHS:F15–49 2900	0, prim., sec., sec.+	27.7	48.9	-17	-37	-32	-40	-	Westoff and Ochoa (1991)
Trinidad and Tobago, 1987	H	H	N	DHS:F15–49 2617	0, prim., sec., sec.+	16.1	14.8	2	-3	1	-5	7	Westoff and Ochoa (1991)

a Refers to the difference between the rates for women with no education compared with women at each successively higher level of education.
b See Introduction to appendices for discussion of the various types of relationships.
c See Bibliography for full citation.
d Refers to all women in the sample.
e Refers to women with no education in the sample.

Notes: Unmet need for contraception is measured as the proportion of couples who want no more children and are fecund but are not practising contraception. See Introduction to appendices for list of abbreviations and technical notes on the appendix.

Appendix K. *Studies addressing the relationship between women's education and contraceptive knowledge*

Site and survey date	Levels of: Per capita income	Female literacy rate	Gender disparity in literacy	Sample type; universe (sex and age); size	Education variable (years of schooling); (method, if means n/a)	Percentage with contraceptive knowledge among: All women[d]	Unedu-cated women[e]	Percentage difference between uneducated and better educated women[a] by years of schooling 1-3	4-6	7+	10+	Direction of relation-ship[b]	Author (date)[c]
A. Sub-Saharan Africa													
Botswana[†] 1988	H	M	M	DHS:F15-49 4368	0, 1-3, 4-6, 7-9, 10+	94.4	85.2	12	13	14	15	+	United Nations (1995)
Burundi[†] 1987	L	L	W	DHS:F15-49 3970	0, 1-3, 4-6, 7-9, 10+	63.3	60.1	15	17	33	30	+	United Nations (1995)
Ghana[†] 1988	L	M	M	DHS:F15-49 4488	0, 1-3, 4-6, 7-9, 10+	76.8	60.6	22	25	33	34	+	United Nations (1995)
Kenya[†] 1989	L	M	M	DHS:F15-49 7150	0, 1-3, 4-6, 7-9, 10+	91.3	82.8	7	11	15	17	+	United Nations (1995)
Liberia[†] 1986	M	L	W	DHS:F15-49 5239	0, 1-3, 4-6, 7-9, 10+	69.5	61.6	21	27	34	37	+	United Nations (1995)
Mali[†] 1987	L	L	W	DHS:F15-49 3200	0, 1-3, 4-6, 7-9, 10+	28.8	23.1	19	31	67	77	+	United Nations (1995)
Mauritius[†] 1991	H	H	N	F15-44 5262	0 to prim., comp. prim., sec., comp. prim.+	99.1	98.2	—[f]	1	2	n/a	0	Ministry of Health (1992)
Nigeria, Ilorin 1983-4				CMW 15-35 913	0, prim., sec., sec.+	75.6	58.2	26	—[f]	32	36	+	Oni (1985)
Nigeria[†] 1990	L	L	W	DHS:F15-49 8781	0, prim., sec.+	41.2	26.7	34	38	57	n/a	+	Federal Office of Statistics (1992)
Senegal[†] 1986	M	L	W	DHS:F15-49 4415	0, 1-3, 4-6, 7-9, 10+	68.6	64.7	6	30	34	34	+	United Nations (1995)
Togo[†] 1988	L	L	W	DHS:F15-49 3360	0, 1-3, 4-6, 7-9, 10+	81.4	75.6	11	19	23	22	+	United Nations (1995)
Uganda, Ankole 1984				EMW 15-49 683	0, 1-4, 5+	15.8	11.4	8	18	—[f]	n/a	+	Ntozi and Kabera (1991)
Uganda[†] 1988-9	L	L	W	DHS:F15-49 4730	0, 1-3, 4-6, 7-9, 10+	78.5	68.0	13	18	27	31	+	United Nations (1995)
United Rep. of Tanzania[†] 1991-2	L	H	N	DHS:F15-49 9238	0, comp. prim., sec.+	80.2	68.7	17	21	30	n/a	+	Ngallaba et al. (1993)

Location / Year			Sample	Education categories								Source
Zimbabwe† 1988–9	M	M	DHS:F15–49 42C1	0, 1–3, 4–6, 7–9, 10+	97.8	94.0	3	5	6	6	rev. 7	United Nations (1995)
B. North Africa and the Middle East												
Egypt† 1988–9	M	W	DHS:F15–49 8911	0, 1–3, 4–6, 7–9, 10+	97.8	96.5	2	3	3	3	0	United Nations (1995)
Morocco† 1987	M	W	DHS:F15–49 5982	0, 1–3, 4–6, 7–9, 10+	97.5	97.0	3	3	3	3	0	United Nations (1995)
Sudan† 1989–90	L	W	DHS:F15–49 5860	0, comp. prim., sec.+	70.8	54.2	37	38	43	n/a	+	Ministry of Econ. and Natl. Planning (1991)
Tunisia† 1988	M	M	DHS:F15–49 4184	0, 1–3, 4–6, 7–9, 10+	98.8	98.1	1	2	2	2	0	United Nations (1995)
C. East and South-East Asia												
Indonesia† 1987	M	N	DHS:F15–49 11894	0, 1–3, 4–6, 7–9, 10+	93.1	80.8	13	17	19	19	+	United Nations (1995)
Philippines 1983, 1988			F15–49 Rural: 1983 <35: 2673	Years	n/a	n/a	n/a	n/a	n/a	n/a	0.165*	Raymundo et al. (1993)
			Rural: 1988 <35: 3722								0.264*	
Thailand† 1987	H	N	DHS:F15–49 6775	0, 1–3, 4–6, 7–9, 10+	99.4	96.1	3	4	4	4	0	United Nations (1995)
D. South Asia												
India, Kerala 1980			F15–49 2679	0, 1–4, 5–9, 10+ Years (OLS)	84.0	75.0	14	19	—'	23	+	Zachariah (1984)
					0.32	n/a	n/a	n/a	n/a	n/a	0.3179	
India† 1988–9	L	W	F15–44 (tubectomy) (IUD) correct use: (tubectomy) (IUD) 449'8	0, prim., sec., sec.+	94.9	93.1	4	5	—'	6	rev. 7	Operations Research Group (1990)
					55.4	38.9	31	44	—'	56	+	
India, Tamil Nadu 1970			CMW 35–44 766	Years (OLS)	52.8	42.6	19	25	—'	29	0.1025	Jejeebhoy (1991)
1980			258		30.2	16.9	22	36	—'	54	0.0757	
India, Maharashtra 1983–4			CMW 15–44 1956	0, prim., middle, sec.+ (methods known)[a]	2.9	2.6	23	38	62	n/a	+	United Nations (1993)

Appendix K. (cont.)

Site and survey date	Levels of: Per capita income	Female literacy rate	Gender disparity in literacy	Sample type; universe (sex and age); size	Education variable (years of schooling); (method, if means n/a)	Percentage with contraceptive knowledge among: All women[d]	Uneducated women[e]	Percentage difference between uneducated and better educated women[a] by years of schooling 1–3	4–6	7+	10+	Direction of relationship[b]	Author (date)[c]
India, Maharashtra 1992–3				DHS:F15–49 4106	0, prim. to middle, middle comp., sec.+	97.8	96.5	2	—'	3	3	0	Population Research Centre, Gokhale Institute et al. (1994)
India, Tamil Nadu 1992				DHS:F15–49 3948	0, prim. to middle, middle comp., sec.+	99.1	98.7	1	—'	1	1	0	Population Research Centre, Gandhigram Institute et al. (1994)
India, Uttar Pradesh 1992–3				DHS:F15–49 11438	0, prim. to middle, middle comp., sec.+	95.2	94	4	—'	6	6	rev. 7	Population Research Centre, Lucknow University et al. (1994)
Pakistan 1987	L	L		EMW 15–52 1000	0, 1–9, 10+	n/a	89.0	0	—'	3	3	0	Sathar and Kazi (1990)
Pakistan[†] 1991			W	DHS:F15–49 6611	0, prim., comp. prim., sec.+	77.2	73.0	19	21	22	n/a	+	National Institute of Population Studies (1992)
Sri Lanka[†] 1987	L	H	N	DHS:F15–49 5865	0, 1–3, 4–6, 7–9, 10+	98.7	96.2	2	2	3	4	0	United Nations (1995)
E. Latin America and the Caribbean													
Bolivia[†] 1989	M	M	M	DHS:F15–49 7923	0, 1–3, 4–6, 7–9, 10+	68.4	32.0	31	43	61	64	+	United Nations (1995)
Brazil[†] 1986	H	M	N	DHS:F15–44 5892	0, 1–3, 4–6, 7–9, 10+	99.8	99.6	0	0	0	0	0	United Nations (1995)
Colombia[†] 1986	H	H	N	DHS:F15–49 5329	0, 1–3, 4–6, 7–9, 10+	99.3	95.8	4	4	4	4	0	United Nations (1995)

Dominican Rep.[†] 1986	M	M	N	DHS:F15–49	7649	0, 1–3, 4–6, 7–9, 10+	99.3	95.5	4	4	4	4	0	United Nations (1995)
Ecuador[†] 1987	M	H	N	DHS:F15–49	4713	0, 1–3, 4–6, 7–9, 10+	90.0	65.7	17	27	32	33	+	United Nations (1995)
El Salvador[†] 1985	M	M	N	DHS:F15–49	5207	0, 1–3, 4–6, 7–9, 10+	93.0	85.6	7	11	13	14	+	United Nations (1995)
Guatemala[†] 1987	M	M	M	DHS:F15–49	5160	0, 1–3, 4–6, 7–9, 10+	72.5	55.2	27	39	44	45	+	United Nations (1995)
Haiti[†] 1989	L	M	M	DHS:F15–49	1996	0, 1–3, 4–6, 7+	81.3	79.5	−2	2	10	n/a	rev. 7	Cayemittes et al. (1991)
Mexico[†] 1987	H	H	N	DHS:F15–49	9310	0, 1–3, 4–6, 7–9, 10+	93.3	74.5	18	23	25	26	+	United Nations (1995)
Peru[†] 1986	H	M	N	DHS:F15–49	4999	0, 1–3, 4–6, 7–9, 10+	86.4	58.2	23	32	41	41	+	United Nations (1995)
Trinidad and Tobago[†] 1987	H	H	N	DHS:F15–49	3806	0, 1–3, 4–6, 7–9, 10+	98.7	94.7	−1	4	5	5	rev. 7	United Nations (1995)

[a] Refers to the difference between the rates for women with no education compared with women at each successively higher level of education (1–3 years, 4–6 years, and so on).
[b] See Introduction to appendices for discussion of the various types of relationships.
[c] See Bibliography for full citation.
[d] Refers to all women in the sample or in the sub-sample, if there was one.
[e] Refers to women with no education in the sample or in the sub-sample, if these was one.
[f] Merged with next level; if data are given for classes 1–3 and 4–6 together, results are shown under the lower category, 1–3.
[g] Dependent variable is the mean number of methods known.
[h] Studies included in Tables 8.4, 8.5, and 8.6.
* Statistically significant.

Notes: Unless otherwise indicated, contraceptive knowledge is defined as the proportions aware of at least one method by which fertility can be controlled. See Introduction to appendices for list of abbreviations and technical notes on the appendix. For studies in which more than one set of numbers are provided, see column headed 'Sample type' for the sub-population to which the rates refer, and column headed 'Site and survey date' if different years.

Appendix L. *Percentage contribution of each proximate determinant to the difference between potential and actual fertility, for various educational levels*

Site and survey date	Survey	Level of:			Percentage of reduction in potential fertility among:											
		Per capita income	Female literacy rate	Gender disparity in literacy	Uneducated women, due to:			Women with 1–3 years of schooling, due to:			Women with 4–6 years of schooling, due to:			Women with 7+ years of schooling, due to:		
(1)	(2)	(3)	(4)	(5)	Ci (6)	Cm (7)	Cc (8)	Ci (9)	Cm (10)	Cc (11)	Ci (12)	Cm (13)	Cc (14)	Ci (15)	Cm (16)	Cc (17)
A. Sub-Saharan Africa																
Botswana† 1988	DHS	H	M	M	33.9	52.0	14.1	30.0	54.8	15.1	28.8	55.7	15.5	18.7	55.1	26.2
Burundi† 1987	DHS	L	L	W	61.6	33.6	4.8	65.3	27.4	7.3	50.9	40.3	8.8	38.5	46.2	15.3
Ghana 1979–80	WFS				71.7	21.4	7.0	51.2	34.9	13.9	56.0	31.6	12.4	43.6	35.5	21.0
Ghana† 1988	DHS	L	M	M	74.0	19.2	6.8	62.2	30.4	7.3	60.5	27.3	12.2	48.1	37.9	14.0
Kenya† 1977–8	WFS				68.7	25.8	5.6	62.4	28.2	9.3	55.4	32.6	12.0	32.4	43.0	24.6
Kenya† 1988–9	DHS	L	M	M	61.1	23.0	15.8	50.4	30.6	19.0	41.3	28.0	30.8	27.6	42.7	29.7
Lesotho† 1977	WFS	M	M	M	63.3	34.8	1.9	60.0	36.3	3.7	59.6	35.0	5.3	41.9	50.4	7.7
Liberia† 1986	DHS	M	L	W	68.2	28.0	3.8	55.7	38.2	6.1	45.9	50.9	3.2	25.9	46.9	27.1
Mali† 1987	DHS	L	L	W	89.0	7.9	3.1	80.9	12.4	6.7	84.1	6.3	9.6	51.5	14.2	34.3
Nigeria† 1983	Other	L	L	W	84.3	14.9	0.8	68.8	26.3	5.0	50.4	38.6	11.0	32.9	45.1	22.0
Senegal 1978	WFS				77.9	19.5	2.6	33.5	13.2	53.2	51.9	48.1	0.0	36.3	63.7	0.0
Senegal† 1986	DHS	M	L	W	77.5	14.7	7.8	58.1	35.7	6.2	36.4	51.5	12.1	23.1	59.8	17.1
Togo† 1988	DHS	L	L	W	65.6	12.1	22.3	52.6	22.5	24.9	50.2	27.2	22.6	30.9	42.8	26.3
Uganda† 1988–9	DHS	L	L	W	71.0	27.6	1.4	59.6	34.9	5.5	50.1	41.5	8.4	33.3	52.6	14.1

	Survey														
Zimbabwe† 1988-9	DHS	M	M	M	42.8	14.5	42.8	41.1	17.8	41.1	35.5	29.0	35.5	32.0	36.0	32.0
B. North Africa and the Middle East																
Egypt† 1988-9	DHS	M	L	W	47.1	18.4	34.5	42.0	10.6	47.4	27.8	18.0	54.3	21.7	15.6	62.8
Jordan† 1976	WFS	H	M	M	50.2	31.0	18.8	40.4	20.6	38.9	25.8	32.3	42.0	12.1	43.3	44.6
Morocco† 1987	DHS	M	L	W	39.5	21.0	39.5	25.2	14.1	60.7	14.3	17.2	68.5	10.9	10.0	79.1
Sudan† 1978-9	WFS	L	L	W	63.9	33.8	2.3	48.8	39.5	11.8	44.3	42.1	13.6	29.2	43.4	27.4
Syrian Arab Rep.†, 1978	WFS	H	L	W	45.9	39.0	15.1	27.8	35.6	36.7	25.9	36.6	37.4	13.6	46.9	39.5
Tunisia† 1988	DHS	H	M	M	36.7	13.7	49.6	27.8	15.3	56.9	13.3	14.3	72.4	14.5	12.9	72.6
C. East and South-East Asia																
Fiji 1974	WFS	M	M	M	34.5	n/a	65.5	20.8	n/a	79.2	34.2	n/a	65.8	30.2	n/a	69.8
Indonesia 1976	WFS				73.1	n/a	26.9	64.4	n/a	35.6	61.3	n/a	38.7	43.4	n/a	56.6
Indonesia† 1991	DHS	M	M	N	45.6	13.3	41.1	41.5	7.8	50.7	36.0	12.6	51.4	24.5	13.8	61.7
Malaysia† 1974	WFS	H	M	M	18.4	52.5	29.1	13.1	47.6	39.4	12.1	46.6	41.3	5.9	58.9	35.2
Philippines† 1978	WFS	M	H	N	41.4	50.7	7.9	44.4	36.5	19.2	31.8	39.2	29.0	13.4	52.4	34.3
Rep. of Korea†, 1974	WFS	H	H	N	40.7	34.5	24.8	40.7	31.9	27.4	35.3	41.0	23.7	22.7	50.6	26.7
Thailand 1975	WFS				54.6	n/a	45.4	52.0	n/a	48.0	53.7	n/a	46.3	26.5	n/a	73.5
Thailand† 1987	DHS	H	H	N	22.8	13.2	64.0	24.5	8.3	67.2	19.1	9.2	71.6	15.1	12.6	72.3
D. South Asia																
Bangladesh† 1975-6	WFS	L	L	W	80.4	13.0	6.6	75.1	11.5	13.5	74.8	9.3	15.9	37.3	23.5	39.1
Nepal 1976	WFS	L	L	W	96.6	n/a	3.4	91.3	n/a	8.7	82.5	n/a	17.5	73.8	n/a	26.2
Pakistan† 1975	WFS	L	L	W	68.9	26.4	4.7	53.4	30.9	15.7	50.9	37.2	11.9	20.7	67.3	12.0
Sri Lanka 1975	WFS				76.8	n/a	23.2	72.3	n/a	27.7	64.9	n/a	35.1	56.1	n/a	43.9

Appendix L. (cont.)

(1) Site and survey date	(2) Survey	Level of:			Percentage of reduction in potential fertility among:											
		(3) Per capita income	(4) Female literacy rate	(5) Gender disparity in literacy	Uneducated women, due to:			Women with 1–3 years of schooling, due to:			Women with 4–6 years of schooling, due to:			Women with 7+ years of schooling, due to:		
					Ci (6)	Cm (7)	Cc (8)	Ci (9)	Cm (10)	Cc (11)	Ci (12)	Cm (13)	Cc (14)	Ci (15)	Cm (16)	Cc (17)
Sri Lanka† 1987	DHS	L	H	N	29.5	18.5	52.0	24.6	13.9	61.5	25.5	12.5	62.0	26.3	12.3	61.5
E. Latin America and the Caribbean																
Bolivia† 1989	DHS	M	M	M	49.5	43.2	7.3	47.0	34.6	18.4	38.5	38.5	23.0	23.3	43.8	32.9
Brazil† 1986	DHS	H	M	N	11.6	30.2	58.1	13.2	27.6	59.1	5.8	31.4	62.8	6.1	40.3	53.6
Colombia 1976	WFS				28.7	37.6	33.7	19.9	43.5	36.6	12.2	43.2	44.6	5.5	46.8	47.7
Colombia† 1986	DHS	H	H	N	13.7	35.1	51.2	16.5	30.7	52.8	12.3	30.7	56.9	6.0	43.7	50.4
Costa Rica† 1976	WFS	H	H	N	10.6	39.0	50.4	9.8	31.9	58.3	5.5	36.1	58.4	4.2	46.1	49.7
Dominican Rep., 1975	WFS				33.0	33.4	33.6	25.4	35.1	39.5	17.5	36.4	46.1	6.3	51.3	42.4
Dominican Rep.†, 1986	DHS	M	M	N	33.6	25.4	41.0	24.0	29.0	47.0	16.9	32.1	51.0	11.8	48.3	39.9
Ecuador† 1987	DHS	M	H	N	49.4	36.4	14.2	37.5	26.4	36.1	29.8	28.6	41.6	18.1	41.2	40.7
El Salvador† 1989	DHS	M	M	N	38.8	23.8	37.4	31.6	22.7	45.7	21.7	28.4	49.9	15.9	39.3	44.8
Guatemala† 1987	DHS	M	M	M	63.3	26.8	10.0	44.8	31.6	23.6	27.9	38.5	33.6	14.4	45.1	40.5
Guyana† 1975	WFS	L	H	N	34.5	27.7	37.8	21.7	15.8	62.5	23.6	26.2	50.1	13.9	43.8	42.3
Haiti† 1977	WFS	L	M	M	42.4	45.8	11.9	27.1	49.1	23.7	20.2	52.4	27.4	10.7	57.3	32.0
Jamaica† 1975–6	WFS	H	H	N	57.0	31.4	11.6	22.7	18.2	59.1	24.5	29.8	45.6	16.3	32.8	50.8
Mexico 1977	WFS				42.0	37.6	20.4	28.7	38.8	32.5	15.8	43.3	40.8	4.4	47.9	47.7

1976 Mexico†	DHS	H	N	48.5	21.9	29.6	30.3	20.5	49.2	12.1	28.7	59.1	7.1	42.1	50.8
1987 Panama†	WFS	H	N	25.1	25.9	48.9	29.0	26.4	44.6	17.3	29.8	52.9	3.6	43.6	52.8
1975–6 Paraguay†	WFS	H	N	39.1	35.5	25.3	31.5	42.6	25.9	19.5	46.2	34.3	8.8	50.1	41.0
1979 Peru	WFS	H		48.9	39.1	12.0	38.1	38.5	23.4	21.1	41.5	37.4	8.8	55.1	36.2
1977–8 Peru†	DHS	M	N	50.0	34.7	15.3	40.1	35.9	24.0	29.7	35.8	34.5	13.6	43.2	43.2
1986 Trinidad and Tobago	WFS			24.5	34.0	41.4	16.8	19.8	63.4	22.4	28.6	49.0	10.0	34.6	55.4
1977 Trinidad and Tobago†	DHS	H	N	0.0	28.9	71.1	7.7	40.8	51.6	14.1	34.8	51.1	10.5	35.1	54.4
1987 Venezuela†	WFS	M	N	26.3	36.4	37.3	23.1	29.6	47.2	12.3	35.8	51.9	4.4	48.8	46.8
1977															

Notes:

Cols. 6, 9, 12, and 15 calculated as: $100 - \ln(Ci)/\{\ln(Ci) + \ln(Cc) + \ln(Cm)\}$

Cols. 7, 10, 13, and 16 calculated as: $100 - \ln(Cm)/\{\ln(Ci) + \ln(Cc) + \ln(Cm)\}$

Cols. 8, 11, 14, and 17 calculated as: $100 - \ln(Cc)/\{\ln(Ci) + \ln(Cc) + \ln(Cm)\}$

Sources:

Values of Ci, Cm, and Cc (Bongaarts indices) for women at each level of education are taken from United Nations (1995) for all DHS-based studies, from Casterline *et al.* (1984) for all WFS-based studies, and from Oni (1985) for Nigeria. See Bibliography for full citation.

Glossary

Couple protection rate The contraceptive prevalence rate or the proportion of eligible couples (with the women aged 15–49) who use a non-terminal method of contraception or one of whom has been sterilized. The couple protection rate is usually estimated indirectly from family planning programme data.

Demographic transition and fertility transition The transition over time from high levels of fertility and mortality, through a stage in which mortality declines but fertility remains generally high, to a stage in which both fertility and mortality levels decline until a final stage in which both levels are low.

Enrolment ratio The ratio of students enrolled in particular grades to the number of children in the appropriate age group. (In some cases, the ratio can exceed 100: if, for example, over-age students are retained in a lower grade, they appear in the numerator but not the denominator.)

Hazards rate, proportional hazards model Appropriate in the study of one-time non-renewable events, such as first-marriage formation, the timing of the first birth. The proportional hazards models combine life-table and regression analysis in a multivariate context.

Intervening variable A factor through which education affects fertility, such as those relating to the supply of children, the demand for children, costs of and obstacles to contraception, and actual contraceptive use.

Literacy rate Percentage of persons, usually aged 15 and over, who can read and write.

Logistic regression analysis When the dependent variable is dichotomous, i.e. cannot be ordered, the usual assumptions underlying the linear model do not hold. In such cases, logistic regression analysis rather than ordinary least-squares analysis is appropriate. A dichotomous dependent variable is, for example, one in which responses are 'yes' or 'no'. In the analysis reported in Chapter 7, the dependent variable is whether or not the woman wanted additional children.

Lisrel analysis Lisrel is short for 'linear structural relations'. It is one of several multivariate statistical techniques used for studying the causal relationship of several independent variables to one dependent variable. In Chapter 8, the intention is to examine the determinants of knowledge of modern contraception; the independent variables include female schooling, ethnic background, and rural–urban residence.

Multivariate study A study of the causal relationship of more than one independent variables to one dependent variable. Many statistical techniques are used to distinguish the relative effects of multiple independent variables, including multiple regression analysis, path analysis, and lisrel analysis.

Proximate determinants of fertility The immediate determinants of fertility, defined by J. Bongaarts ('A Framework for Analyzing the Proximate Determinants of Fertility' (1978) and 'The Fertility-Inhibiting Effects of the Intermediate Fertility Variables' (1982)) to include four components—proportions married, use of contraception, abortion, and lactational infecundability.

Singulate mean age at marriage Calculated from census data on the proportions who are single, by age.

Total fertility rate   The number of children that would be born per woman, if she were to live to the end of her child-bearing years and bear children at each age in accordance with the age-specific fertility rates.

Unmet need for contraception   Unmet need is measured as the proportion of couples who want no more children and are fecund but are not practising contraception.

Zero-order correlation   A correlation that measures the relationship between two variables, one independent and one dependent variable. The zero-order correlation measures the extent to which change in one variable, such as women's literacy, is associated with change in another variable, such as the fertility rate. Zero-order correlations range from 0 (no association) to + or – 1.0, meaning a perfect correlation, with an increase of 1 per cent in one variable being associated with a similar change (increase if the sign is + and decrease if it is –) in the dependent variable.

Bibliography

Abou-Gamrah, H., 'Fertility Levels and Differentials by Mother's Education in Some Countries of the ECWA Region', in *Determinants of Fertility in Some African and Asian Countries*, Research Monograph Series No. 10 (Cairo, Cairo Demographic Centre, 1982).

Acuna, O. M., 'La mujer en la familia y el valor de los hijos', in *Seminario Nacional de Demografía*, Direction General de Estadistica y Censos (San Jose, Departamento de Publicaciones, 1981), 112–29.

Adewuyi, A. A., 'Education and Fertility: The Nigerian Case', *Ife Social Sciences Review*, 9/1 and 2 (1986), 29–45.

—— and Isiugo-Abanihe, U. C., 'Regional Patterns and Correlates of Birth Interval Length in Nigeria', Research Note No. 107 (Canberra, Department of Demography, Research School of Social Sciences, Australian National University, 1990).

Ahmad, O. B., Eberstein, I. W., and Sly, D. F., 'Proximate Determinants of Child Mortality in Liberia', *Journal of Biosocial Science*, 23/3 (July 1991), 313–25.

Akande, B., 'Some Socio-cultural Factors Influencing Fertility Behaviour: A Case Study of Yoruba Women', *Biology and Society*, 6/4 (Dec. 1989), 165–70.

Akin, J. S., Griffin, C. C., Guilkey, D. K., and Popkin, B. M., 'The Demand for Primary Health-Care Services in the Bicol Region of the Philippines', *Economic Development and Cultural Change*, 34 (1986), 755–82.

Al-Bustan, M., and Kohli, B. R., 'Socio-economic and Demographic Factors Influencing Breast-feeding Among Kuwaiti Women', *Genus*, 44/1–2 (Jan.–June 1988), 265–77.

Alsuwaigh, S. A., 'Women in Transition: The Case of Saudi Arabia', *Journal of Comparative Family Studies*, 20/1 (1989), 67–78.

Amin, Sajeda, 'The Correlates of Female Education and Fertility in Rural Bangladesh', paper presented at the Workshop on Female Education, Autonomy and Fertility Change in South Asia, New Delhi, Apr. 1993.

Anker, R., 'Problems of Interpretation and Specification in Analysing Fertility Differentials: Illustrated with Kenyan Survey Data', in G. M. Farooq and G. B. Simmons (eds.), *Fertility in Developing Countries: An Economic Perspective on Research and Policy Issues* (Geneva, International Labour Office, 1985).

Aryal, R. H., 'Socioeconomic and Cultural Differentials in Age at Marriage and the Effect on Fertility in Nepal', *Journal of Biosocial Science*, 23/2 (1991), 167–78.

Azelmat, M., Ayad, M., and Bilhachmia, H., *Maroc enquête nationale sur la planification familiale, la fécondité et la santé de la population au Maroc 1987* (Columbia, Md., Westinghouse, 1989).

Bailey, M., 'Differential Fertility by Religious Group in Rural Sierra Leone', *Journal of Biosocial Science*, 18 (1986), 7–85.

Balk, Deborah, 'Individual and Community Aspects of Fertility and Women's Status in Rural Bangladesh', *Population Studies*, 48 (1994), 21–45.

Bankole, A., 'Maternal Employment and Infant Mortality: An Examination of the Role of Breastfeeding as an Intermediate Factor', *Biology and Society*, 6/1 (1989), 19–26.

Barrera, A., 'The Role of Maternal Schooling and Its Interaction with Public Health

Programmes in Child Health Production', *Journal of Development Economics*, 32 (1990), 69–91.

Barrett, R. E., Bridges, W. P., Semyonov, M., and Gao, X, 'Female Labor Force Participation in Urban and Rural China', *Rural Sociology*, 56/1 (Spring 1991), 1–21.

Basu, A. M., 'Household Influences on Childhood Mortality: Evidence from Historical and Recent Mortality Trends', *Social Biology*, 34/3–4 (1987), 187–205.

—— 'Is Discrimination in Food Really Necessary for Explaining Sex Differentials in Childhood Mortality?', *Population Studies*, 43 (1989), 193–210.

—— 'Culture and the Status of Women in North and South India', in S. N. Singh, M. K. Premi, P. S. Bhatia, and A. Bose (eds.), *Population Transition in India*, ii (New Delhi, B. R. Publishing House, 1989).

—— *Culture, the Status of Women, and Demographic Behaviour: Illustrated with the Case of India* (Oxford, Clarendon Press, 1992).

—— 'Female Education, Autonomy and Fertility Change: What Do These Words Mean in South Asia?', paper presented at the Workshop on Female Education, Autonomy and Fertility Change in South Asia, New Delhi, Apr. 1993.

—— and Basu, K., 'Women's Economic Roles and Child Survival: The Case of India', *Health Transition Review*, 1/1 (1991), 83–103.

Beckman, L. J., 'Communication, Power, and the Influence of Social Networks on Couple Decisions on Fertility', in R. A. Bulatao and R. D. Lee (eds.), *Determinants of Fertility in Developing Countries* (New York, Academic Press, 1983).

Behm, Hugo,'Socio-economic Determinants of Mortality in Latin America', in World Health Organization, *Socioeconomic Determinants and Consequences of Mortality* (Geneva, World Health Organization, 1980).

Belize, Ministry of Health, *1991 Belize Family Health Survey: Final Report* (Atlanta, Ga., US Department of Health and Human Services, Public Health Service, Centers for Disease Control, Center for Chronic Disease Prevention and Health Promotion, Division of Reproductive Health, 1992).

Berelson, B., 'Beyond Family Planning', *Studies in Family Planning*, 38 (1969), 1–16.

Bhargava, P. K., and Saxena, P. C., 'Female Work Participation and Age at Marriage in an Urban Setting', in K. Srinivasan and S. Mukerji (eds.), *Dynamics of Population and Family Welfare* (Bombay, Himalaya Publishing House, 1985).

Bhuiya, A., and Streatfield, K., 'Mothers' Education and Survival of Female Children in a Rural Area of Bangladesh', *Population Studies*, 45 (1991), 253–64.

—— —— and Meyer, P., 'Mothers' Hygienic Awareness, Behaviour and Knowledge of Major Childhood Diseases in Matlab, Bangladesh', in J. Caldwell, S. Findley, P. Caldwell, G. Santow, W. Cosford, J. Braid, and D. Broars-Freeman (eds.), *What We Know About Health Transition: The Cultural, Social and Behavioural Determinants of Health*, i (Canberra, Health Transition Centre, Australian National University, 1990).

—— —— and Sarder, A. M., 'Mother's Education and Knowledge of Major Childhood Diseases in Matlab, Bangladesh', in International Union for the Scientific Study of Population (IUSSP), *Proceedings of the International Population Conference, Montreal*, iv (Liège, International Union for the Scientific Study of Population, 1993).

Bicego, G. T., and Boerma, T., 'Maternal Education and Child Survival: A Comparative Analysis of DHS Data', paper presented at the Demographic and Health Surveys World Conference, Washington, DC, Aug. 1991.

Birdsall, N., 'Public Inputs and Child Schooling in Brazil', *Journal of Development Economics*, 18 (1985), 67–86.

—— and Cochrane, S. H., 'Education and Parental Decision Making: A Two-Generation Approach', in L. Anderson and D. M. Windham (eds.), *Education and Development* (Lexington, Mass., D. C. Heath, 1982).

—— and Griffin, C. C., 'Fertility and Poverty in Developing Countries', *Journal of Policy Modeling*, 10/1 (1988), 29–55.

Blau, D. M., 'Investments in Child Nutrition and Women's Allocation of Time in Developing Countries', *Yale Economic Growth Center Discussion Paper* (New Haven, Economic Growth Center, Yale University, 1981).

Bledsoe, C., 'The Politics of Polygyny in Mende Education and Child Fosterage Transactions', in B. D. Miller (ed.), *Sex and Gender Hierarchies* (Cambridge, Cambridge University Press, 1988).

—— 'School Fees and the Marriage Process for Mende Girls in Sierra Leone', in P. R. Sanday and R. G. Goodenough (eds.), *Beyond the Second Sex: New Directions in the Anthropology of Gender* (Philadelphia, University of Pennsylvania, 1990).

Boerma, J. Ties, Sommerfelt, A., and Rutstein, Shea, *Childhood Morbidity and Treatment Patterns*, Demographic and Health Surveys, Comparative Studies No. 4 (Columbia, Md., Institute for Resource Development, 1991).

—— Sommerfelt, A. Elisabeth, Rutstein, Shea O., and Rojas, Guillermo, *Immunisation: Levels, Trends and Differentials*, Demographic and Health Surveys, Comparative Studies No. 4 (Columbia, Md., Institute for Resource Development, 1990).

Bongaarts, J., 'A Framework for Analyzing the Proximate Determinants of Fertility', *Population and Development Review*, 4/1 (1978), 105–32.

—— 'The Fertility-Inhibiting Effects of the Intermediate Fertility Variables', *Studies in Family Planning*, 13/6–7 (1982), 179–89.

—— and Lightbourne, R., 'Wanted Fertility in Latin America: Trends and Differentials in Seven Countries', paper prepared for the Seminar on Fertility Transition in Latin America, sponsored by the IUSSP Committee on Comparative Analysis of Fertility and Family Planning in collaboration with CELADE and CENEP, Buenos Aires, 3–6 Apr. 1990.

Briscoe, J., *et al.*, 'Underlying and Proximate Determinants of Child Health: The Cebu Longitudinal Health and Nutrition Study', *American Journal of Epidemiology*, 133/2 (1991), 185–201.

Bulatao, R. A., 'Reducing Fertility in Developing Countries: A Review of Determinants and Policy Levers', World Bank Staff Working Papers No. 680 (Washington, DC, The World Bank, 1984).

—— and Lee, R. D. (eds.), *Determinants of Fertility in Developing Countries*, 2 vols. (New York, Academic Press, 1983).

Bustillo, Ines, 'Latin America', in E. M. King and M. A. Hill (eds.), *Women's Education in Developing Countries: Barriers, Benefits and Policy* (Washington, DC, The World Bank, Education and Employment Division, Population and Human Resources Department, Sept. 1991).

Cain, M., 'Perspectives on Family and Fertility in Developing Countries', *Population Studies*, 36/2 (July 1982), 159–75.

—— 'Patriarchal Structure and Demographic Change', in Nora Federici, Karen Oppenheim Mason, and Solvi Sogner (eds.), *Women's Position and Demographic Change* (Oxford, Oxford University Press, 1993).

—— Khanam, S. R., and Nahar, S., 'Class, Patriarchy and Women's Work in Bangladesh', *Population and Development Review*, 5/3 (1979).

Caldwell, J. C., 'Toward a Restatement of Demographic Transition Theory', *Population and Development Review*, 2/3–4 (1976).

—— 'Education as a Factor in Mortality Decline: An Examination of Nigerian Data', *Population Studies*, 33/3 (1979), 395–413.

—— 'The Mechanisms of Demographic Change in Historical Perspective', *Population Studies*, 35/1 (Mar. 1981), 5–27.

—— 'Maternal Education as a Factor in Child Mortality', *World Health Forum*, 2/1 (1981), 75–8.

—— *Theory of Fertility Decline* (London, Academic Press, 1982).

—— 'Mass Education as a Determinant of the Timing of Fertility Decline', in J. C. Caldwell (ed.), *Theory of Fertility Decline* (London, Academic Press, 1982).

—— 'The Transition from Familial to Labour Market Production and the Social Implications', in J. C. Caldwell (ed.), *Theory of Fertility Decline* (London, Academic Press, 1982).

—— 'The Wealth Flows Theory of Fertility Decline', in J. C. Caldwell (ed.), *Theory of Fertility Decline* (London, Academic Press, 1982).

—— 'Family Change and Demographic Change: The Reversal of the Veneration Flow', in K. Srinivasan and S. Mukerji (eds.), *Dynamics of Population and Family Welfare* (Bombay, Himalaya Publishing House, 1987).

—— 'Cultural and Social Factors Influencing Mortality Levels in Developing Countries', *Annals*, 510 (July 1990), 44–59.

—— and Caldwell, P., 'The Achieved Small Family: Early Fertility Transition in an African City', *Studies in Family Planning*, 9/1 (Jan. 1978)), 2–18.

—— —— 'Cause and Sequence in the Reduction of Postnatal Abstinence in Ibadan City, Nigeria', in H. J. Page and R. Lesthaeghe (eds.), *Child-spacing in Tropical Africa: Traditions and Change* (London, Academic Press, 1981).

—— and McDonald, P., 'Influence of Maternal Education on Infant and Child Mortality: Levels and Causes', paper presented at the IUSSP International Population Conference, Manila, 1981.

—— —— 'Influence of Maternal Education on Infant and Child Mortality: Levels and Causes', *Health Policy and Education*, 2 (1982), 251–67.

—— Reddy, P. H., and Caldwell, P., 'The Causes of Demographic Change in Rural South India: A Micro Approach', *Population Development Review*, 8/4 (Dec. 1982), 689–727.

—— —— —— 'The Causes of Marriage Change in South India', *Population Studies*, 37 (1983), 343–61.

—— —— —— 'The Social Component of Mortality Decline: An Investigation in South India Employing Alternative Methodologies', *Population Studies*, 37 (1983), 185–205.

—— —— —— 'Educational Transition in Rural India', *Population and Development Review*, 11/1 (Mar. 1985), 29–51.

—— Gajanayake, I., Caldwell, B., and Caldwell, P., 'Is Marriage Delay a Multiphasic Response to Pressures for Fertility Decline? The Case of Sri Lanka' (not dated).

—— Gaminiratne, K. H. W., Caldwell, P., de Silva, S., Caldwell, B., Weeraratne, N., and Silva, P., 'The Role of Traditional Fertility Regulation in Sri Lanka', *Studies in Family Planning*, 18/1 (Jan.–Feb. 1987), 1–21.

—— Findley, S., Caldwell, P., Santow, G., Cosford, W., Braid, J., and Broars-Freeman, D. (eds.), *What We Know About Health Transition: The Cultural, Social and Behavioural Determinants of Health*, 2 vols. (Canberra, Health Transition Centre, Australian National University, 1990).

Caldwell, P., and Caldwell, J. C., 'The Function of Child-spacing in Traditional Societies and the Direction of Change', in H. J. Page and R. Lesthaeghe (eds.), *Child-spacing in Tropical Africa: Traditions and Change* (London, Academic Press, 1981).

Casterline, J. B., Singh, S., Cleland, J., and Ashurst, H., 'The Proximate Determinants of Fertility', *World Fertility Survey Comparative Studies Cross National Summaries*, No. 39 (Voorburg, Netherlands, International Statistical Institute, Nov. 1984).

Castro, L. S. E., Caceres, H. J. M., and Salguero, J. C., *1988 Family Health Survey, El Salvador*, Final English Language Report' (Atlanta, Ga., US Department of Health and Human Services, Public Health Service, Centers for Disease Control, Center for Chronic Disease Prevention and Health Promotion, Division of Reproductive Health, 1989).

Castro-Martin, T., and Juarez, F., 'Women's Education and Fertility in Latin America: Exploring the Significance of Education for Women's Lives', paper presented at the International Population Conference (International Union for the Scientific Study of Population), Montreal, 24 Aug.–1 Sept. 1993.

Cayemittes, M., Augustin, A., and Rival, A., *1989 Haiti National Contraceptive Prevalence Survey* (Atlanta, Ga., US Department of Health and Human Services, Public Health Service, Centers for Disease Control, Center for Chronic Disease Prevention and Health Promotion, Division of Reproductive Health, 1991).

Cebu Study Team, 'Underlying and Proximate Determinants of Child Health: The Cebu Longitudinal Health and Nutrition Study', *American Journal of Epidemiology*, 133/2 (1991), 185–201.

Centro de Estudios de Poblacion y Paternidad Responsable, *Ecuador encuesta demografica y de salud familiar 1987* (Columbia, Md., Westinghouse, 1988).

Chackiel, J., and Schkolnik, S., 'America Latina: Transicion de la fecondidad en el periodo 1950-1990', paper presented at the Seminar on Fertility Transition in Latin America, organized by IUSSP Committee on Comparative Analysis of Fertility and Family Planning in collaboration with CELADE and CENEP, Buenos Aires, 3–6 Apr. 1990.

Chandrashekaran, C. 'Cultural Patterns in Relation to Family Planning in India', *Proceedings of the Third International Conference on Planned Parenthood*, Bombay, India, Family Planning Association of India, 1952.

Chaudhury, R. H., 'The Influence of Female Education, Labour Force Participation and Age at Marriage on Fertility Behaviour in Bangladesh', *Social Biology*, 31/1–2 (1984), 59–74.

Chayovan, N., Kamnuansilpa, P., and Knodel, J., *Thailand Demographic and Health Survey 1987* (Columbia, Md., Westinghouse, 1988).

Chernichovsky, D., 'Socioeconomic and Demographic Aspects of School Enrollment and Attendance in Rural Botswana', *Economic Development and Cultural Change*, 33/2 (Jan. 1985), 319–32.

—— and Meesook, O. A., 'School Enrollment in Indonesia', World Bank Staff Working Papers No. 746 (Washington, DC, The World Bank, 1985).

Chhabra, R. (1982), 'Status of Women in India', *Population of India*, Country Monograph Series No. 10 (United Nations, Economic and Social Commission for Asia and the Pacific, 1982).

Chieh-Johnson, D., Cross, A. R., Way, A. A., and Sullivan, J. M., *Liberia Demographic and Health Survey 1986* (Columbia, Md., Westinghouse, 1988).

Chowdhury, A., 'Factors Influencing Infant Survival in Rural Bangladesh', *Glimpse*, 4 (1982), 9–10.

Chowdhury, A., Khan, Atiqur Rahman, and Chen, Lincoln C., 'Experience in Pakistan and Bangladesh', in Samuel H. Preston (ed.), *The Effects of Infant and Child Mortality on Fertility* (New York, Academic Press, 1978).

Cleland, J., 'Maternal Education and Child Survival: Further Evidence and Explanations', in J. Caldwell, S. Findley, P. Caldwell, G. Santow, W. Cosford, J. Braid, and D. Broars-Freeman (eds.), *What We Know About Health Transition: The Cultural, Social and Behavioural Determinants of Health* (Canberra, Health Transition Centre, Australian National University, 1990).

—— 'Large Data-Sets and the Relationships Between "Women's Status" and Fertility in South Asia', paper presented at the Workshop on Female Education, Autonomy and Fertility Change in South Asia, New Delhi, Apr. 1993.

—— and Rodriguez, G., 'The Effect of Parental Education on Marital Fertility in Developing Countries', *Population Studies*, 42 (1988), 419–42.

—— and van Ginneken, J. K., 'Maternal Education and Child Survival in Developing Countries: The Search for Pathways of Influence', *Social Science and Medicine*, 27/12 (1988), 1357–68.

—— and Wilson, C., 'Demand Theories of the Fertility Transition: An Iconoclastic View', *Population Studies*, 41/1 (1987), 5–30.

——, Bicego, G., and Fegan, G., 'Socioeconomic Inequalities in Childhood Mortality: The 1970s to the 1980s', *Health Transition Review*, 2/1 (1992).

Cochrane, S. H., *Fertility and Education: What Do We Really Know?* (Baltimore and London, The Johns Hopkins University Press, 1979).

—— 'Effects of Education and Urbanization on Fertility', in R. A. Bulatao and R. D. Lee (eds.), *Determinants of Fertility in Developing Countries*, ii (New York, Academic Press, 1983).

—— and Farid, S. M., *Fertility in Sub-Saharan Africa: Analysis and Explanation* (Washington, DC, The World Bank, 1989).

—— —— 'Socio-economic Differentials in Fertility and Their Explanation', in G. T. F. Acsadi, G. J. Acsadi, and R. A. Bulatao (eds.), *Population Growth and Reproduction in Sub-Saharan Africa: Technical Analysis of Fertility and Its Consequences* (Washington, DC, The World Bank, 1990).

—— and Jamison, D. T., 'Educational Attainment and Achievement in Rural Thailand', in A. Summers (ed.), *New Directions for Testing and Measurement: Productivity Assessment in Education*, No. 15 (San Francisco, Jossey-Bass, 1982).

—— and Nandwani, K., 'The Determinants of Fertility in 22 Villages of Northern Thailand', Discussion Paper No. 81-59 (Washington, DC, The World Bank, Population and Human Resources Division, 1981).

—— Leslie, J., and O'Hara, D. J., 'Parental Education and Child Health: Intracountry Evidence', *Health Policy and Education*, 2 (1982), 213–50.

——, Mehra, K., and Osheba, I. S., 'The Educational Participation of Egyptian Children', in A. M. Hallouda, S. Farid, and S. H. Cochrane (eds.), *Egypt: Demographic Responses to Modernization* (Cairo, Central Agency for Public Mobilisation and Statistics, 1988).

—— O'Hara, D. J., and Leslie, J., *The Effects of Education on Health*, Staff Working Paper No. 405 (Washington, DC, The World Bank, 1980).

Consejo Nacional de Poblacion y Familia, *Republica Dominicana encuesta demografica y de salud DHS 1986* (Columbia, Md., Westinghouse, 1987).

Cordova, Rosa Maria, 'Instituciones sociales y reproduccion' (Mexico, Centro de Estudios Demograficos y de Desarrollo Urbano de El Colegio de Mexico, 1991).

Das Gupta, M., 'Selective Discrimination Against Female Children in Rural Punjab, India', *Population and Development Review*, 13/1 (Mar. 1987), 77–100.

—— 'Death Clustering, Mother's Education and the Determinants of Child Mortality in Rural Punjab, India', *Population Studies*, 44 (1990), 489–505.

DaVanzo, J., 'Infant Mortality and Economic Development: The Case of Malaysia', in *Proceedings of the International Population Conference, Florence, 1985*, ii, (Liège, International Union for the Scientific Study of Population, 1985).

—— 'Infant Mortality and Socioeconomic Development: Evidence from Malaysian Household Data', *Demography*, 25/4, (Nov. 1988), 581–95.

—— Butz, W. P., and Habicht, J. P., 'How Biological and Behavioral Influences on Mortality in Malaysia Vary During the First Year of Life', *Population Studies*, 37/3 (1983).

Demographic and Health Surveys Program, *Women's Education: Findings from Demographic and Health Surveys*, prepared for the World Conference on Education for All, Bangkok, Thailand (Columbia, Md., Mar. 1990).

De Vos, Susan, *The Old-Age Security Value of Children in the Philippines and Taiwan*, Papers of the East–West Population Institute, No. 60-G (Honolulu, East–West Center, 1984).

Dixon, Ruth B., 'Women's Rights and Fertility', *Reports on Population/Family Planning*, No. 17 (Jan. 1975).

Do Valle Silva, N., Helena, M., Henriques, F. J., and de Souza, A., 'The Determinants of the Demand for Children: Supply of Children and Costs of Fertility Regulation', in *An Analysis of Reproductive Behaviour in Brazil*, DHS Further Analysis Series No. 6 (Columbia, Md., DHS, 1990).

Dyson, Tim, and Moore, Mick, 'On Kinship Structure, Female Autonomy and Demographic Behaviour in India', *Population and Development Review*, 9 (Mar. 1983), 35–60.

Easterlin, Richard A., 'An Economic Framework for Fertility Analysis', *Studies in Family Planning*, 6 (Mar. 1975), 54–63.

—— 'The Economics and Sociology of Fertility: A Synthesis', in Charles Tilly (ed.), *Historical Studies of Changing Fertility* (Princeton, Princeton University Press, 1978).

—— 'Modernization and Fertility: A Critical Essay', in R. A. Bulatao and R. D. Lee (eds.), *Determinants of Fertility in Developing Countries*, ii (New York, Academic Press, 1983).

—— and Crimmins, Eileen M., *The Fertility Revolution: A Supply–Demand Analysis* (Chicago, University of Chicago Press, 1985).

Edigbola, A. K., 'The Effect of Modernisation on Family Size and Reproductive Attitude of Yoruba Women, Nigeria', *Demography India*, 17/2 (1988), 227–41.

Edmonston, B., 'Community Variations in Infant and Child Mortality in Rural Jordan', *Journal of Developing Areas*, 71 (1983), 473–89.

Eelens, F., and Donne, L., 'The Proximate Determinants of Fertility in Sub-Saharan Africa', Interuniversity Programme in Demography (IPD) Working Paper, 1985-3 (Brussels, Vrije Universiteit, 1985), as quoted in T. P. Schultz, 'Returns to Women's Education', in E. M. King and M. A. Hill (eds.), *Women's Education in Developing Countries: Barriers, Benefits and Policy* (Washington, DC, The World Bank, Education and Employment Division, Population and Human Resources Department, September 1991).

Egypt, National Population Council, *Egypt Demographic and Health Survey 1992: Preliminary Report* (Columbia, Md., Macro International Inc., Mar. 1993).

Eisemon, T. O., Patel, V. L., and Sena, S. O., 'Uses of Formal and Informal Knowledge in the Comprehension of Instructions for Oral Rehydration Therapy in Kenya', *Social Science and Medicine*, 25/11 (1987), 1225–34.

Elo, I. T., 'Utilization of Maternal Health-care Services in Peru: The Role of Women's Education', *Health Transition Review*, 2/1 (1992), 49–69.

El-Sanabary, N., 'Middle East and North Africa', in E. M. King and M. A. Hill (eds.), *Women's Education in Developing Countries: Barriers, Benefits and Policy* (Washington, DC, The World Bank, Education and Employment Division, Population and Human Resources Department, Sept. 1991).

Emereuwaonu, E. U., 'Determinants of Fertility: A Regression Analysis of Kenya Data', *Genus*, 40/3–4 (July–Dec. 1984), 77–96.

Farah, Abdul-Aziz, and Preston, S. H., 'Child Mortality Differentials in Sudan', *Population And Development Review*, 8/2, (June 1982), 365–83.

Faust, K., Bach, R., Gadalla, S., Khattab, H., and Gulick, J., 'Mass Education, Islamic Revival, and the Population Problem in Egypt', *Journal of Comparative Family Studies*, 22/3 (1991), 329–41.

Federici, Nora, Mason, Karen Oppenheim, and Sogner, Solvi (eds.), *Women's Position and Demographic Change* (Oxford, Oxford University Press, 1993).

Fernandez, R., 'Analysis of Information About Mother–Child Care Taken from Fertility Surveys in Latin America' (Voorberg, International Statistical Institute, 1984), unpub.

Fernando, D. F. S., 'Female Educational Attainment and Fertility', *Journal of Biosocial Science*, 9 (1977), 339–51.

Feyisetan, B. J., 'Postpartum Sexual Abstinence, Breastfeeding and Childspacing Among Yoruba Women in Urban Nigeria', *Social Biology*, 37/1–2 (1990), 110–27.

—— and Bankole, A., 'Mate Selection and Fertility in Urban Nigeria', *Journal of Comparative Family Studies*, 22/3 (Autumn 1991), 273–92.

—— and Togunde, O., 'Fertility and Indices of Women's Status: A Study of Relationships in Nigeria', *Genus*, 44/1-2 (Jan.–June 1988), 229–46.

Flegg, A. T., 'Inequality of Income, Illiteracy and Medical Care as Determinants of Infant Mortality in Underdeveloped Countries, *Population Studies*, 36/3 (1982), 441–58.

Florez, C. E., and Hogan, D. P., 'Women's Status and Infant Mortality in Rural Colombia', *Social Biology*, 37/3–4 (1990), 188–203.

Fosu, G. B., 'Disease Classification in Rural Ghana: Framework and Consequences for Health Behaviour', *Social Science and Medicine*, 15B (1981), 471–82.

Freedman, R., Zhenyu, X., Bohua, Li, and Lavely, W. R., 'Education and Fertility in Two Chinese Provinces: 1967–1970 to 1979–1982', *Asia-Pacific Population Journal*, 3/1 (Mar. 1988), 3–30.

—— —— —— —— 'Local Area Variations in Reproductive Behaviour in the People's Republic of China, 1973–1982' *Population Studies*, 42 (1988), 39–57.

Gadalla, S., McCarthy, J., and Kak, N., 'The Determinants of Fertility in Rural Egypt: A Study of Menoufia and Beni-suef Governorates', *Journal of Biosocial Science*, 19 (1987), 195–207.

Gage-Brandon, A. J., and Meekers, D., 'The Changing Dynamics of Family Formation: Women's Status and Nuptiality in Togo', paper presented at the seminar on Women and Demographic Change in Sub-Saharan Africa, sponsored by the IUSSP Committee on Gender and Population, Dakar, Senegal, 3–6 Mar. 1993.

Gaisie, K., Cross, A. R., and Nsemukila, G., *Zambia Demographic and Health Survey 1992* (Columbia, Md., Macro International Inc., 1993).

Galal el Din, Mohamed El Awad, 'The Economic Value of Children in Rural Sudan', in J. C. Caldwell (ed.), *The Persistence of High Fertility: Population Prospects in the Third World*, pt. 2 (Canberra, Department of Demography, Australian National University, 1977).

Garcia, B., and de Oliveira, O., 'The Effects of Variation and Change in Female Economic Roles upon Fertility Change in Developing Countries', in International Union for the Scientific Study of Population, *Proceedings of the International Population Conference, New Delhi* (Liège, International Union for the Scientific Study of Population, 1989).

—— —— 'Maternity and Work in Mexico in the Late Eighties', in M. Bronfman, B. Garcia, F. Juarez, O. de Oliveira and J. Quilodran, *Social Sectors and Reproduction in Mexico*, DHS Further Analysis Series No. 7 (Columbia, Md., and New York, Institute for Development/Macro Systems Inc. and The Population Council, Apr. 1990).

Ghana Statistical Service, *Ghana Demographic and Health Survey 1988* (Columbia, Md., Macro Systems Inc., 1989).

Goldstein, R. L., 'Students in Saris: College Education in the Lives of Young Indian Women', *Journal of Asian and African Studies*, 5/3 (July 1970), 192–201.

Goodburn, E., Ebrahim, G. J., and Senapati, S., 'Strategies Educated Mothers Use to Ensure the Health of Their Children', *Journal of Tropical Pediatrics*, 36/5 (Oct. 1990), 235–9.

Greenhalgh, Susan, 'Sexual Stratification: The Other Side of Growth with Equity in East Asia', *Population and Development Review*, 11/2 (June 1985), 265–314.

Guilkey, D. K., Popkin, B. M., Flieger, W., and Akin, J. S., 'Changes in Breast-feeding in the Philippines, 1973–1983', *Social Science and Medicine*, 31/12 (1990), 1365–75.

Haile, Azbaha, 'Fertility Conditions in Gondar, Northwestern Ethiopia: An Appraisal of Current Status', *Studies in Family Planning*, 21/2 (Mar./Apr. 1990), 110–17.

Haines, M. R., and Avery, R. C., 'Differentials in Infant and Child Mortality in Costa Rica, 1968–73', *Population Studies*, 36 (1982), 31–44.

Hatti, N., and Ohlsson, R., 'Impact of Education on Age at Marriage', *Demography India*, 14/2 (July–Dec. 1985), 159–73.

Heath, K., Costa-Martinez, D. D., and Sheon, A. R., *Trinidad and Tobago Demographic and Health Survey 1987* (Columbia, Md., Westinghouse, 1988).

Henry, L., 'Some Data on Natural Fertility', *Eugenics Quarterly*, 8/1 (1961), 81–91.

Heredia, R., Palacios, M., Rodriguez, W., and Ojida, G., *Colombia encuesta de prevalencia demografia y salud 1986* (Columbia, Md., Westinghouse, 1988).

Hobcraft, J. N., 'Child Spacing and Child Mortality', in IRD/Macro International Inc., *Proceedings of the Demographic and Health Surveys World Conference, Washington D.C., 1991*, ii (Columbia, Md., 1991).

—— 'Women's Education, Child Welfare and Child Survival', paper presented at the United Nations Expert Group Meeting on Population and Women, Gaborone, Botswana, 22–26 June 1992.

—— McDonald, J. W., and Rutstein, S. O., 'Socio-economic Factors in Infant and Child Mortality: A Cross-national Comparison', *Population Studies*, 38 (1984), 193–223.

—— —— —— 'Demographic Determinants of Infant and Early Child Mortality: A Comparative Analysis', *Population Studies*, 39 (1985), 363–85.

Holian, J., 'The Effect of Female Education on Marital Fertility in Different Size Communities of Mexico', *Social Biology*, 31/3–4 (1984), 298–307.

Huq, M. N. and Cleland, John, *Bangladesh Fertility Survey 1989 Main Report* (Dhaka, National Institute of Population Research and Training, 1990).

India, Government of, Registrar General, *Census of India 1981: Fertility and Child Mortality Estimates of Tamil Nadu*, Occasional Paper No. 4 of 1987 (New Delhi, 1987).

—— *Census of India 1981: Fertility and Child Mortality Estimates of Rajasthan*, Occasional Paper No. 5 of 1987 (New Delhi, 1987).

India, Government of, Registrar General, *Census of India 1981: Fertility and Child Mortality Estimates of Madhya Pradesh*, Occasional Paper No. 7 of 1987 (New Delhi, 1987).

—— *Census of India 1981: Fertility and Child Mortality Estimates of Karnataka*, Occasional Paper No. 11 of 1987 (New Delhi, 1987).

—— *Census of India: Advance Report on Age at Marriage Differentials in India 1984*, Occasional Paper No. 2 of 1988 (New Delhi, 1988).

—— *Census of India 1981: Fertility and Child Mortality Estimates of Maharashtra*, Occasional Paper No. 3 of 1988 (New Delhi, 1988).

Indonesia, Central Bureau of Statistics, National Family Planning Coordinating Board and Ministry of Health, *Indonesia Demographic and Health Survey 1991* (Columbia, Md., Macro International Inc., 1992).

Inkeles, A., and Smith, D., *On Becoming Modern: Individual Change in Six Countries* (Cambridge, Mass., Harvard University Press, 1974).

Jain, A., and Bongaarts, J., 'Breastfeeding: Patterns, Correlates, and Fertility Effects', *Studies in Family Planning*, 12/3 (1981), 79–99.

—— and Nag, M., 'Importance of Female Primary Education for Fertility Reduction in India', *Economic and Political Weekly*, 21/36 (6 Sept. 1986), 1602–8.

Jayaweera, S., 'Women and Education', in *Status of Women: Sri Lanka* (Colombo, University of Colombo, 1979).

Jeffery, P., and Jeffery, R., 'North Indian Relationships: Jats and Sheikhs in Bijnor', paper presented at the Workshop on Female Education, Autonomy and Fertility Change in South Asia, New Delhi, Apr. 1993.

Jejeebhoy, S. J., 'Cohort Consistency in Family Size Preferences: Taiwan, 1965–73', *Studies in Family Planning*, 12/5 (1981), 229–32.

—— 'The Shift from Natural to Controlled Fertility: A Cross-Sectional Analysis of Ten Indian States', *Studies in Family Planning*, 15/4 (July–Aug. 1984), 191–8.

—— 'Women in Rajasthan and Tamil Nadu: A Report of Intensive Village Level Studies' (1989).

—— 'Women's Status and Fertility: Successive Cross-sectional Evidence from Tamil Nadu, India, 1970–80', *Studies in Family Planning*, 22/4 (July–Aug. 1991), 217–30.

—— 'Women's Education, Fertility and the Proximate Determinants of Fertility', paper presented at the United Nations Expert Group Meeting on Population and Women, Gaborone, Botswana, 22–6 June 1992.

—— and Kulkarni, S., 'Reproductive Motivation: A Comparison of Wives and Husbands in Maharashtra, India', *Studies in Family Planning*, 20/5 (Sept.–Oct. 1989), 264–72.

Jensen, A.-M., and Juma, Magdallen N., *Women, Childbearing and Nutrition: A Case Study from Bungoma, Kenya* (Oslo, Norwegian Institute for Urban and Regional Research, 1989).

—— and Khasakhala, A. A., 'Women, Family Planning and Child Mortality: Case-Study of Selected Areas in Kenya, Western and Coast Provinces', in Alhassan Manu (ed.), *Health and Environment in Developing Countries, Proceedings from an International Workshop* (Oslo, Centre for Development and the Environment, Oslo University, 1992).

Joesoef, M. Riduan, Annest, Joseph L., and Ultomo, Budi, 'A Recent Increase of Breast-feeding Duration in Jakarta, Indonesia', *American Journal of Public Health*, 79/1 (1989), 36–8.

Jolly, K. G., 'Differential Fertility Performance by Education, Age at Marriage and Work Status of Women in Delhi Metropolis', *Demography India*, 10/1–2 (1981), 118–25.

Kaijuka, E. M., Kaya, E. Z. A., Cross, A. R., and Loaiza, E., *Uganda Demographic and Health Survey 1988–89* (Columbia, Md., Macro Systems Inc., 1989).

Kanitkar, Tara, Ramesh, B. M., Roy, T. K., Arnold, Fred, and Retherford, Robert D., *National Family Health Survey (MCH and Family Planning): India 1992–93, Introductory Report* (Bombay, International Institute for Population Sciences, 1994).

Kapadia, K. M., *Marriage and Family in India* (Bombay, Oxford University Press, 1958).

Karve, Iravati, *Kinship Organisation in India* (Bombay, Asia Publishing House, 1965).

Kasarda, J. D., Billy, J. O., and West, K., *Status Enhancement and Fertility: Reproductive Responses to Social Mobility and Educational Opportunity* (New York, Academic Press, 1986).

Katjiuanjo, P., Titus, S., Zauana, M., and Boerma, J. Ties, *Namibia Demographic and Health Survey 1992* (Columbia, Md., Macro International Inc., 1993).

Kaufmann, G., Lesthaeghe, R., and Meekers, D., 'Marriage Patterns and Change in Sub-Saharan Africa', in *The Cultural Roots of African Fertility Regimes*, Proceedings of the Ife Conference, 25 Feb.–1 Mar. 1987.

Kenya, National Council for Population and Development, *Kenya Demographic and Health Survey 1989* (Columbia, Md., Macro Systems, Inc., 1989).

Khalifa, A. M., 'The Influence of Wife's Education on Fertility in Rural Egypt', *Journal of Biosocial Science*, 8 (1976), 53–60.

Khan, M. E., and Prasad, C. V. S., *Family Planning Practices in India: Second All-India Survey* (Baroda, Operations Research Group, 1983).

—— Ghosh Dastidar, S. K., and Singh, R., 'Nutrition and Health Practices Among Rural Women: A Case Study of Uttar Pradesh, India', *Journal of Family Welfare*, 33/1 (Sept. 1986), 3–20.

—— Anker, R., Dastidar, S. K. G., and Bairathi, S., 'Inequalities Between Men and Women in Nutrition and Family Welfare Services: An In-Depth Inquiry in an Indian Village', *Social Action*, 38/4 (Oct.–Dec. 1988), 398–417.

Khandker, S. R., 'Determinants of Women's Time Allocation in Rural Bangladesh', *Economic Development and Cultural Change*, 37/1 (1988), 111–26.

Kim, S., and Stinner, W. F., 'Social Origins, Educational Attainment and the Timing of Marriage and First Birth Among Korean Women', *Journal of Marriage and Family*, 42/3 (Aug. 1980), 671–79.

King, E. M., and Hill, M. A., *Women's Education in Developing Countries: Barriers, Benefits and Policy* (Washington, DC, The World Bank, Education and Employment Division, Population and Human Resources Department, 1991).

Knodel, John, and van de Walle, Etienne, 'Lessons from the Past: Policy Implications of Historical Fertility Studies', *Population and Development Review*, 5/2 (1979), 217–45.

—— Chamratrithirong, Aphichat, and Debavalya, N., *Thailand's Reproductive Revolution* (Madison, Wisconsin, University of Wisconsin Press, 1987).

Kohli, K. L., and Al-Omain, M., 'Levels and Trends of Foetal, Infant and Childhood Mortality, and Their Determinants: A Case Study of Kuwait', *Population Bulletin of ECWA*, 22/23 (1982).

Krishnan, P., 'Mortality Decline in India, 1951-1961: Development vs Public Health Programme Hypothesis', *Social Science and Medicine*, 9 (1975), 475–9.

Kritz, M. M., and Gurak, D. T., 'Women's Status, Education and Family Formation in Sub-Saharan Africa', *International Family Planning Perspectives*, 15/3 (Sept. 1989), 100–5.

—— —— 'Women's Economic Independence and Fertility Among the Yoruba', paper presented at the Demographic and Health Surveys World Conference, Washington, DC, Aug. 1991.

Kritz, M. M., and Makinwa-Adebusoye, Paulina, 'Women's Resource Control and Demand for Children in Africa', paper presented at the Seminar on Women and Demographic Change in Sub-Saharan Africa, sponsored by the IUSSP Committee on Gender and Population, Dakar, Senegal, 3–6 Mar. 1993.

Kumari, R., 'Attitude of Girls Towards Marriage and a Planned Family', *Journal of Family Welfare*, 31/3 (Mar. 1985), 53–60.

Lavely, W., Zhenyu, X., Bohua, L., and Freedman, R., 'The Rise in Female Education in China: National and Regional Patterns', *China Quarterly*, 121 (Mar. 1990), 61–93.

Lestede, L. T., Mompati, G. D., Khulumani, P., Lestede, G. N., and Rutenberg, N., *Botswana Family Health Survey, ii, 1988* (Columbia, Md., Westinghouse, 1989).

Lesthaeghe, R., Page, H. J., and Adegbola, O., 'Child-spacing and Fertility in Lagos', in H. J. Page and R. Lesthaeghe (eds.), *Child-spacing in Tropical Africa: Traditions and Change* (London, Academic Press, 1981).

—— Verleye, G., and Jolly, C., 'Female Education and Factors Affecting Fertility in Sub-Saharan Africa', IPD Working Paper 1992-2 (Brussels, c/o Centrum Voor Sociologie, 1992).

—— Vanderhoeft, C., Gaisie, S., and Delaine, G., 'Regional Variation in Components of Child-spacing: The Role of Women's Education', in R. J. Lesthaeghe (ed.), *Reproduction and Social Organisation in Sub-Saharan Africa* (Berkeley, University of California Press, 1989).

LeVine, R. A., 'Women's Schooling, Patterns of Fertility and Child Survival', *Educational Researcher*, 16 (1987), 21–7.

—— LeVine, S. E., Richman, A., and Correa, C. S., *Schooling and Maternal Behaviour in a Mexican City: The Effects on Fertility and Child Survival*, Fertility Determinants Research Notes No. 16 (New York, The Population Council, Feb. 1987).

—— —— —— Uribe, F. Medardo Tapia, Correa, C. S., and Miller, P. M., 'Women's Schooling and Child Care in the Demographic Transition: A Mexican Case Study', *Population and Development Review*, 17/3 (Sept. 1991), 459–96.

Limanonda, B., 'Analysis of Thai Marriage: Attitudes and Behaviour, A Case Study of Women in Bangkok Metropolis', Paper No. 56 (Bangkok, Institute of Population Studies, Chulalongkorn University, 1987).

Lindenbaum, S., 'Maternal Education and Health Care Processes in Bangladesh: The Health and Hygiene of the Middle Classes', in J. Caldwell, S. Findley, P. Caldwell, G. Santow, W. Cosford, J. Braid, and D. Broars-Freeman (eds.), *What We Know About Health Transition: The Cultural, Social and Behavioural Determinants of Health*, i (Canberra, Health Transition Centre, Australian National University, 1990).

—— Chakraborty, M., and Elias, M., *The Influence of Maternal Education on Infant and Child Mortality in Bangladesh*, Special Publication No. 23 (Dhaka, Bangladesh, International Centre for Diarrhoeal Disease Research, 1985).

Mabud, M. A., *Women's Development, Income and Fertility* (Dhaka, Bangladesh, Planning Commission, External Evaluation Unit, 1985).

Majumder, A. K., 'Maternal Factors and Infant and Child Mortality in Bangladesh', *Journal of Biosocial Science*, 20 (1988), 89–98.

Makinwa-Adebusoye, P., 'Changes in the Costs and Benefits of Children to Their Parents: The Changing Cost of Educating Children', paper presented at the Seminar on the Course of Fertility Transition in Sub-Saharan Africa, sponsored by the IUSSP Committee on Comparative Analysis of Fertility and the University of Zimbabwe, Harare, Zimbabwe, 19–22 Nov. 1991.

Malawi, National Statistical Office, *Malawi Demographic and Health Survey 1992: First Report* (Columbia, Md., Macro International Inc., 1993).

Mandelbaum, D. G., *Society in India: Continuity and Change*, 2 vols. (Berkeley, University of California Press, 1970).

——*Human Fertility in India: Social Components and Policy Perspectives* (Berkeley, University of California Press, 1974).

——*Women's Seclusion and Men's Honor: Sex Roles in North India, Bangladesh and Pakistan* (Tucson, University of Arizona Press, 1988).

Martin, L. G., 'Female Education and Fertility in Bangladesh', *Asian and Pacific Population Forum*, 1/3 (May 1987), 1–7.

——Flanagan, D. R., and Klenicki, A. R., 'Evaluation of the Bangladesh Female Secondary Education Scholarship Program and Related Female Education and Employment Initiatives to Reduce Fertility' (Washington, DC, International Science and Technology Institute, Inc., 1985).

Mason, K. O., 'Norms Relating to the Desire for Children', in R. A. Bulatao and R. D. Lee (eds.), *Determinants of Fertility in Developing Countries,* i (New York, Academic Press, 1983).

——*The Status of Women: A Review of Its Relationships to Fertility and Mortality* (New York, Rockefeller Foundation, 1984).

—— 'The Impact of Women's Position on Demographic Change During the Course of Development: What Do We Know?', in Nora Federici, Karen Oppenheim Mason, and Solvi Sogner (eds.) *Women's Position and Demographic Change* (Oxford, Oxford University Press, 1993).

——and Palan, V. T., 'Female Employment and Fertility in Peninsular Malaysia: The Maternal Role Incompatibility Hypothesis Reconsidered', *Demography*, 18/4 (Nov. 1981), 549–75.

——and Taj, A. M., 'Difference Between Women's and Men's Reproductive Goals in Developing Countries', *Population and Development Review*, 14/4 (Dec. 1987), 611–38.

Mauritius, Ministry of Health, *1991 Mauritius Contraceptive Prevalence Survey: Preliminary Report* (Atlanta, Ga., US Department of Health and Human Services, Public Health Service, Centers for Disease Control, 1993).

Mbacke, C., and van de Walle, E., 'Socioeconomic Factors and Access to Health Services as Determinants of Child Mortality', paper presented at the IUSSP Seminar on Mortality and Society in Sub-Saharan Africa, Yaounde, 1987.

McLaren, D. S., 'The Home Environment of the Malnourished-Deprived Child', *Health Policy Education*, 2/91 (1982), quoted in J. Cleland and Jerome K. van Ginneken, 'Maternal Education and Child Survival in Developing Countries: The Search for Pathways of Influence', *Social Science and Medicine*, 27/12 (1988), 1357–68.

Meekers, Dominique, *Report on the IUSSP Seminar on the Course of Fertility Transition in Sub-Saharan Africa*, Harare, Zimbabwe, 19–22 Nov. 1991, IUSSP Papers No. 31 (Liège, International Union for the Scientific Study of Population, 1992).

Mejia-Raymundo, C. M., 'Risk Factors of Breast-feeding Among Filipino Women', *Journal of Biosocial Science*, Supplement 9 (1985), 67–81.

Mencher, J. P., 'Women's Work and Poverty: Women's Contribution to Household Maintenance in South India', in D. Dwyer and J. Bruce (eds.), *A Home Divided: Women and Income in the Third World* (Stanford, Stanford University Press, 1988).

Menon, I. M., 'Education of Muslim Women: Tradition versus Modernity', *Journal of Comparative Family Studies*, 10/1 (1979), 82–9.

Merrick, T. W., 'The Effect of Piped Water on Early Childhood Mortality in Urban Brazil, 1970 to 1976', *Demography*, 22/1 (Feb. 1985), 1–24.

Mhloyi, M. M., 'Fertility Transition in Zimbabwe', paper presented at the Seminar on the Course of Fertility Transition in Sub-Saharan Africa, sponsored by the IUSSP Committee on Comparative Analysis of Fertility and the University of Zimbabwe, Harare, Zimbabwe, 19–22 Nov. 1991.

Minturn, L., 'Changes in the Differential Treatment of Rajput Girls in Khalapur: 1955–1975', *Medical Anthropology*, 8/2 (1984), 127–32.

M'Mange, W. R. M., and Srivastava, M. L., 'Socio-Economic and Demographic Determinants of Family Size in Malawi: A Multivariate Analysis' (University of Malawi, Chancellor College, Demographic Unit, Oct. 1990).

Monteith, R. S., Warren, C. W., Stanziola, E., Urzua, R. L., and Oberle, M. W., 'Use of Maternal and Child Health Services and Immunization Coverage in Panama and Guatemala' *PAHO Bulletin*, 21 (1987), 1–15.

—— Stupp, P., Morris, L., and Montana, E., *Family Planning and Child Survival Survey, Ecuador 1989* (Atlanta, Ga., US Department of Health and Human Services, Centers for Disease Control, National Center for Chronic Disease Prevention and Health Promotion, Division of Reproductive Health, 1992).

Montgomery, M. R., and Cheung, P. P. L., 'First Marriage and Assortative Mating in Singapore' (1991).

—— —— and Sulak, D. B., 'Rates of Courtship and First Marriage in Thailand', *Population Studies*, 42 (1988), 375–88.

Mostajo, N., 'Actitudes de la mujer frente a la fecundidad y uso de metodos anticonceptivos', paper presented at Seminario de Analisis y Capacitacion, Encuesta Mundial de Fecundidad (Santiago de Chile, Centro Latinoamericano de Demografia, 1981).

Namibia, Ministry of Health and Social Services, Central Statistical Office and National Planning Commission, *Namibia Demographic and Health Survey 1992: Preliminary Report* (Columbia, Md., Macro International Inc., 1992).

Nawar, Lalla, Lloyd, Cynthia B., and Ibrahim, Barbara, 'Women's Autonomy and Gender Roles in Egyptian Families', in Carla Makhlouf Obermeyer, *Gender, Family, and Population Policy: Views from the Middle East* (Cairo, American University in Cairo, 1994).

—— El Deeb, B., Nizamuddin, M., and Tourkey, F. G., *Infant and Child Mortality in Egypt* (Cairo, Central Agency for Public Mobilization and Statistics, 1986).

Ndiaye, S., Saar, I., and Ayad, M., *Senegal enquete demographique et de sante au Senegal 1986* (Columbia, Md., Westinghouse, 1988).

Ngallaba, S., Kapiga, S. H., Ruyobya, I., and Boerma, J. Ties, *Tanzania Demographic and Health Survey 1991–92* (Columbia, Md., Macro International Inc., 1993).

Nigeria, Federal Office of Statistics, *Nigeria Demographic and Health Survey 1990* (Columbia, Md., Macro International Inc., 1992).

Ntozi, J. P. M., and Kabera, J. B., 'Family Planning in Rural Uganda: Knowledge and Use of Modern and Traditional Methods in Ankole', *Studies in Family Planning*, 22/2 (Mar.–Apr. 1991), 116–23.

Okafor, C. B., 'Availability and Use of Services for Maternal and Child Health Care in Rural Nigeria', *International Journal of Gynaecology and Obstetrics*, 34/331 (1991), 331–46.

Okojie, C. E. E., 'Fertility Response to Child Survival in Nigeria: An Analysis of Microdata from Bendel State', Center Discussion Paper No. 592 (New Haven, Economic Growth Center, Yale University, 1989).

—— 'Women's Status and Fertility in Bendel State of Nigeria', Center Discussion Paper No. 597 (New Haven, Economic Growth Center, Yale University, Feb. 1990).

—— 'The Relationship Between Women's Status, Proximate Determinants and Fertility in Nigeria', paper presented at the Seminar on Women and Demographic Change in Sub-Saharan Africa, sponsored by the IUSSP Committee on Gender and Population, Dakar, Senegal, 3–6 Mar. 1993.

—— 'Some Inter-relationships Between Maternal Education and Child Survival in Nigeria: Evidence from Household Surveys and Focus Group Discussions', in International Union for the Scientific Study of Population (IUSSP), *Proceedings of the International Population Conference, Montreal*, iv (Liege, International Union for the Scientific Study of Population, 1993).

Omideyi, Adekunbi Kehinde, 'Women's Position, Conjugal Relationships and Fertility Behaviour Among the Yoruba.' *African Population Studies* 4 (Aug. 1990), 20–35.

Oni, G. A., 'Effects of Women's Education on Postpartum Practices and Fertility in Urban Nigeria', *Studies in Family Planning*, 16/6 (Nov.–Dec. 1985), 321–31.

—— and McCarthy, J., 'Contraceptive knowledge and practices in Ilorin, Nigeria: 1983-88', *Studies in Family Planning*, 21/2 (Mar.–Apr. 1990), 104–9.

Operations Research Group, *Family Planning Practices in India: Third All-India Survey* (Baroda, Operations Research Group, 1990).

Oppong, C., 'Women's Roles, Opportunity Costs, and Fertility', in R. A. Bulatao and R. D. Lee (eds.), *Determinants of Fertility in Developing Countries.* i (New York, Academic Press, 1983).

—— and Abu, K., *Seven Roles of Women: Impact of Education, Migration and Employment on Ghanaian Mothers*, Women, Work and Development Series, 13 (Geneva, International Labour Office, 1987).

Orubuloye, I. O., and Caldwell, J. C., 'The Impact of Public Health Services on Mortality: A Study of Mortality Differentials in a Rural Area of Nigeria', *Population Studies*, 29 (1975), 259–72.

—— —— Caldwell, P., and Bledsoe, C. H., 'The Impact of Family and Budget Structure on Health Treatment in Nigeria', *Health Transition Review*, 1/2 (1991), 189–210.

Othman, A., 'The Contraceptive Role of Breastfeeding by Educational Attainment: An Assessment Based on Malaysian Fertility and Family Survey', *Malaysian Journal of Reproductive Health*, 3/1 (1985), 77–83.

Page, H. J., and Lesthaeghe, R. (eds.), *Child-spacing in Tropical Africa: Traditions and Change* (London, Academic Press, 1981).

Pakistan, National Institute of Population Studies, *Pakistan Demographic and Health Survey 1990–1991* (Columbia, Md., Macro International Inc., 1992).

Palloni, A., 'Health Conditions in Latin America and Policies for Mortality Change', in J. Vallin and A. Lopez (eds.), *Health Policy, Social Policy and Mortality Prospects* (Liège, Ordina-International Union for the Scientific Study of Population, 1981).

Population Research Centre, Gokhale Institute of Politics and Economics, Pune, and International Institute for Population Sciences, Bombay, India, *National Family Health Survey: Maharashtra 1992–93* (Bombay, International Institute for Population Sciences, 1994).

Population Research Centre, The Gandhigram Institute of Rural Health and Family Welfare Trust, Tamil Nadu, and International Institute for Population Sciences, Bombay, India, *National Family Health Survey: Tamil Nadu 1992* (Bombay, International Institute for Population Sciences, 1994).

Population Research Centre, Lucknow University, Lucknow, and International Institute for Population Sciences, Bombay, India, *National Family Health Survey: Uttar Pradesh 1992–93* (Bombay, International Institute for Population Sciences, 1994).

Preston, Samuel H. (ed.), *The Effects of Infant and Child Mortality on Fertility* (New York, Academic Press, 1978).

Radcliffe-Brown, A. R., *Structure and Function in Primitive Society* (London, Cohen and West, 1952).

Rao, V. K., and Murty, K. S., 'Covariates of Age at First Birth in Guyana: A Hazards Model Analysis', *Journal of Biosocial Science*, 19 (1987), 427–38.

Rahman, M., Akbar, J., Phillips, J. F., and Becker, S., 'Contraceptive Use in Matlab, Bangladesh: The Role of Gender Preference', *Studies in Family Planning*, 23/4 (July–Aug. 1992), 229–42.

Raymundo, C. M., Perez, A. E., Nazario, M. P., and Mason, K. O., 'Female Education and Fertility in the Philippines: Why the Two Are Linked', paper presented at the International Population Conference (International Union for the Scientific Study of Population), Montreal, 24 Aug.–1 Sept. 1993.

Rehan, N., 'Knowledge, Attitude and Practice of Family Planning in Hausa Women', *Social Science and Medicine*, 18/10 (1984), 839–44.

Richter, K., and Adlakha, A., 'The Effect of Infant and Child Mortality on Subsequent Fertility', *Journal of Population and Social Studies*, 2/1 (July 1989), 43–63.

Rodriguez, G., and Aravena, R., 'Socio-economic Factors and the Transition to Low Fertility in Less Developed Countries: A Comparative Analysis', paper presented at the Demographic and Health Surveys World Conference, Washington, DC, 5–7 Aug. 1991.

—— and Cleland, J., 'Socio-economic Determinants of Marital Fertility in Twenty Countries: A Multivariate Analysis', *World Fertility Survey Conference, Record of Proceedings*, ii (London, World Fertility Survey, 1980).

Roth, E. A., and Kurup, K. B., 'Child Mortality Levels and Survival Patterns from Southern Sudan', *Journal of Biosocial Science*, 22 (1990), 365–72.

Roy, T. K., Rama Rao, G., and Prasad, Rajiva, 'Education, Fertility and Contraception Among Hindus and Roman Catholics in Goa', *Journal of Biosocial Science*, 23 (1991), 353–8.

Rutstein, Shea, and Medica, Vilma, 'The Latin American Experience', in Samuel E. Preston (ed.), *The Effects of Infant and Child Mortality on Fertility* (New York, Academic Press, 1978), 93–112.

Sala-Diakanda, M., 'Fécondité et caractéristiques socio-économiques et culturelles selon le milieu d'habitat au Zaire', *Canadian Studies in Population*, 9 (1982), 45–69.

Salaff, J. W., 'The Status of Unmarried Hong Kong Women and the Social Factors Contributing to Their Delayed Marriage', *Population Studies*, 30/3 (1976), 391–412.

—— *Working Daughters of Hong Kong: Filial Piety or Power in the Family?* (Cambridge, Cambridge University Press, 1981).

—— and Wong, A. K., 'Chinese Women at Work: Work Commitment and Fertility in the Asian Setting', in S. Kupinsky (ed.), *The Fertility of Working Women* (New York, Praeger Publishers, 1977).

Sathar, Z. A., 'Does Female Education Affect Fertility Behaviour in Pakistan?', *The Pakistan Development Review*, 23/4 (1984), 573-90.

—— 'Intervening Variables', in Iqbal Alam and Betzy Dinesen (eds.), *Fertility in Pakistan: A Review of Findings from the Pakistan Fertility Survey* (Voorburg, Netherlands, International Statistical Institute, 1984).

—— 'Women's Status and Fertility in Pakistan: The Most Recent Evidence' (New York, United Nations Population Division, 1992).

—— 'Women's Education and Autonomy as Factors in Fertility Change in Pakistan: Some Empirical Findings', paper presented at the Workshop on Female Education, Women's Autonomy and Fertility Change in South Asia, New Delhi, India, Apr. 1993.

—— 'The Processes by Which Female Education Affects Fertility and Child Survival', in International Union for the Scientific Study of Population (IUSSP), *Proceedings of the International Population Conference, Montreal*, iv (Liège, International Union for the Scientific Study of Population, 1993).

—— and Kazi, Shahnaz, 'Women, Work and Reproduction in Karachi', *International Family Planning Perspectives*, 16/2 (June 1990), 66–9 and 80.

—— and Kiani, M. F. K., 'Delayed Marriages in Pakistan', *The Pakistan Development Review*, 25/4 (1986), 535–52.

—— and Mason, K. O., 'Why Female Education Affects Reproductive Behaviour in Urban Pakistan', revision of the paper presented at the 1989 XXI General Conference of the IUSSP, New Delhi, India (1993).

—— Crook, Nigel, Callum, Christine, and Kazi, Shahnaz, 'Women's Status and Fertility Change in Pakistan', *Population and Development Review*, 14/3 (Sept. 1988), 415–32.

Schoemaker, J., 'Participacion laboral femenina y fecundidad en Paraguay', paper presented at Seminario de Analisis y Capacitacion, Encuesta Mundial de Fecundidad (Santiago de Chile, Centro Latinoamericano de Demografia, 1981).

Schuler, S. R., Meekers, D., and Hashemi, S. M., 'The Impact of Women's Participation in Credit Programs on Family Planning in Rural Bangladesh' (Mass. and Va., John Snow, Inc., JSI Research and Training Institute, not dated).

Schultz, T. P., 'Interpretations of the Relations Among Mortality, Economics of the Household and the Health Environment', *Socio-economic Determinants and Consequences of Mortality Differences* (Geneva, World Health Organization, 1980).

—— *Women and Development: Objectives, Frameworks, and Policy Interventions*, Policy, Planning and Research Working Papers: WPS 200, (Washington, DC, The World Bank, Population and Human Resources Department, 1989).

—— 'Returns to Women's Education', in E. M. King and M. A. Hill (eds.), *Women's Education in Developing Countries: Barriers, Benefits and Policy* (Washington DC, The World Bank, Education and Employment Division, Population and Human Resources Department, Sept. 1991).

Seetharamu, A. S., and Ushadevi, M. D., *Education in Rural Areas* (New Delhi, Ashish Publishing House, 1985).

Segamba, L., Ndikumasabo, V., Makinson, C., and Ayad, M., *Burundi enquête démographique et de santé au Burundi 1987* (Columbia, Md.. Westinghouse, 1988).

Sembajwe, Israel S. L., *Fertility and Infant Mortality Amongst the Yoruba in Western Nigeria* (Canberra, Australian National University Press, 1981).

Shah, N. M., 'Education: Level, Enrollment, Facilities and Attitudes', in Nasra Shah (ed.), *Pakistan Women* (Islamabad, Pakistani Institute of Development Economics, 1986).

—— and Bulatao, E. Q., 'Purdah and Family Planning in Pakistan', *International Family Planning Perspectives*, 7/1 (Mar. 1981), 32–7.

Shain, R. N., and Jennings, V. H., 'The Influence of Sex Roles on Fertility', in R. N. Shain and C. J. Pauerstein (eds.), *Fertility Control, Biologic and Behavioural Aspects* (Hagerstown, Md., Harper and Row, 1980).

Shapiro, D., and Tambashe, O., 'Women's Employment, Education and Contraceptive

Behavior in Kinshasa', paper presented at the Seminar on the Course of Fertility Transition in Sub-Saharan Africa, sponsored by the IUSSP Committee on Comparative Analysis of Fertility and the University of Zimbabwe, Harare, Zimbabwe, 19–22 Nov. 1991.

Sharma, Ravi K., Rutstein, Shea O., Labbok, Miriam, Ramos, Gilberto, and Effendi, Sofian, 'A Comparative Analysis of Trends and Differentials in Breastfeeding: Findings from DHS Surveys', paper presented at the Annual Meeting of the Population Association of America, Toronto, May 1990.

Singh, Susheela, Casterline, John B., and Cleland, John, 'The Proximate Determinants of Fertility: Sub-national Variations, *Population Studies*, 39/1 (Mar. 1985), 113–35.

Smith, Peter C., 'The Impact of Age at Marriage and Proportions Marrying on Fertility', in R. A. Bulatao and R. D. Lee (eds.), *Determinants of Fertility in Developing Countries*, ii (New York, Academic Press, 1983).

Smock, A. C., *Women's Education in Developing Countries: Opportunities and Outcomes* (New York, Praeger Publishers, 1981).

Sommerfelt, A. E., Boerma, J. T., Ochoa, L. H., and Rutstein, S. O., *Maternal and Child Health in Bolivia: Report on the In-depth DHS Survey in Bolivia, 1989* (Columbia, Md., Institute for Resource Development/Macro Systems, Inc., 1991).

Sri Lanka, Ministry of Plan Implementation, Department of Census and Statistics, *Sri Lanka Demographic and Health Survey 1987* (Columbia, Md., Institute for Resource Development, 1988).

Srinivas, M. N., *Social Change in Modern India* (Bombay, Asia Publishing House, 1966).

Standing, Guy, 'Women's Work Activity and Fertility', in R. A. Bulatao and R. D. Lee (eds.), *Determinants of Fertility in Developing Countries*, i (New York, Academic Press, 1983).

Stephens, P. W., *The Relationship Between the Level of Household Sanitation and Child Mortality: An Examination of Ghanaian Data*, African Demography Working Paper No. 10 (Philadelphia, Population Studies Center, University of Pennsylvania, 1984).

Streatfield, K., Singarimbun, M., and Diamond, I., 'Maternal Education and Child Immunization', *Demography*, 27/3 (Aug. 1990), 447–55.

——— ——— and Singarimbun, I., 'The Impact of Maternal Education on the Use of Child Immunisation and Other Health Services', *International Population Dynamics Program Research Note on Child Survival*, No. 8CS (Canberra, Australian National University, 1986).

Suarez, F., 'Peru: Formacion de la familia y su efecto sobre la participacion laboral de la mujer', paper presented at Seminario de Analisis y Capacitacion, Encuesta Mundial de Fecundidad (Santiago de Chile, Centro Latinoamericano de Demografia, 1981).

Subbarao, K., and Raney, L., *Social Gains from Female Education: A Cross-National Study*, The World Bank, Policy Research Working Papers, Women in Development, WPS 1045 (Washington, DC, The World Bank, Population and Human Resource Department, 1992).

Sudan, Ministry of Economic and National Planning, Department of Statistics, *Sudan Demographic and Health Survey 1989–90* (Columbia, Md., Macro International Inc., 1991).

Sundar, R., 'The Status of Women and Family Planning Acceptance: Some Field Results', *Journal of Family Welfare*, 36/2 (June 1990), 60–8.

Tagoe, Eva, 'Maternal Education and Infant/Child Morbidity in Ghana: The Case of Diarrhoea, Evidence from the Ghana D.H.S.', paper presented at the Seminar on Women and Demographic Change in Sub-Saharan Africa, sponsored by the IUSSP Committee on Gender and Population, Dakar, Senegal, 3–6 Mar. 1993.

Taucher, Erica, 'Effects of Decreasing Fertility on Infant Mortality Levels', Infant Mortality and Health Studies, Technical Study 57e (Ottawa, International Development Research Centre, 1989).

Tekce, B., and Shorter, F. C., 'Determinants of Child Mortality: A Study of Squatter Settlements in Jordan', *Population and Development Review*, 10 (suppl.) (1984), 257–80.

Tienda, M., 'Community Characteristics, Women's Education and Fertility in Peru', *Studies in Family Planning*, 15/4 (July–Aug. 1984), 162–9.

Tilak, J. B. G., 'East Asia', in E. M. King and M. A. Hill (eds.), *Women's Education in Developing Countries: Barriers, Benefits and Policy* (Washington DC, The World Bank, Education and Employment Division, Population and Human Resources Department, Sept. 1991).

Traore, B., Konate, M., and Stanton, C., *Mali enquête démographique et de santé au Mali 1987* (Columbia, Md., Westinghouse, 1989).

Trussell, J., and Hammerslough, C., 'A Hazard-Model Analysis of the Covariates of Infant and Child Mortality in Sri Lanka', *Demography*, 20/1 (1983), 1–26.

Tsui, A., De Clerque, J., and Mangani, N., 'Maternal and Socio-Demographic Correlates of Child Morbidity in Bas-Zaire: The Effects of Maternal Reporting', *Social Science and Medicine*, 26 (1988), 701–13.

—— Stupp, P., de Silva, V., and de Silva, S., 'Young Women's Work and Family Formation: A District Study in Sri Lanka', paper prepared for the Annual Meeting of the Population Association of America, Toronto, 3–5 May 1990.

Tsuya, N. O., and Choe, M. K., 'Trends and Covariates of Infant and Child Mortality in Rural China: The Case of Jilin Province', paper presented at the Annual Meeting of the Population Association of America, Baltimore, 29 Mar.–1 Apr. 1989.

Tucker, K., and Sanjur, D., 'Maternal Employment and Child Nutrition in Panama', *Social Science and Medicine*, 26/6 (1988), 605–12.

United Nations, *The Determinants and Consequences of Population Trends* (New York, United Nations, 1973).

—— *Socio-economic Differentials in Child Mortality in Developing Countries* (New York, Department of International Economic and Social Affairs, United Nations, 1985).

—— *Fertility Behaviour in the Context of Development: Evidence from the World Fertility Survey*, Population Studies No. 100 (New York, Department of International Economic and Social Affairs, United Nations, 1987).

—— *The World's Women 1970–1990: Trends and Statistics* (New York, United Nations, 1991).

—— *Child Mortality in Developing Countries*, E.91.XIII.13 (New York, United Nations, 1991).

—— 'The Impact of Mother's Education on Infant and Child Mortality in Selected Countries in the ESCWA Region', paper presented at the United Nations Expert Group Meeting on Population and Women, Gaborone, Botswana, 22–6 June 1992.

—— 'Women's Education and Employment and Linkages with Population', paper presented at the United Nations Expert Group Meeting on Population and Women, Gaborone, Botswana, 22–6 June 1992.

—— 'Population and Women: A Review of Issues and Trends', paper presented at the United Nations Expert Group Meeting on Population and Women, Gaborone, Botswana, 22–6 June 1992.

—— *Women's Education and Fertility Behaviour: A Case-study of Rural Maharashtra, India* (New York, United Nations, 1993).

—— *Women's Education and Fertility Behaviour: Recent Evidence from the Demographic and Health Surveys* (New York, United Nations, 1995).

United Nations Children's Fund, *The State of the World's Children 1992* (Oxford, Oxford University Press, 1992).

United Nations Development Programme, *Human Development Report, 1993* (Oxford and New Delhi, Oxford University Press, 1993).

United Nations Educational, Scientific and Cultural Organization, *Statistical Yearbook, 1988* (Paris, United Nations, 1988).

—— *Statistical Yearbook, 1990* (Paris, UNESCO, 1991).

Van de Walle, F., and Ouaidou, N., 'Status and Fertility Among Urban Women in Burkina Faso', *International Family Planning Perspectives*, 11/2 (June 1985), 60–4.

—— and Van de Walle, E., 'Woman's Autonomy and Fertility', in Nora Federici, Karen Oppenheim Mason, and Solvi Sogner (eds.), *Women's Position and Demographic Change* (Oxford, Oxford University Press, 1993).

Visaria, Leela, 'Female Autonomy and Fertility Behaviour: An Exploration of Gujarat Data', in International Union for the Scientific Study of Population (IUSSP), *Proceedings of the International Population Conference, Montreal*, iv (Liège, International Union for the Scientific Study of Population, 1993).

—— 'Regional Variations in Female Autonomy and Fertility Behaviour in India', paper presented at the Workshop on Female Education, Autonomy and Fertility Change in South Asia, New Delhi, Apr. 1993.

Vlassoff, C., 'Unmarried Adolescent Females in Rural India: A Study of the Social Impact of Education', *Journal of Marriage and the Family*, 42/2 (May 1980), 427–36.

—— 'The Status of Women in Rural India: A Village Study', *Social Action*, 32/4 (Oct.–Dec. 1982), 380–407.

—— 'Against the Odds: The Changing Impact of Education on Female Autonomy and Fertility in an Indian Village', paper presented at the Workshop on Female Education, Autonomy and Fertility Change in South Asia, New Delhi, Apr. 1993.

Vlassoff, Michael, and Vlassoff, Carol, 'Old Age Security and the Utility of Children in Rural India' *Population Studies*, 34 (Nov. 1980), 487–99.

Wainerman, C. H., 'The Impact of Education on the Female Labour Force in Argentina and Paraguay', *Comparative Education Review*, 24/2 (June 1980), S180–S195.

Ware, H., 'Effects of Maternal Education, Women's Roles and Child Care on Child Mortality', *Population and Development Review*, 10 (suppl.) (1984), 191–214.

Warren, C. W., 'Fertility Determinants in Puerto Rico', *Studies in Family Planning*, 18/1, (Jan.–Feb. 1987), 42–8.

Weinberger, M. B., 'The Relationship Between Women's Education and Fertility: Selected Findings from the World Fertility Surveys', *International Family Planning Perspectives*, 13/2 (June 1987), 35–46.

—— Lloyd, C., and Blanc, A. K., 'Women's Education and Fertility: A Decade of Change in Four Latin American Countries', *International Family Planning Perspectives*, 15/1 (Mar. 1989), 4–14.

Westoff, C., and Moreno, L., 'The Demand for Family Planning: Estimates for Developing Countries', paper presented at the International Union for the Scientific Study of Population Seminar of the Committee on the Comparative Analysis of Family Planning and Fertility, Tunisia, 26–30 June 1989.

—— and Ochoa, L. H., 'Unmet Need and the Demand for Family Planning', Demographic and Health Surveys Comparative Studies No. 5 (Columbia, Md., Institute for Resource Development, July 1991).

—— and Pebley, A., 'Alternative Measures of Unmet Need for Family Planning in

Developing Countries', *International Family Planning Perspectives*, 7/4 (1981), 126–36.
—— Potter, R. G., Jr., and Sagi, Philip C., *The Third Child: A Study in the Prediction of Fertility* (Princeton, Princeton University Press, 1963).
Whyte, S. R., and Kariuki, P. W., 'Malnutrition and Gender Relations in Western Kenya', *Health Transition Review*, 1/2 (1991), 171–87.
Wolfe, B. L., and Behrman, J. R., 'Determinants of Child Mortality, Health and Nutrition in a Developing Country', *Journal of Development Economics*, 11 (1982), 163–93.
—— —— 'Who Is Schooled in Developing Countries? The Roles of Income, Parental Schooling, Sex, Residence and Family Size', *Economics of Education Review*, 3/3 (1984), 231-45.
—— —— 'Women's Schooling and Children's Health: Are the Effects Robust with Adult Sibling Control for the Women's Childhood Background?', *Journal of Health Economics*, 6 (1987), 239–54.
Wong, E. L., Popkin, B. M., Guilkey, D. K., and Akin, J. S., 'Accessibility, Quality of Care and Prenatal Care Use in the Philippines', *Social Science and Medicine*, 24 (1987), 927–44.
Yates, B. A., 'African Reactions to Education: The Congolese Case', *Comparative Education Review*, 15 (1971), 158–71.
Yohannes, A. G., and Streatfield, K., 'Utilisation of Health Facilities for Child Illness in Ethiopia 1983', *Child Survival Research Note*, 19CS (Canberra, Australian National University, 1988).
Zachariah, K. C., 'The Anomaly of the Fertility Decline in India's Kerala State: A Field Investigation', World Bank Staff Working Papers No. 700 (Washington, DC, The World Bank, 1984).
Zanamwe, L., 'The Relationship Between Fertility and Child Mortality in Zimbabwe', in *Proceedings of the African Population Conference, Dakar, Senegal, 7–12 Nov. 1988*, ii (Liège, International Union for the Scientific Study of Population, 1988).
Zhao, Jianmin, and Sun, Jinghua, 'Education and Fertility of Women of Child-bearing Age', in China Population Implementation Centre (CMC) (comp.), *Analysis of China's National One-per-Thousand Population Fertility Sampling Survey* (Beijing, China, 1984), 84–7.

Index

Key: *Italic* page number indicates figure or table; **boldface** number indicates boxed material

Printed in the United States
144565LV00001B/26/A